the dreaming

by
Queenie Chan

TOKYOPOP®

HAMBURG // LONDON // LOS ANGELES // TOKYO

The Dreaming Vol. 1
Written and Illustrated by Queenie Chan

Production Artists - Lucas Rivera and Jason Milligan
Cover Design - Anne Marie Horne
Copy Editors - Peter Ahlstrom, Eric Althoff,
and Hope Donovan

Editor - Carol Fox
Digital Imaging Manager - Chris Buford
Production Managers - Jennifer Miller and Mutsumi Miyazaki
Managing Editor - Lindsey Johnston
VP of Production - Ron Klamert
Publisher and E.I.C. - Mike Kiley
President and C.O.O. - John Parker
C.E.O. - Stuart Levy

A 🔴 **TOKYOPOP**® Manga

TOKYOPOP Inc.
5900 Wilshire Blvd. Suite 2000
Los Angeles, CA 90036

E-mail: info@TOKYOPOP.com
Come visit us online at www.TOKYOPOP.com

ISBN: 1-59816-382-5

First TOKYOPOP printing: December 2005

10 9 8 7 6 5 4 3 2 1

Printed in the USA

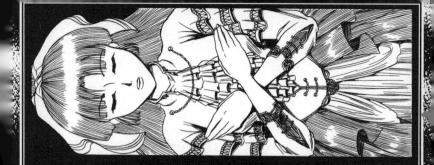

Table of Contents

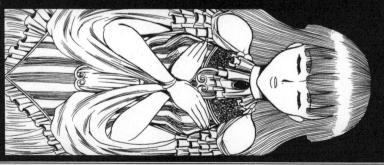

For my
Mum
Susan,
and
my
Dad
Marco.

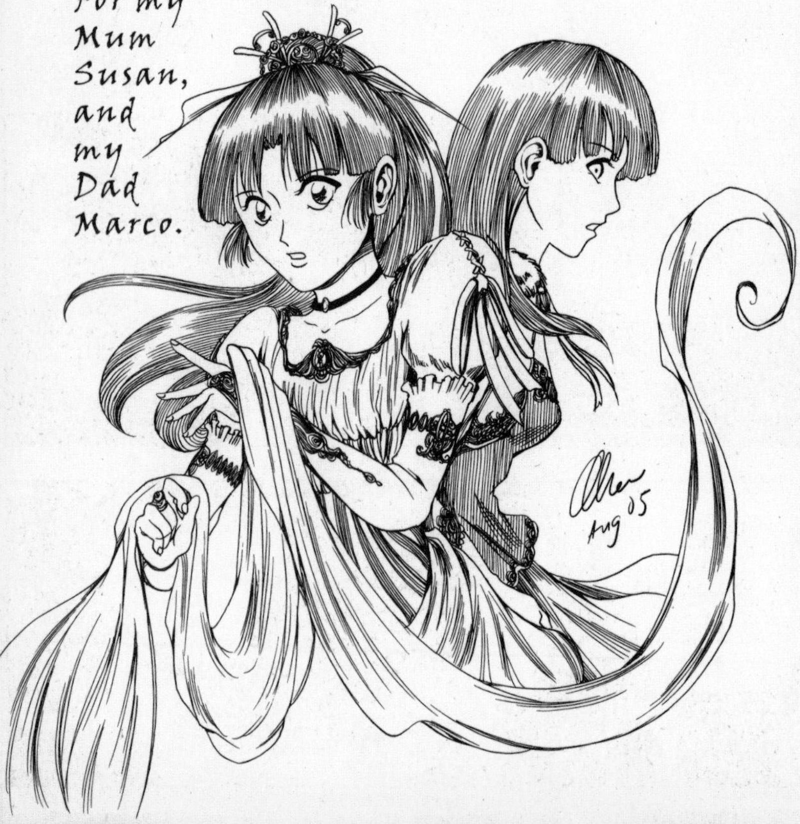
Aug 05

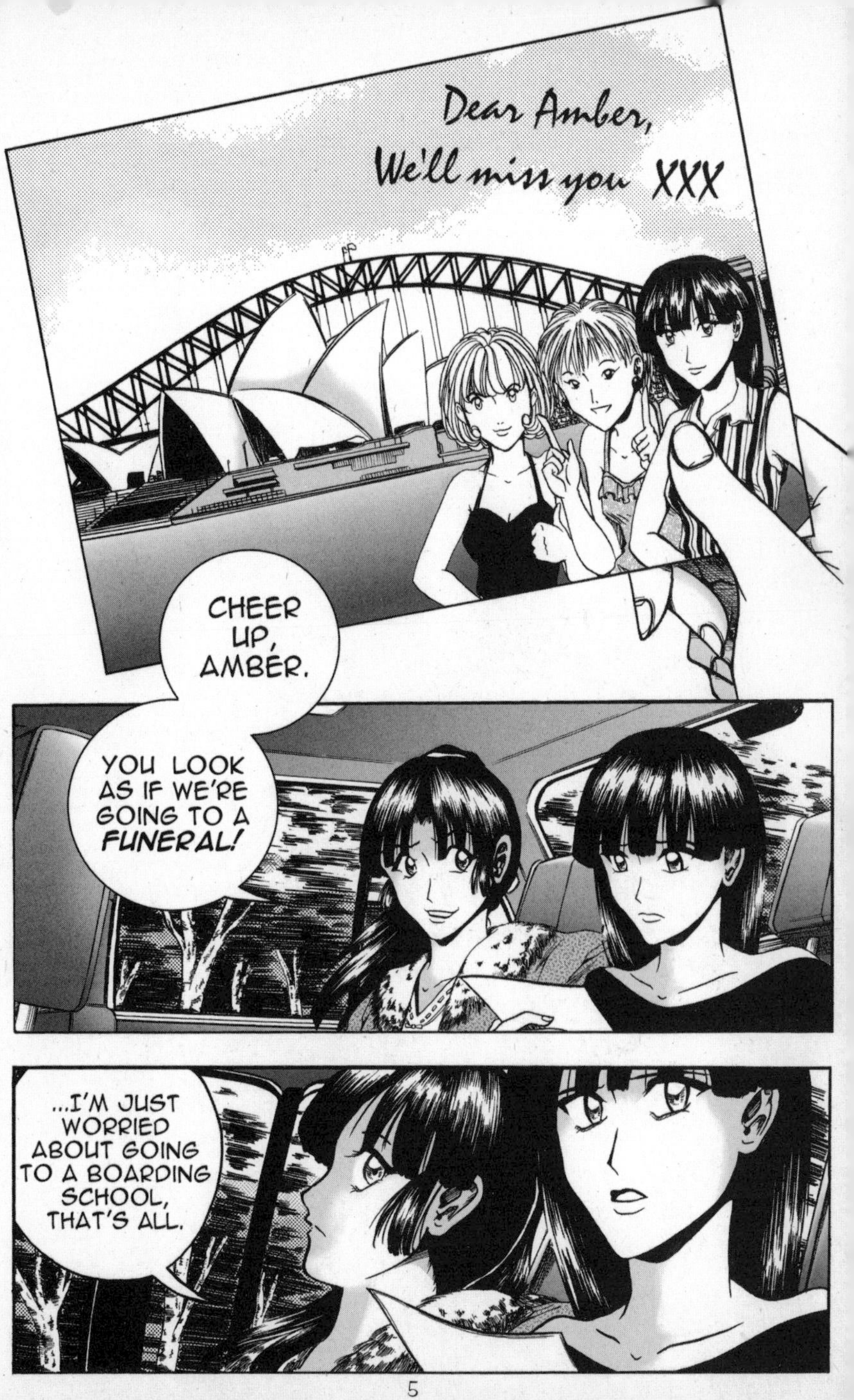
Dear Amber,
We'll miss you XXX
CHEER UP, AMBER.
YOU LOOK AS IF WE'RE GOING TO A FUNERAL!
...I'M JUST WORRIED ABOUT GOING TO A BOARDING SCHOOL, THAT'S ALL.

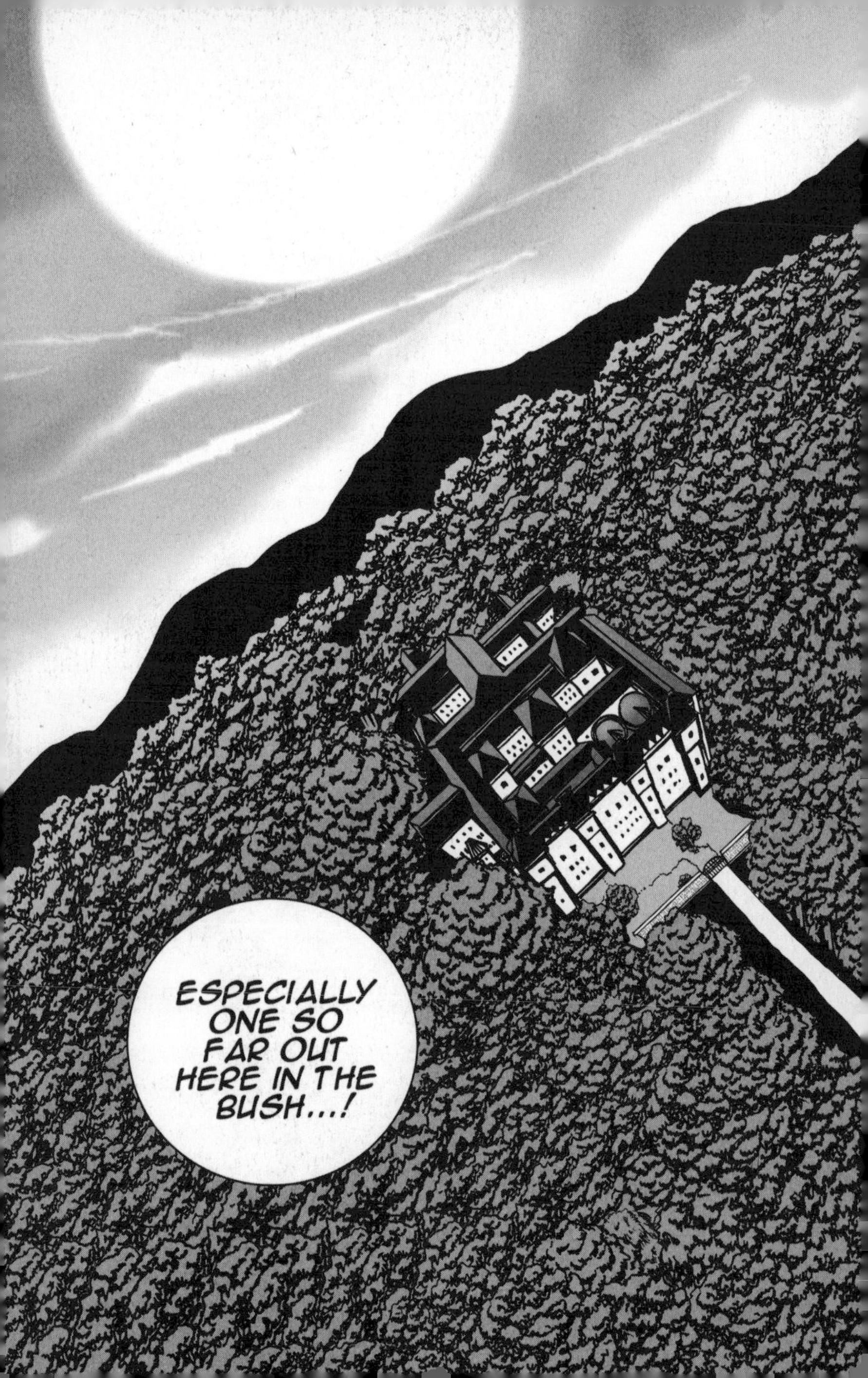
ESPECIALLY ONE SO FAR OUT HERE IN THE BUSH...!

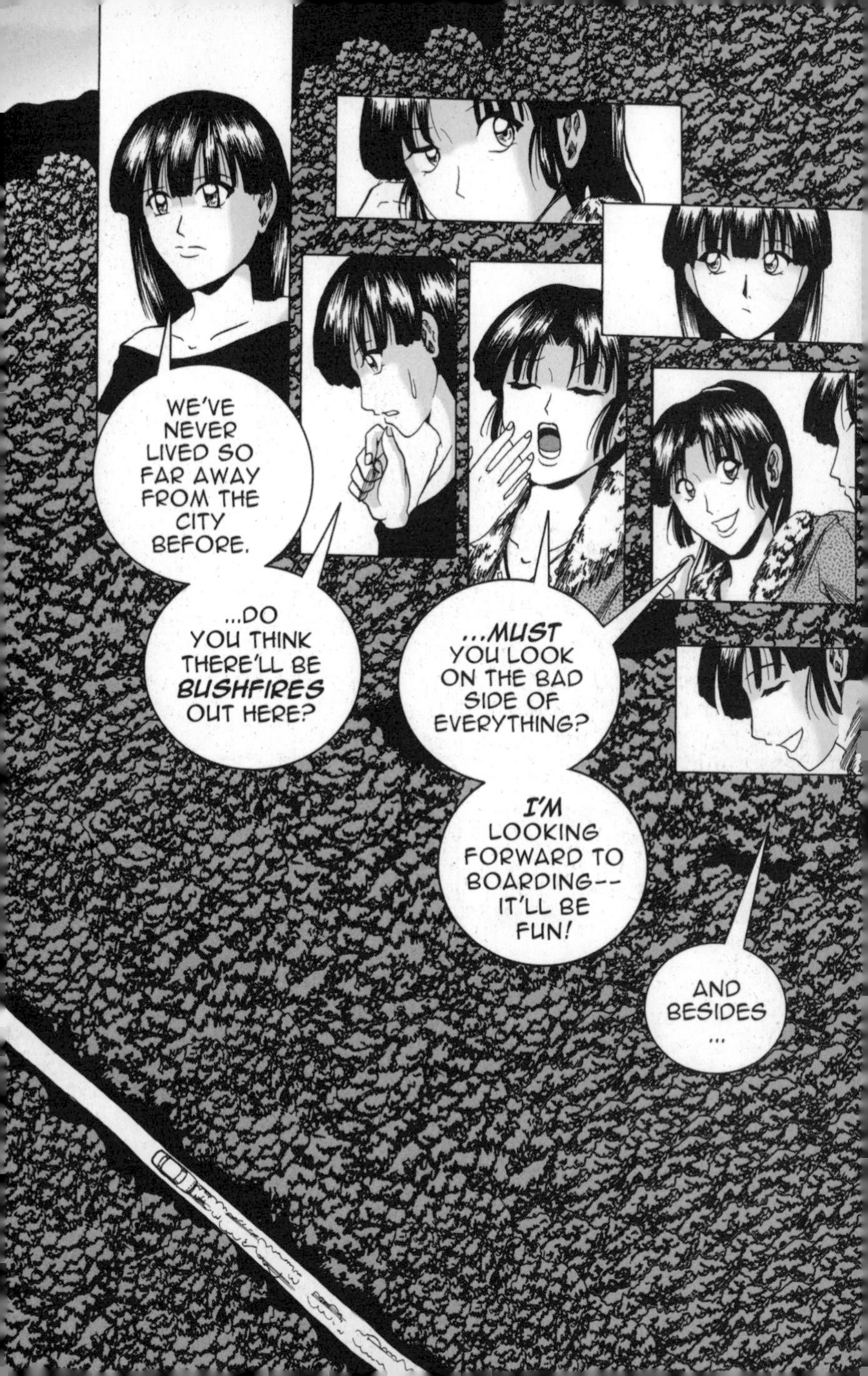
WE'VE NEVER LIVED SO FAR AWAY FROM THE CITY BEFORE.
...DO YOU THINK THERE'LL BE *BUSHFIRES* OUT HERE?
...MUST YOU LOOK ON THE BAD SIDE OF EVERYTHING?
I'M LOOKING FORWARD TO BOARDING-- IT'LL BE FUN!
AND BESIDES ...

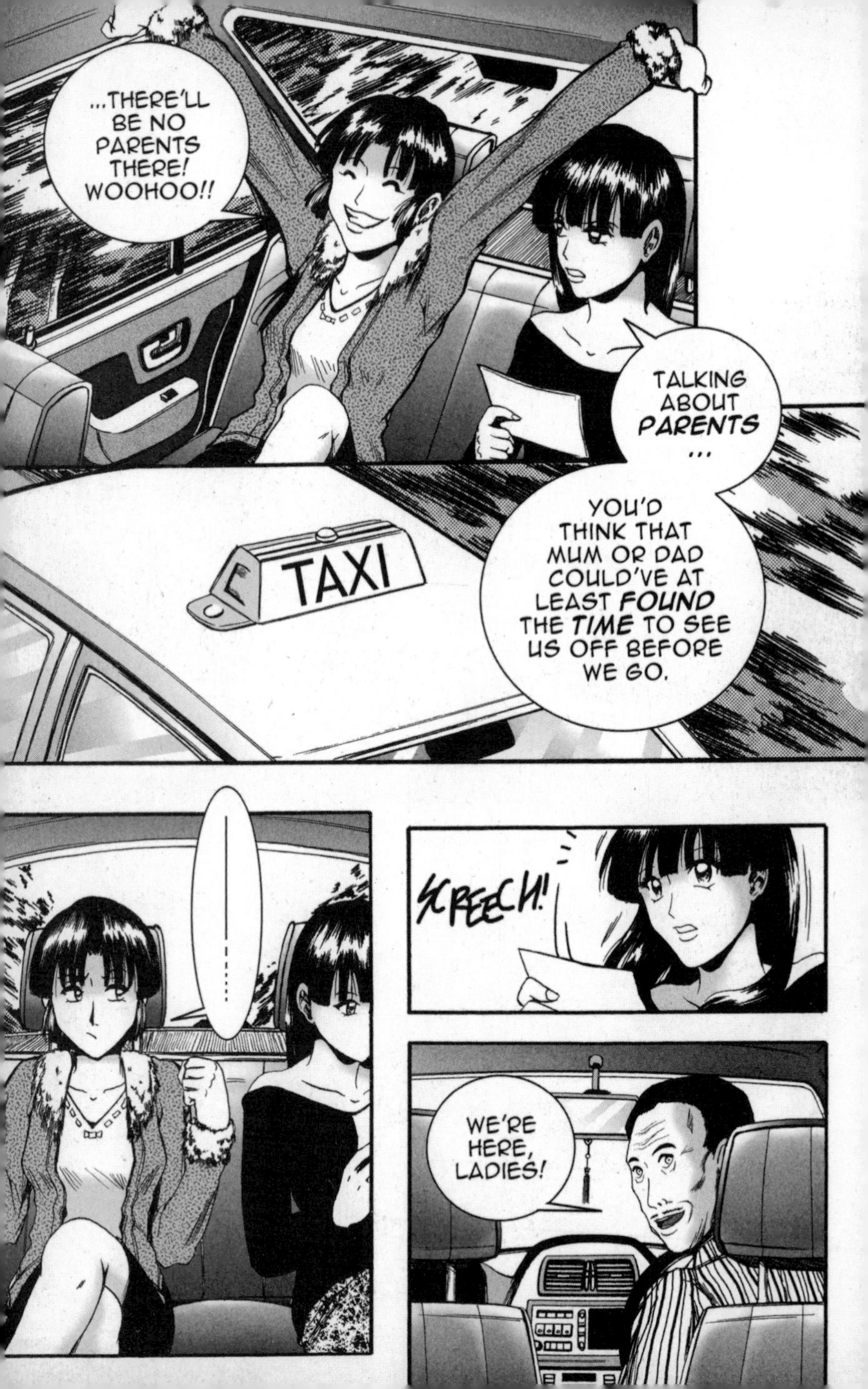
...THERE'LL BE NO PARENTS THERE! WOOHOO!!
TALKING ABOUT PARENTS ...
YOU'D THINK THAT MUM OR DAD COULD'VE AT LEAST FOUND THE TIME TO SEE US OFF BEFORE WE GO.
TAXI
......
SCREECH!
WE'RE HERE, LADIES!

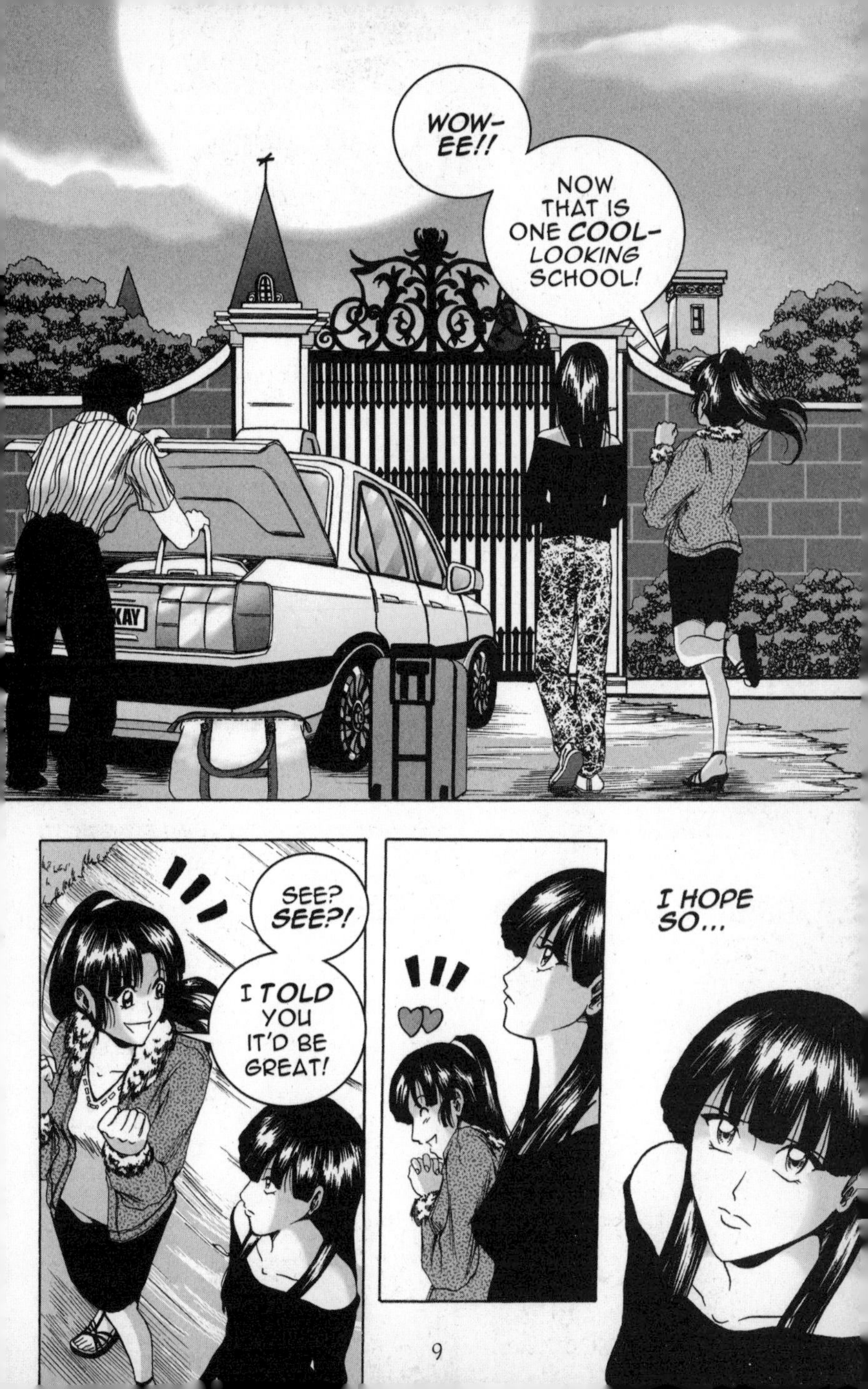
WOW-EE!!
NOW THAT IS ONE COOL-LOOKING SCHOOL!
SEE? SEE?!
I TOLD YOU IT'D BE GREAT!
I HOPE SO...

Chapter 1
A New School

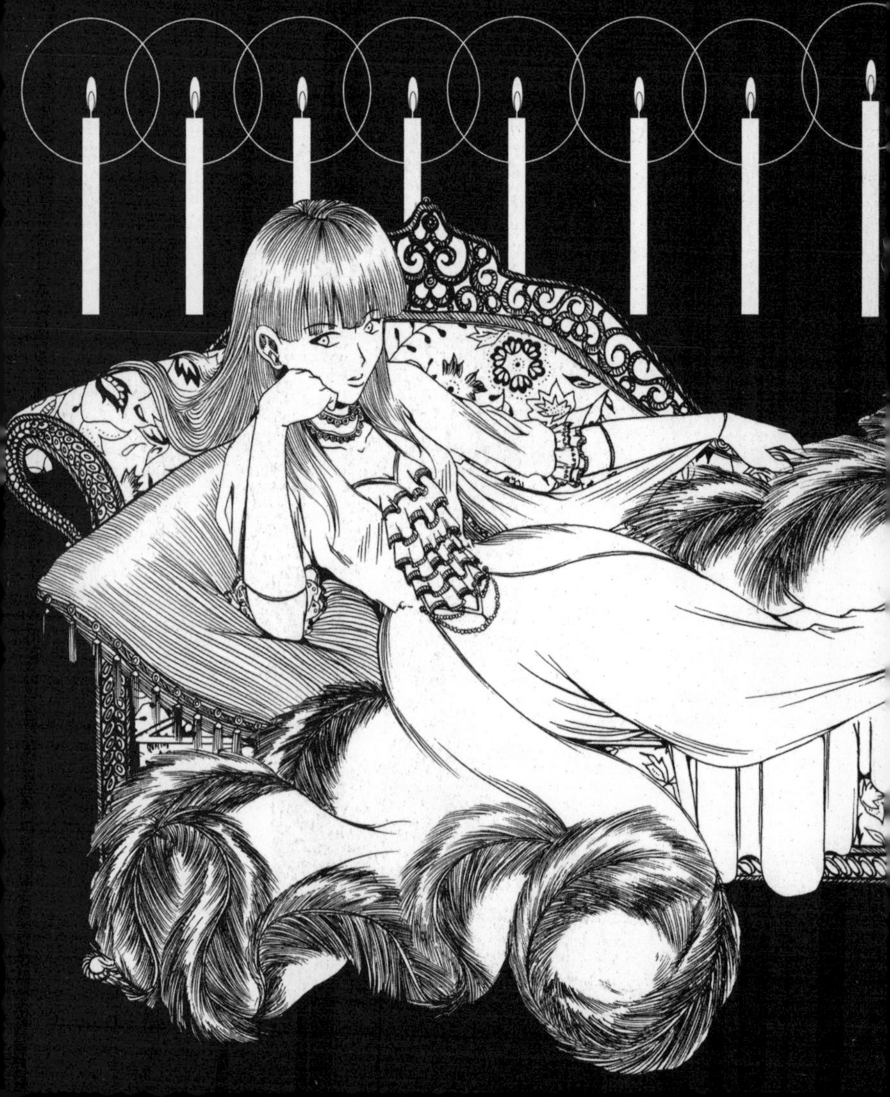

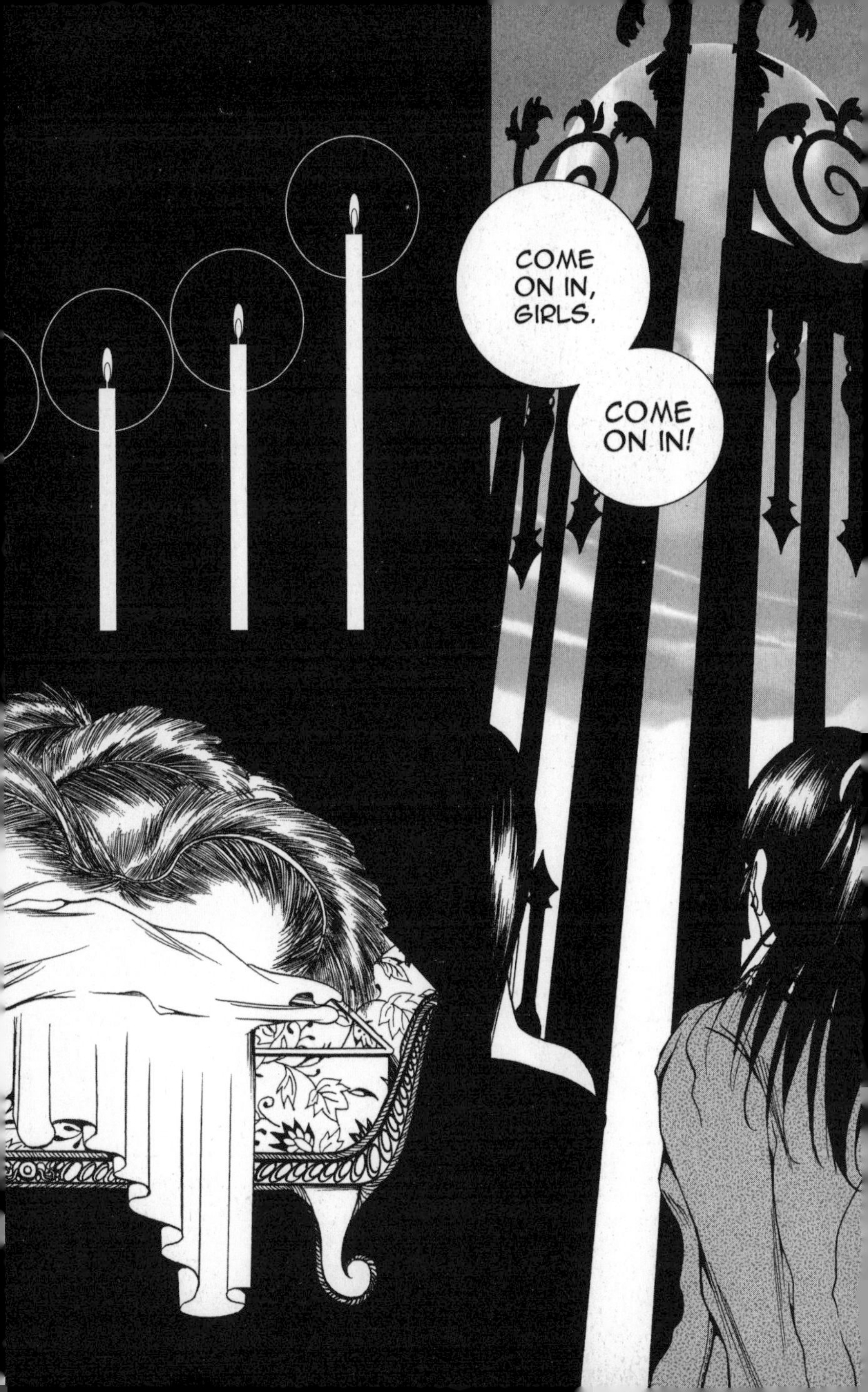
COME ON IN, GIRLS.
COME ON IN!

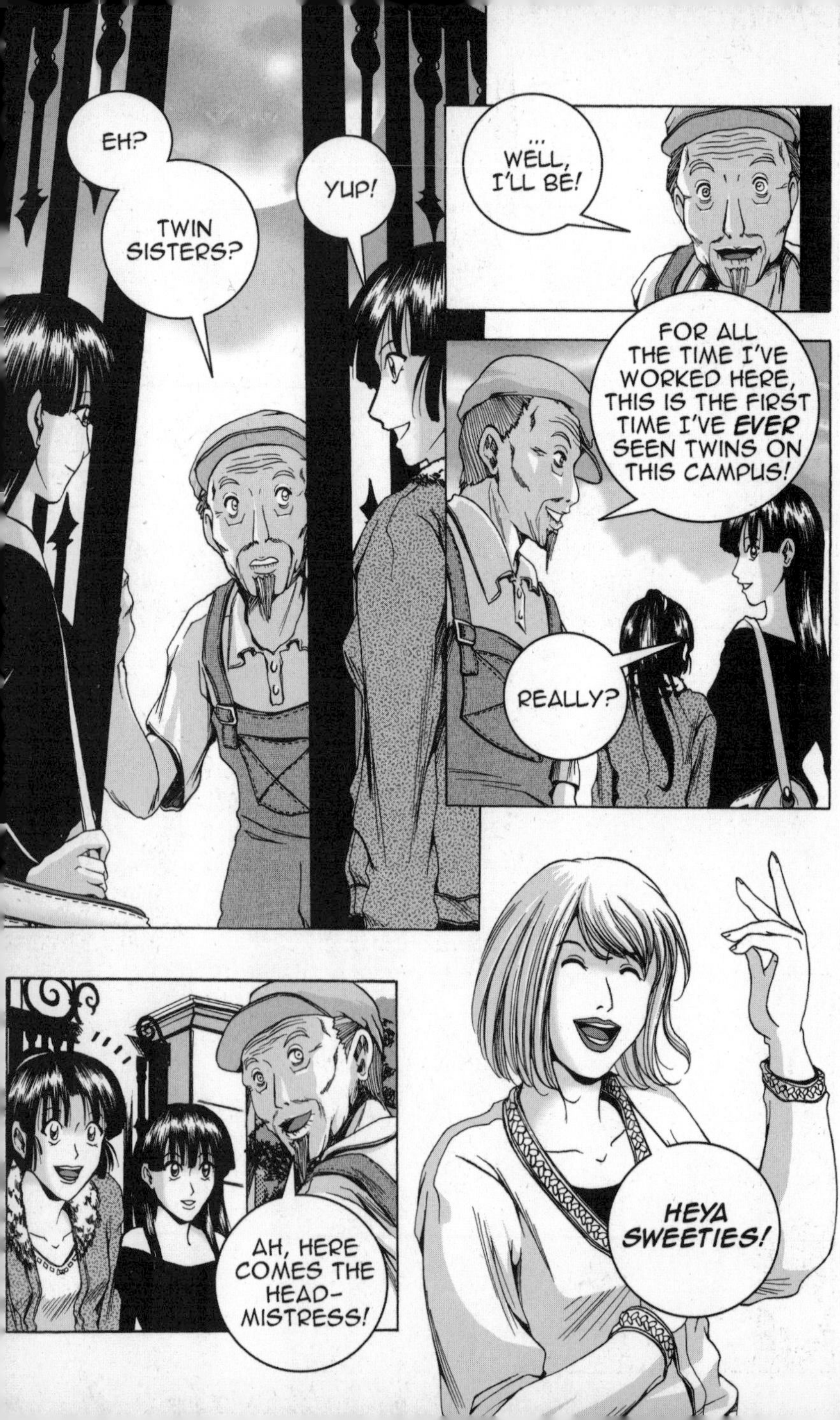
EH?
TWIN SISTERS?
YUP!
... WELL, I'LL BE!
FOR ALL THE TIME I'VE WORKED HERE, THIS IS THE FIRST TIME I'VE *EVER* SEEN TWINS ON THIS CAMPUS!
REALLY?
AH, HERE COMES THE HEAD-MISTRESS!
HEYA SWEETIES!

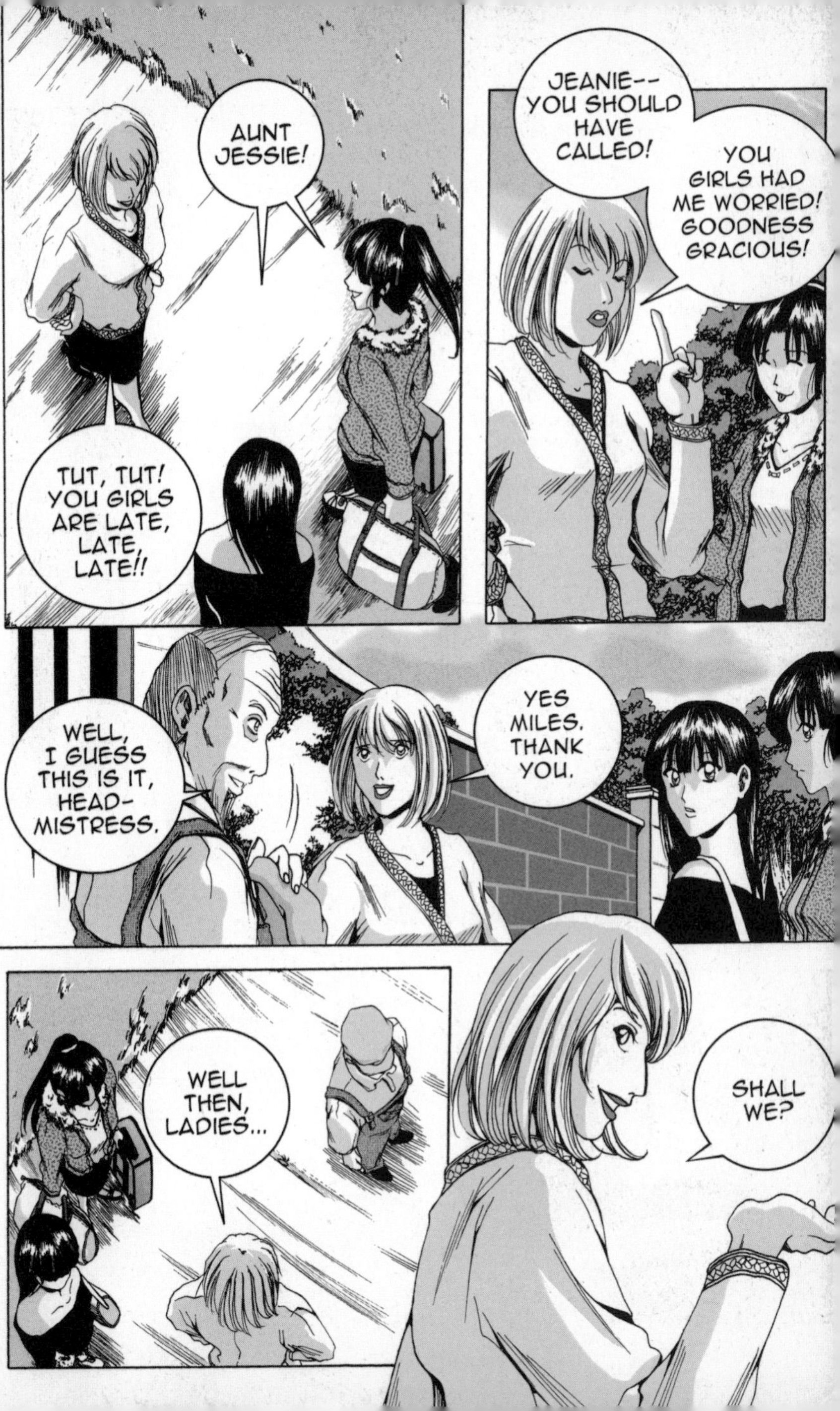
AUNT JESSIE!
TUT, TUT! YOU GIRLS ARE LATE, LATE, LATE!!
JEANIE-- YOU SHOULD HAVE CALLED!
YOU GIRLS HAD ME WORRIED! GOODNESS GRACIOUS!
WELL, I GUESS THIS IS IT, HEAD-MISTRESS.
YES MILES. THANK YOU.
WELL THEN, LADIES...
SHALL WE?

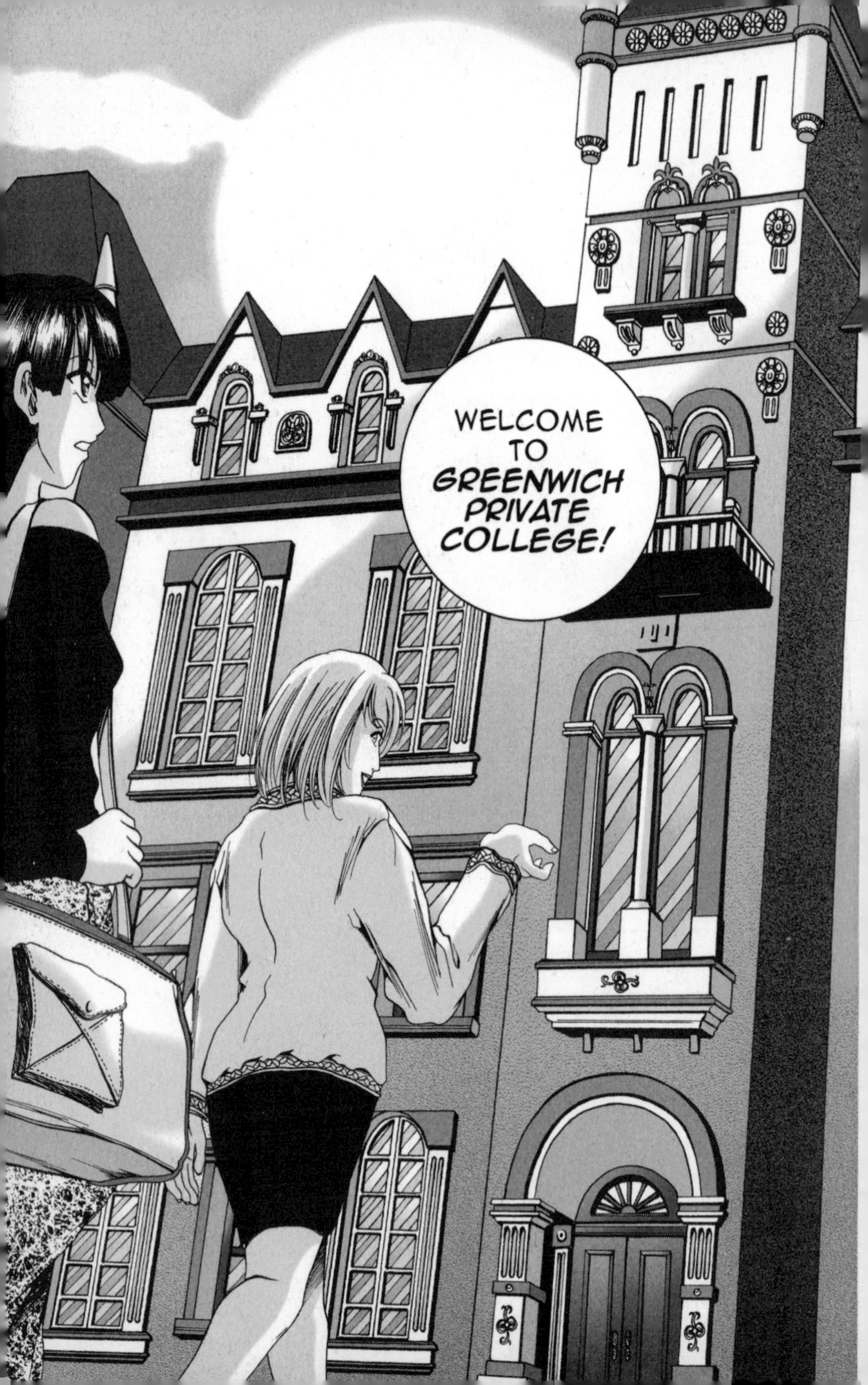
WELCOME TO GREENWICH PRIVATE COLLEGE!

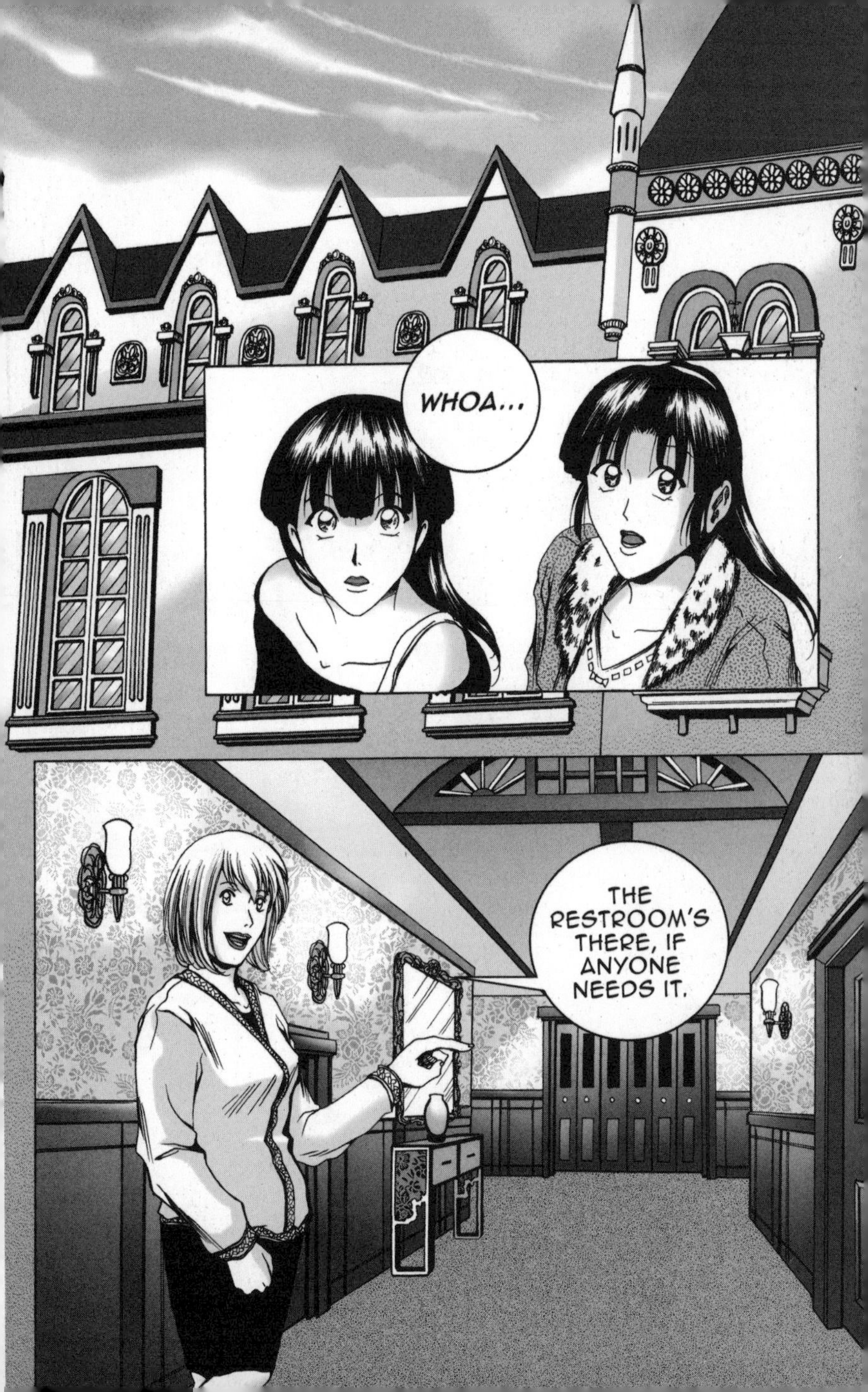
WHOA...
THE RESTROOM'S THERE, IF ANYONE NEEDS IT.

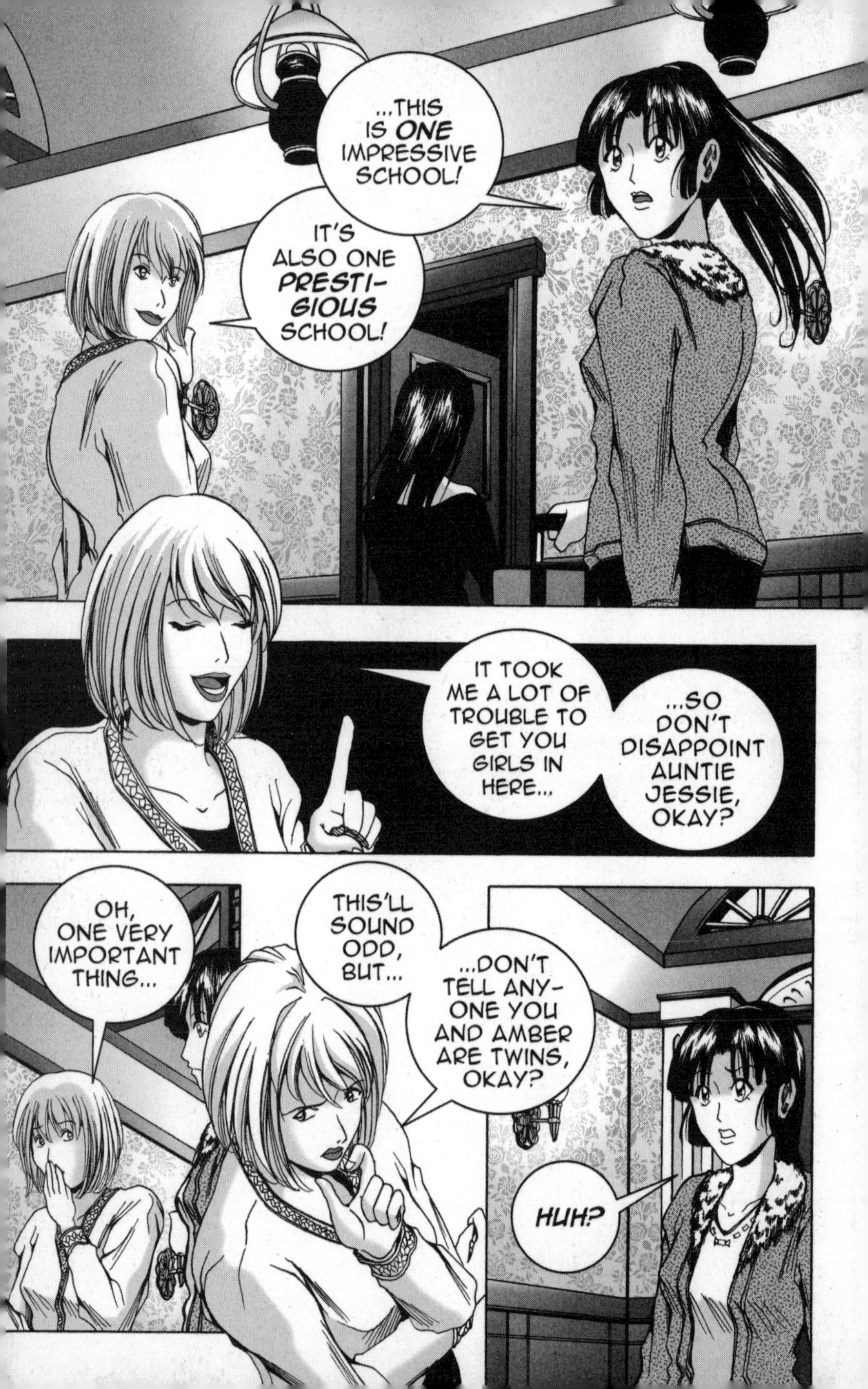
...THIS IS *ONE* IMPRESSIVE SCHOOL!
IT'S ALSO ONE *PRESTIGIOUS* SCHOOL!
IT TOOK ME A LOT OF TROUBLE TO GET YOU GIRLS IN HERE...
...SO DON'T DISAPPOINT AUNTIE JESSIE, OKAY?
OH, ONE VERY IMPORTANT THING...
THIS'LL SOUND ODD, BUT...
...DON'T TELL ANYONE YOU AND AMBER ARE TWINS, OKAY?
HUH?

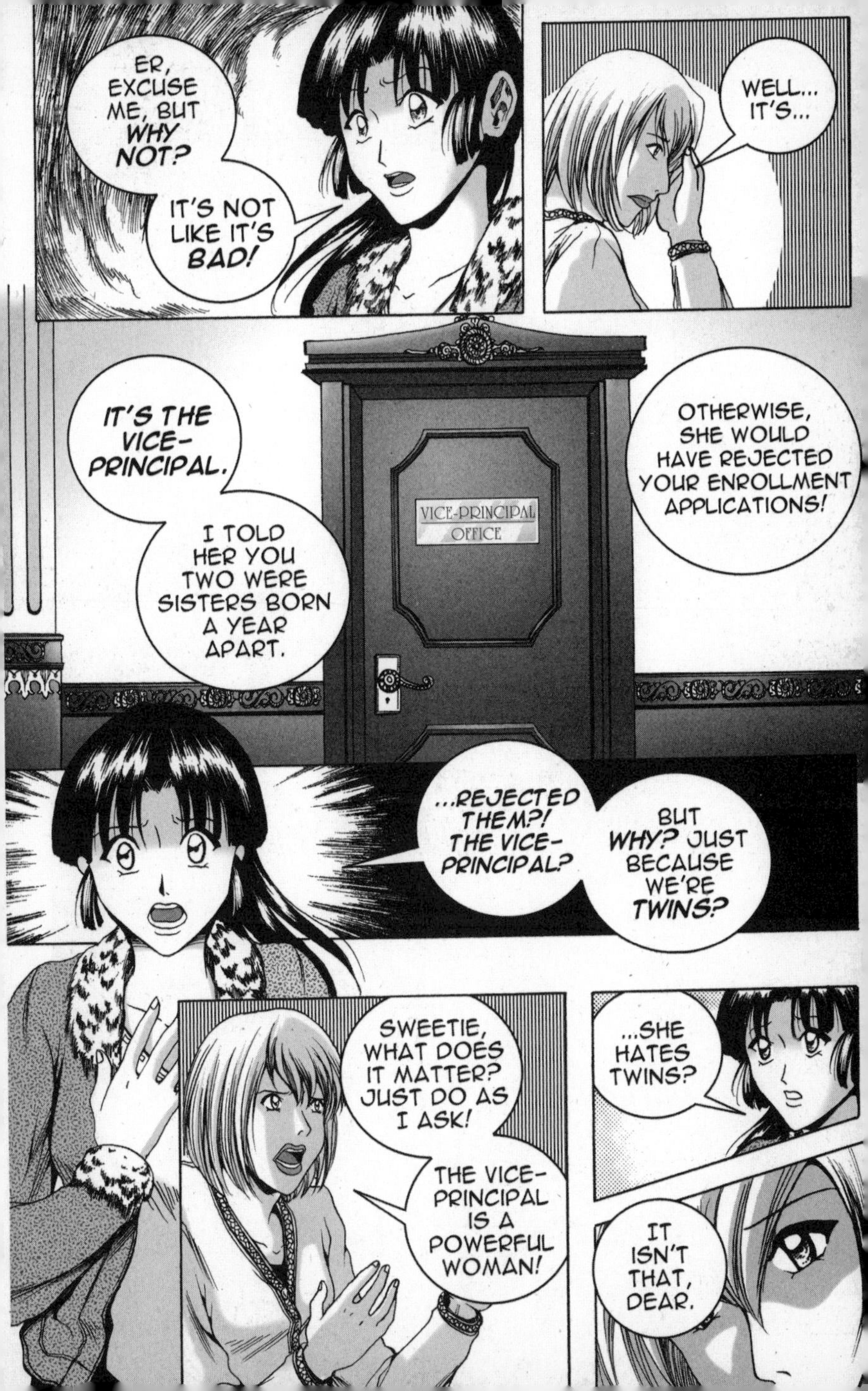
ER, EXCUSE ME, BUT WHY NOT?
IT'S NOT LIKE IT'S BAD!
WELL... IT'S...
IT'S THE VICE-PRINCIPAL.
I TOLD HER YOU TWO WERE SISTERS BORN A YEAR APART.
VICE-PRINCIPAL OFFICE
OTHERWISE, SHE WOULD HAVE REJECTED YOUR ENROLLMENT APPLICATIONS!
...REJECTED THEM?! THE VICE-PRINCIPAL?
BUT WHY? JUST BECAUSE WE'RE TWINS?
SWEETIE, WHAT DOES IT MATTER? JUST DO AS I ASK!
THE VICE-PRINCIPAL IS A POWERFUL WOMAN!
...SHE HATES TWINS?
IT ISN'T THAT, DEAR.

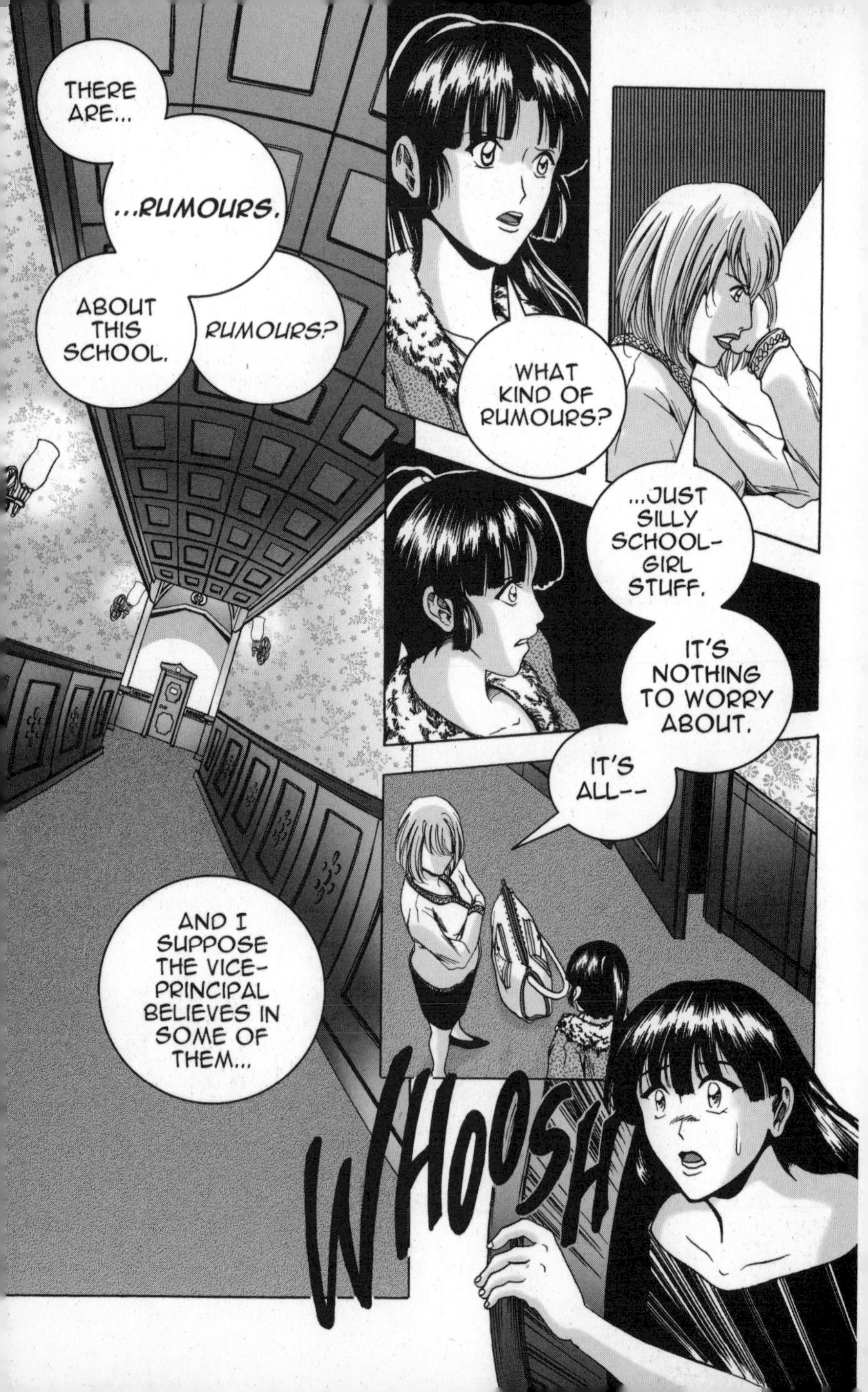
THERE ARE...
...RUMOURS.
RUMOURS?
ABOUT THIS SCHOOL.
WHAT KIND OF RUMOURS?
...JUST SILLY SCHOOL-GIRL STUFF.
IT'S NOTHING TO WORRY ABOUT.
IT'S ALL--
AND I SUPPOSE THE VICE-PRINCIPAL BELIEVES IN SOME OF THEM...
WHOOSH

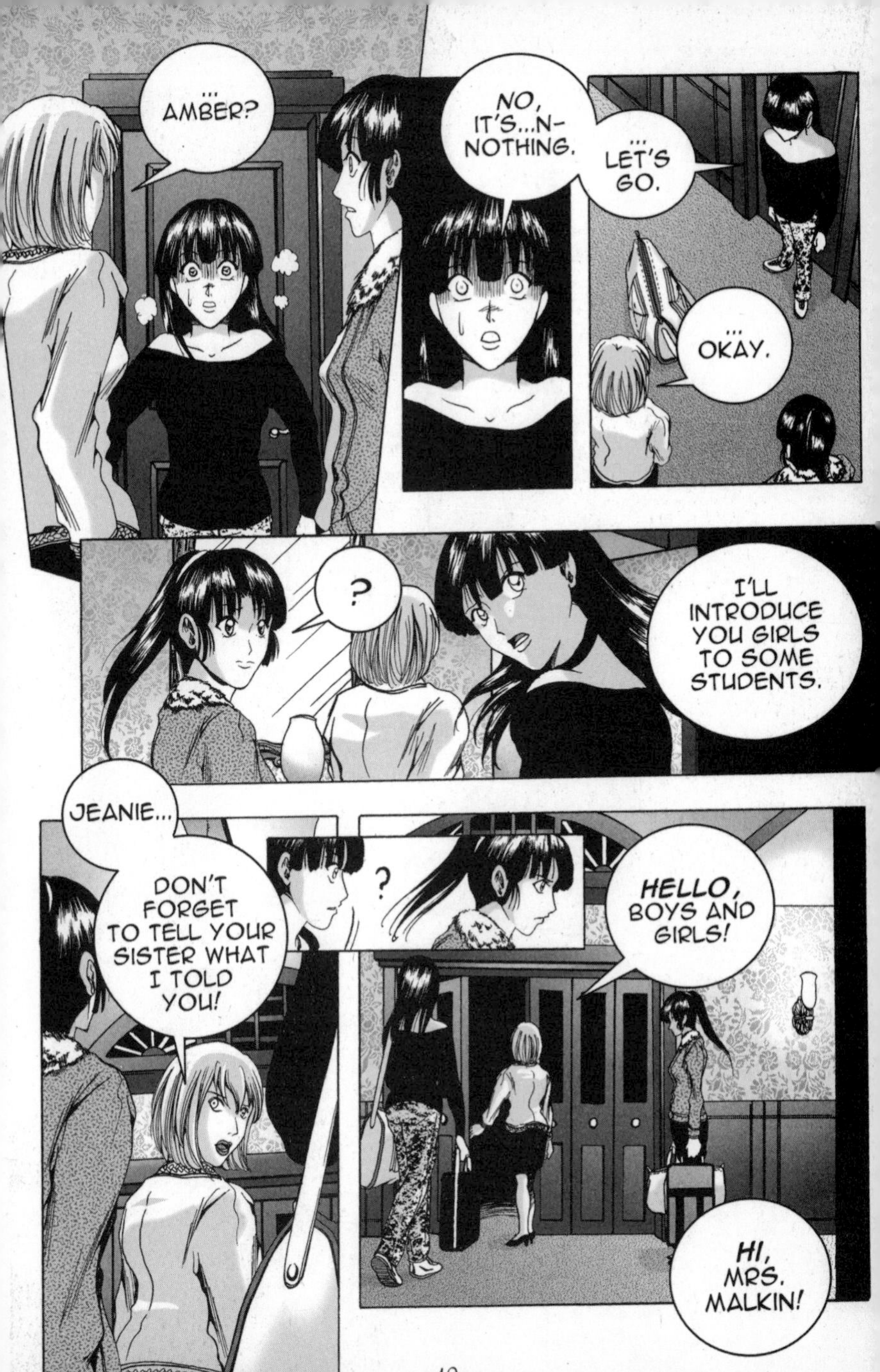
...AMBER?
NO, IT'S...N-NOTHING.
...LET'S GO.
...OKAY.
?
I'LL INTRODUCE YOU GIRLS TO SOME STUDENTS.
JEANIE...
DON'T FORGET TO TELL YOUR SISTER WHAT I TOLD YOU!
?
HELLO, BOYS AND GIRLS!
HI, MRS. MALKIN!

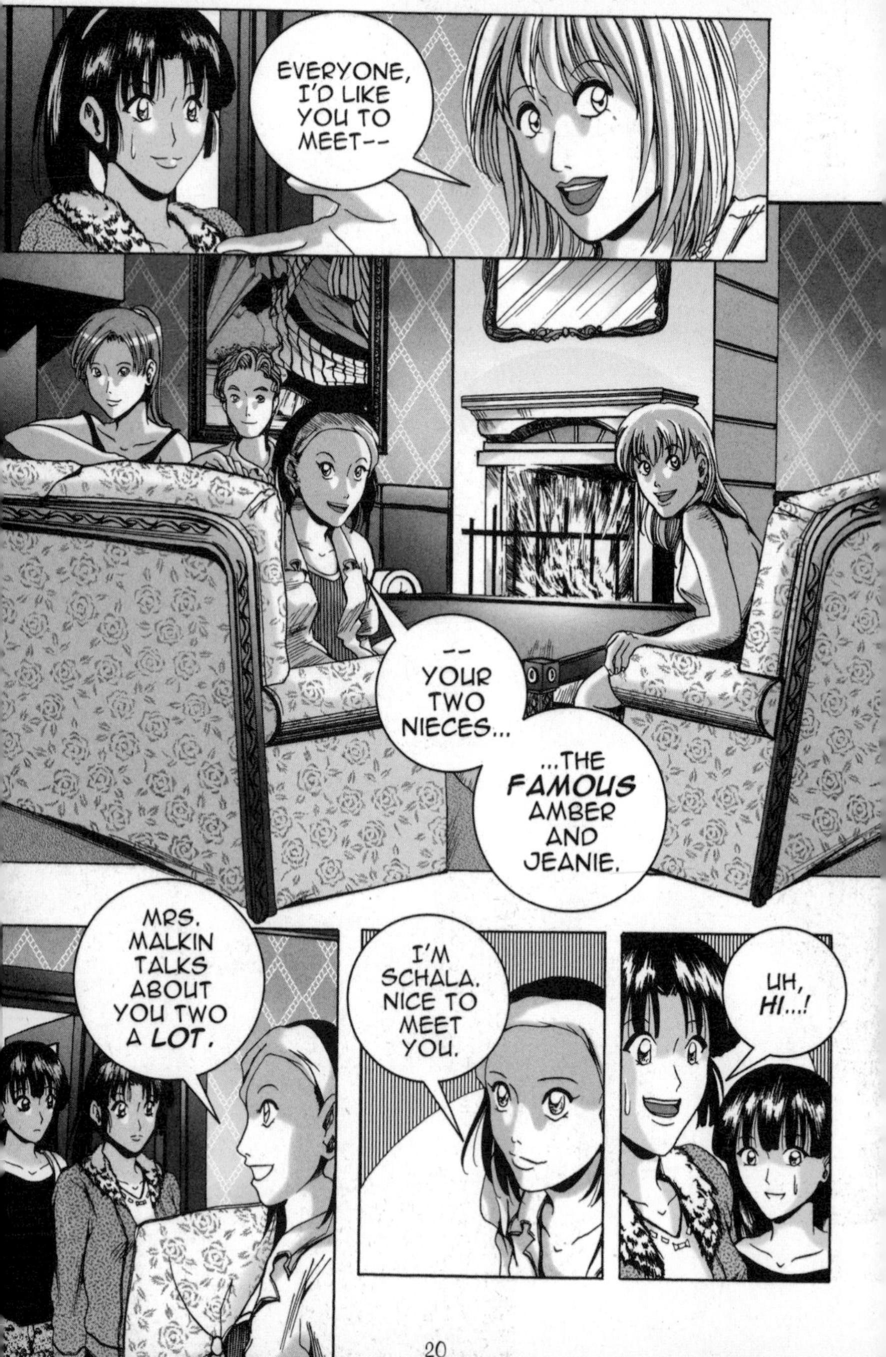
EVERYONE, I'D LIKE YOU TO MEET--
--YOUR TWO NIECES...
...THE *FAMOUS* AMBER AND JEANIE.
MRS. MALKIN TALKS ABOUT YOU TWO A *LOT*.
I'M SCHALA. NICE TO MEET YOU.
UH, *HI*...!

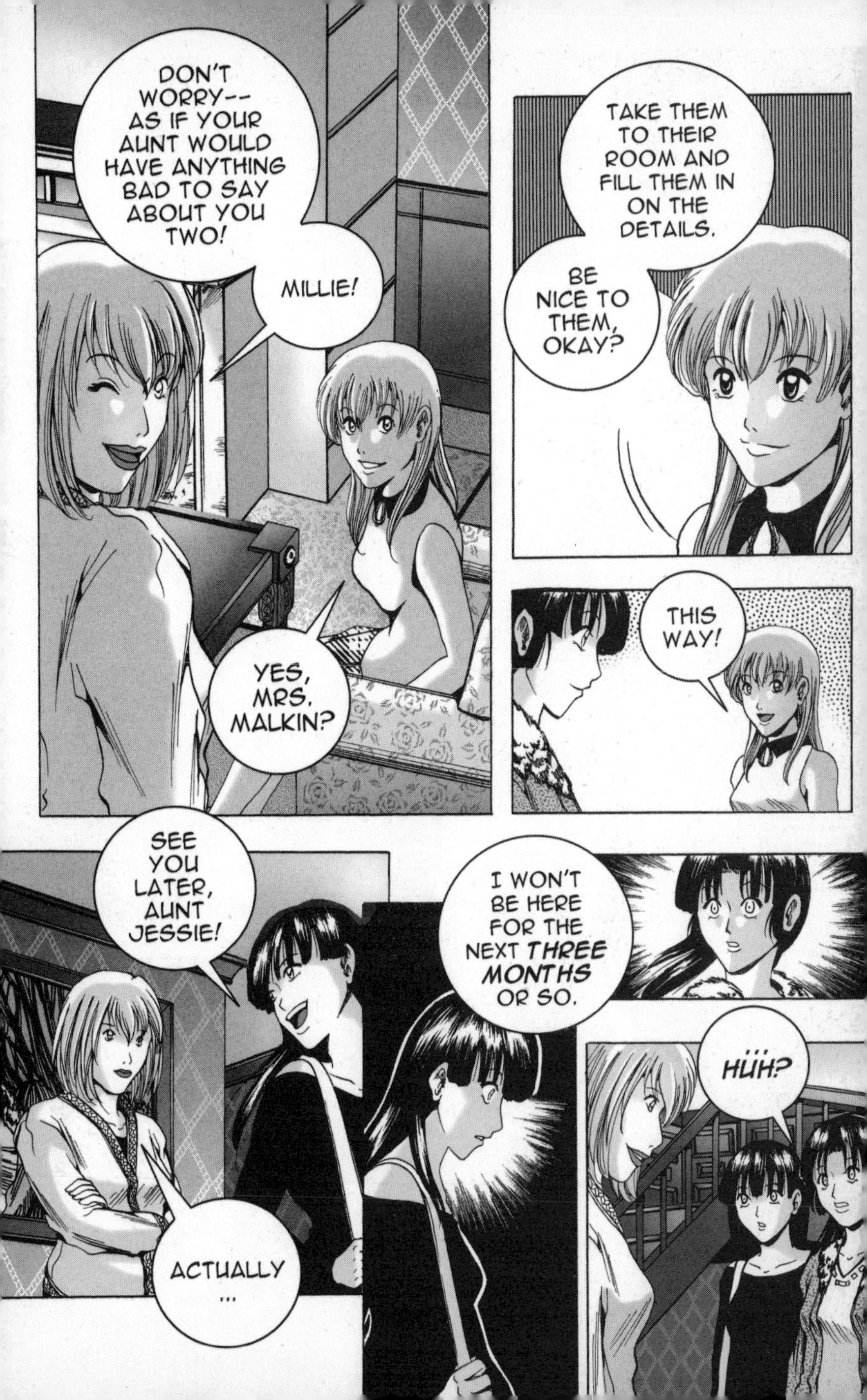
DON'T WORRY-- AS IF YOUR AUNT WOULD HAVE ANYTHING BAD TO SAY ABOUT YOU TWO!
MILLIE!
YES, MRS. MALKIN?
TAKE THEM TO THEIR ROOM AND FILL THEM IN ON THE DETAILS.
BE NICE TO THEM, OKAY?
THIS WAY!
SEE YOU LATER, AUNT JESSIE!
ACTUALLY ...
I WON'T BE HERE FOR THE NEXT *THREE MONTHS* OR SO.
... *HÜH?*

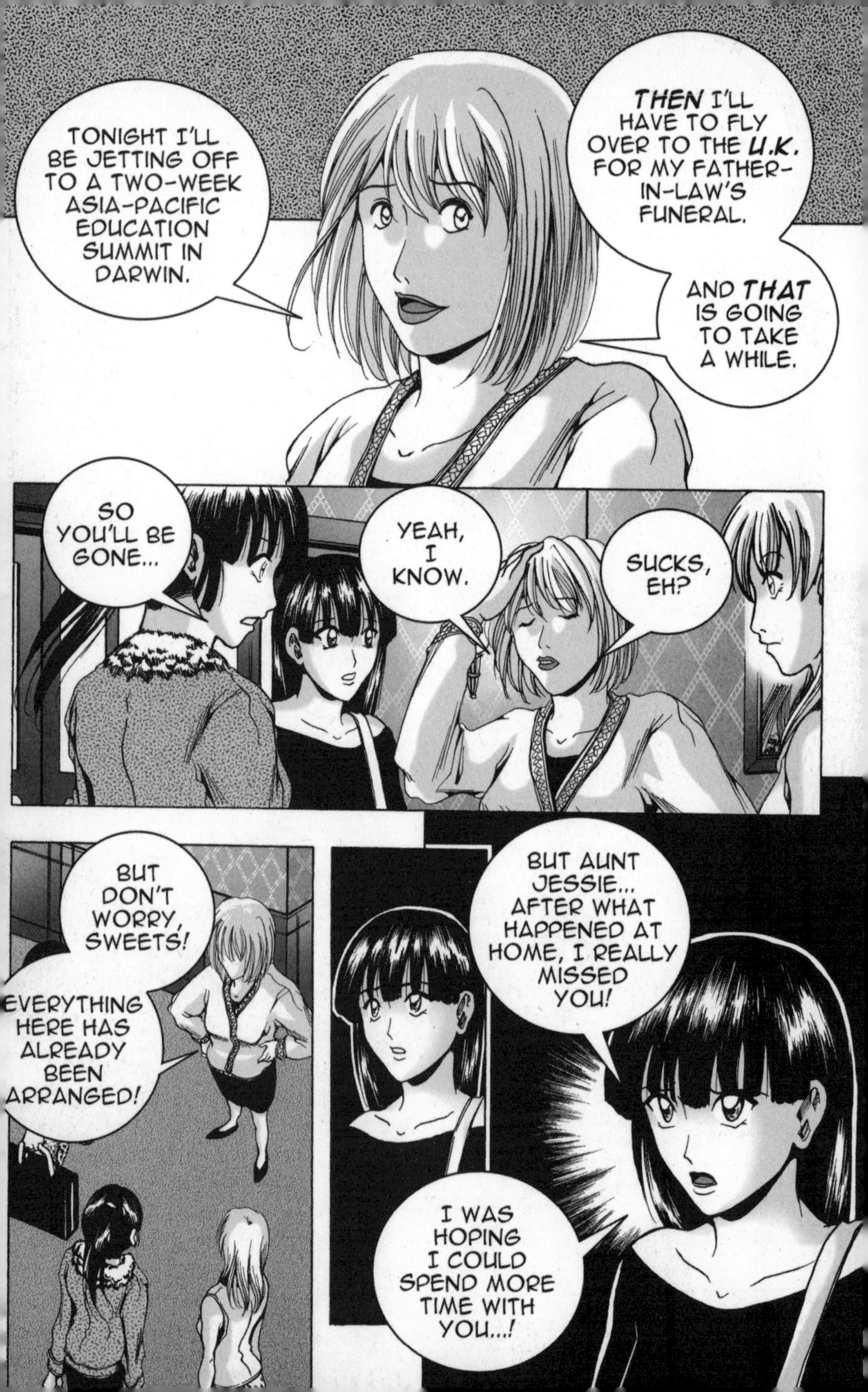
TONIGHT I'LL BE JETTING OFF TO A TWO-WEEK ASIA-PACIFIC EDUCATION SUMMIT IN DARWIN.
THEN I'LL HAVE TO FLY OVER TO THE U.K. FOR MY FATHER-IN-LAW'S FUNERAL.
AND THAT IS GOING TO TAKE A WHILE.
SO YOU'LL BE GONE...
YEAH, I KNOW.
SUCKS, EH?
BUT DON'T WORRY, SWEETS!
EVERYTHING HERE HAS ALREADY BEEN ARRANGED!
BUT AUNT JESSIE... AFTER WHAT HAPPENED AT HOME, I REALLY MISSED YOU!
I WAS HOPING I COULD SPEND MORE TIME WITH YOU...!

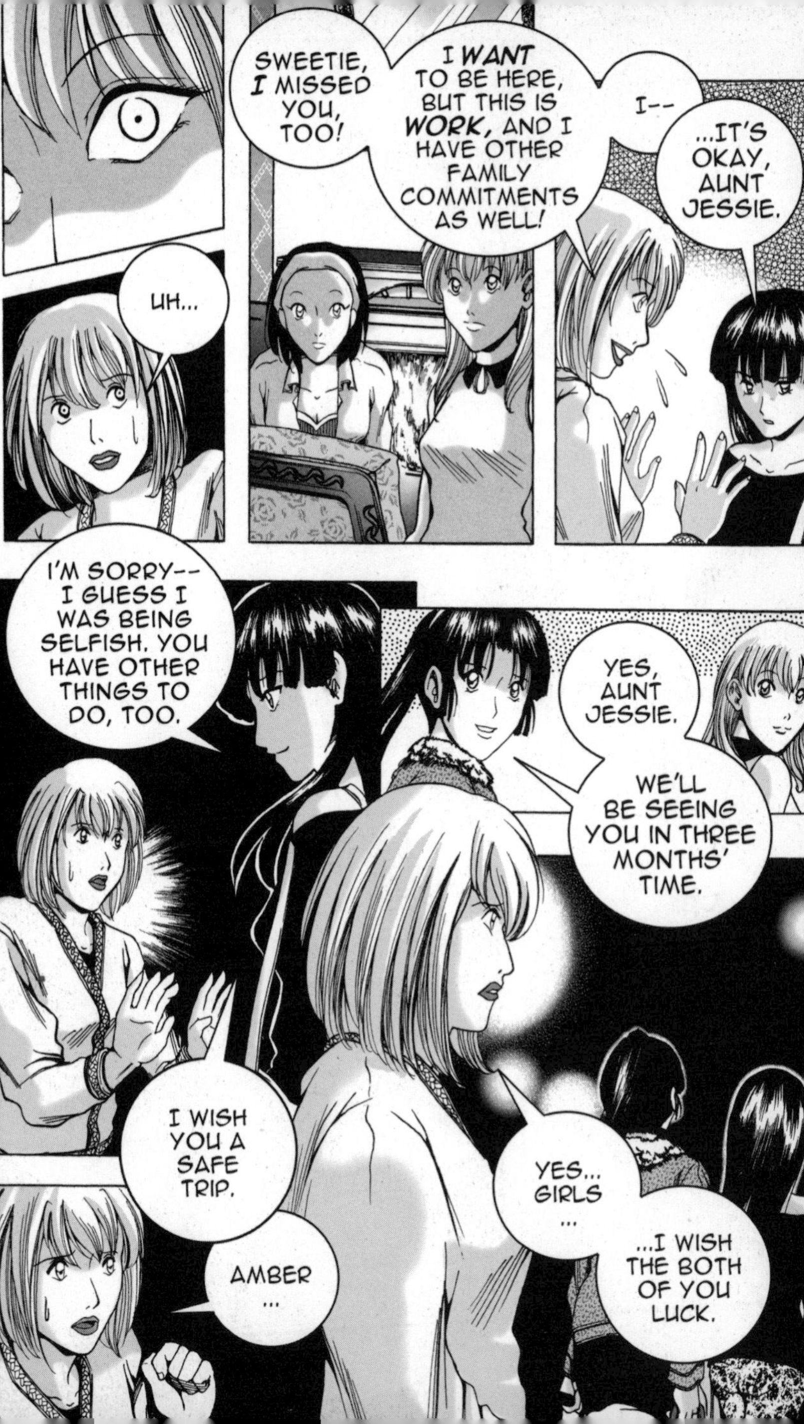
UH...
SWEETIE, I MISSED YOU, TOO!
I WANT TO BE HERE, BUT THIS IS WORK, AND I HAVE OTHER FAMILY COMMITMENTS AS WELL!
I--
...IT'S OKAY, AUNT JESSIE.
I'M SORRY-- I GUESS I WAS BEING SELFISH. YOU HAVE OTHER THINGS TO DO, TOO.
YES, AUNT JESSIE.
WE'LL BE SEEING YOU IN THREE MONTHS' TIME.
I WISH YOU A SAFE TRIP.
YES... GIRLS ...
...I WISH THE BOTH OF YOU LUCK.
AMBER ...

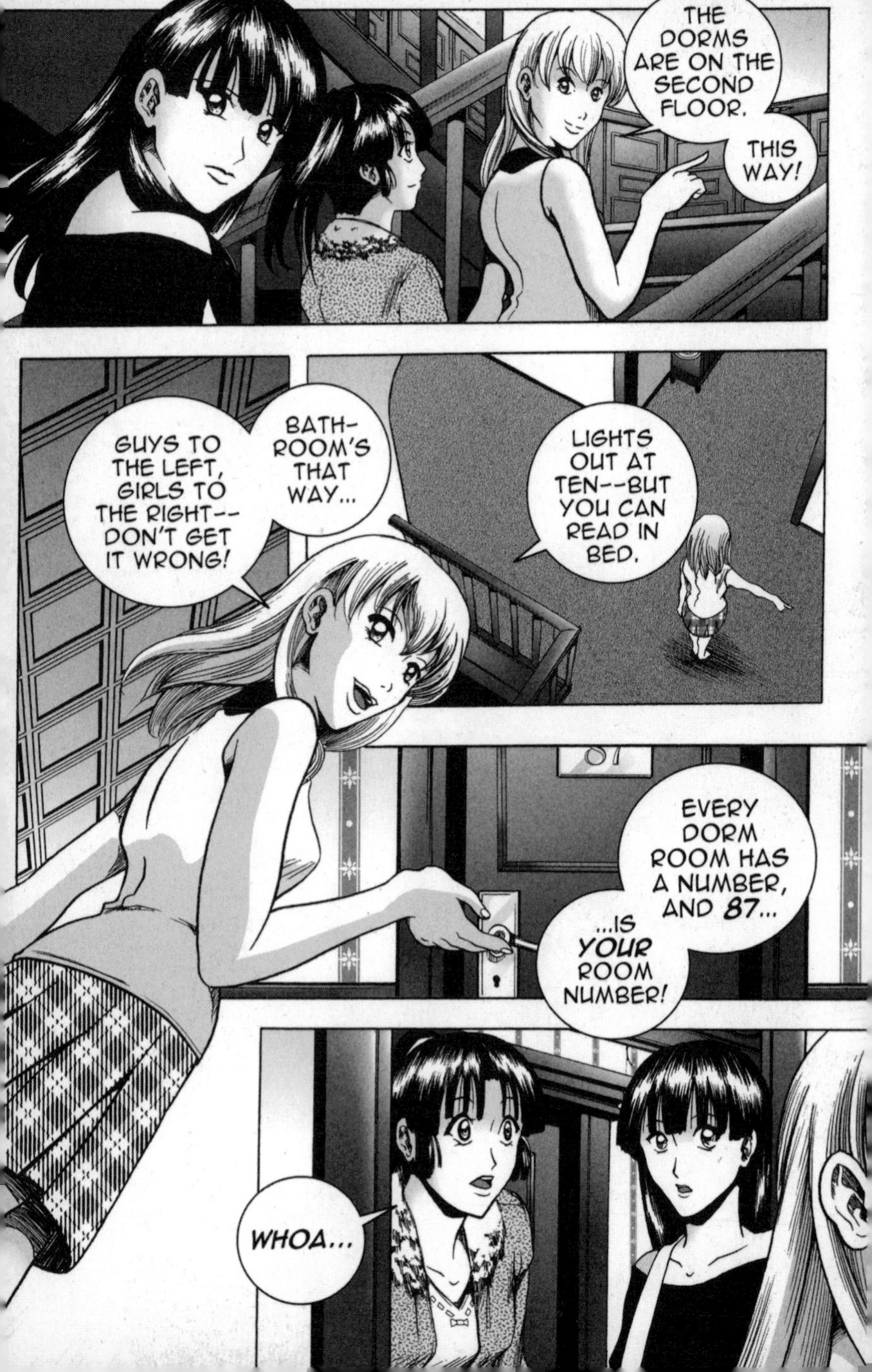
THE DORMS ARE ON THE SECOND FLOOR.
THIS WAY!
LIGHTS OUT AT TEN--BUT YOU CAN READ IN BED.
BATH-ROOM'S THAT WAY...
GUYS TO THE LEFT, GIRLS TO THE RIGHT--DON'T GET IT WRONG!
EVERY DORM ROOM HAS A NUMBER, AND 87...
...IS YOUR ROOM NUMBER!
WHOA...

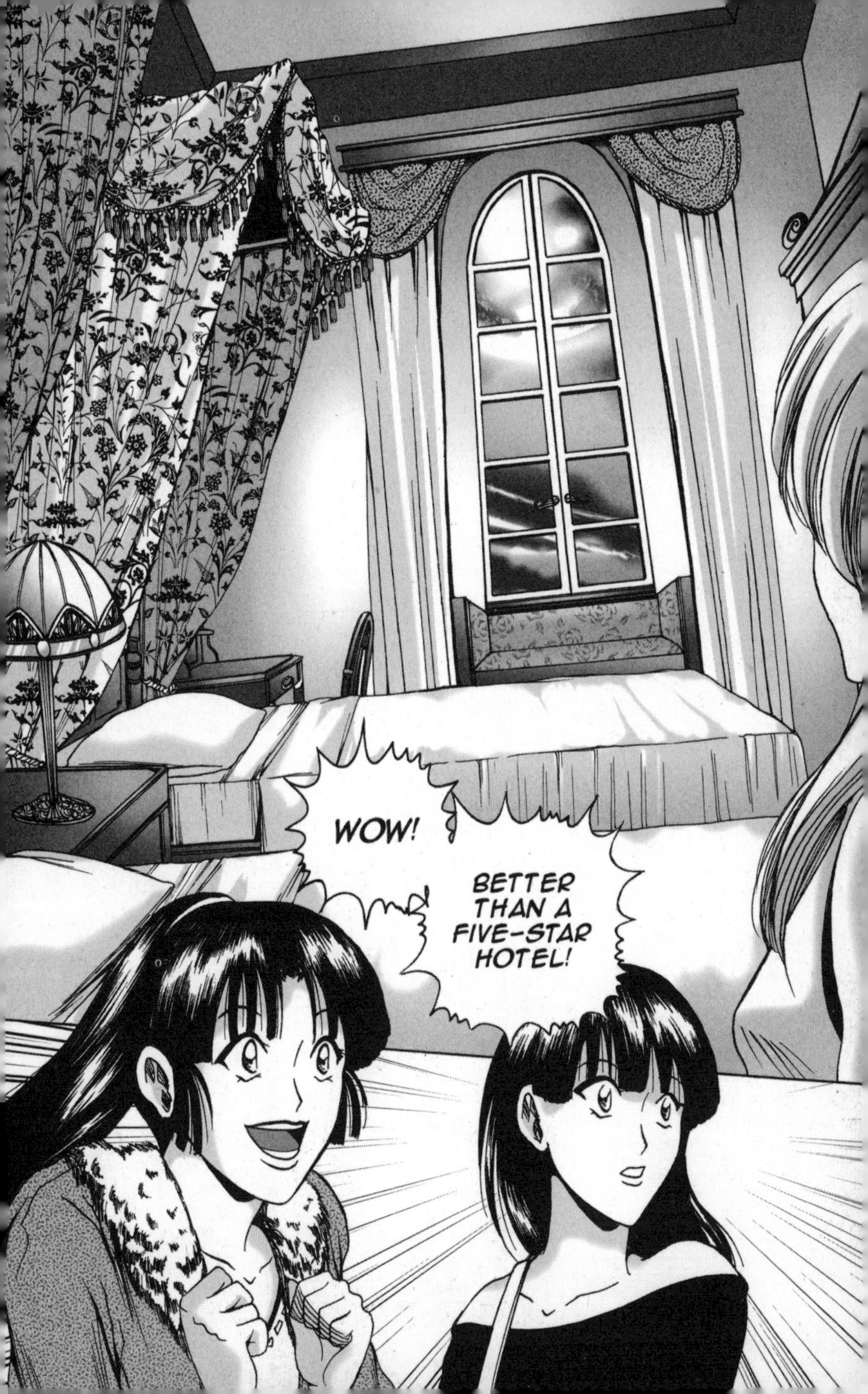
WOW!
BETTER THAN A FIVE-STAR HOTEL!

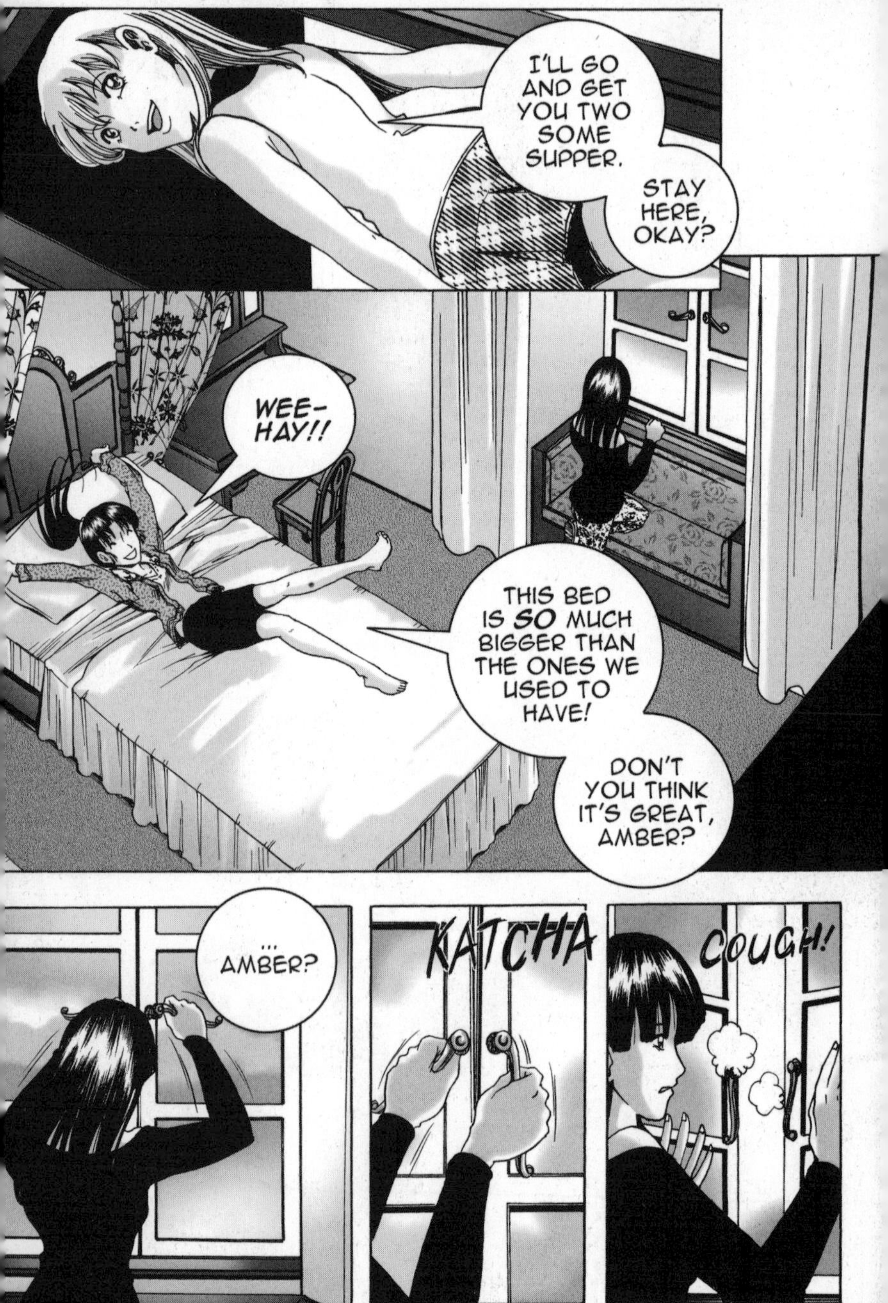
I'LL GO AND GET YOU TWO SOME SUPPER.
STAY HERE, OKAY?
WEE-HAY!!
THIS BED IS SO MUCH BIGGER THAN THE ONES WE USED TO HAVE!
DON'T YOU THINK IT'S GREAT, AMBER?
... AMBER?
KATCHA
COUGH!

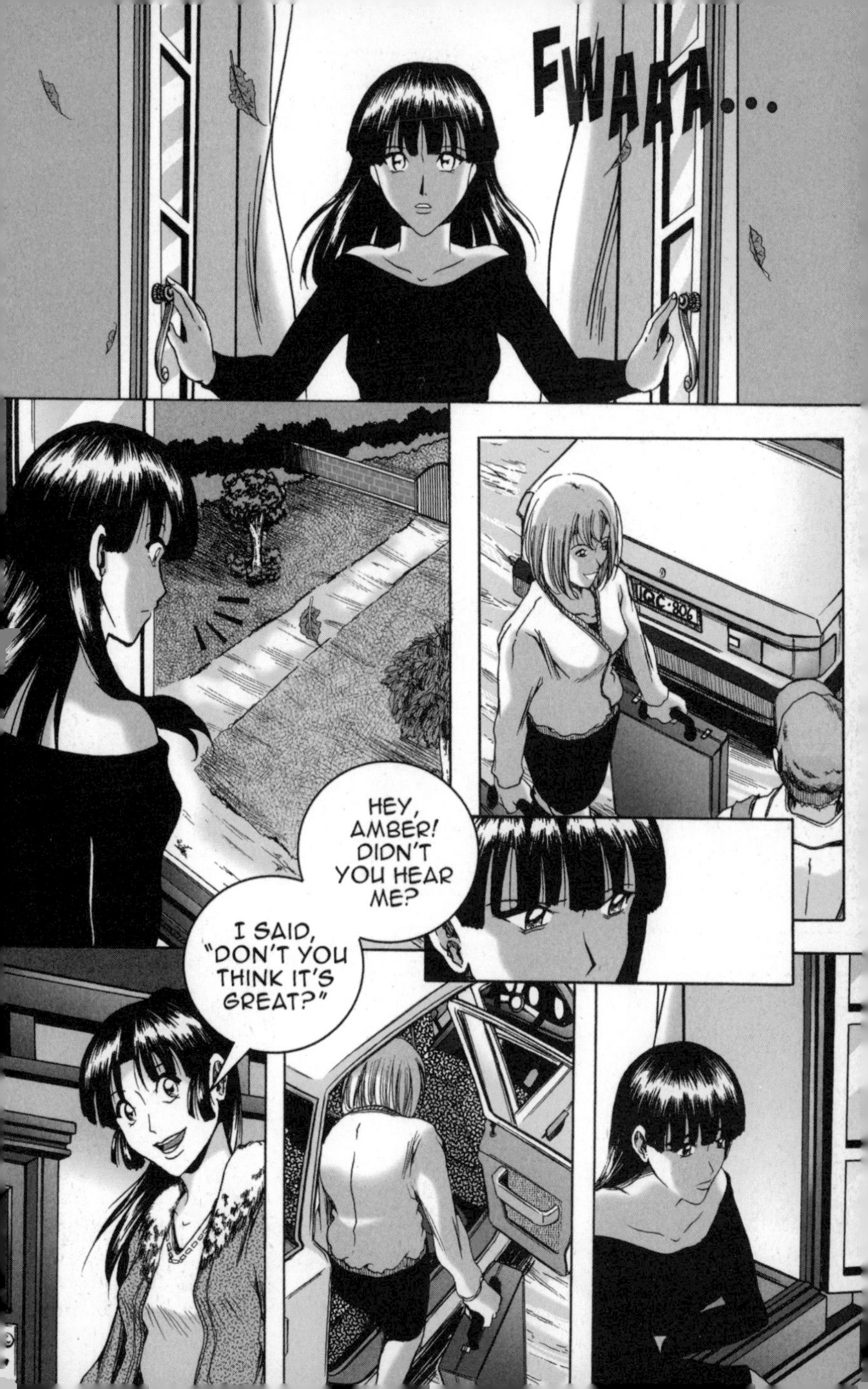
FWAAA...
HEY, AMBER! DIDN'T YOU HEAR ME?
I SAID, "DON'T YOU THINK IT'S GREAT?"

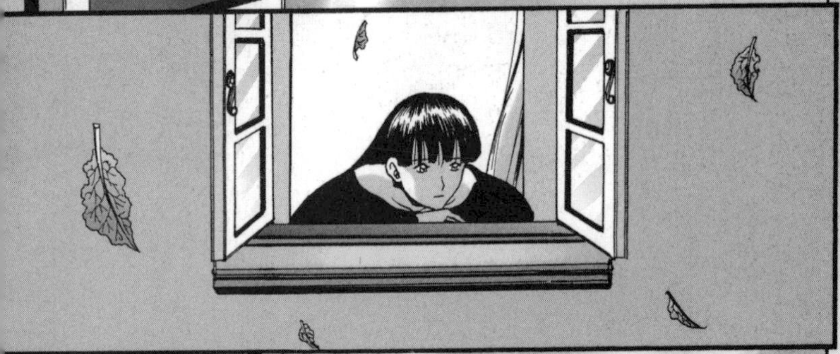

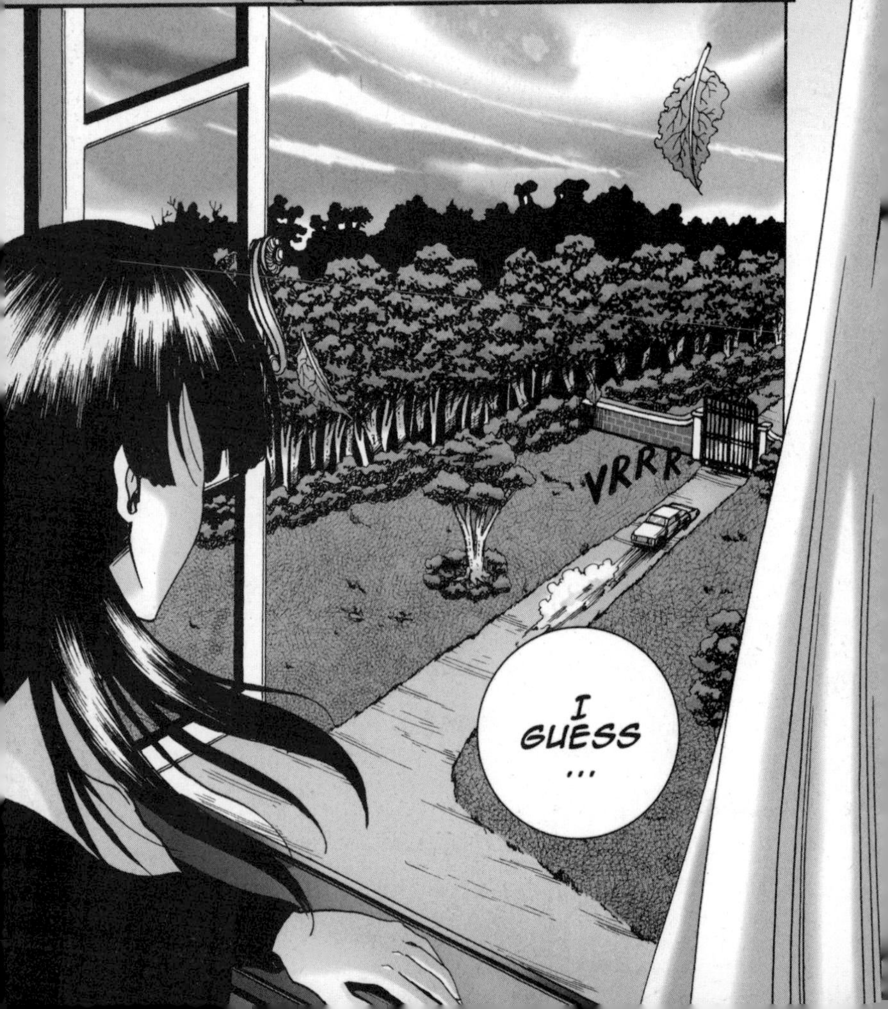
VRRR
I GUESS ...

Chapter 2
The Door

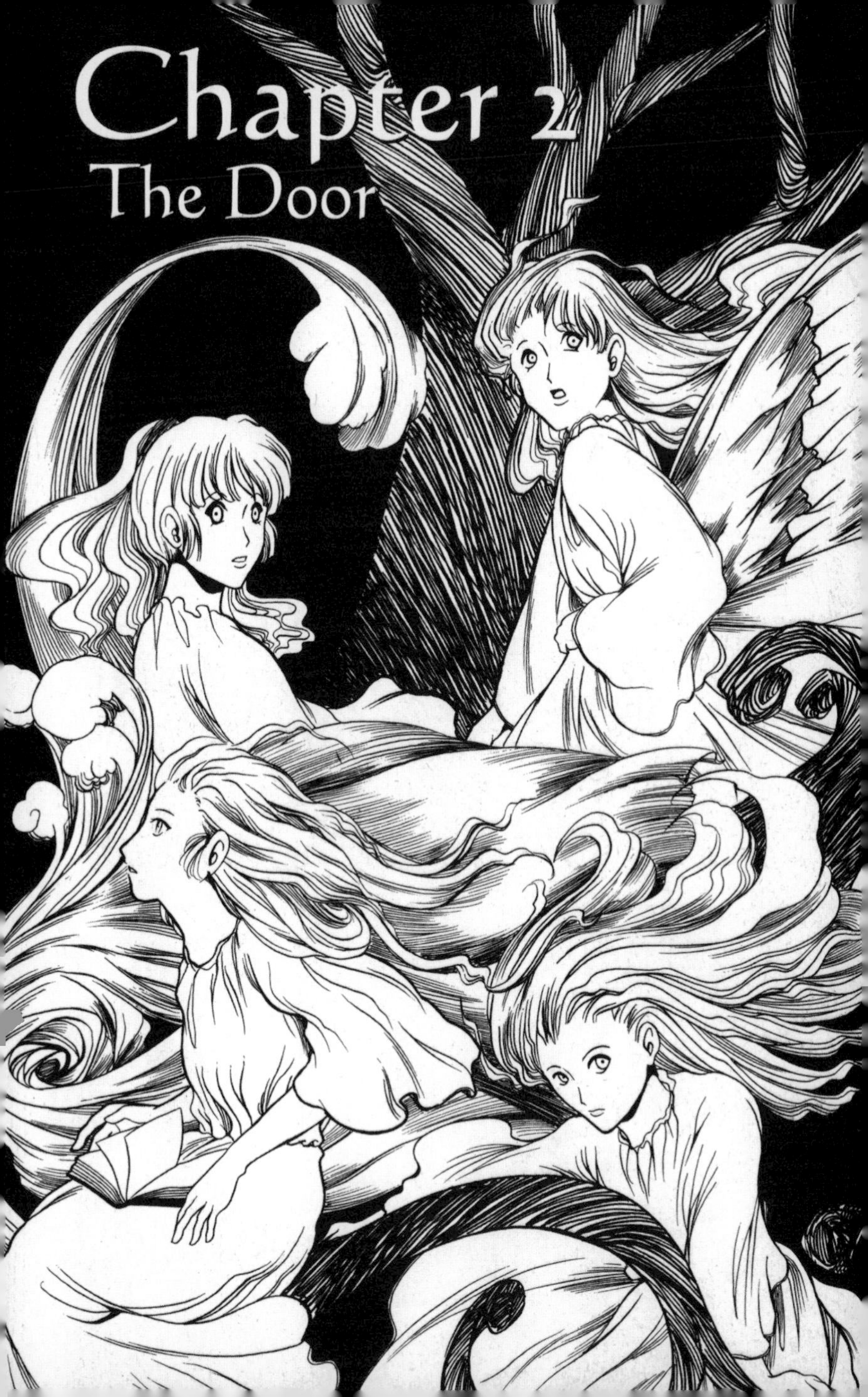

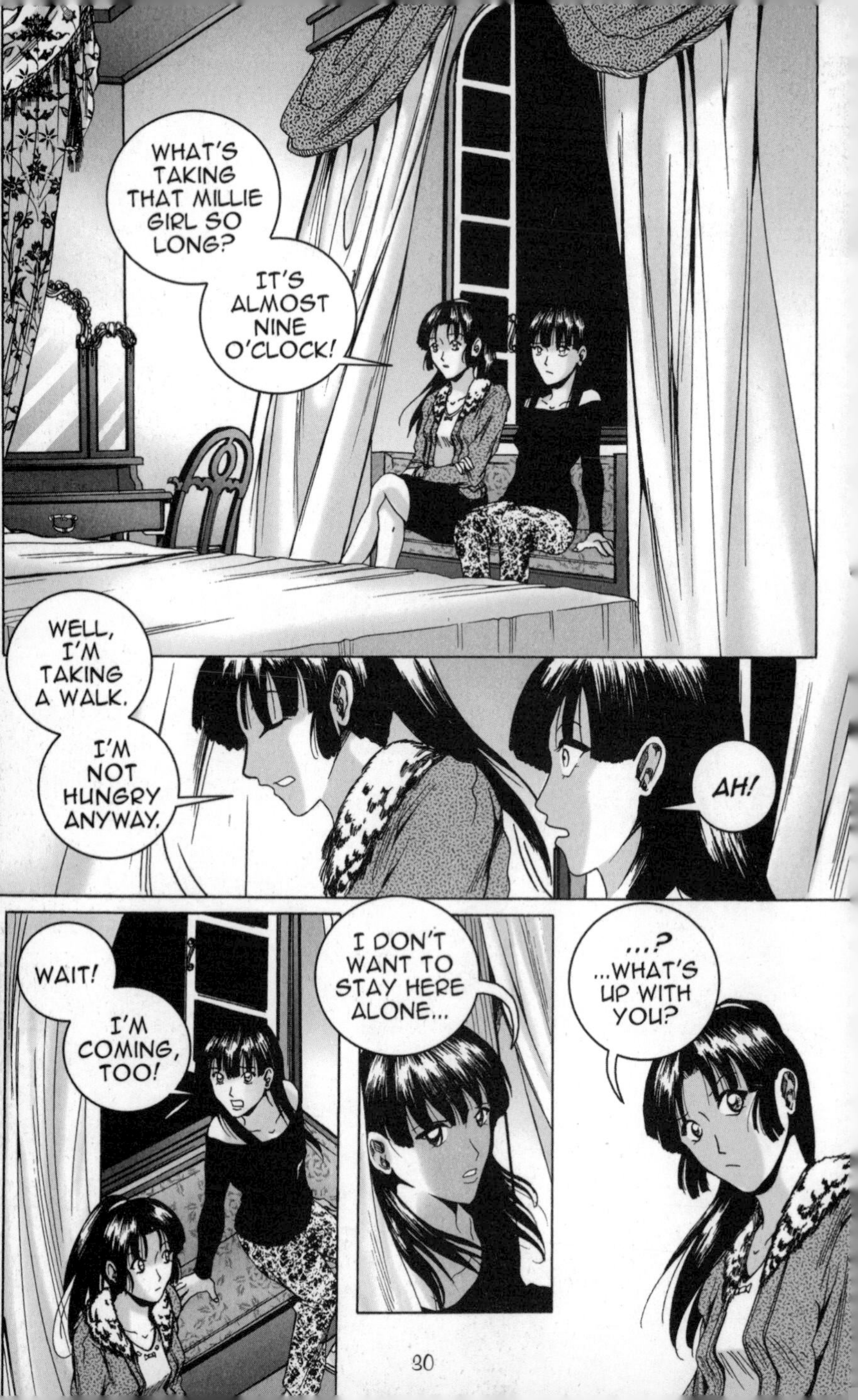
WHAT'S TAKING THAT MILLIE GIRL SO LONG?
IT'S ALMOST NINE O'CLOCK!
WELL, I'M TAKING A WALK.
I'M NOT HUNGRY ANYWAY.
AH!
WAIT!
I'M COMING, TOO!
I DON'T WANT TO STAY HERE ALONE...
...?
...WHAT'S UP WITH YOU?

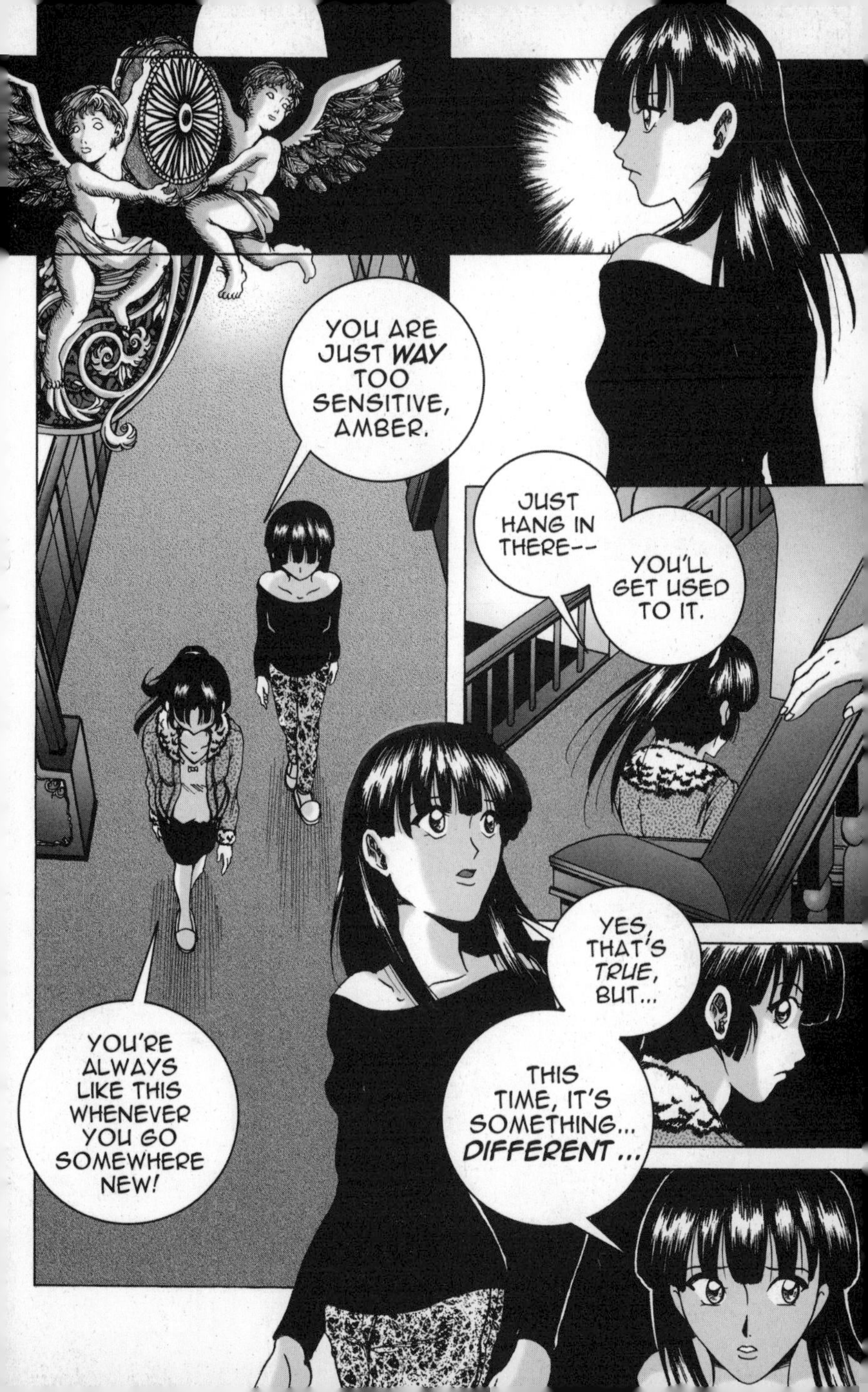
YOU ARE JUST WAY TOO SENSITIVE, AMBER.
YOU'RE ALWAYS LIKE THIS WHENEVER YOU GO SOMEWHERE NEW!
JUST HANG IN THERE--
YOU'LL GET USED TO IT.
YES, THAT'S TRUE, BUT...
THIS TIME, IT'S SOMETHING... DIFFERENT...

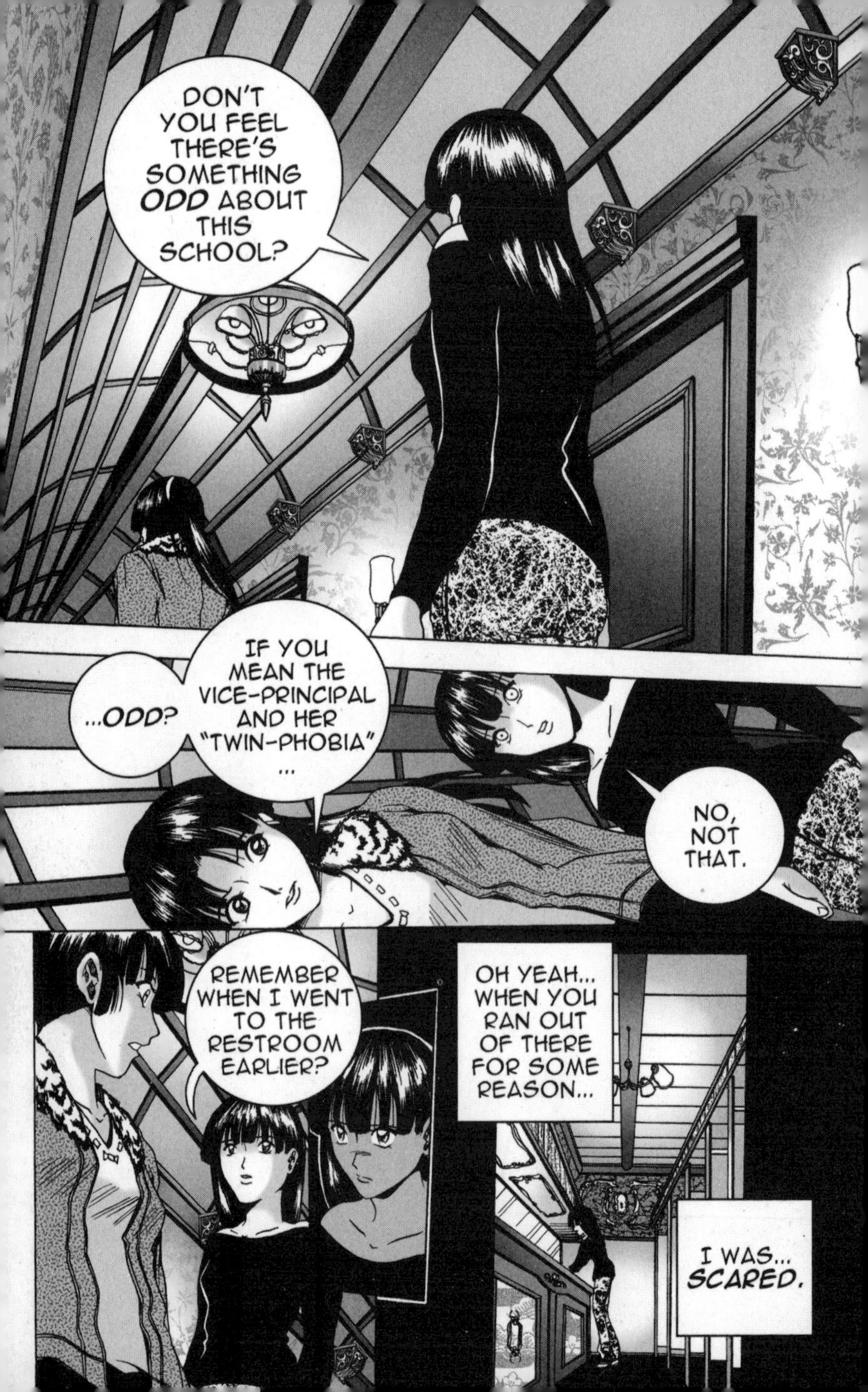
DON'T YOU FEEL THERE'S SOMETHING ODD ABOUT THIS SCHOOL?
...ODD?
IF YOU MEAN THE VICE-PRINCIPAL AND HER "TWIN-PHOBIA" ...
NO, NOT THAT.
REMEMBER WHEN I WENT TO THE RESTROOM EARLIER?
OH YEAH... WHEN YOU RAN OUT OF THERE FOR SOME REASON...
I WAS... SCARED.

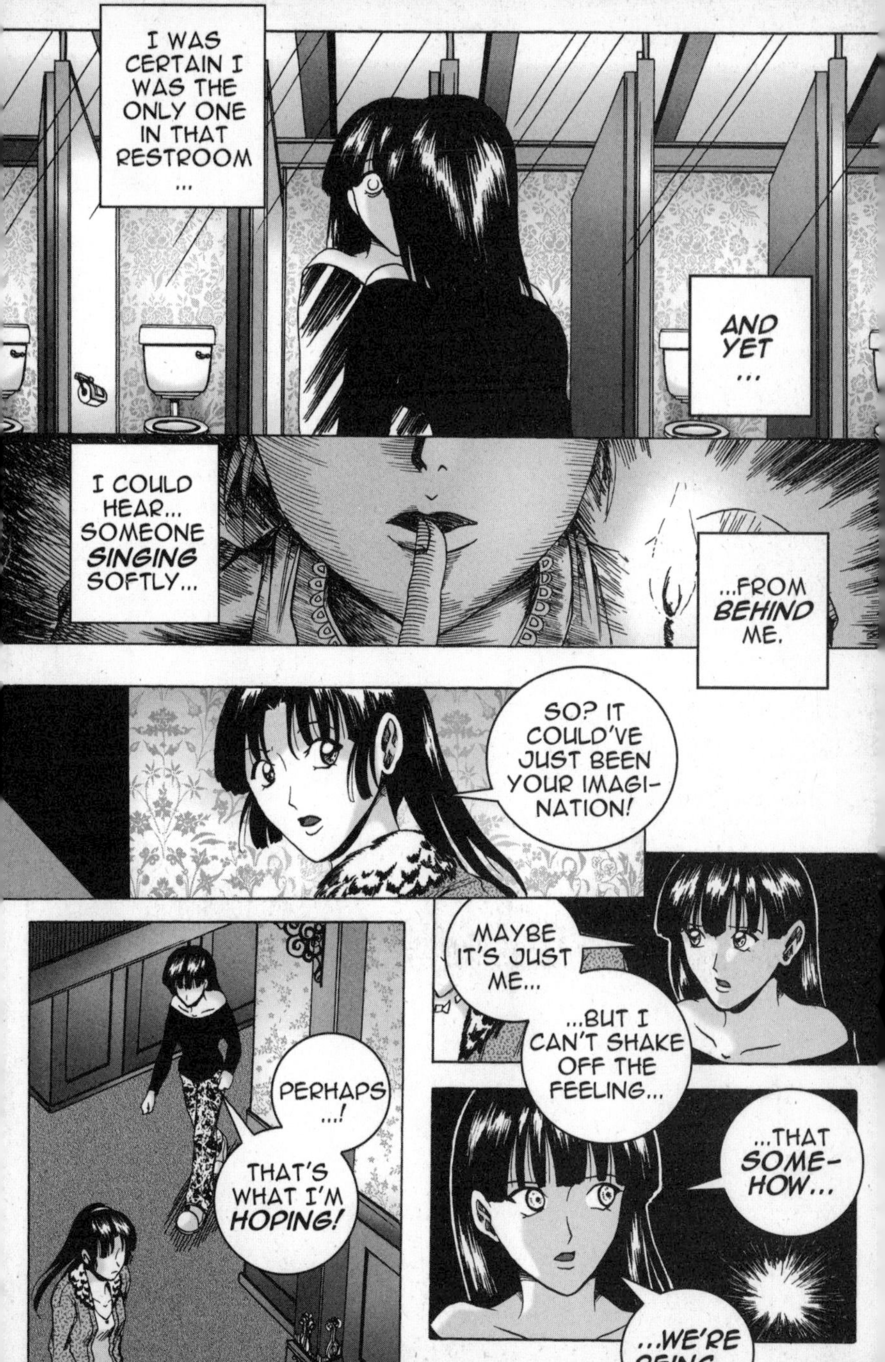
I WAS CERTAIN I WAS THE ONLY ONE IN THAT RESTROOM ...
AND YET ...
I COULD HEAR... SOMEONE SINGING SOFTLY...
...FROM BEHIND ME.
SO? IT COULD'VE JUST BEEN YOUR IMAGINATION!
MAYBE IT'S JUST ME...
...BUT I CAN'T SHAKE OFF THE FEELING...
...THAT SOMEHOW...
...WE'RE BEING...
PERHAPS ...!
THAT'S WHAT I'M HOPING!

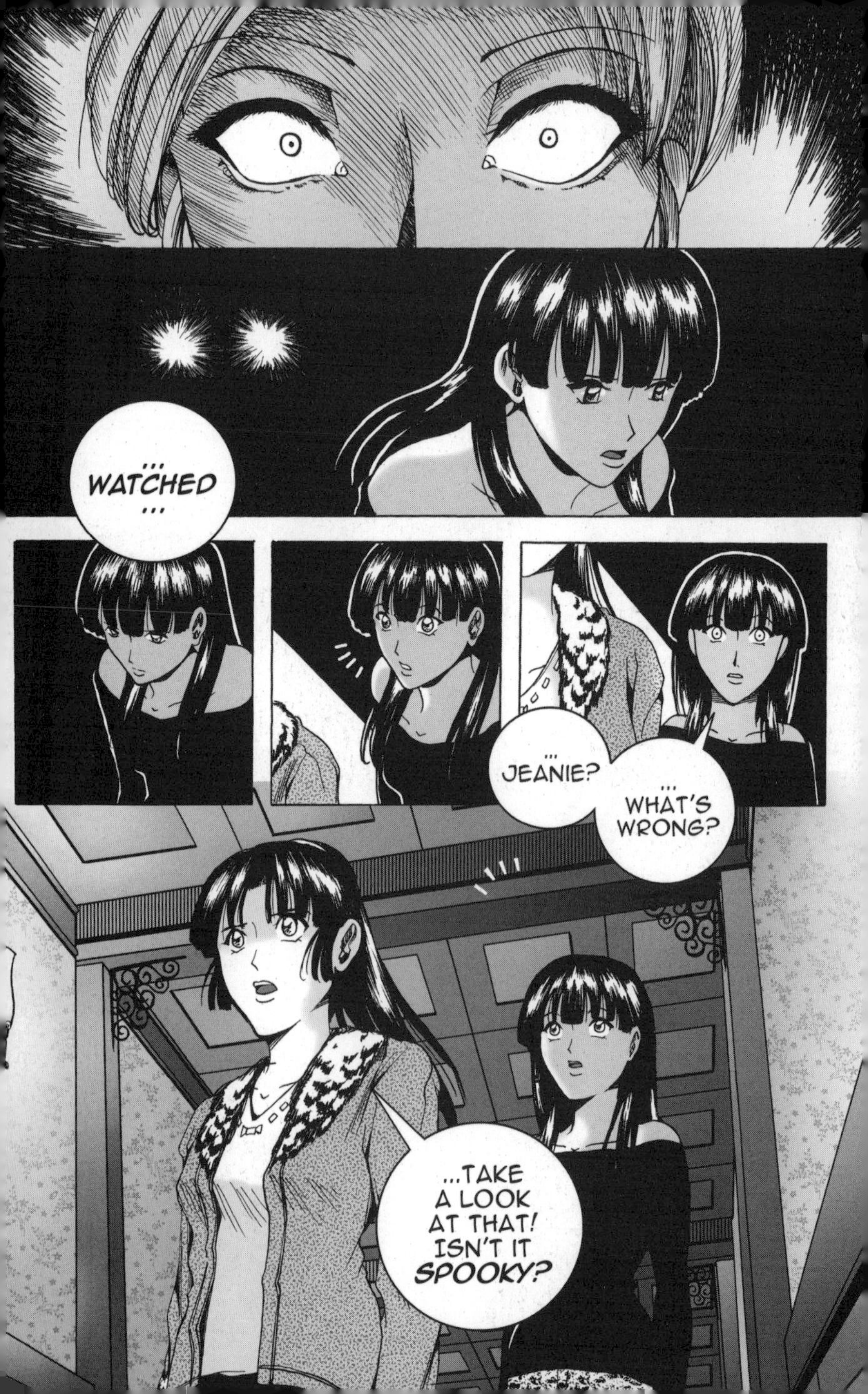
...WATCHED...
...JEANIE?
...WHAT'S WRONG?
...TAKE A LOOK AT THAT! ISN'T IT *SPOOKY?*

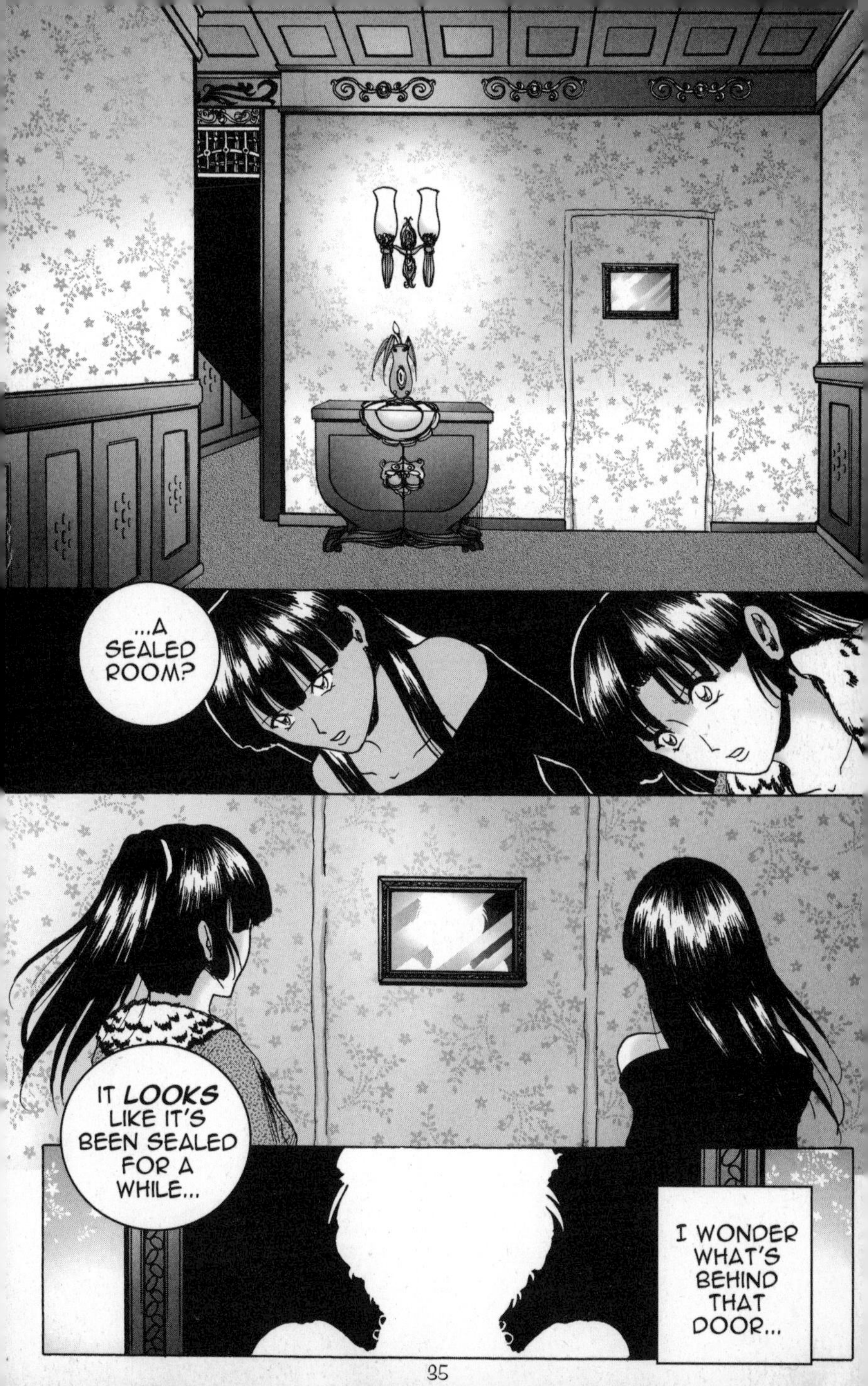
...A SEALED ROOM?
IT LOOKS LIKE IT'S BEEN SEALED FOR A WHILE...
I WONDER WHAT'S BEHIND THAT DOOR...

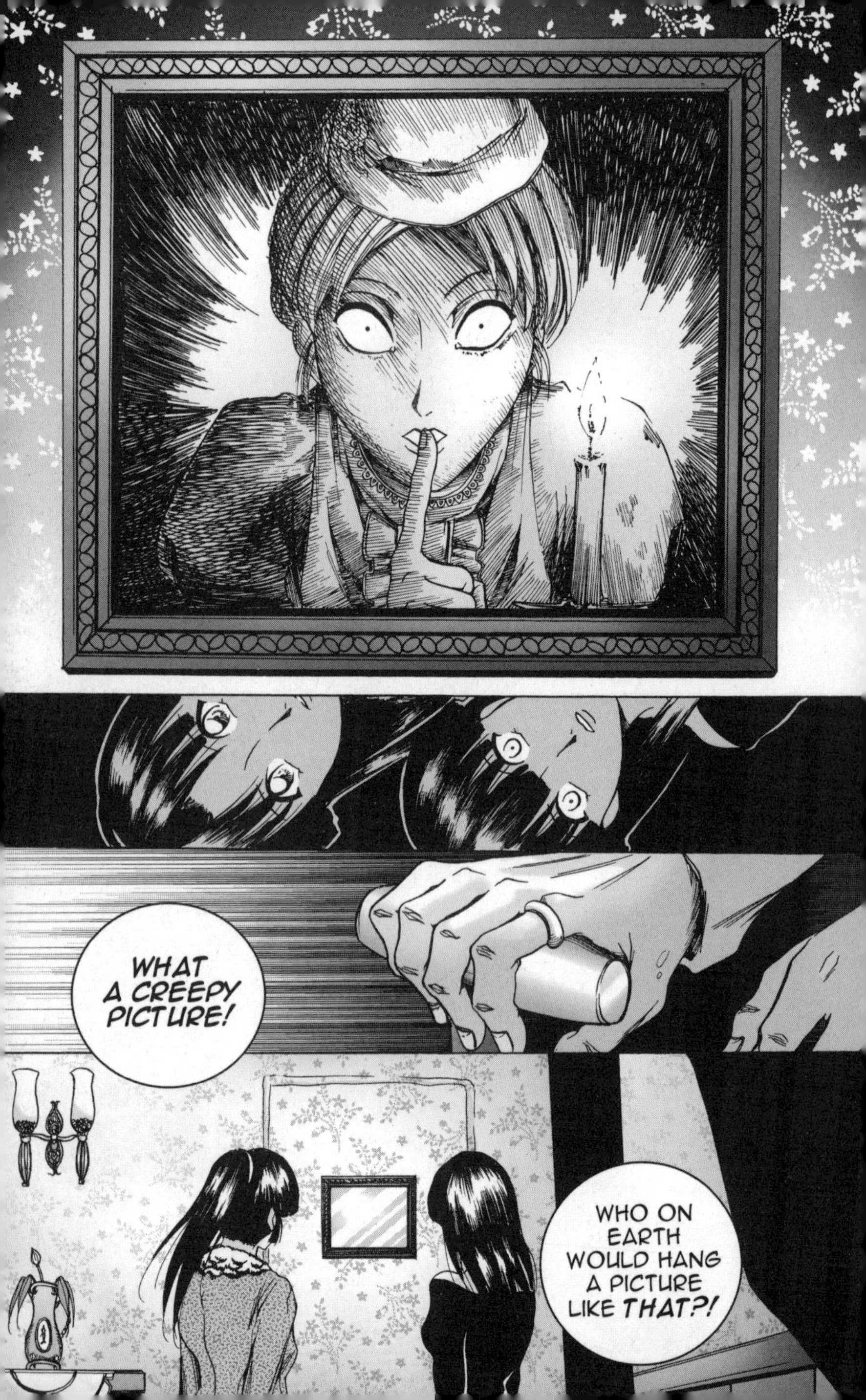
WHAT A CREEPY PICTURE!
WHO ON EARTH WOULD HANG A PICTURE LIKE *THAT?!*

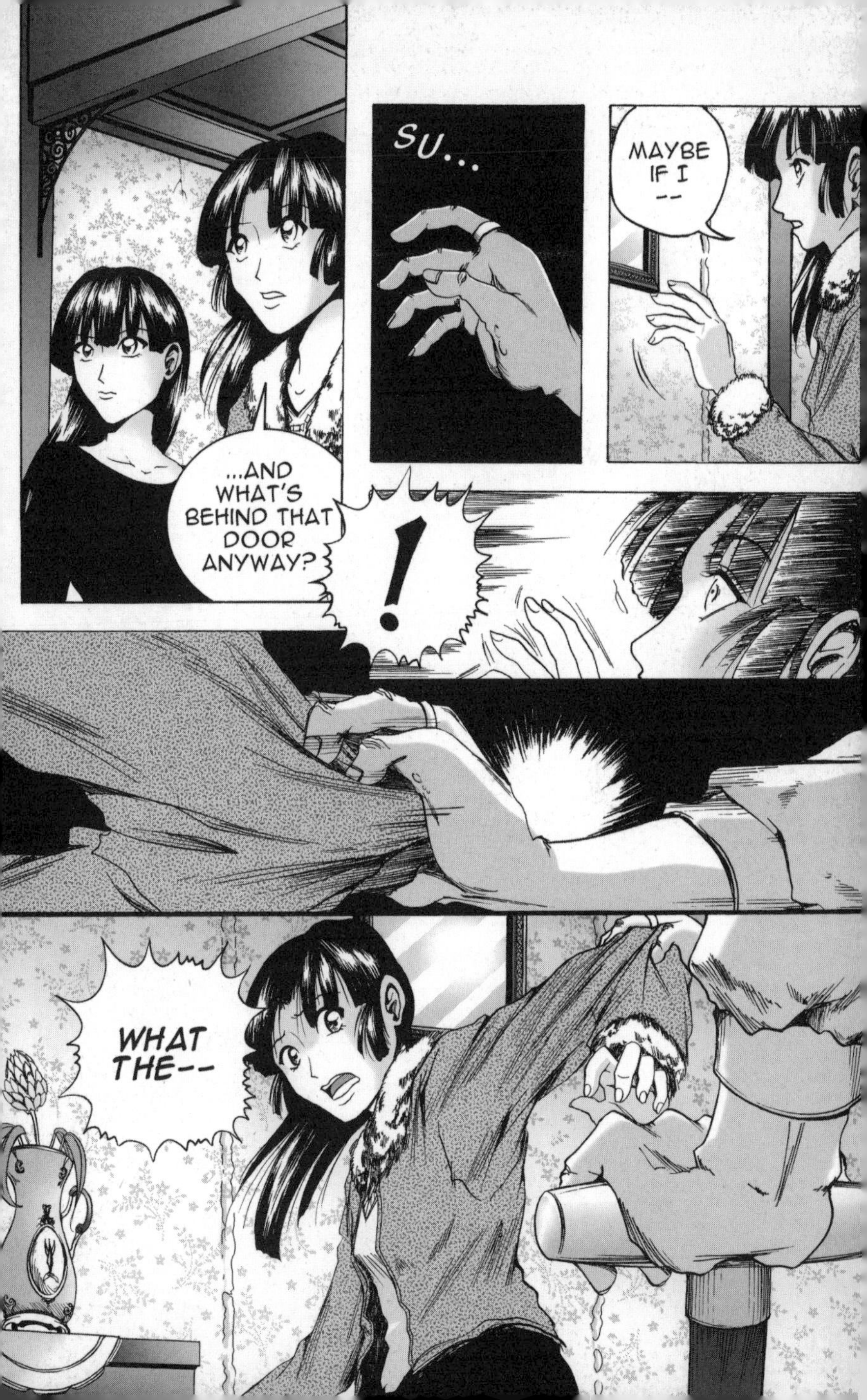
MAYBE IF I --
SU...
!
...AND WHAT'S BEHIND THAT DOOR ANYWAY?
WHAT THE--

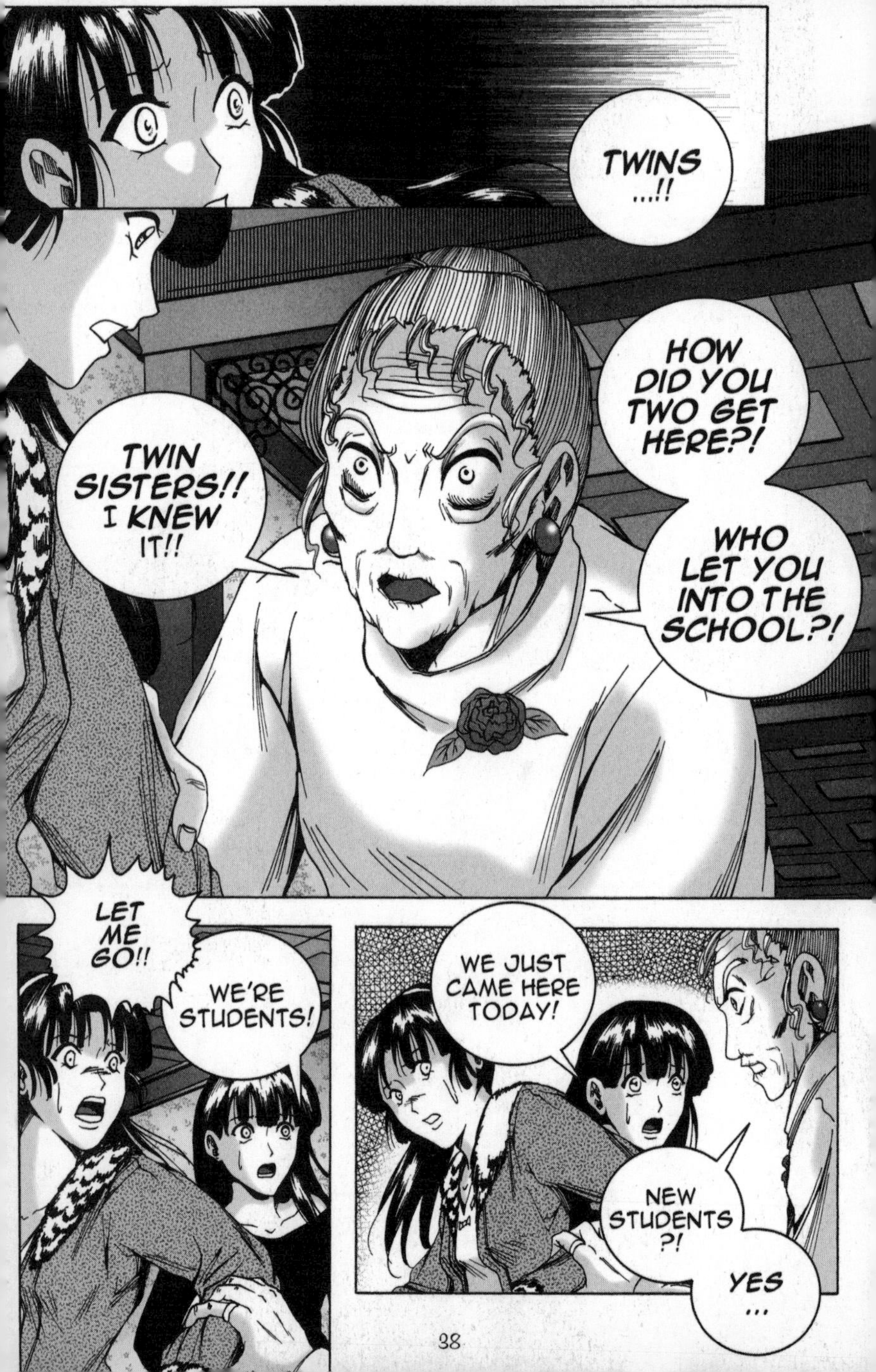
TWINS ...!!
TWIN SISTERS!! I KNEW IT!!
HOW DID YOU TWO GET HERE?!
WHO LET YOU INTO THE SCHOOL?!
LET ME GO!!
WE'RE STUDENTS!
WE JUST CAME HERE TODAY!
NEW STUDENTS ?!
YES ...

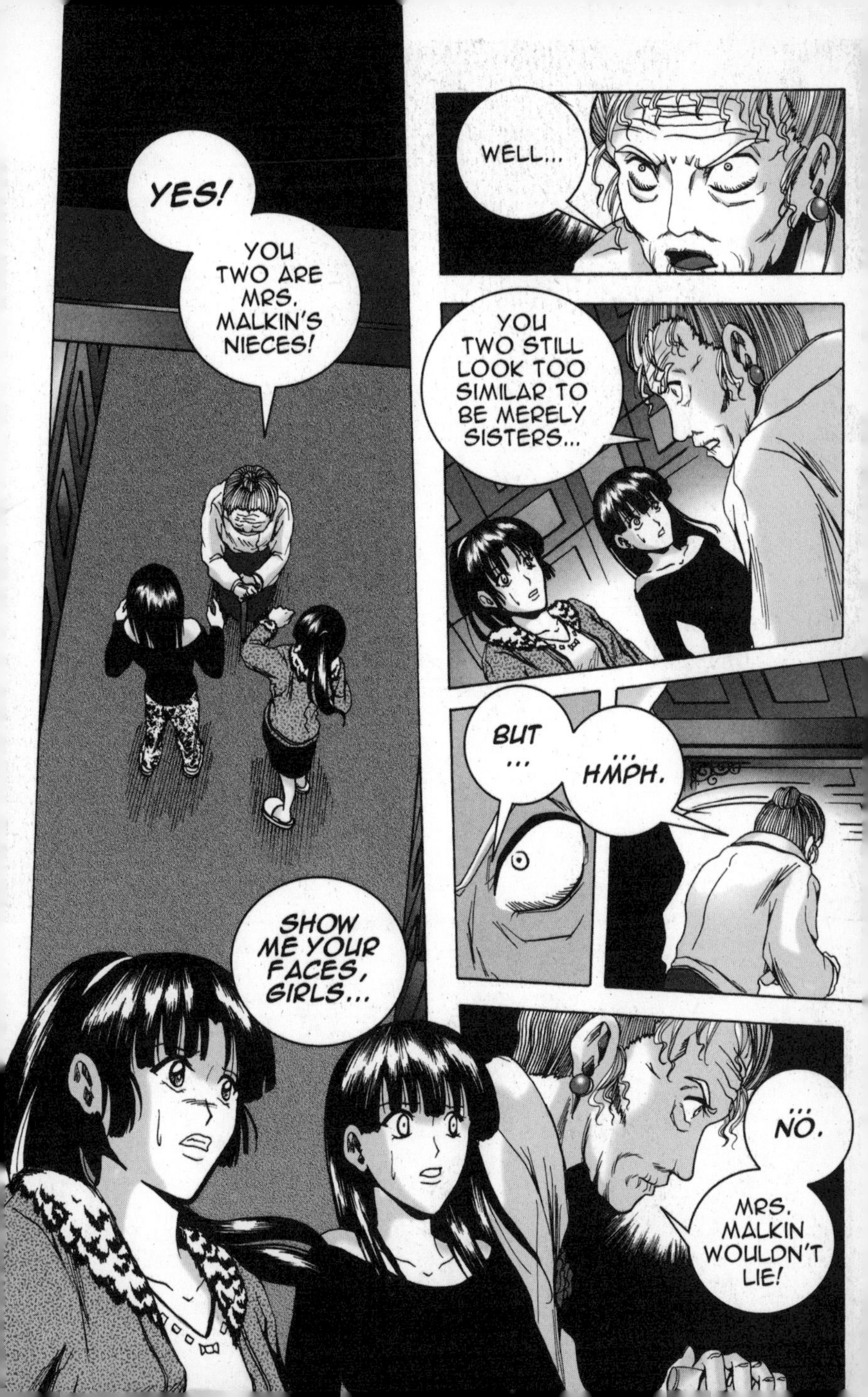
YES!
YOU TWO ARE MRS. MALKIN'S NIECES!
SHOW ME YOUR FACES, GIRLS...
WELL...
YOU TWO STILL LOOK TOO SIMILAR TO BE MERELY SISTERS...
BUT ...
... HMPH.
... NO.
MRS. MALKIN WOULDN'T LIE!

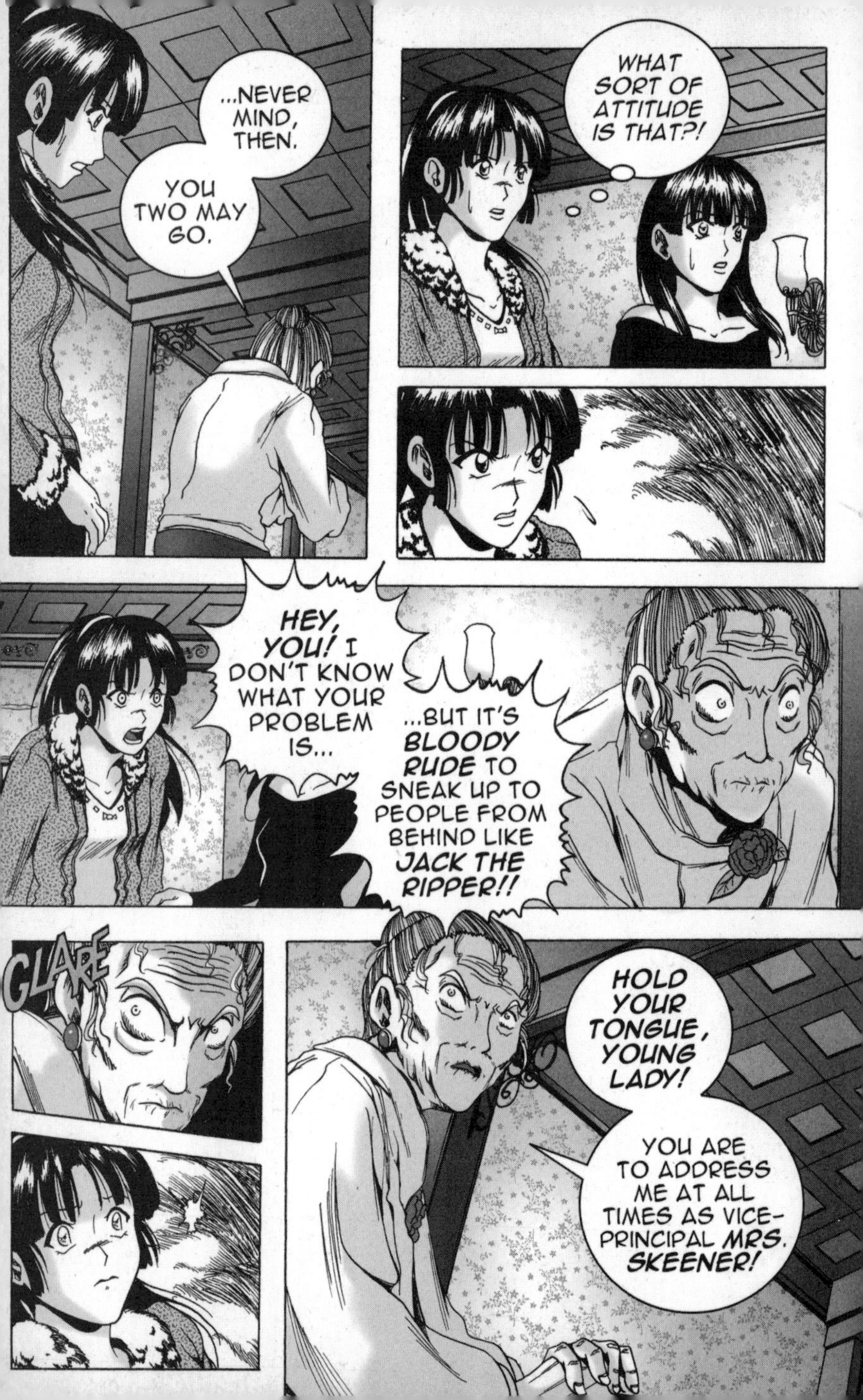
...NEVER MIND, THEN.
YOU TWO MAY GO.
WHAT SORT OF ATTITUDE IS THAT?!
HEY, YOU! I DON'T KNOW WHAT YOUR PROBLEM IS...
...BUT IT'S BLOODY RUDE TO SNEAK UP TO PEOPLE FROM BEHIND LIKE JACK THE RIPPER!!
GLARE
HOLD YOUR TONGUE, YOUNG LADY!
YOU ARE TO ADDRESS ME AT ALL TIMES AS VICE-PRINCIPAL MRS. SKEENER!

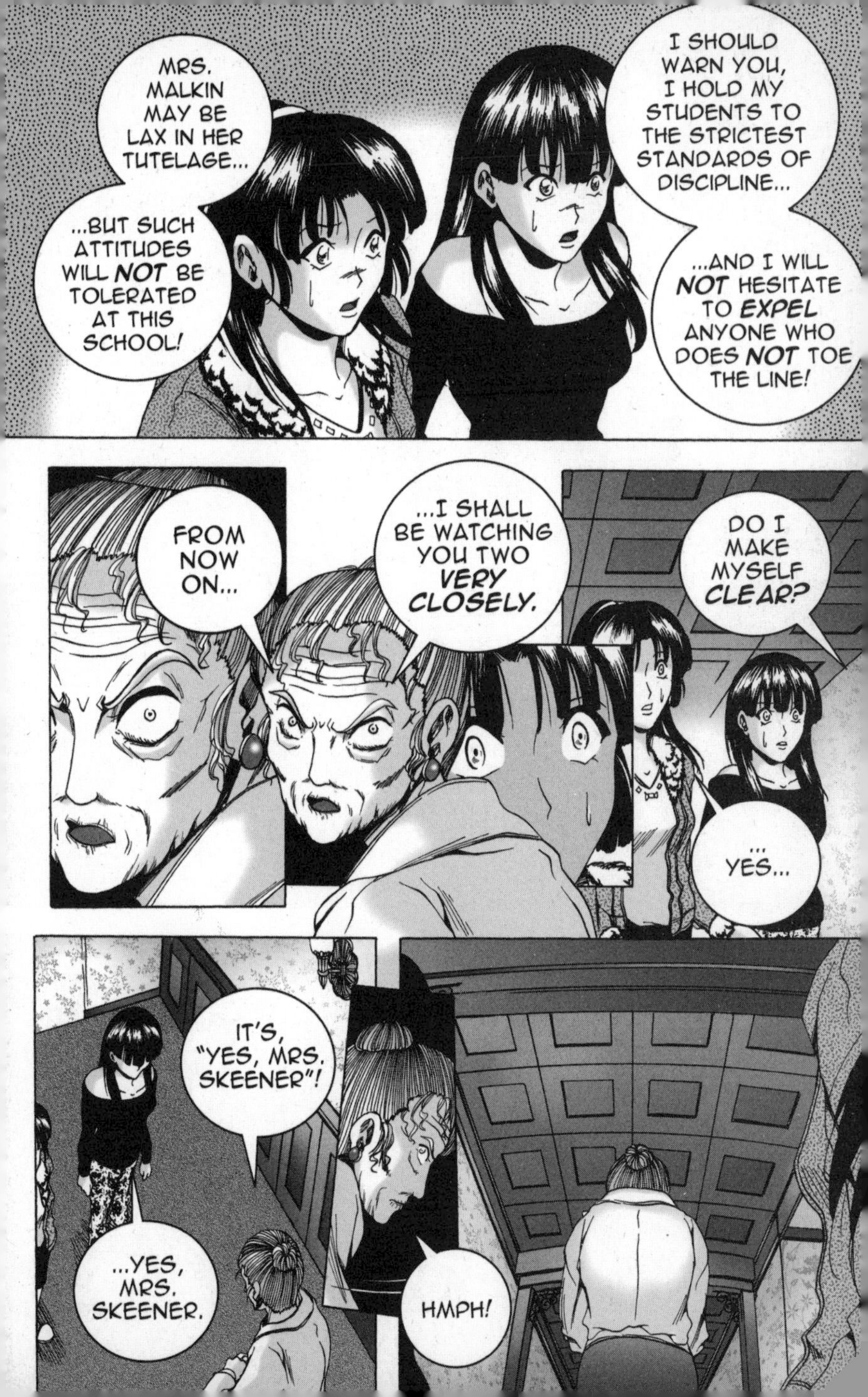
MRS. MALKIN MAY BE LAX IN HER TUTELAGE...
...BUT SUCH ATTITUDES WILL NOT BE TOLERATED AT THIS SCHOOL!
I SHOULD WARN YOU, I HOLD MY STUDENTS TO THE STRICTEST STANDARDS OF DISCIPLINE...
...AND I WILL NOT HESITATE TO EXPEL ANYONE WHO DOES NOT TOE THE LINE!
FROM NOW ON...
...I SHALL BE WATCHING YOU TWO VERY CLOSELY.
DO I MAKE MYSELF CLEAR?
... YES...
IT'S, "YES, MRS. SKEENER"!
...YES, MRS. SKEENER.
HMPH!

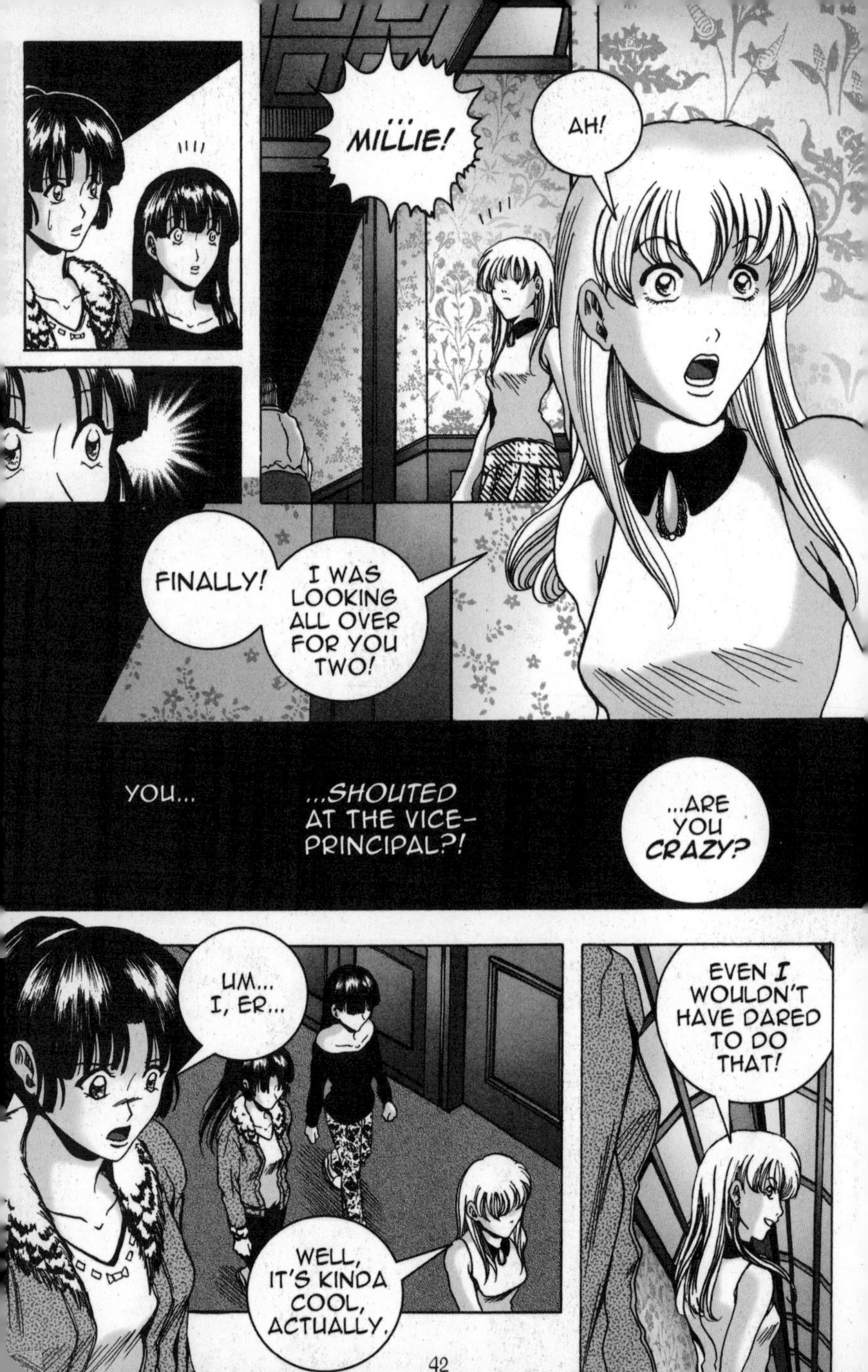
...MILLIE!
AH!
FINALLY!
I WAS LOOKING ALL OVER FOR YOU TWO!
YOU...
...SHOUTED AT THE VICE-PRINCIPAL?!
...ARE YOU CRAZY?
UM... I, ER...
WELL, IT'S KINDA COOL, ACTUALLY.
EVEN I WOULDN'T HAVE DARED TO DO THAT!

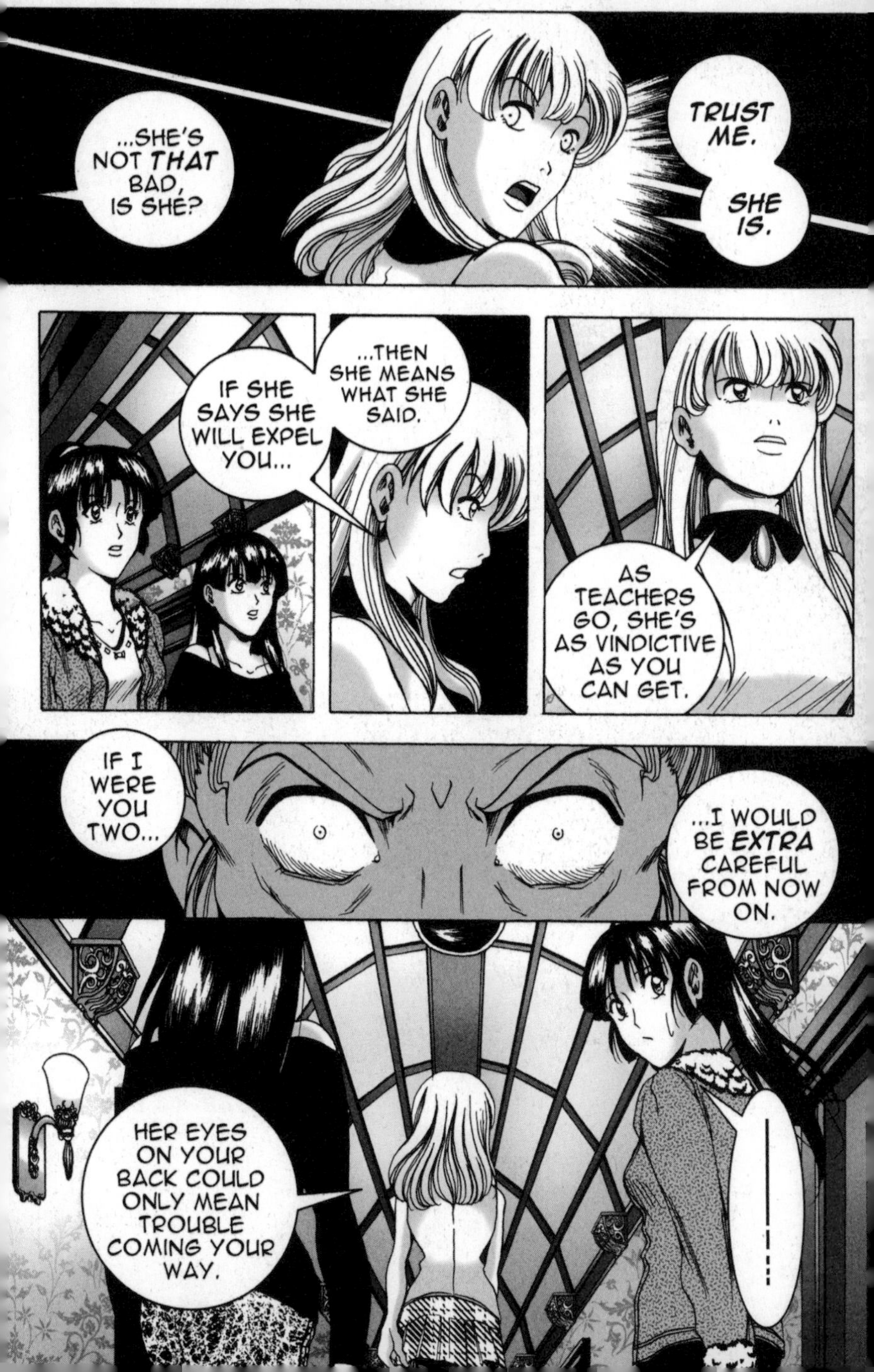
...SHE'S NOT **THAT** BAD, IS SHE?
TRUST ME.
SHE IS.
IF SHE SAYS SHE WILL EXPEL YOU...
...THEN SHE MEANS WHAT SHE SAID.
AS TEACHERS GO, SHE'S AS VINDICTIVE AS YOU CAN GET.
IF I WERE YOU TWO...
...I WOULD BE **EXTRA** CAREFUL FROM NOW ON.
HER EYES ON YOUR BACK COULD ONLY MEAN TROUBLE COMING YOUR WAY.
......

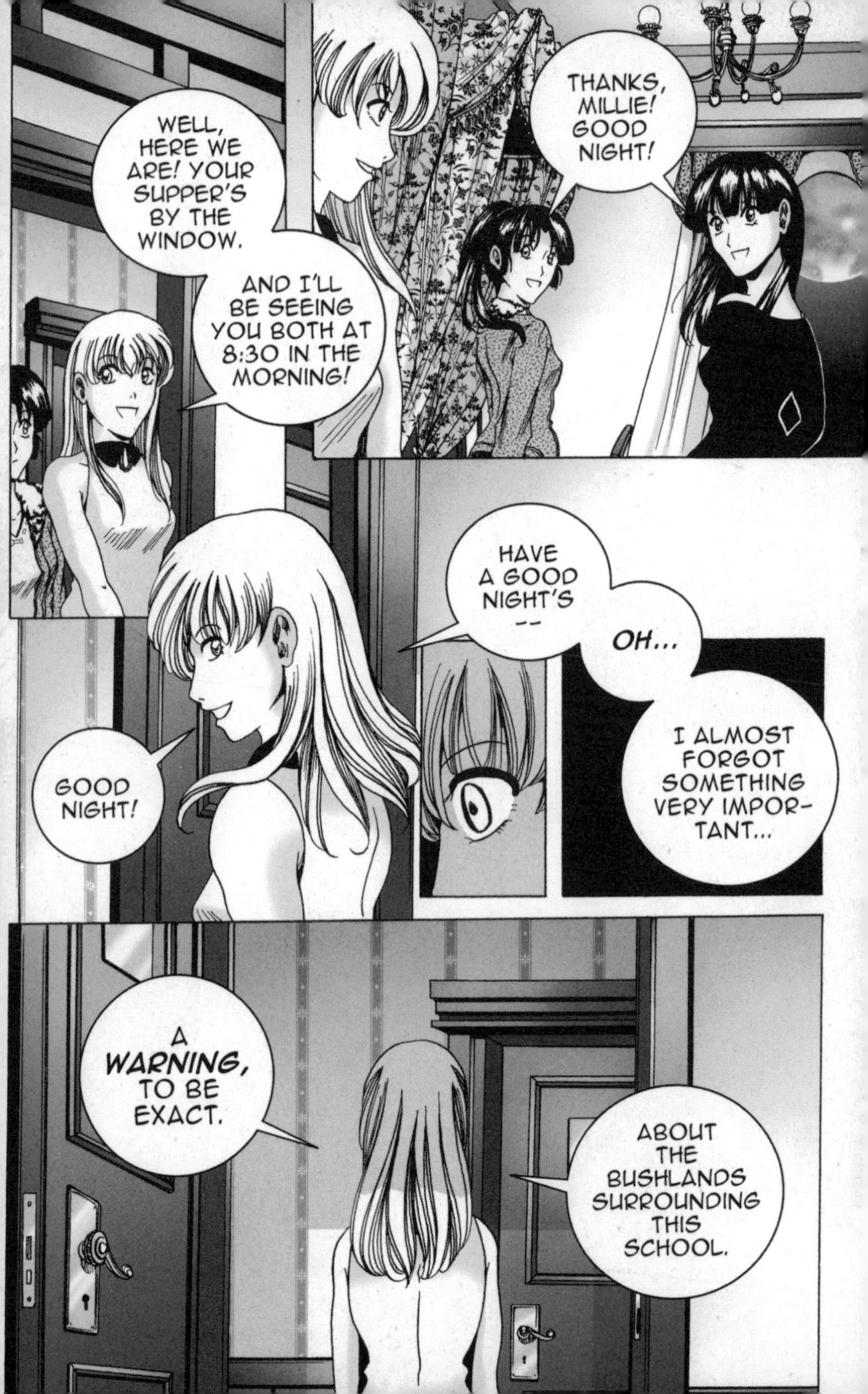
WELL, HERE WE ARE! YOUR SUPPER'S BY THE WINDOW.
AND I'LL BE SEEING YOU BOTH AT 8:30 IN THE MORNING!
THANKS, MILLIE! GOOD NIGHT!
HAVE A GOOD NIGHT'S --
GOOD NIGHT!
OH...
I ALMOST FORGOT SOMETHING VERY IMPOR-TANT...
A *WARNING,* TO BE EXACT.
ABOUT THE BUSHLANDS SURROUNDING THIS SCHOOL.

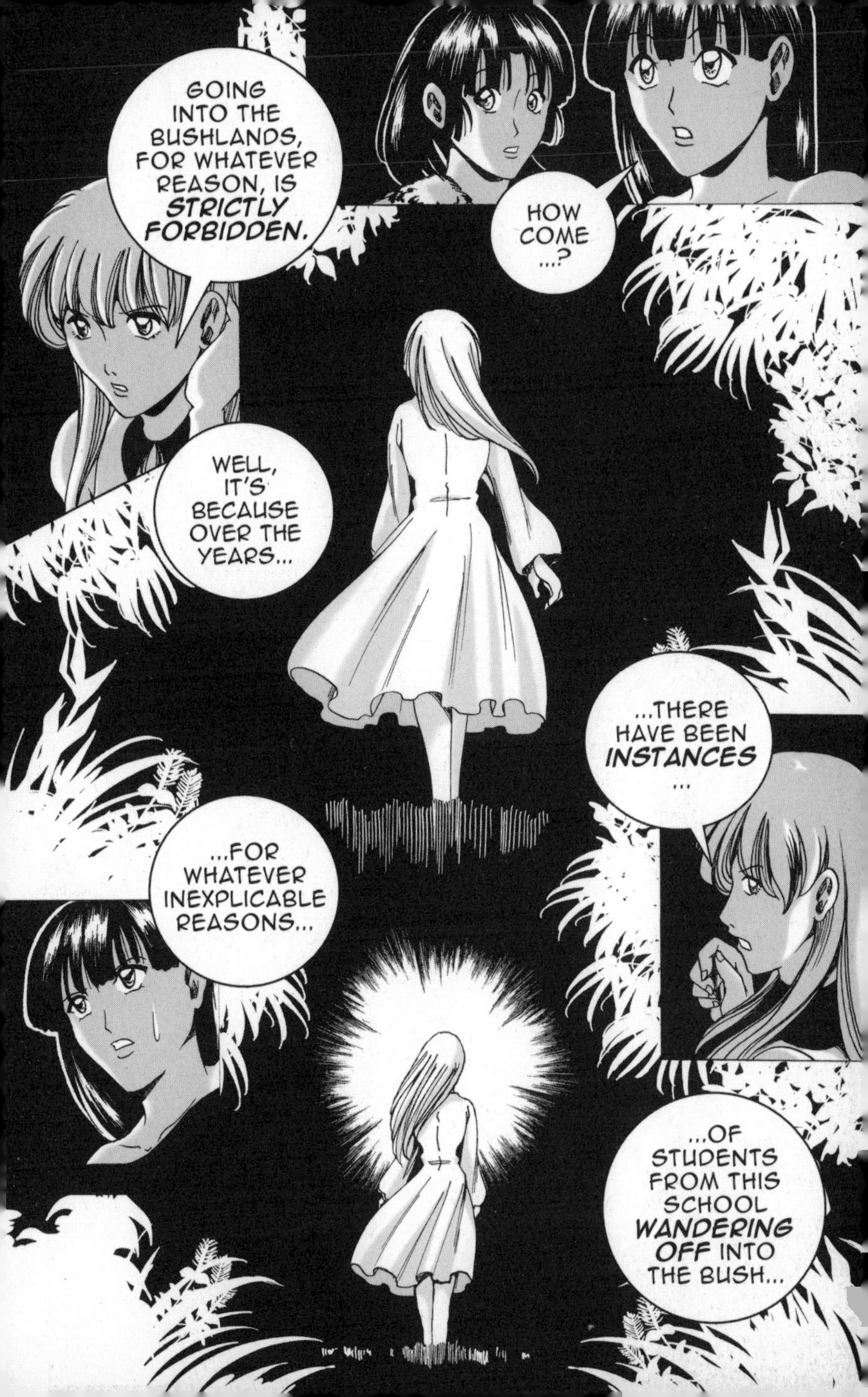
GOING INTO THE BUSHLANDS, FOR WHATEVER REASON, IS STRICTLY FORBIDDEN.
HOW COME ...?
WELL, IT'S BECAUSE OVER THE YEARS...
...THERE HAVE BEEN INSTANCES ...
...FOR WHATEVER INEXPLICABLE REASONS...
...OF STUDENTS FROM THIS SCHOOL WANDERING OFF INTO THE BUSH...

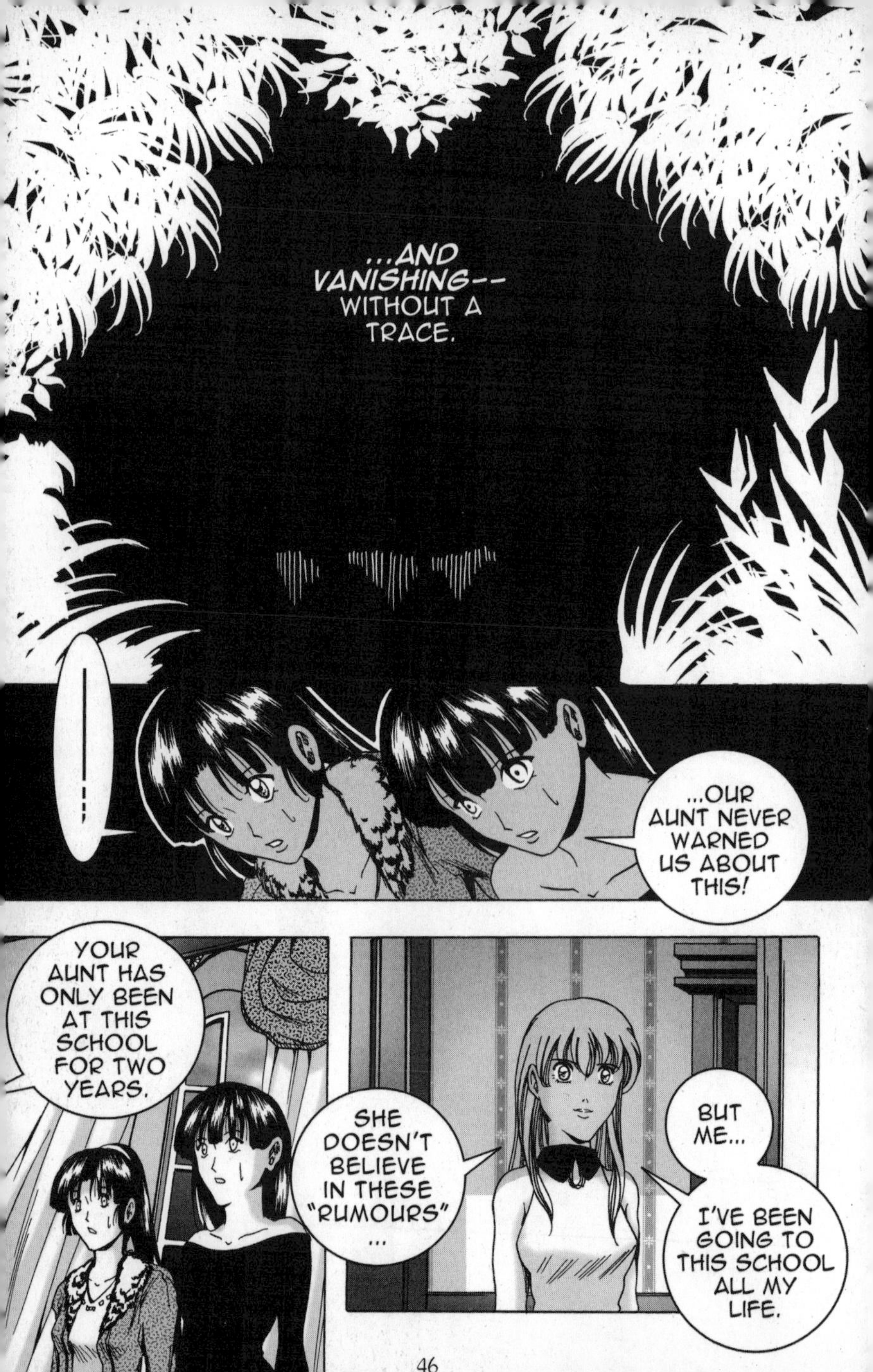
...AND VANISHING-- WITHOUT A TRACE.
...OUR AUNT NEVER WARNED US ABOUT THIS!
YOUR AUNT HAS ONLY BEEN AT THIS SCHOOL FOR TWO YEARS.
SHE DOESN'T BELIEVE IN THESE "RUMOURS" ...
BUT ME...
I'VE BEEN GOING TO THIS SCHOOL ALL MY LIFE.

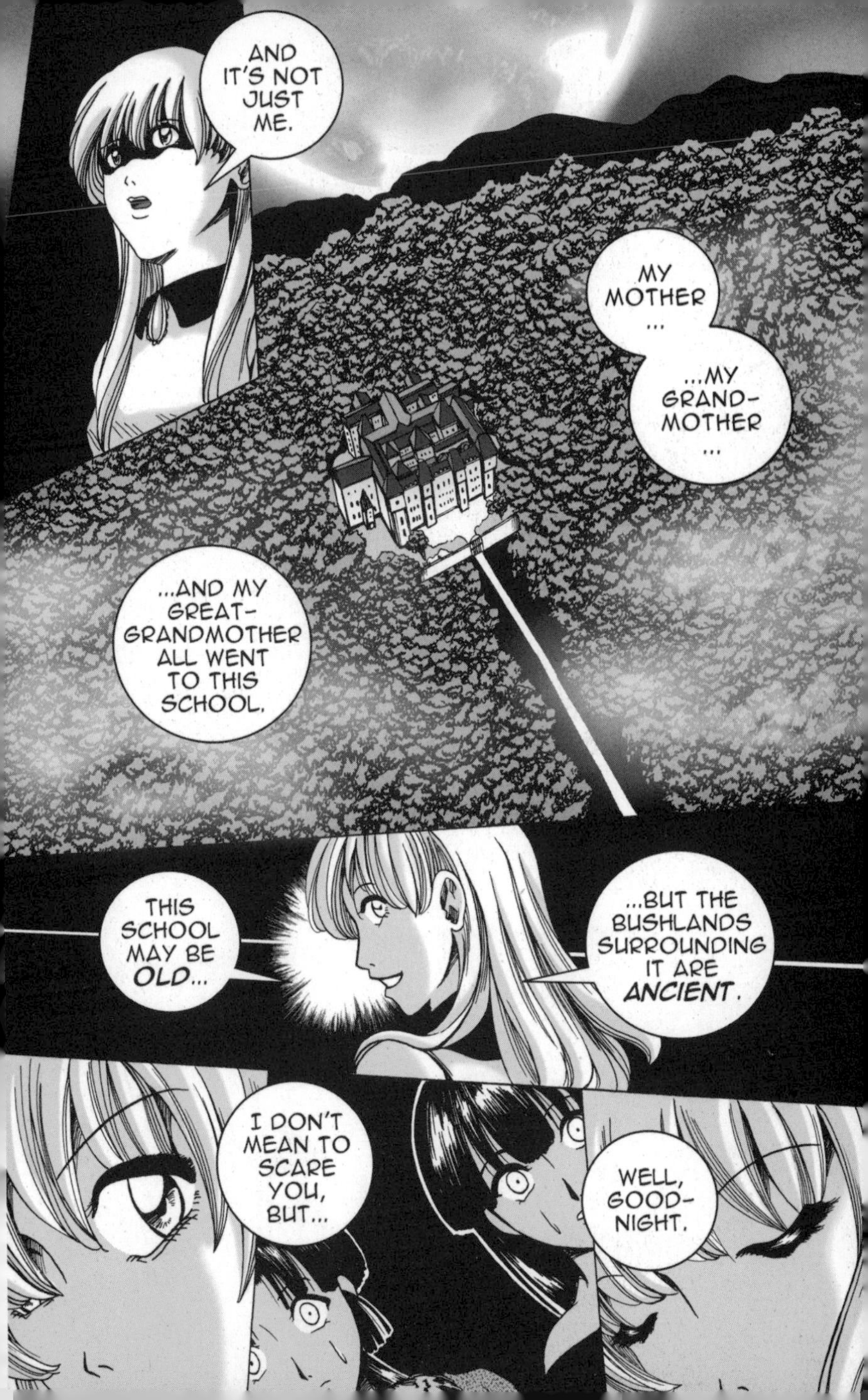
AND IT'S NOT JUST ME.
MY MOTHER ...
...MY GRANDMOTHER ...
...AND MY GREAT-GRANDMOTHER ALL WENT TO THIS SCHOOL.
THIS SCHOOL MAY BE *OLD*...
...BUT THE BUSHLANDS SURROUNDING IT ARE *ANCIENT*.
I DON'T MEAN TO SCARE YOU, BUT...
WELL, GOOD-NIGHT.

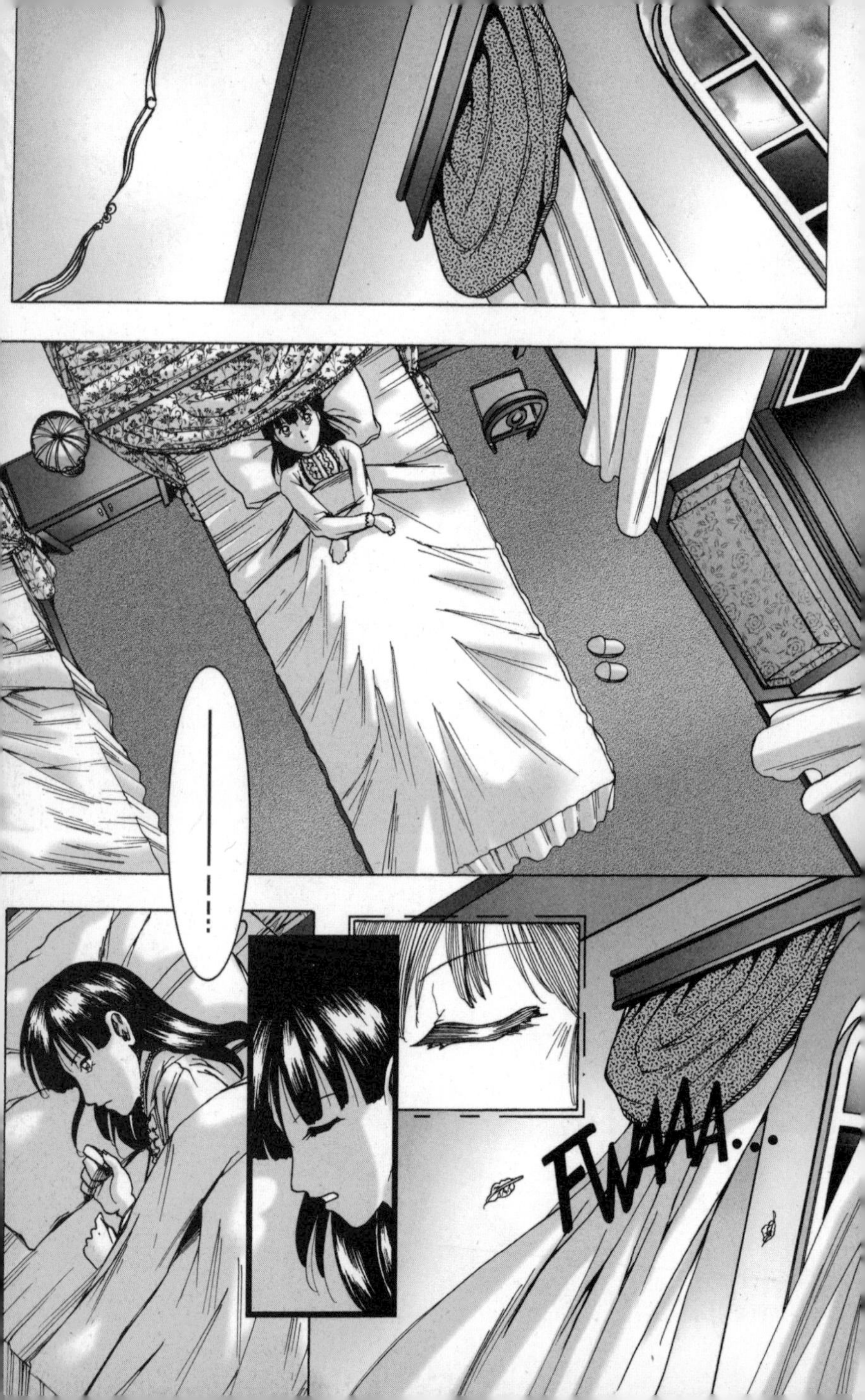
——……
FWAAA...

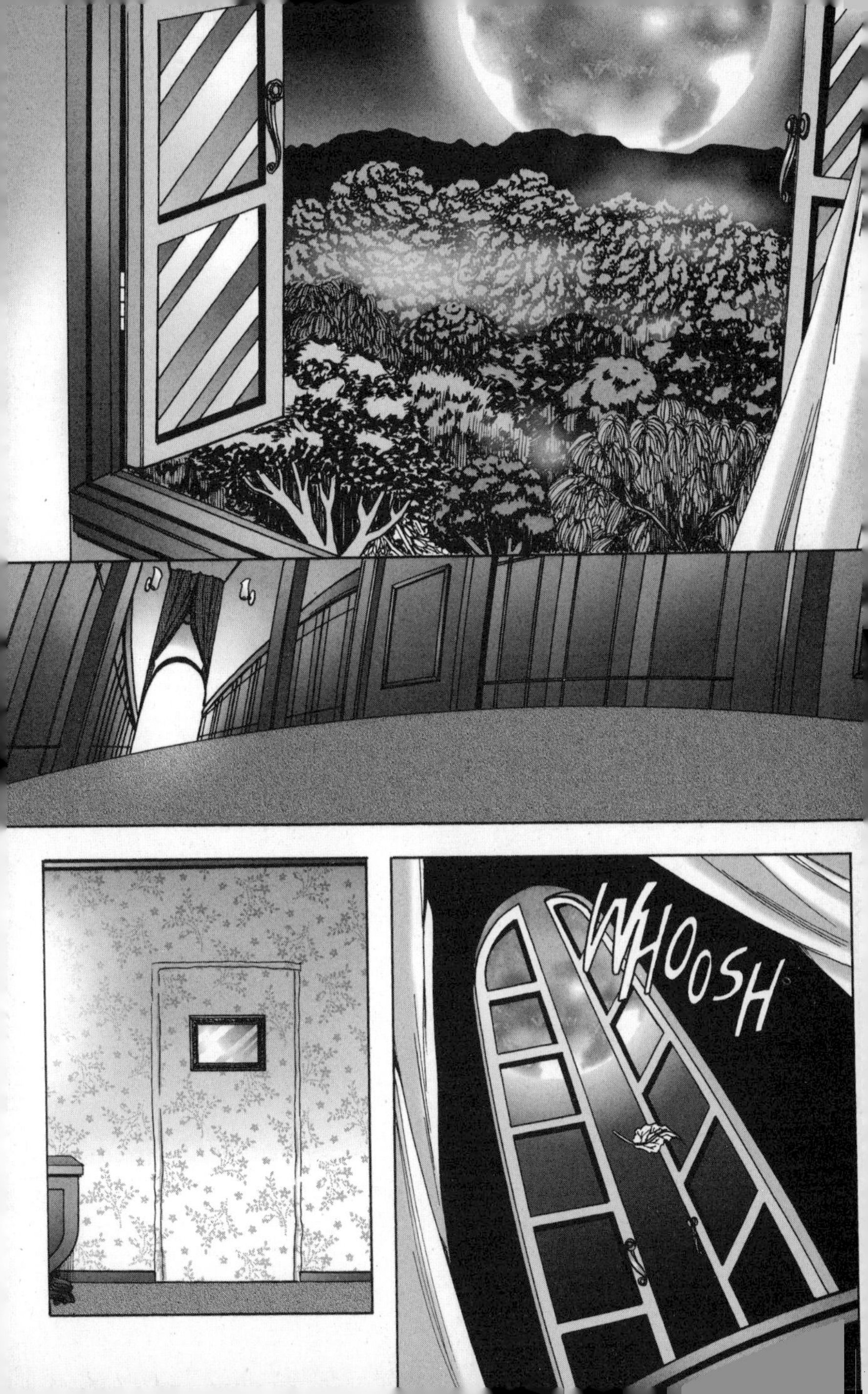
WHOOSH

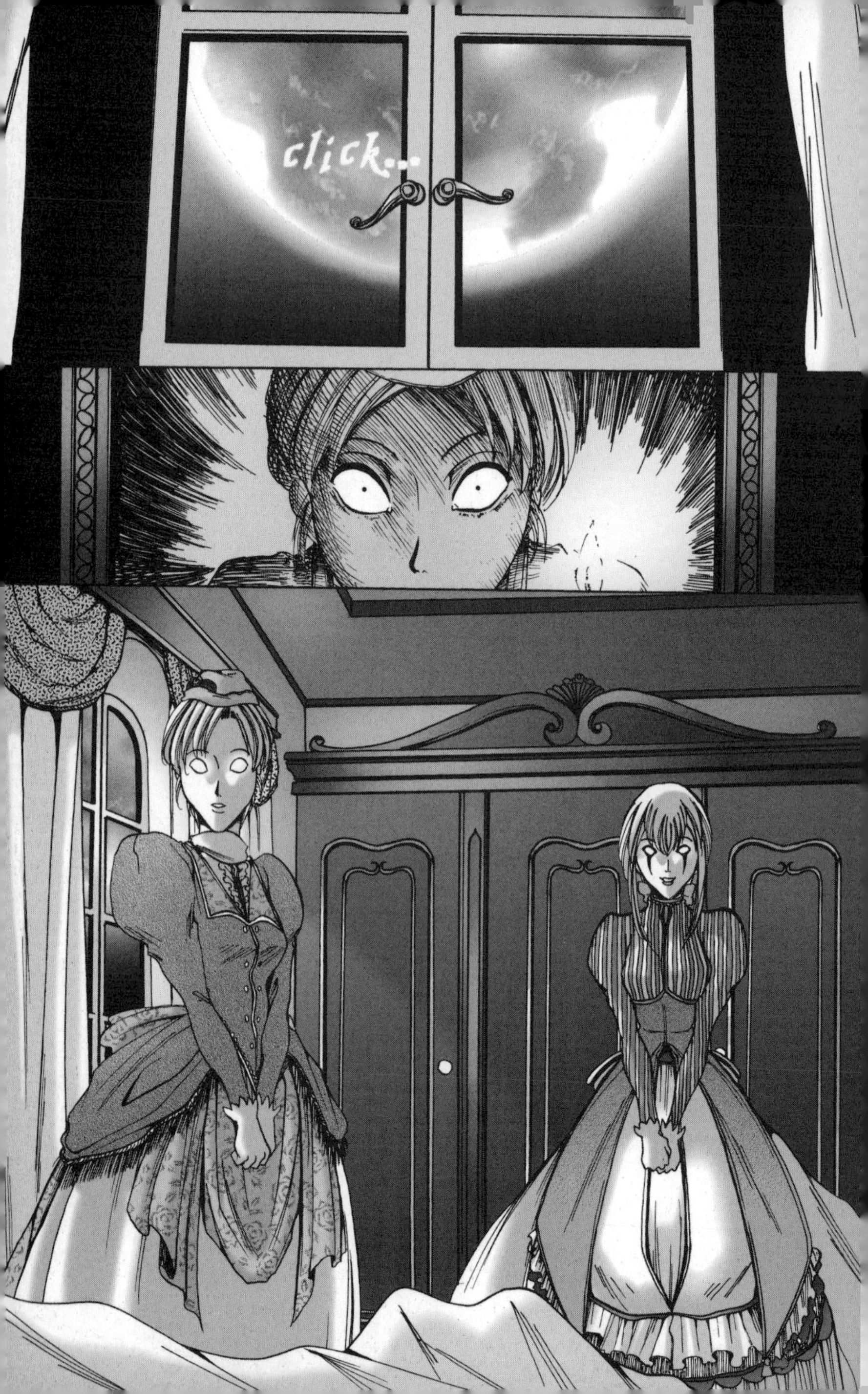
click...

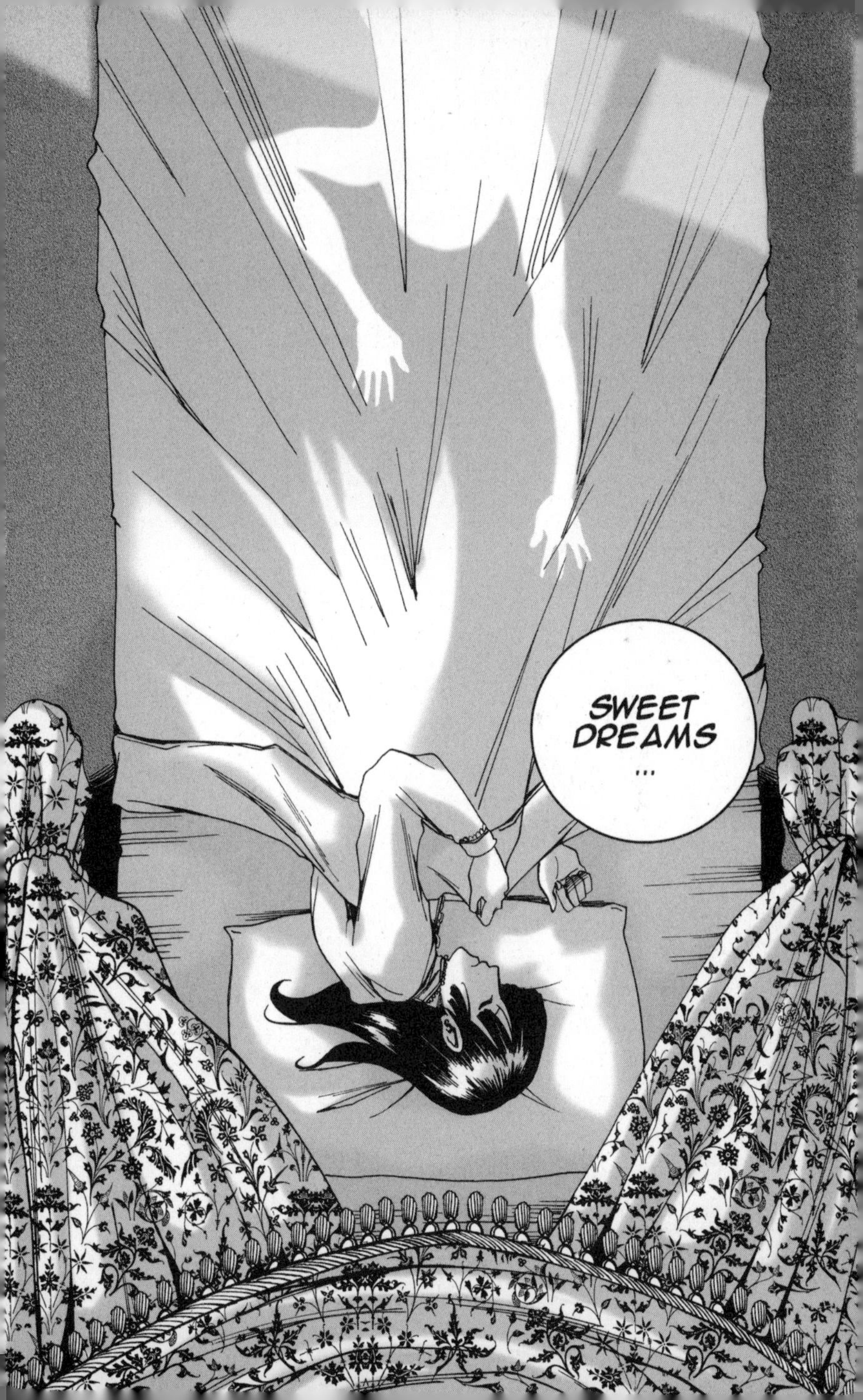
SWEET DREAMS ...

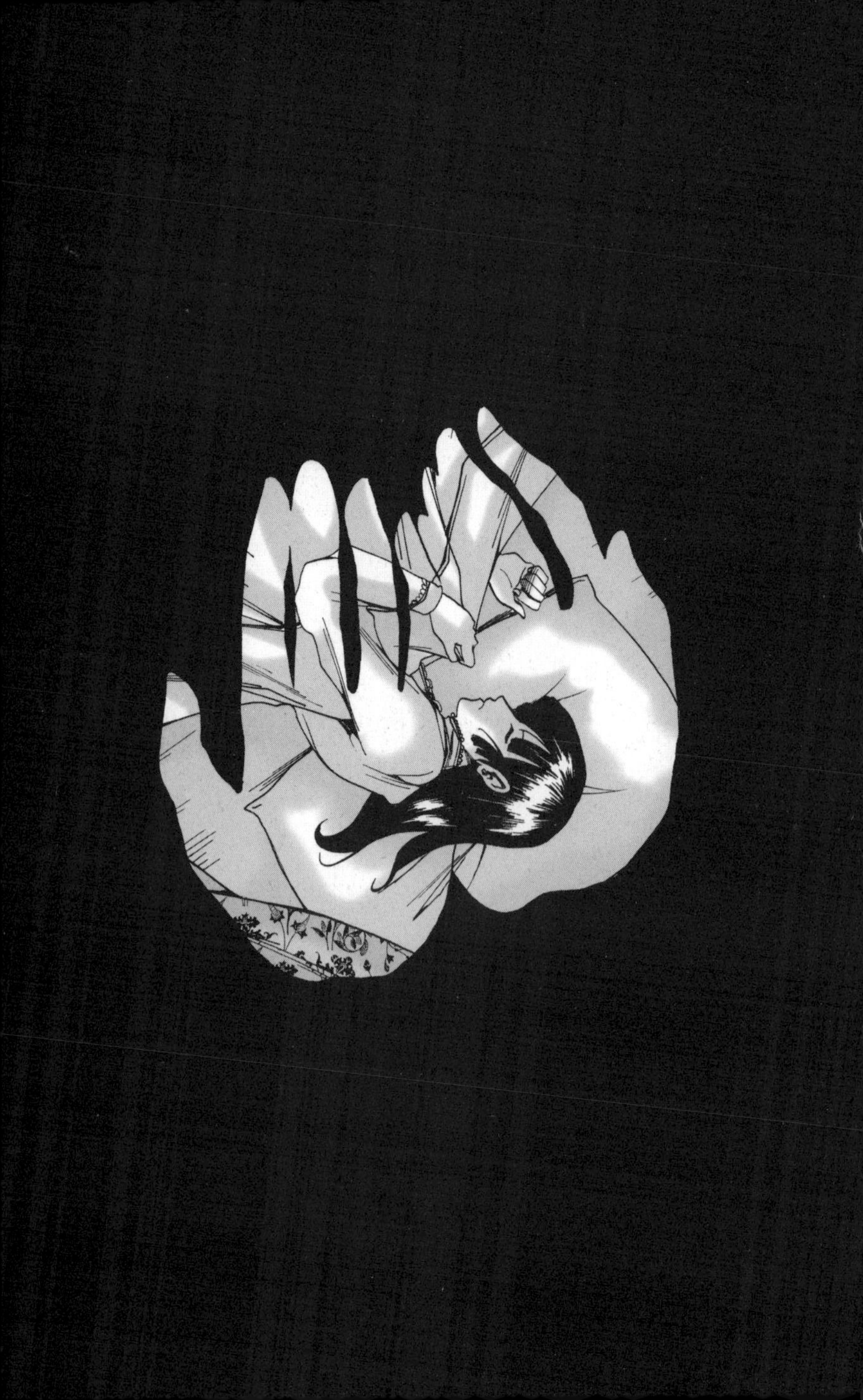

Chapter 3
The Dreaming

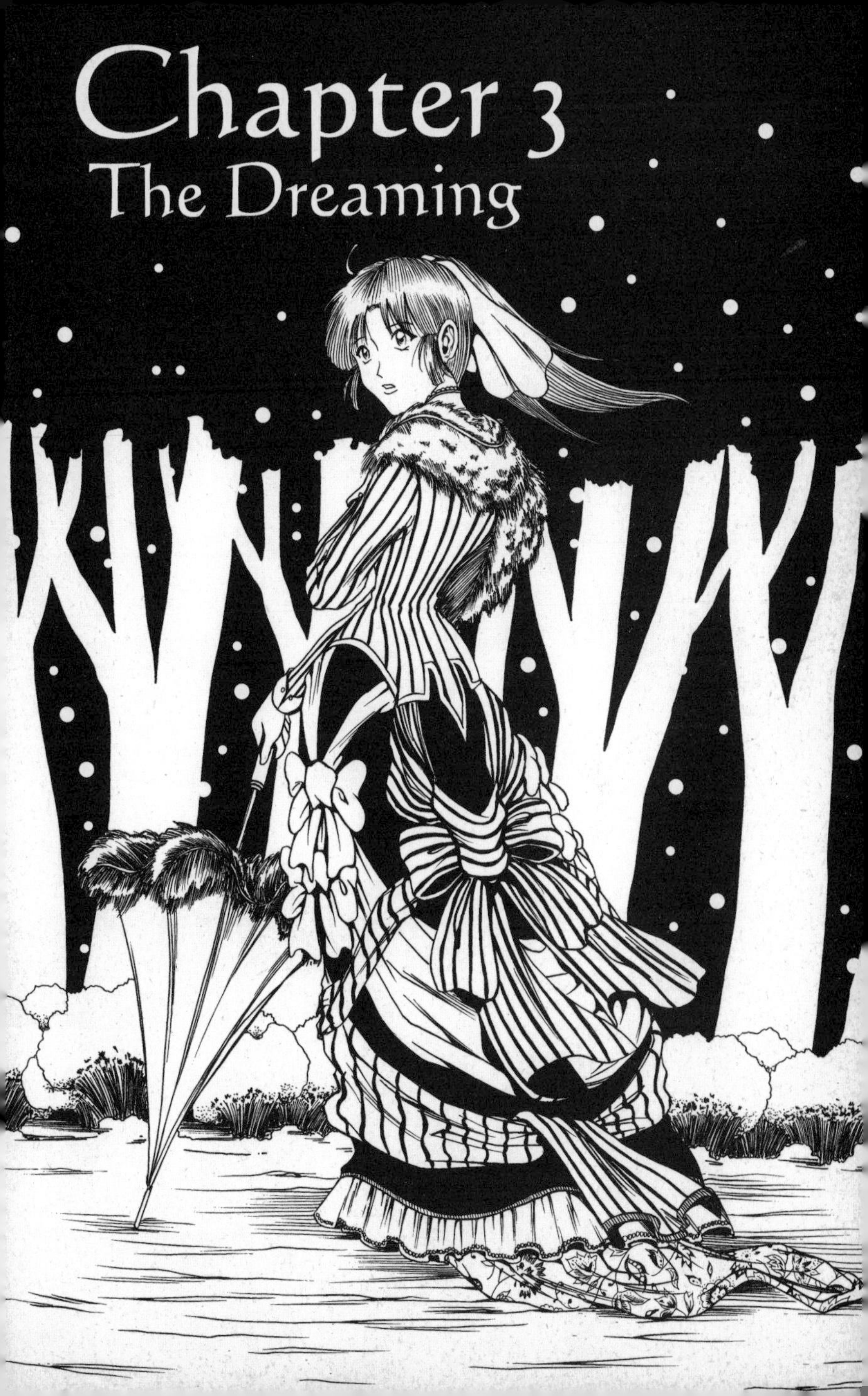

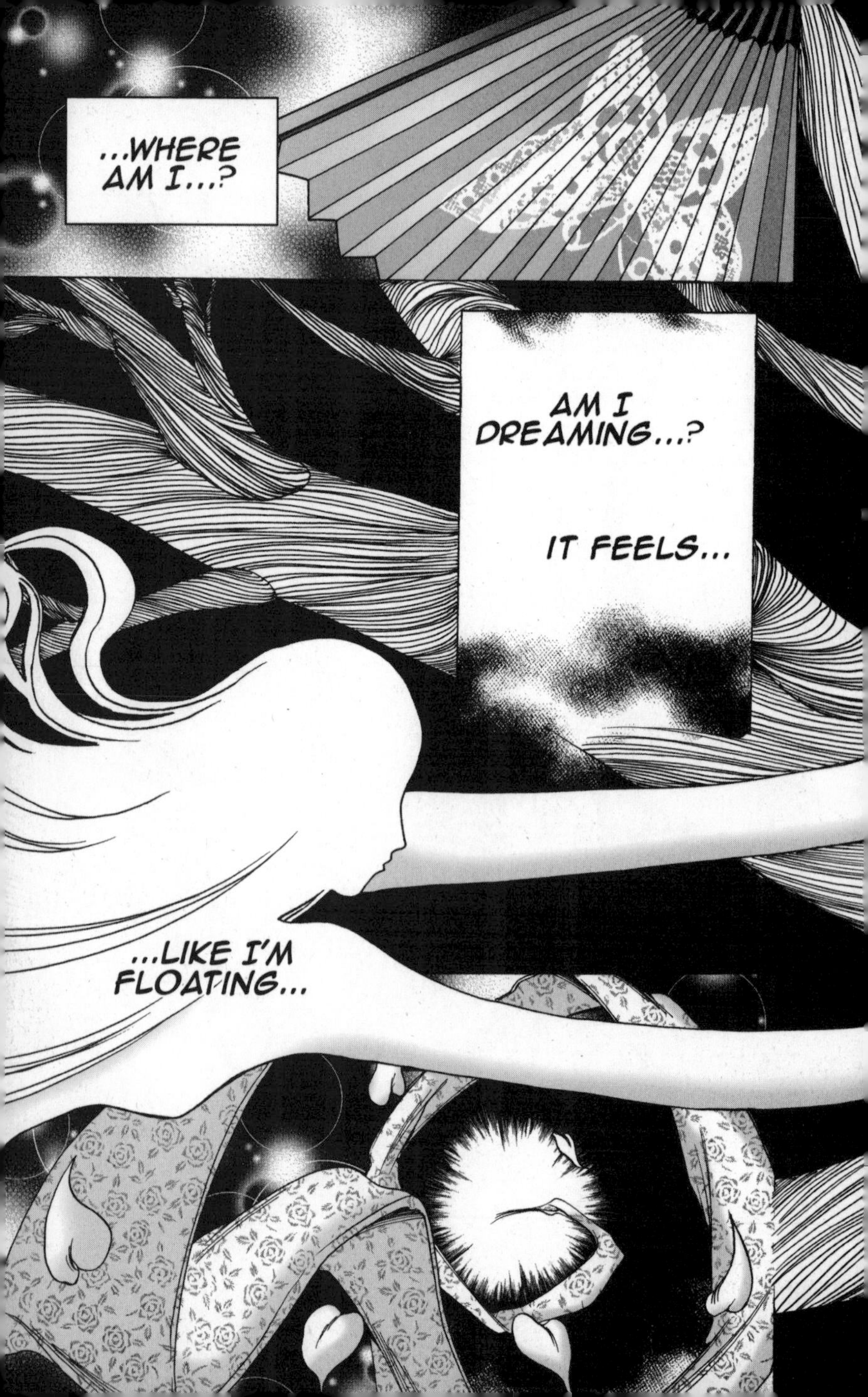
...WHERE AM I...?
AM I DREAMING...?
IT FEELS...
...LIKE I'M FLOATING...

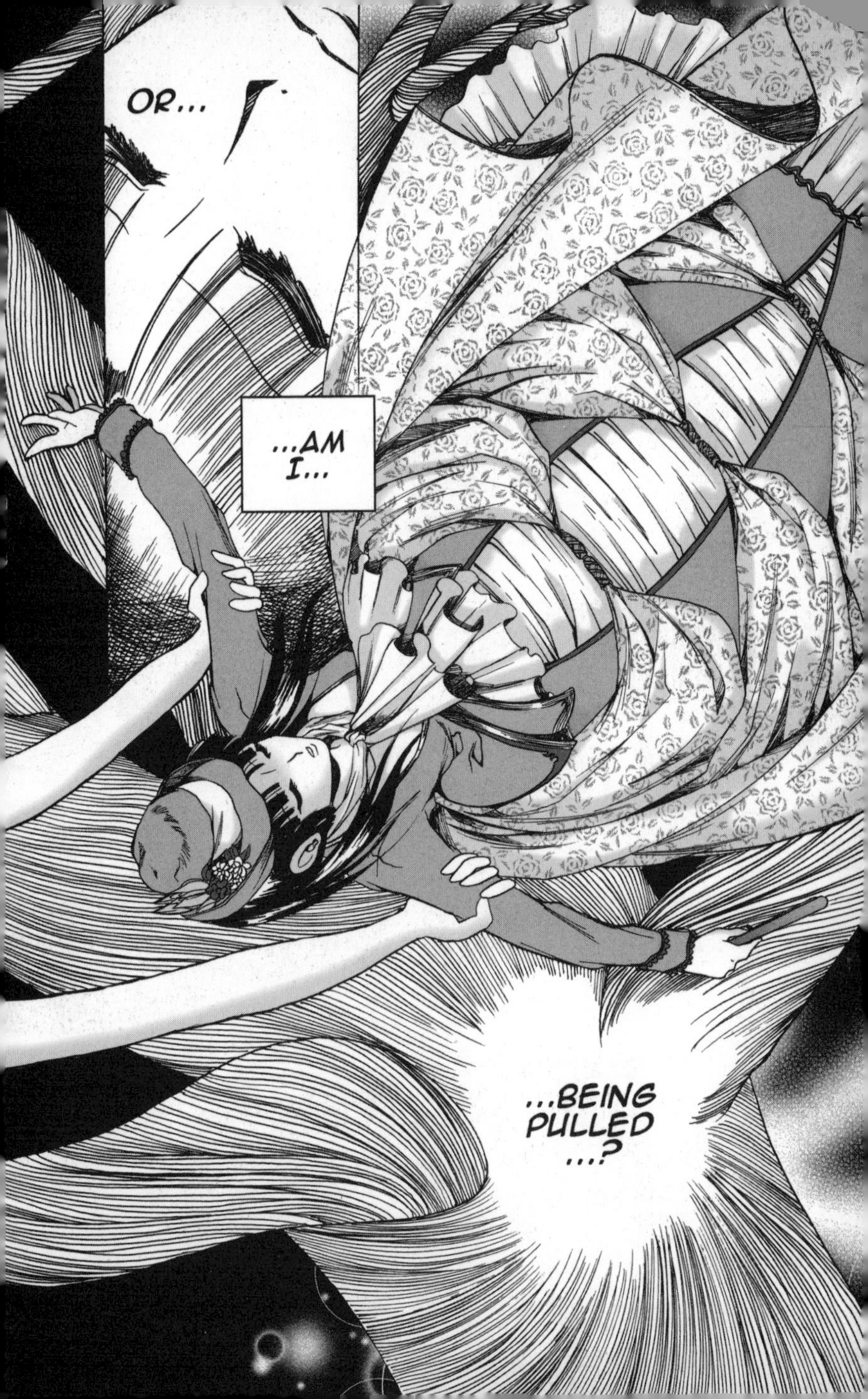
OR...
...AM I...
...BEING PULLED ...?

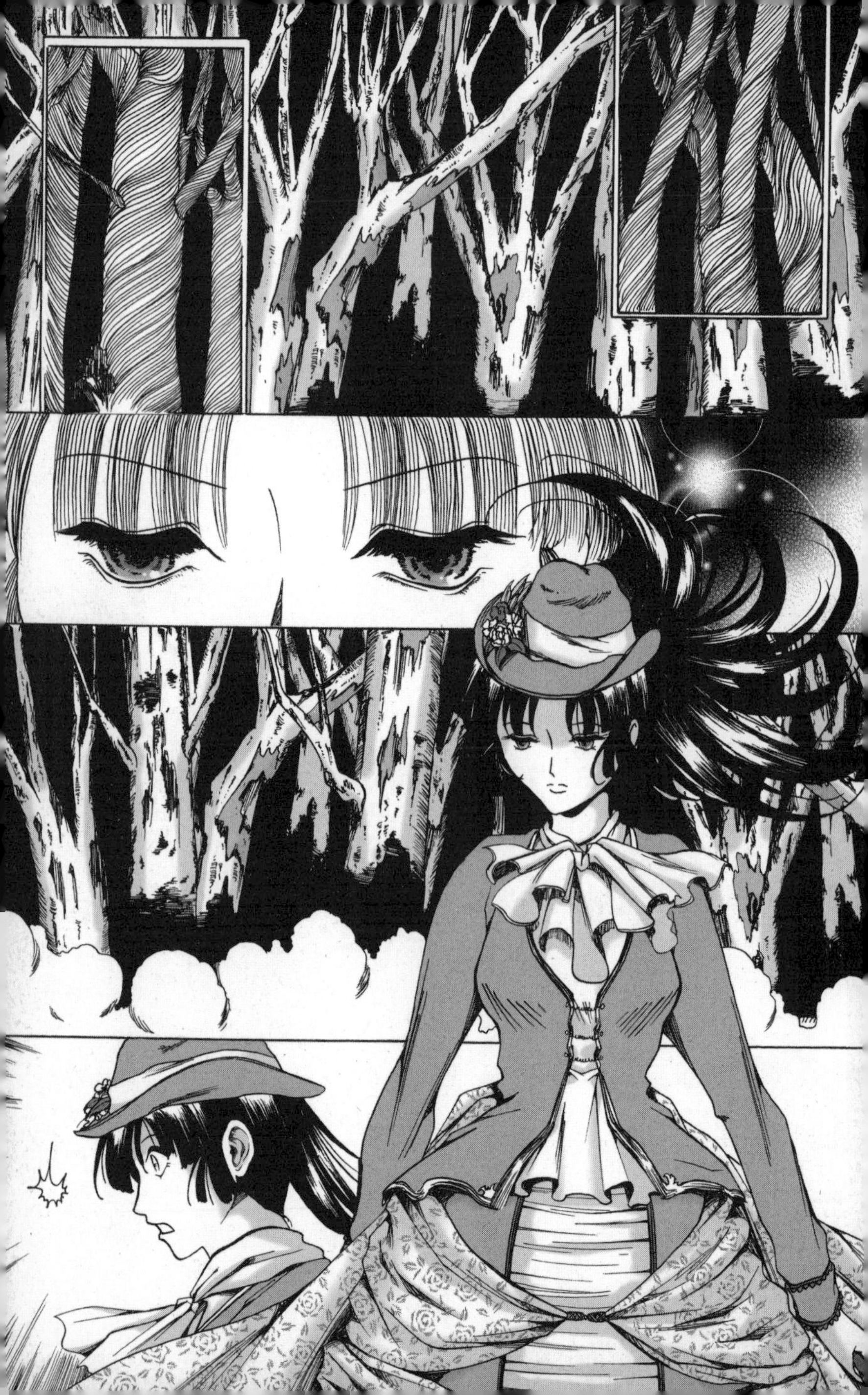

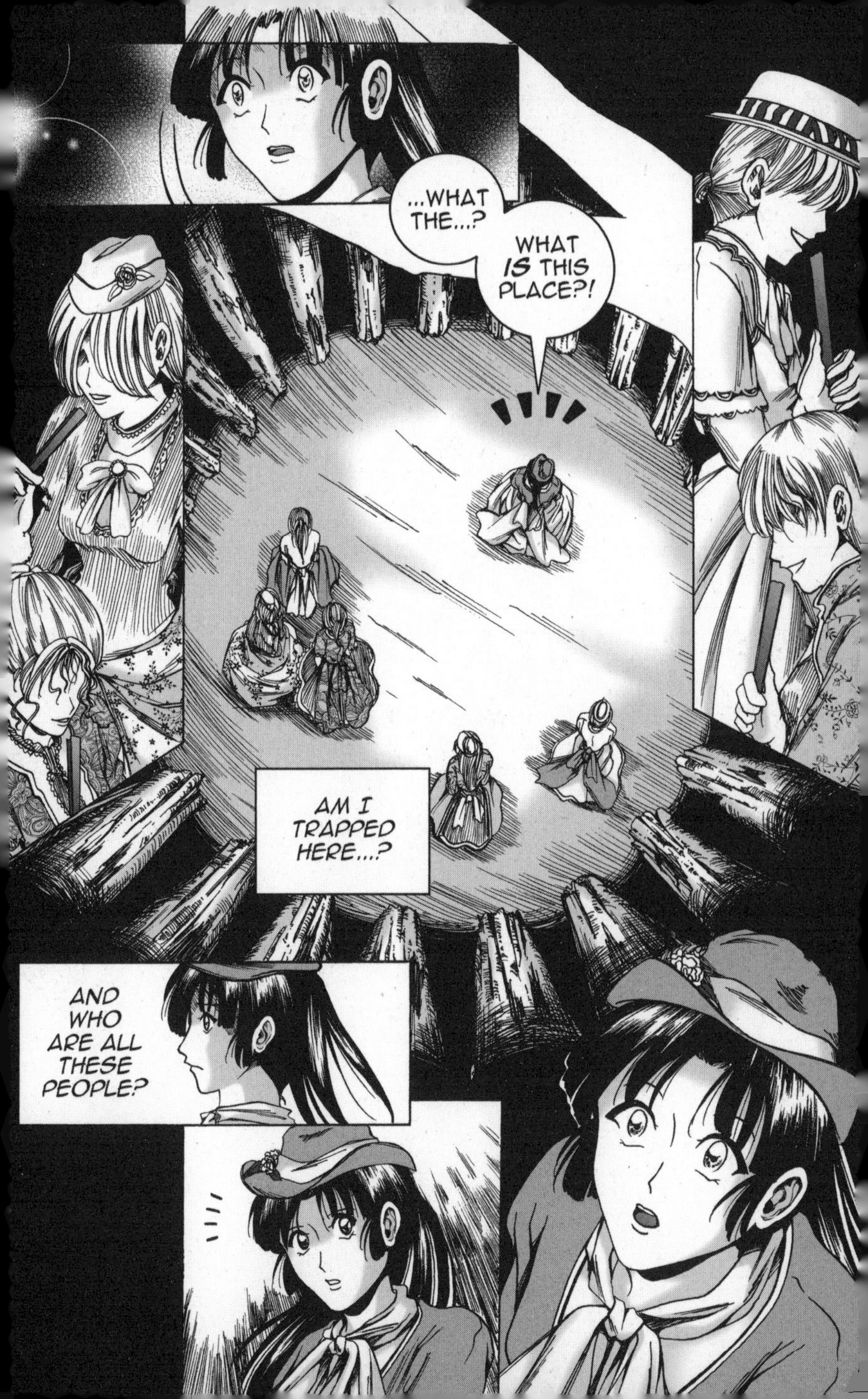
...WHAT THE...?
WHAT *IS* THIS PLACE?!
AM I TRAPPED HERE...?
AND WHO ARE ALL THESE PEOPLE?

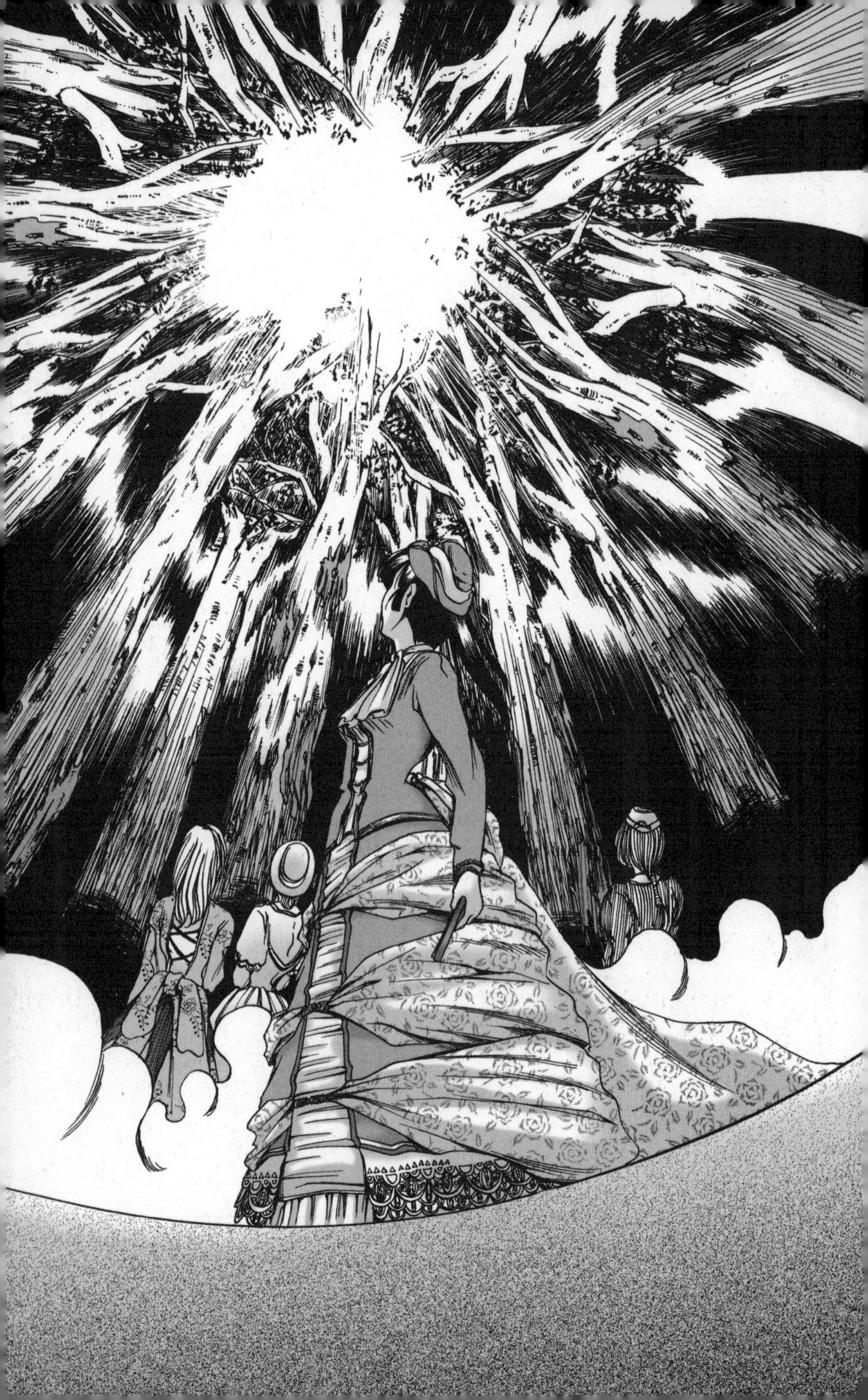

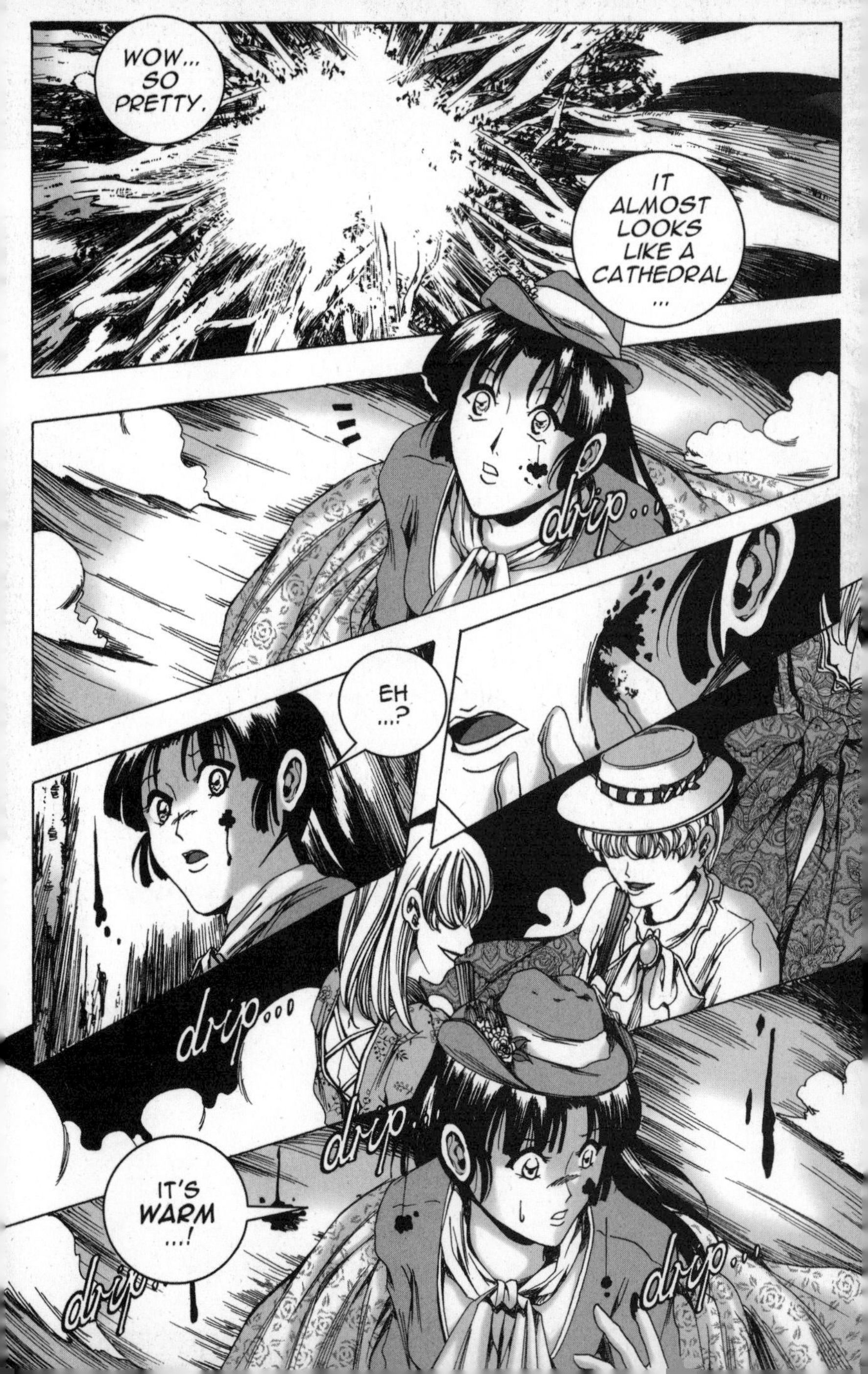
WOW... SO PRETTY.
IT ALMOST LOOKS LIKE A CATHEDRAL ...
drip...
EH ...?
drip...
drip...
IT'S WARM ...!
drip...
drip...

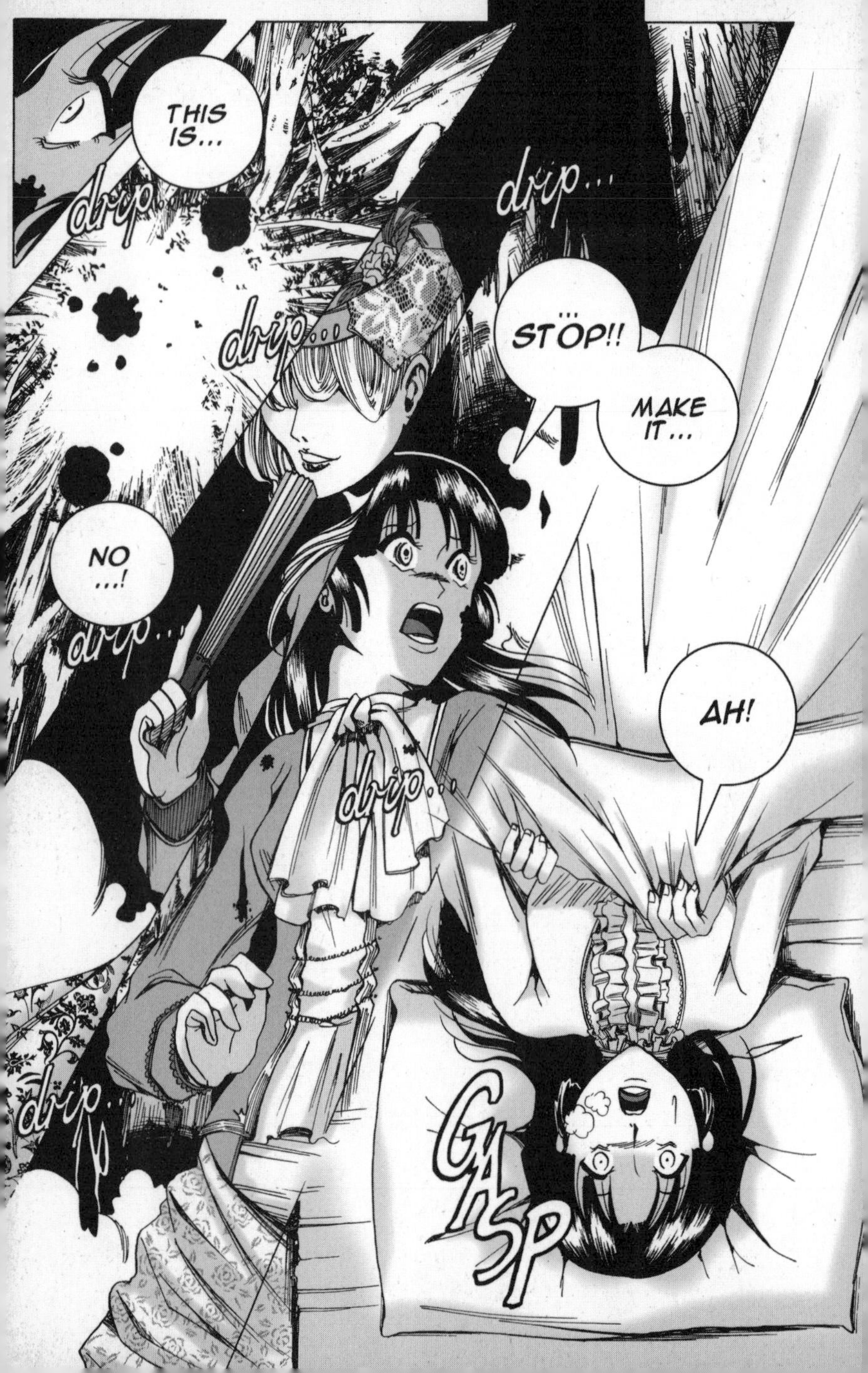
drip...
MAKE IT...
...STOP!!
THIS IS...
drip...
drip...
NO...!
drip...
AH!
drip...
drip...
GASP

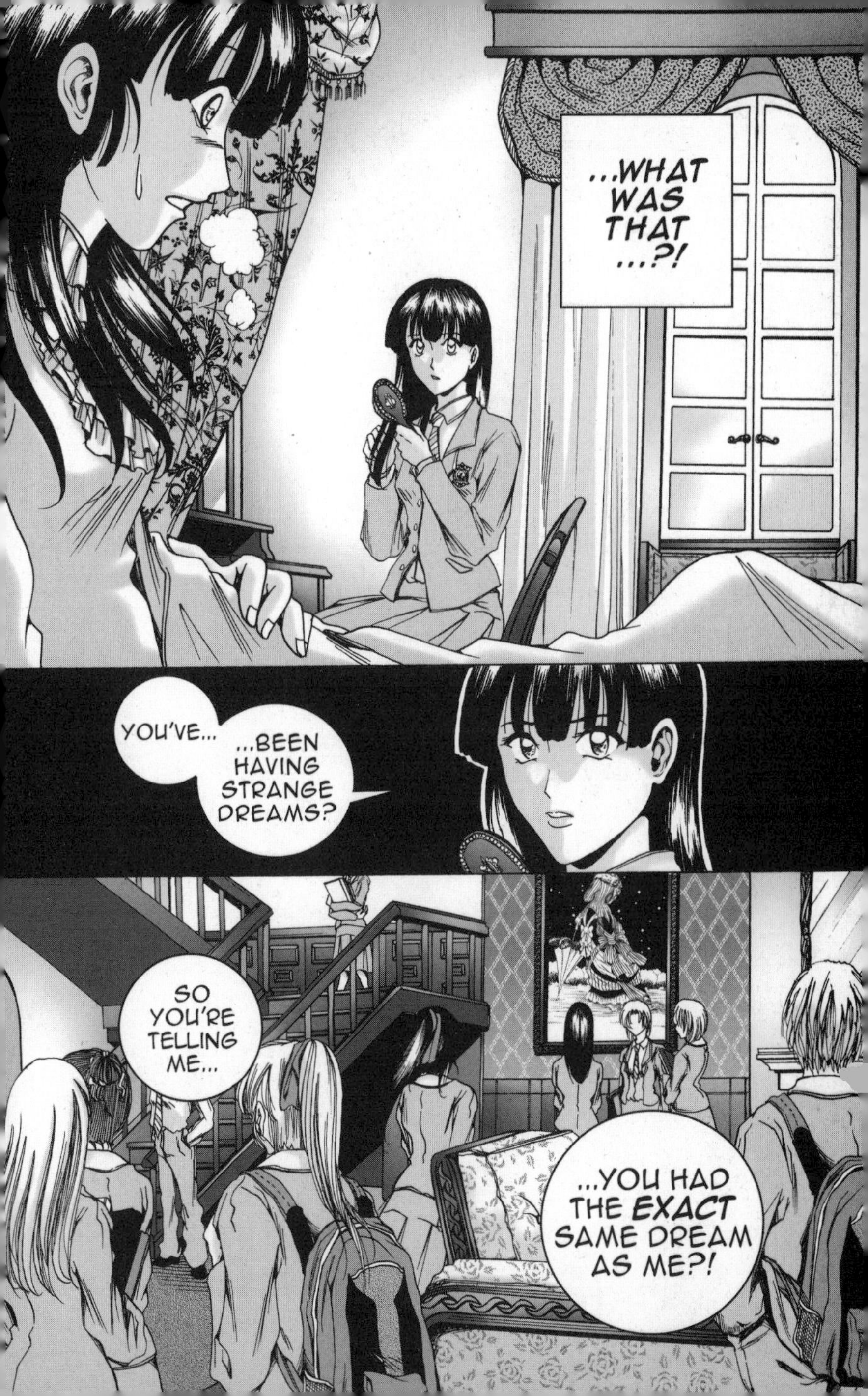
...WHAT WAS THAT ...?!
YOU'VE...
...BEEN HAVING STRANGE DREAMS?
SO YOU'RE TELLING ME...
...YOU HAD THE **EXACT** SAME DREAM AS ME?!

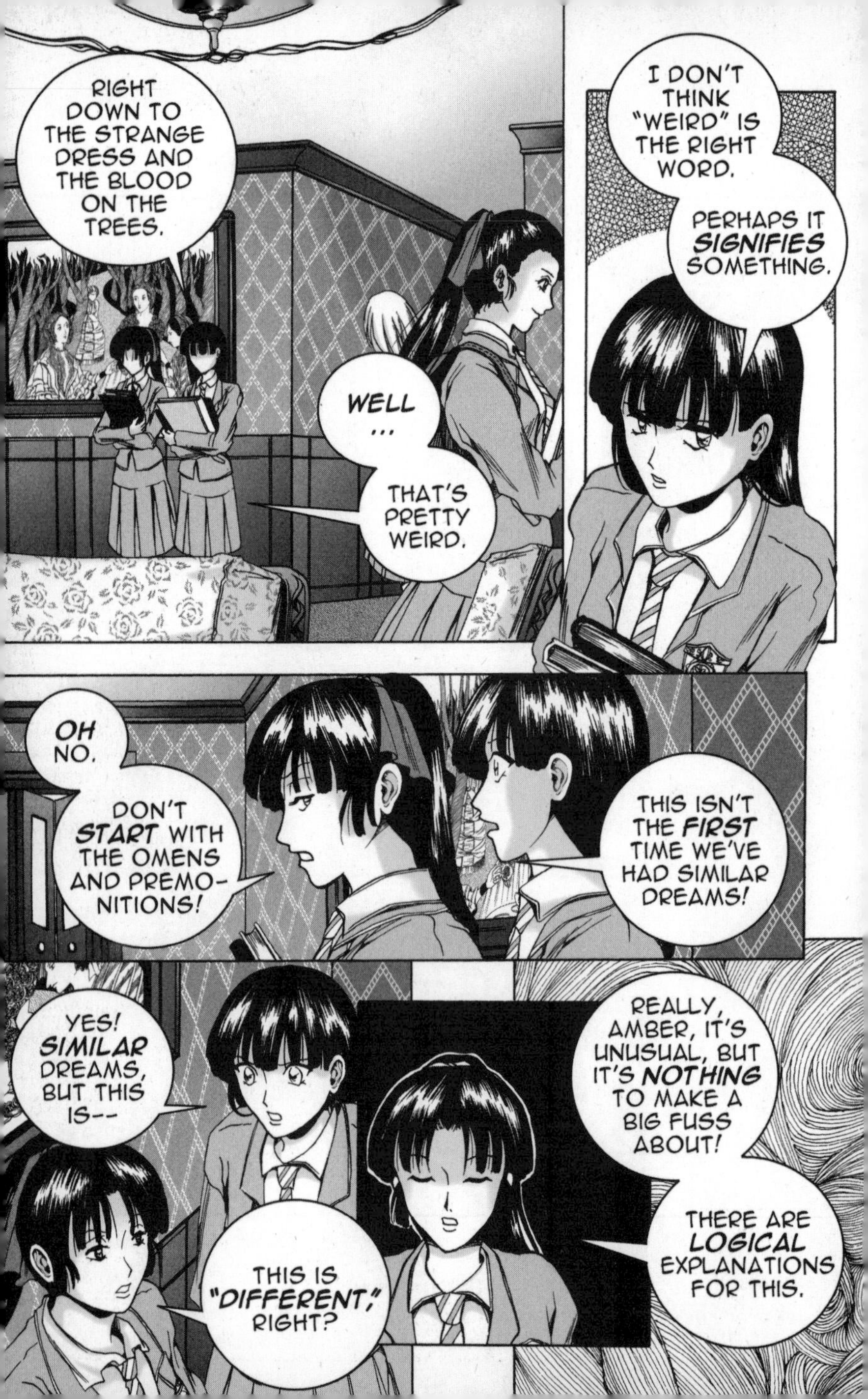
RIGHT DOWN TO THE STRANGE DRESS AND THE BLOOD ON THE TREES.
WELL ...
THAT'S PRETTY WEIRD.
I DON'T THINK "WEIRD" IS THE RIGHT WORD.
PERHAPS IT *SIGNIFIES* SOMETHING.
OH NO.
DON'T *START* WITH THE OMENS AND PREMONITIONS!
THIS ISN'T THE *FIRST* TIME WE'VE HAD SIMILAR DREAMS!
YES! *SIMILAR* DREAMS, BUT THIS IS--
THIS IS "*DIFFERENT*," RIGHT?
REALLY, AMBER, IT'S UNUSUAL, BUT IT'S *NOTHING* TO MAKE A BIG FUSS ABOUT!
THERE ARE *LOGICAL* EXPLANATIONS FOR THIS.

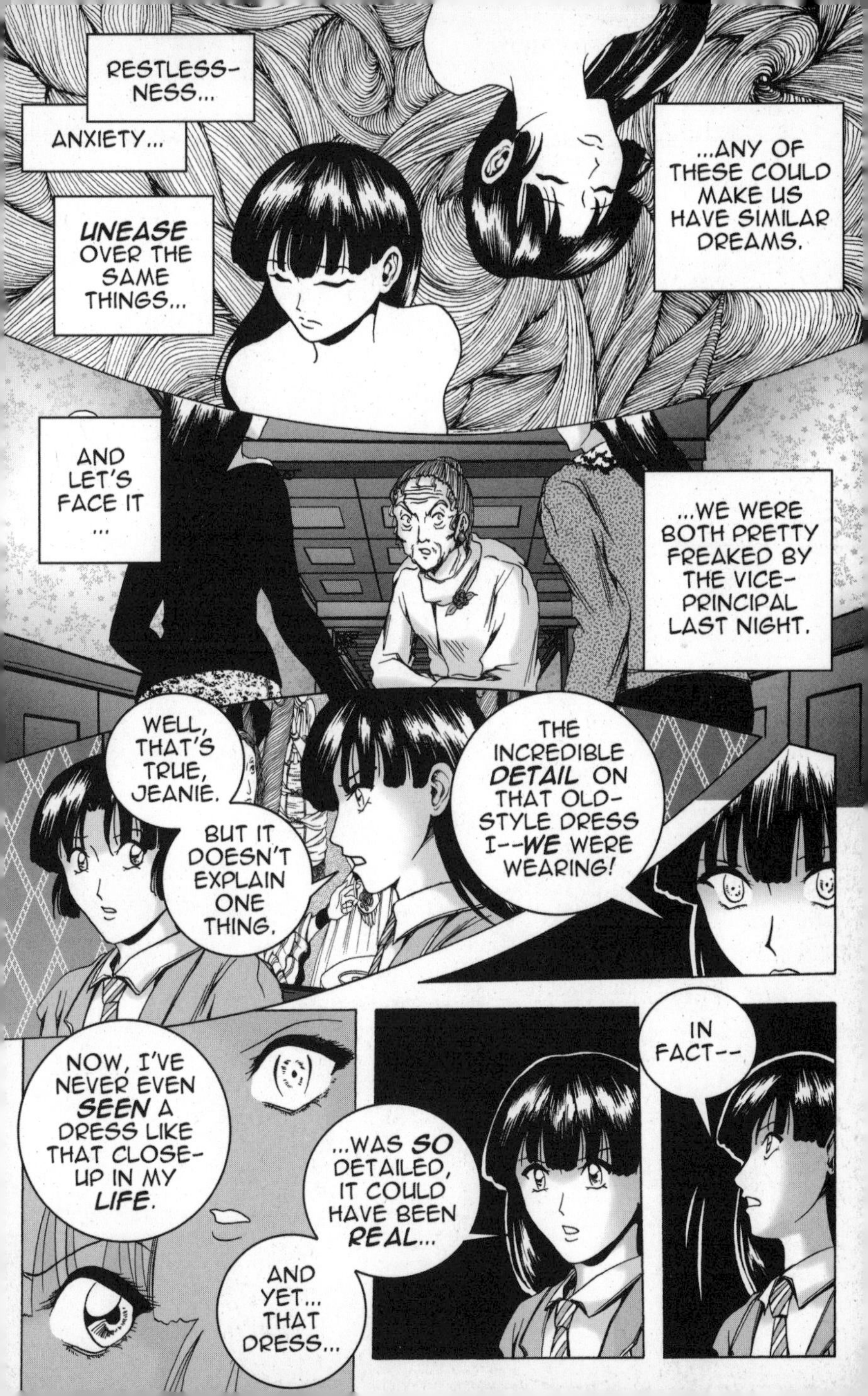
RESTLESS-NESS...
ANXIETY...
UNEASE OVER THE SAME THINGS...
...ANY OF THESE COULD MAKE US HAVE SIMILAR DREAMS.
AND LET'S FACE IT ...
...WE WERE BOTH PRETTY FREAKED BY THE VICE-PRINCIPAL LAST NIGHT.
WELL, THAT'S TRUE, JEANIE.
BUT IT DOESN'T EXPLAIN ONE THING.
THE INCREDIBLE DETAIL ON THAT OLD-STYLE DRESS I--WE WERE WEARING!
NOW, I'VE NEVER EVEN SEEN A DRESS LIKE THAT CLOSE-UP IN MY LIFE.
AND YET... THAT DRESS...
...WAS SO DETAILED, IT COULD HAVE BEEN REAL...
IN FACT--

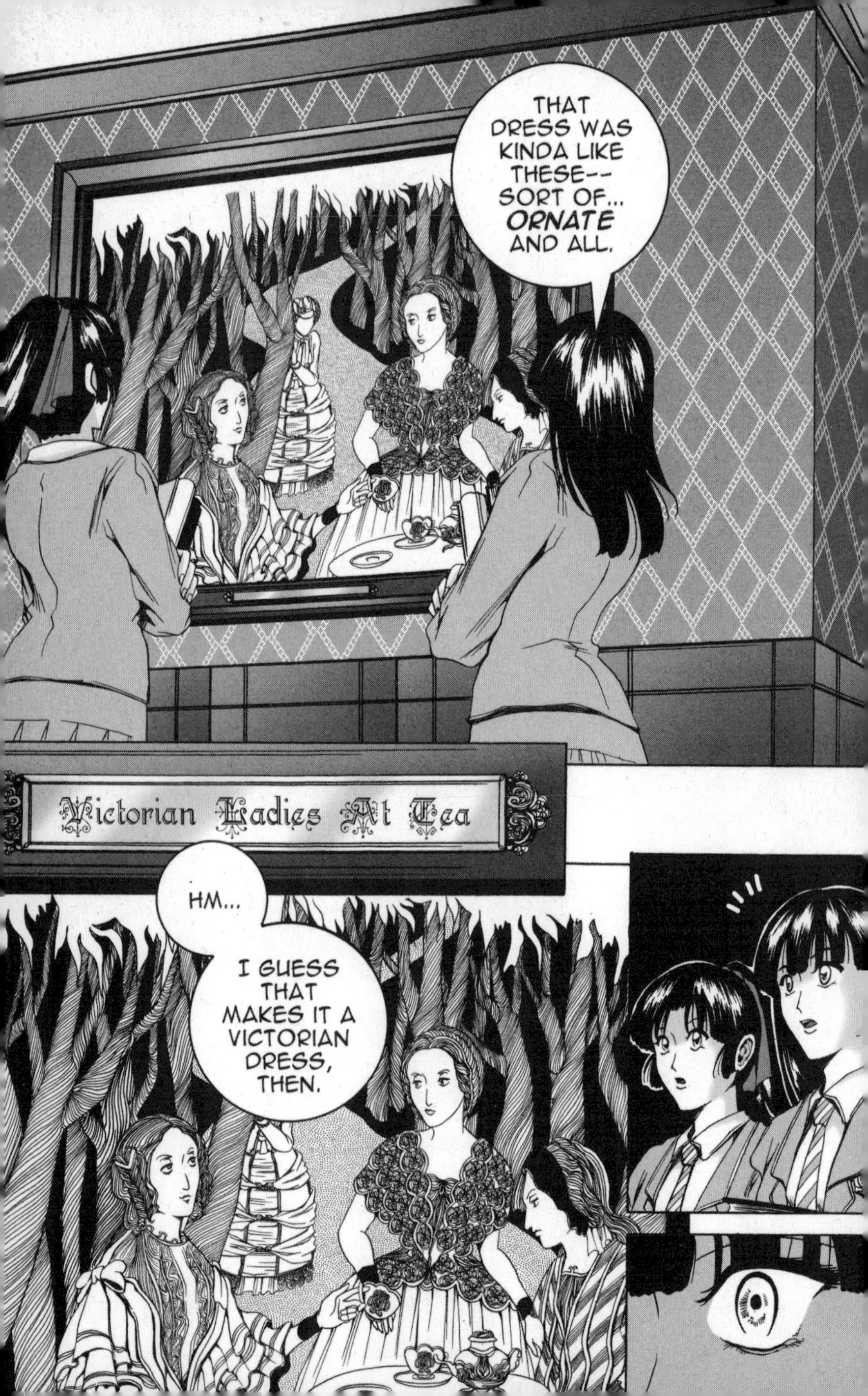
THAT DRESS WAS KINDA LIKE THESE-- SORT OF... *ORNATE* AND ALL.
Victorian Ladies At Tea
HM...
I GUESS THAT MAKES IT A VICTORIAN DRESS, THEN.

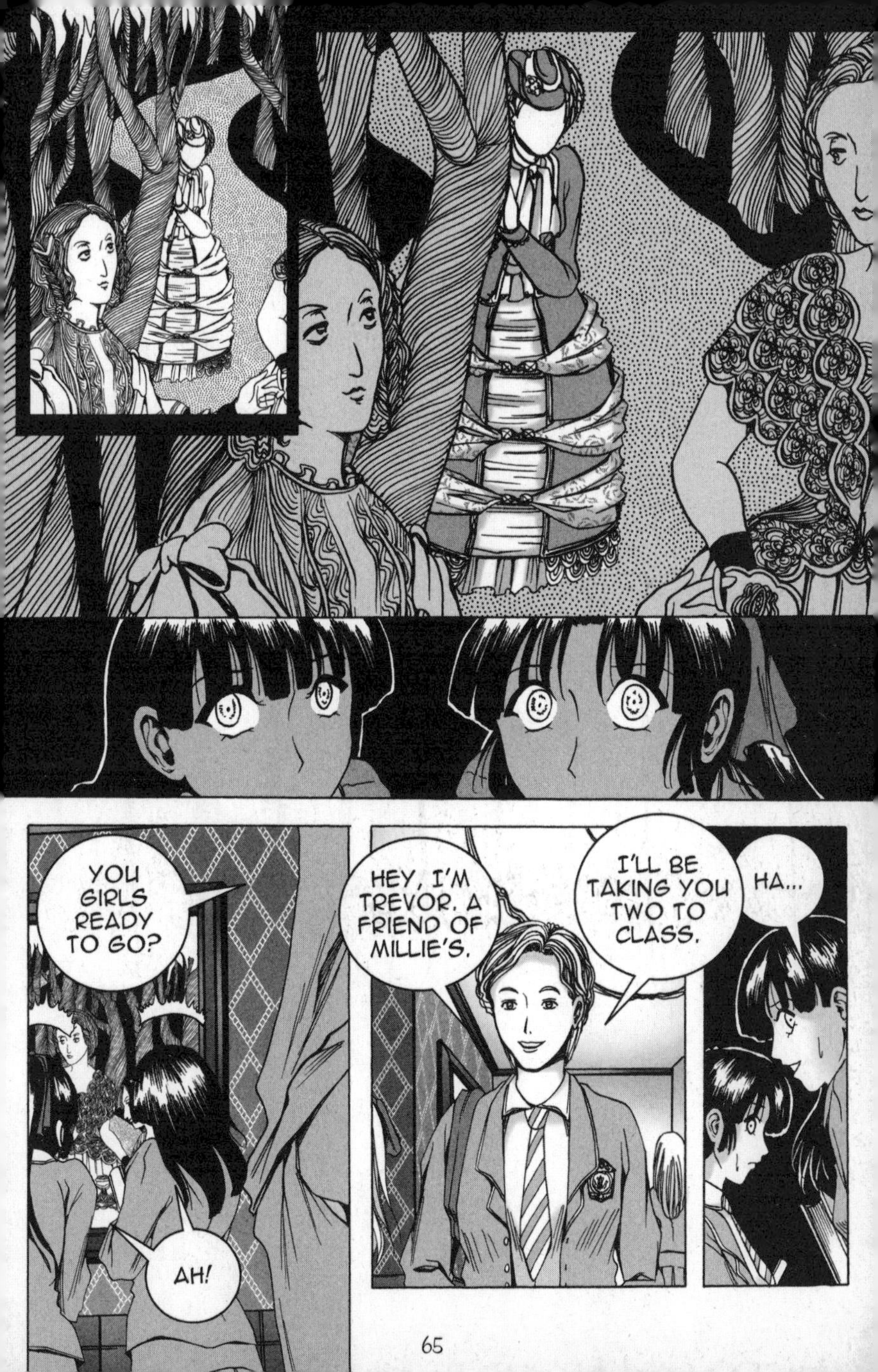
YOU GIRLS READY TO GO?
AH!
HEY, I'M TREVOR. A FRIEND OF MILLIE'S.
I'LL BE TAKING YOU TWO TO CLASS.
HA...

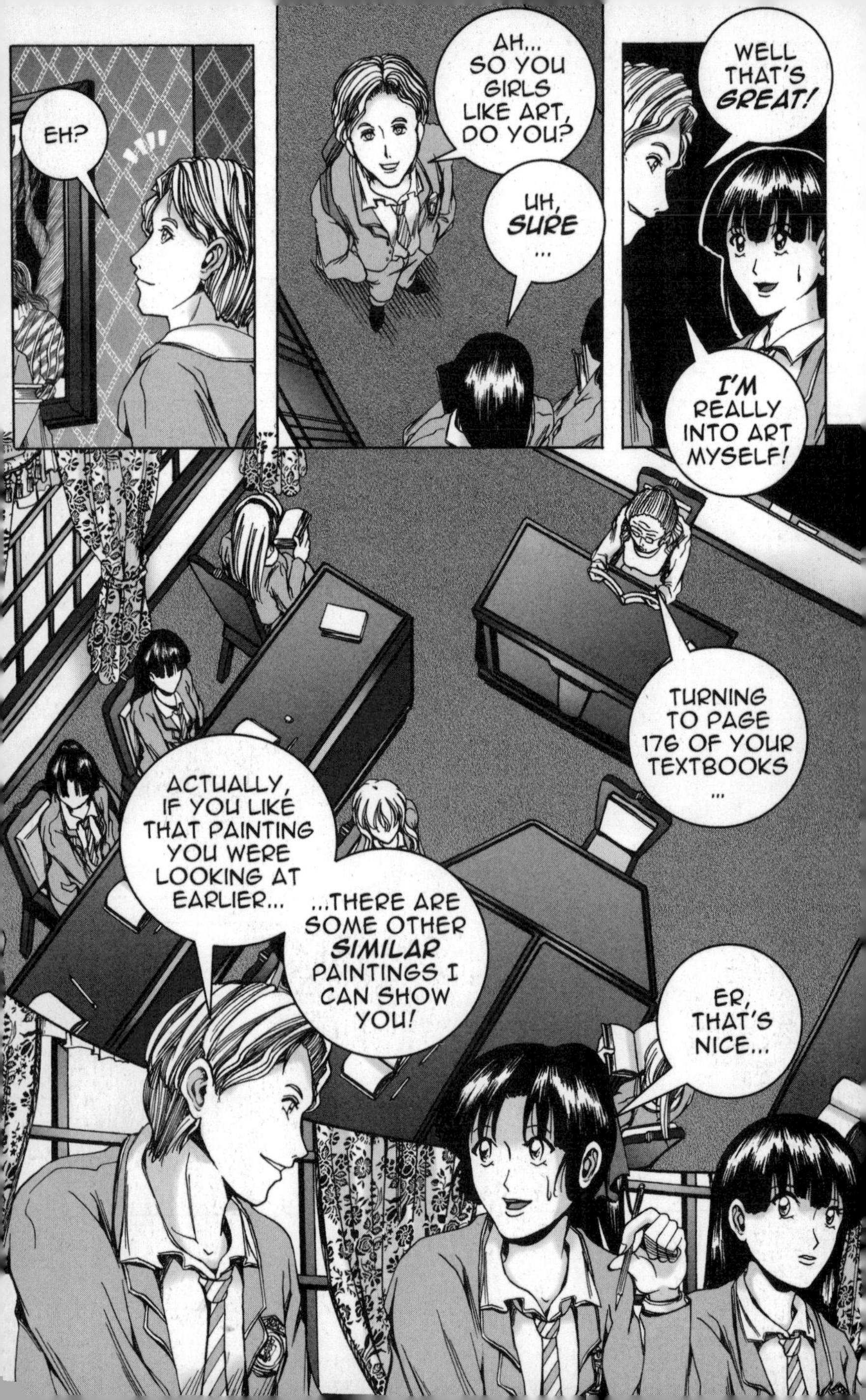
EH?
AH... SO YOU GIRLS LIKE ART, DO YOU?
UH, SURE ...
WELL THAT'S GREAT!
I'M REALLY INTO ART MYSELF!
TURNING TO PAGE 176 OF YOUR TEXTBOOKS ...
ACTUALLY, IF YOU LIKE THAT PAINTING YOU WERE LOOKING AT EARLIER...
...THERE ARE SOME OTHER SIMILAR PAINTINGS I CAN SHOW YOU!
ER, THAT'S NICE...

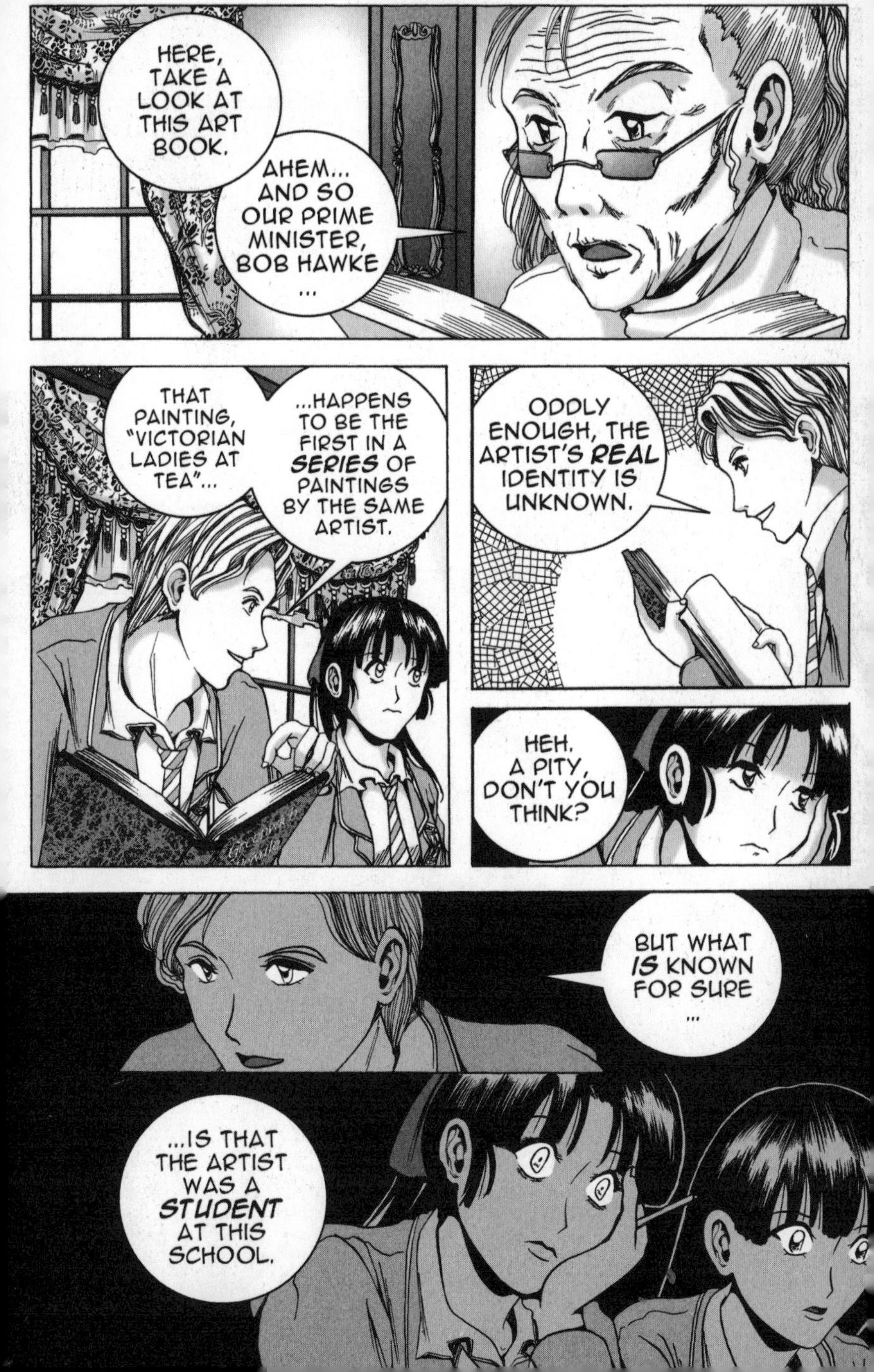
HERE, TAKE A LOOK AT THIS ART BOOK.
AHEM... AND SO OUR PRIME MINISTER, BOB HAWKE ...
THAT PAINTING, "VICTORIAN LADIES AT TEA"...
...HAPPENS TO BE THE FIRST IN A SERIES OF PAINTINGS BY THE SAME ARTIST.
ODDLY ENOUGH, THE ARTIST'S REAL IDENTITY IS UNKNOWN.
HEH. A PITY, DON'T YOU THINK?
BUT WHAT IS KNOWN FOR SURE ...
...IS THAT THE ARTIST WAS A STUDENT AT THIS SCHOOL.

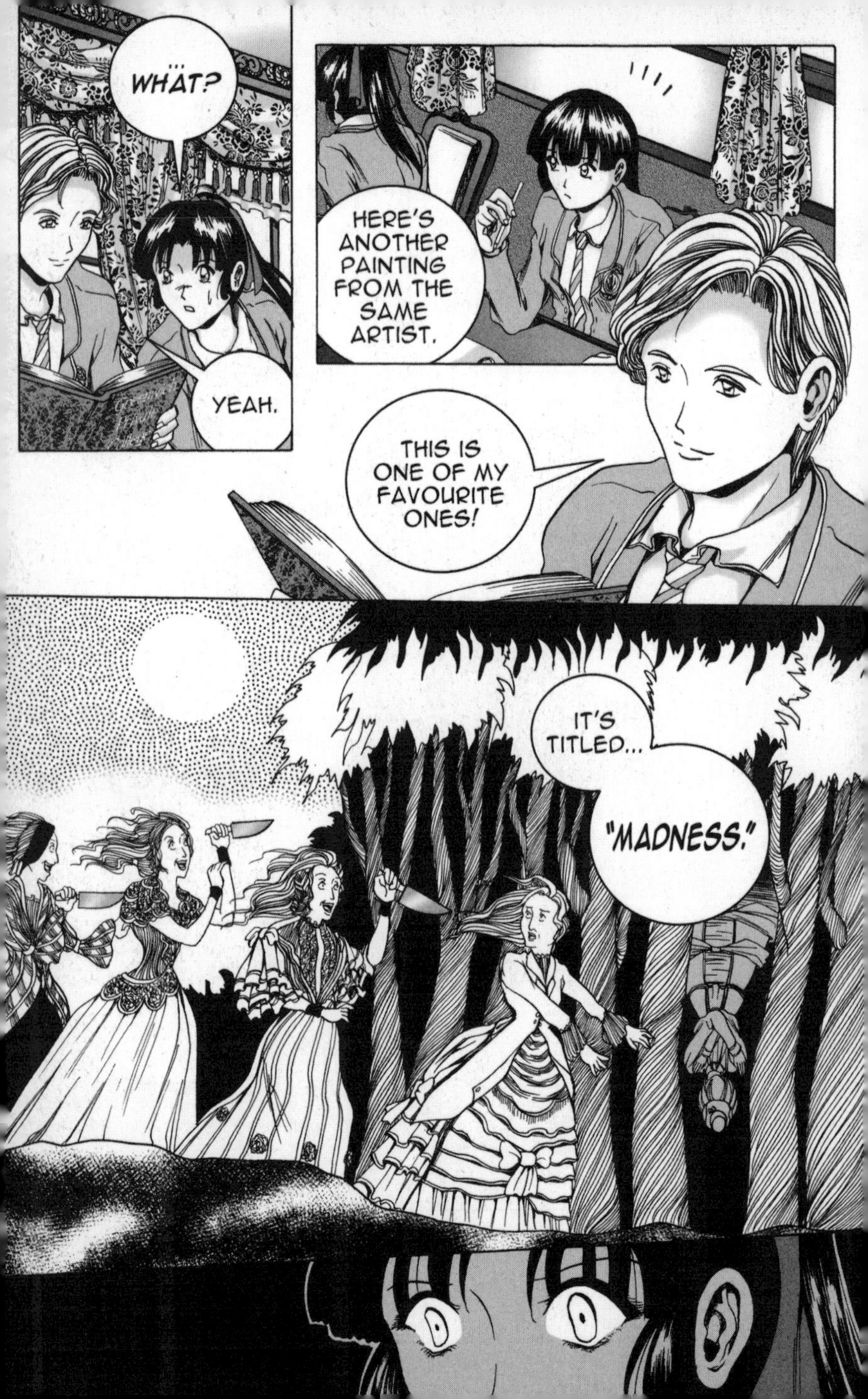
HERE'S ANOTHER PAINTING FROM THE SAME ARTIST.
... WHAT?
YEAH.
THIS IS ONE OF MY FAVOURITE ONES!
IT'S TITLED...
"MADNESS."

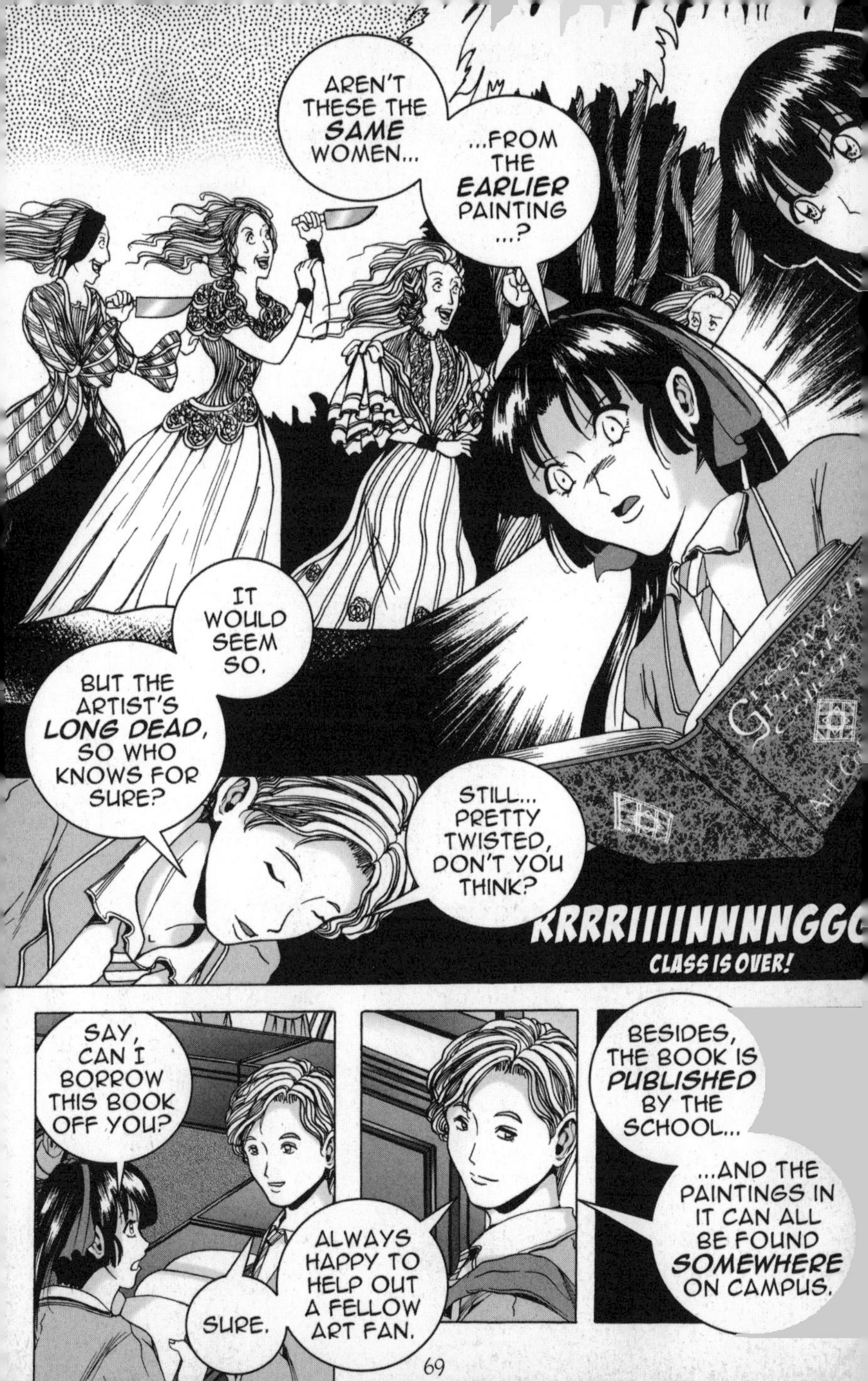
AREN'T THESE THE SAME WOMEN...
...FROM THE EARLIER PAINTING ...?
IT WOULD SEEM SO.
BUT THE ARTIST'S LONG DEAD, SO WHO KNOWS FOR SURE?
STILL... PRETTY TWISTED, DON'T YOU THINK?
KRRRIIIINNNNGGG
CLASS IS OVER!
SAY, CAN I BORROW THIS BOOK OFF YOU?
SURE.
ALWAYS HAPPY TO HELP OUT A FELLOW ART FAN.
BESIDES, THE BOOK IS PUBLISHED BY THE SCHOOL...
...AND THE PAINTINGS IN IT CAN ALL BE FOUND SOMEWHERE ON CAMPUS.

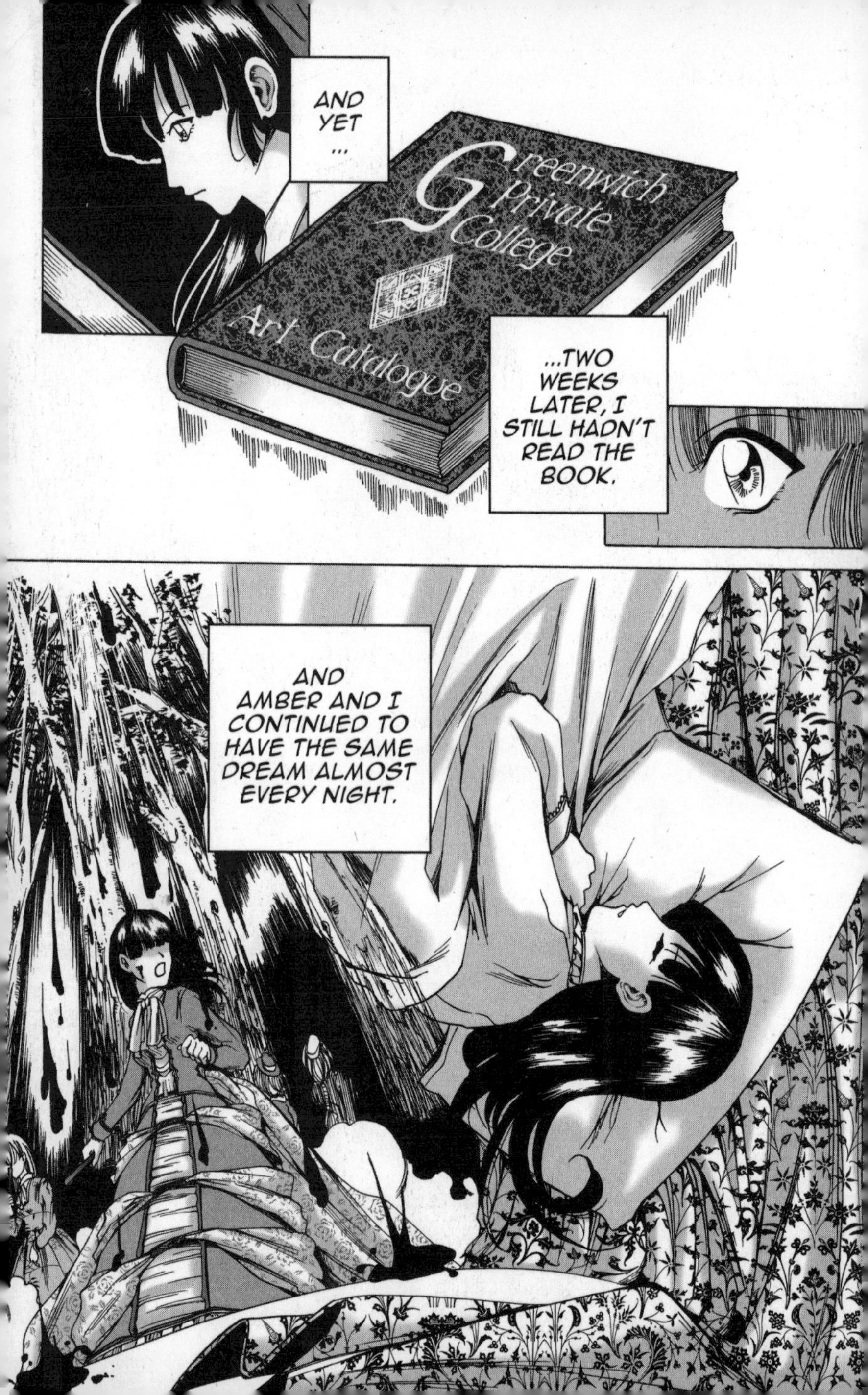
AND YET ...
Greenwich Private College
Art Catalogue
...TWO WEEKS LATER, I STILL HADN'T READ THE BOOK.
AND AMBER AND I CONTINUED TO HAVE THE SAME DREAM ALMOST EVERY NIGHT.

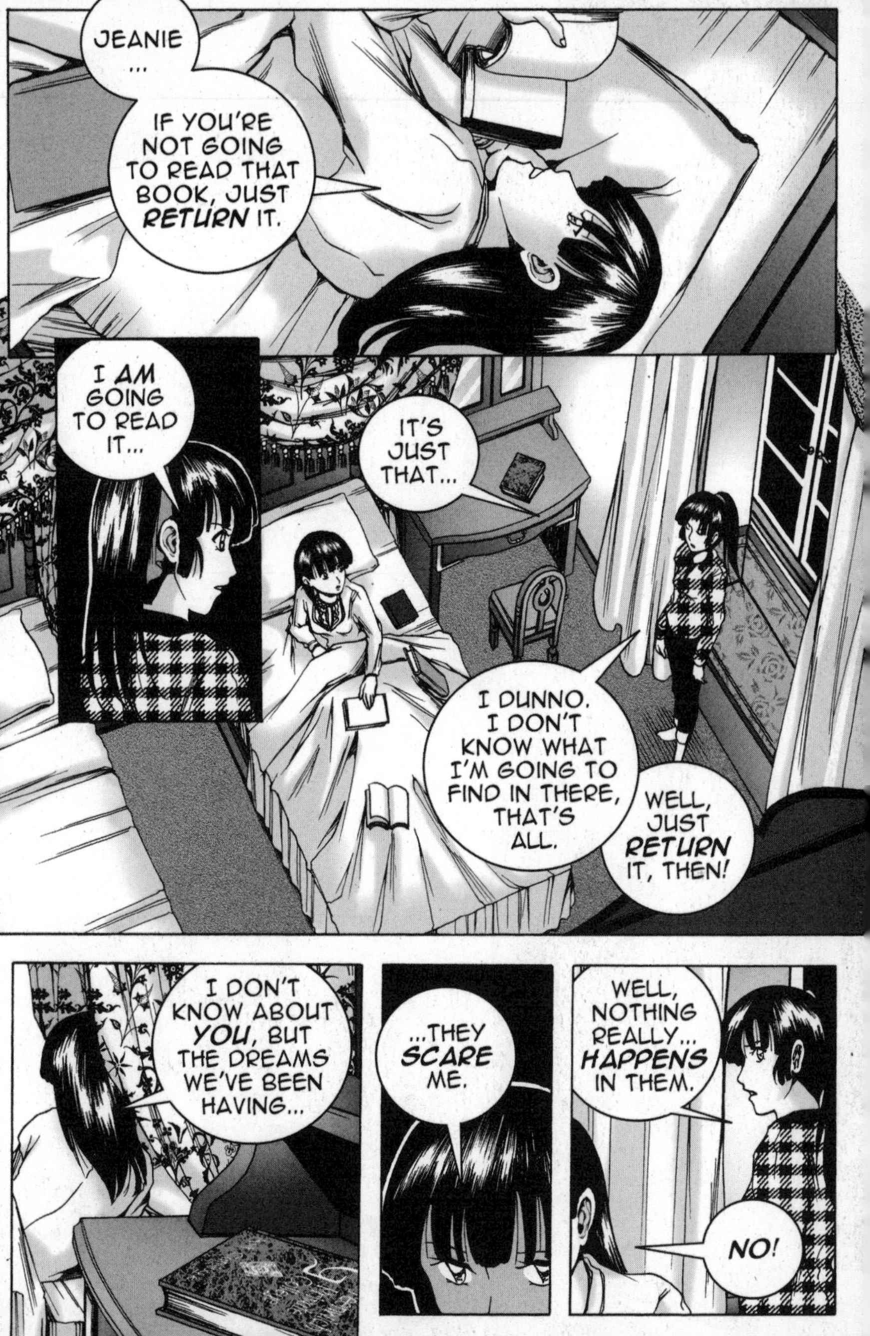
JEANIE ...
IF YOU'RE NOT GOING TO READ THAT BOOK, JUST RETURN IT.
I AM GOING TO READ IT...
IT'S JUST THAT...
I DUNNO. I DON'T KNOW WHAT I'M GOING TO FIND IN THERE, THAT'S ALL.
WELL, JUST RETURN IT, THEN!
I DON'T KNOW ABOUT YOU, BUT THE DREAMS WE'VE BEEN HAVING...
...THEY SCARE ME.
WELL, NOTHING REALLY... HAPPENS IN THEM.
NO!

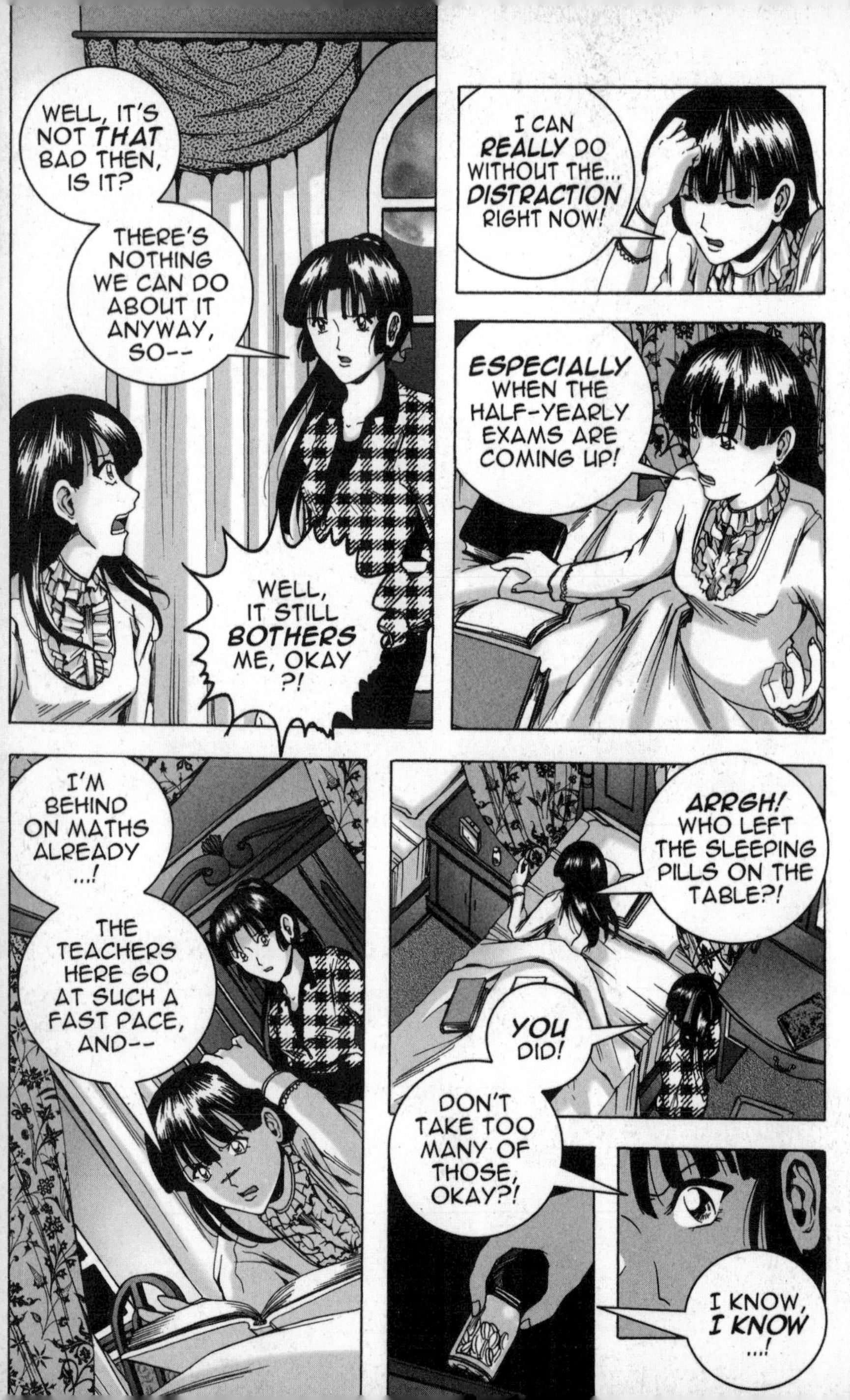
WELL, IT'S NOT *THAT* BAD THEN, IS IT?
THERE'S NOTHING WE CAN DO ABOUT IT ANYWAY, SO--
WELL, IT STILL *BOTHERS* ME, OKAY ?!
I CAN *REALLY* DO WITHOUT THE... *DISTRACTION* RIGHT NOW!
ESPECIALLY WHEN THE HALF-YEARLY EXAMS ARE COMING UP!
I'M BEHIND ON MATHS ALREADY ...!
THE TEACHERS HERE GO AT SUCH A FAST PACE, AND--
ARRGH! WHO LEFT THE SLEEPING PILLS ON THE TABLE?!
YOU DID!
DON'T TAKE TOO MANY OF THOSE, OKAY?!
I KNOW, *I KNOW* ...!

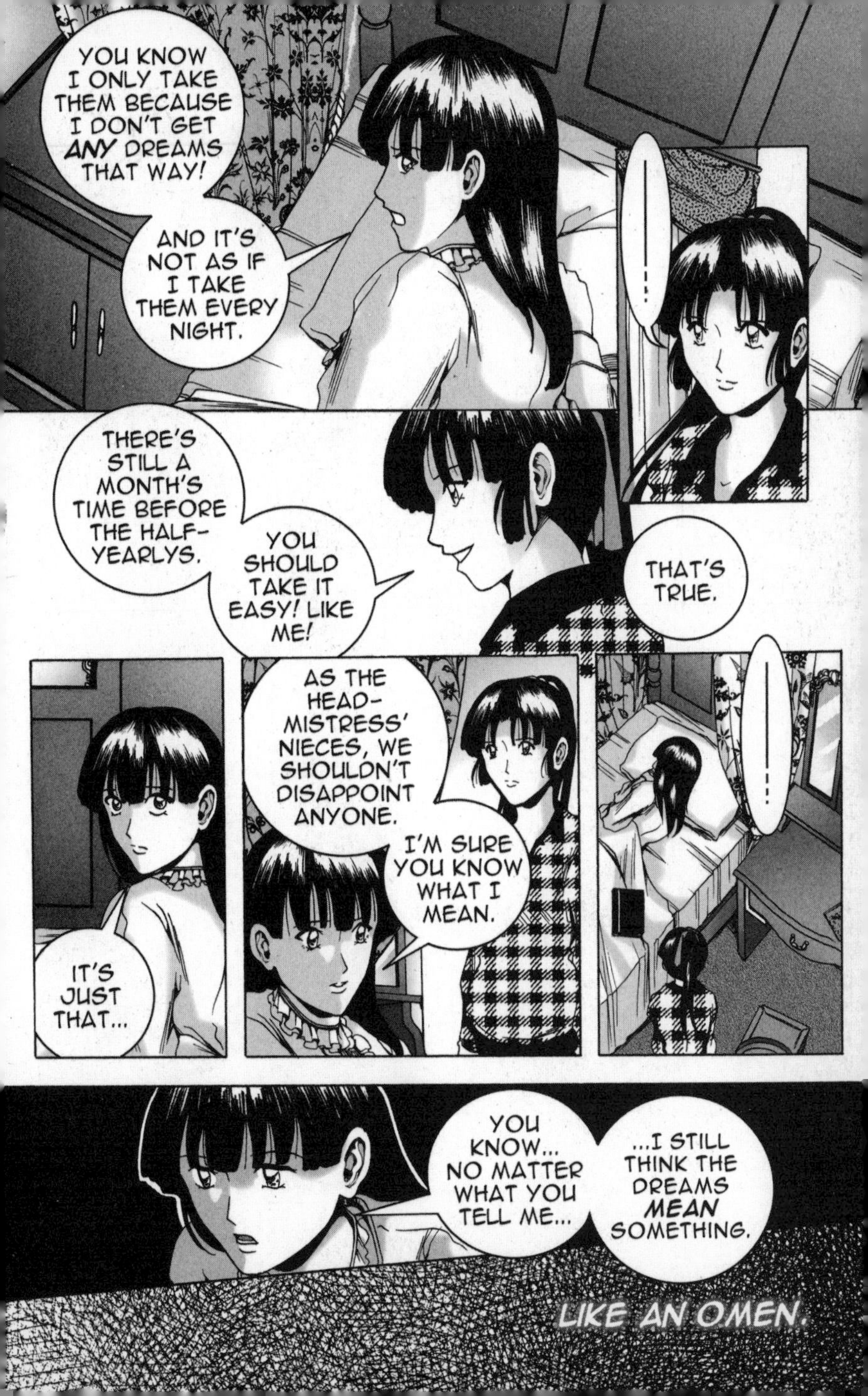
YOU KNOW I ONLY TAKE THEM BECAUSE I DON'T GET ANY DREAMS THAT WAY!
AND IT'S NOT AS IF I TAKE THEM EVERY NIGHT.
......
THERE'S STILL A MONTH'S TIME BEFORE THE HALF-YEARLYS.
YOU SHOULD TAKE IT EASY! LIKE ME!
THAT'S TRUE.
IT'S JUST THAT...
AS THE HEAD-MISTRESS' NIECES, WE SHOULDN'T DISAPPOINT ANYONE.
I'M SURE YOU KNOW WHAT I MEAN.
......
YOU KNOW... NO MATTER WHAT YOU TELL ME...
...I STILL THINK THE DREAMS MEAN SOMETHING.
LIKE AN OMEN.

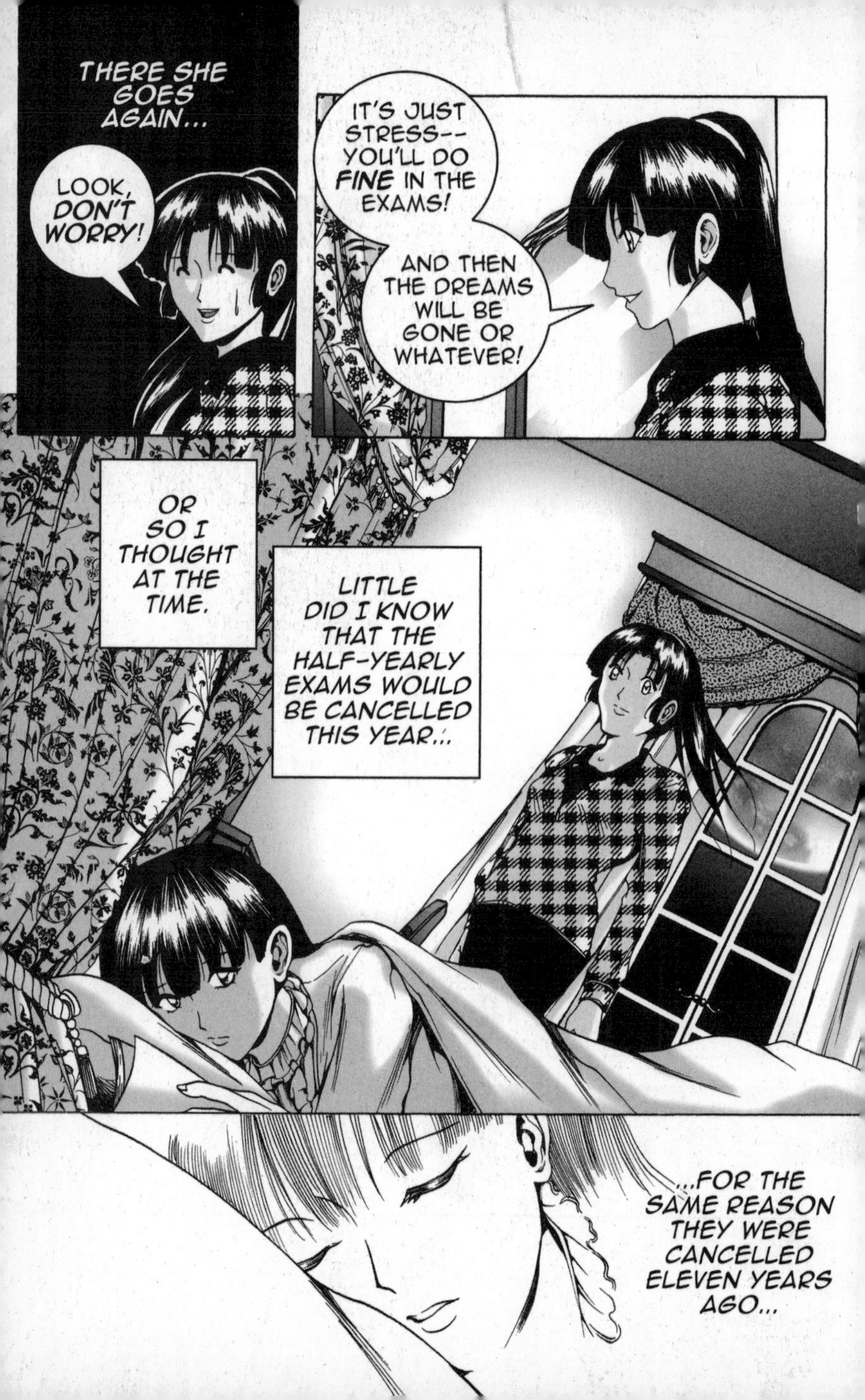
THERE SHE GOES AGAIN...
LOOK, DON'T WORRY!
IT'S JUST STRESS-- YOU'LL DO FINE IN THE EXAMS!
AND THEN THE DREAMS WILL BE GONE OR WHATEVER!
OR SO I THOUGHT AT THE TIME.
LITTLE DID I KNOW THAT THE HALF-YEARLY EXAMS WOULD BE CANCELLED THIS YEAR...
...FOR THE SAME REASON THEY WERE CANCELLED ELEVEN YEARS AGO...

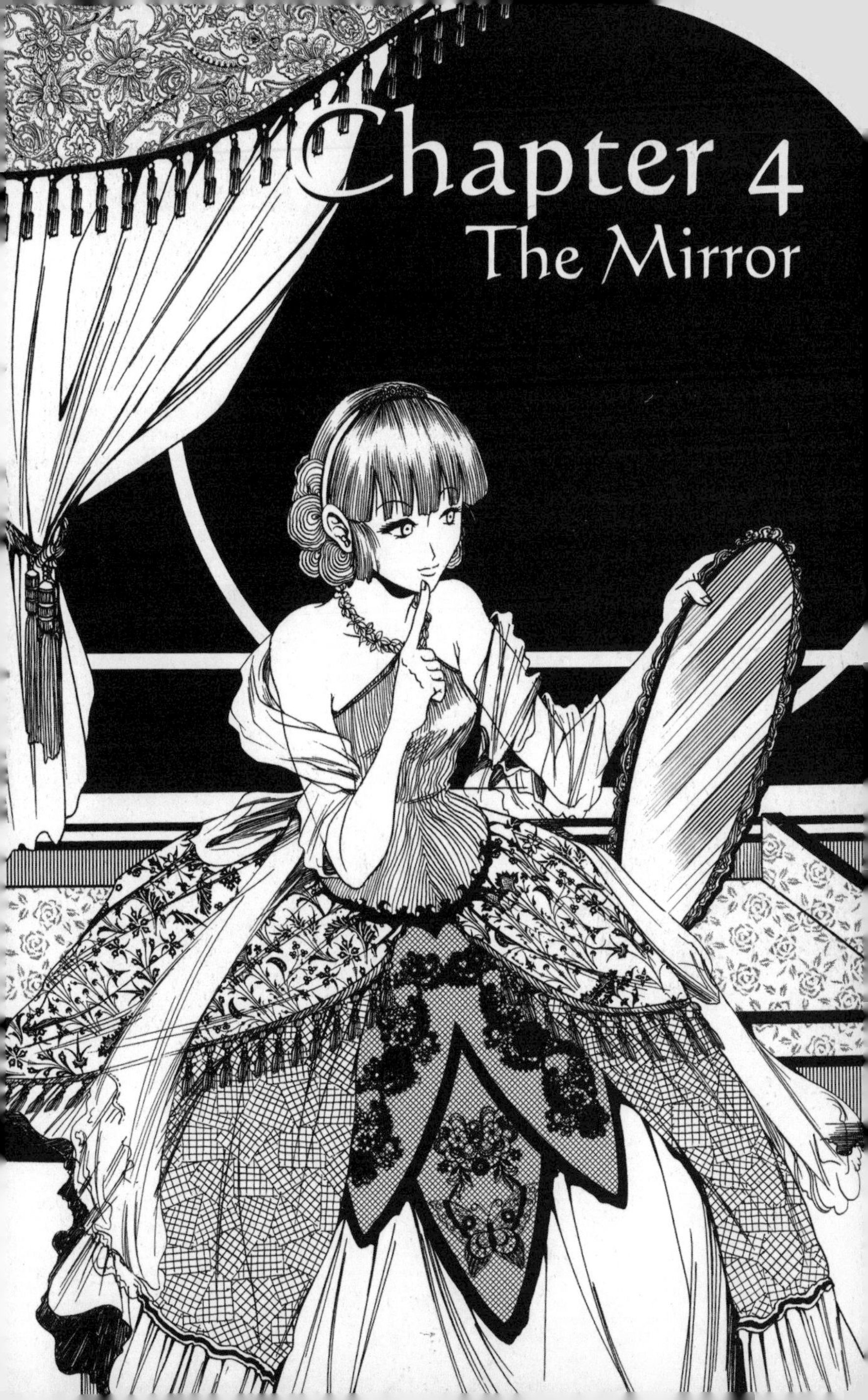
Chapter 4
The Mirror

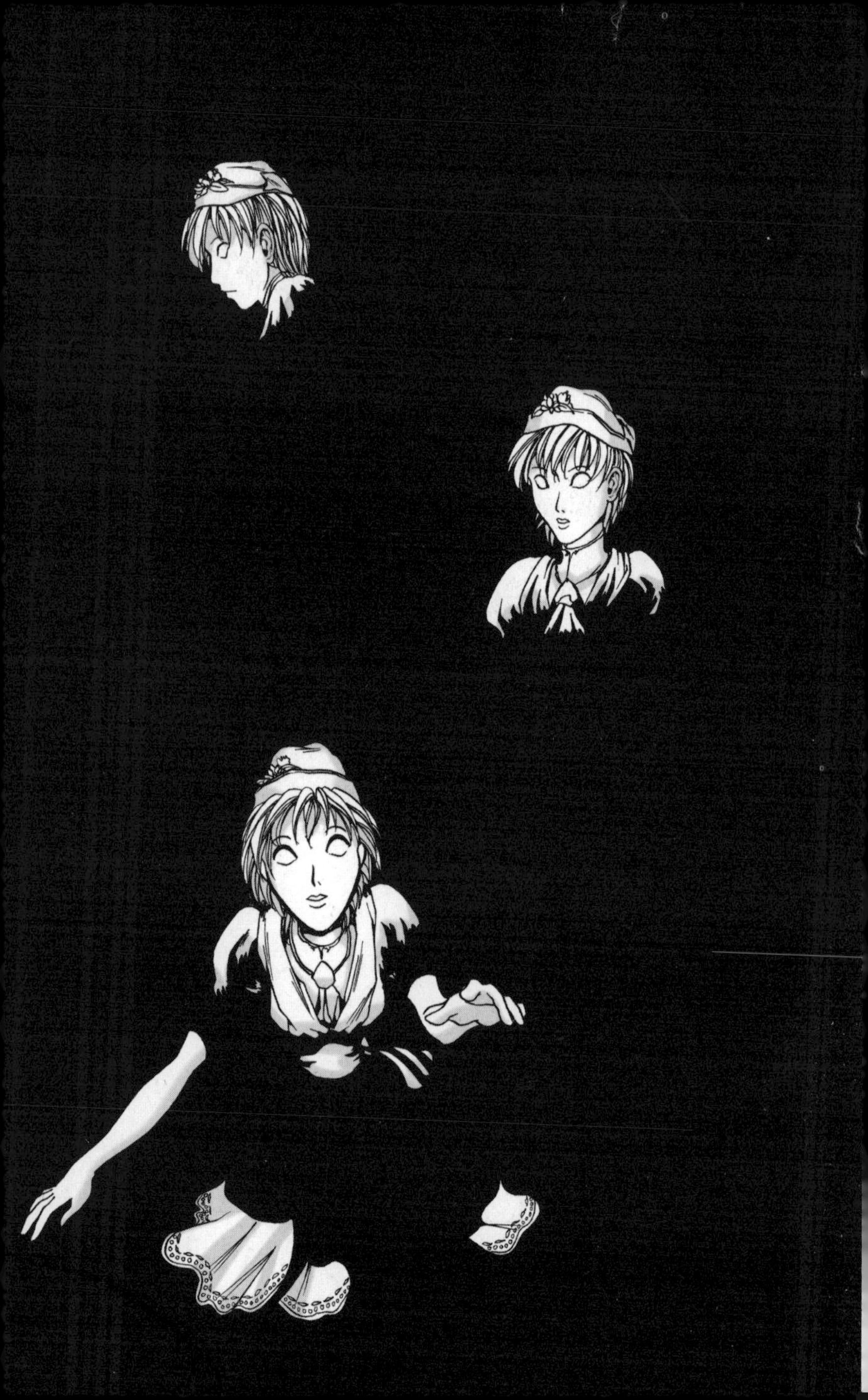

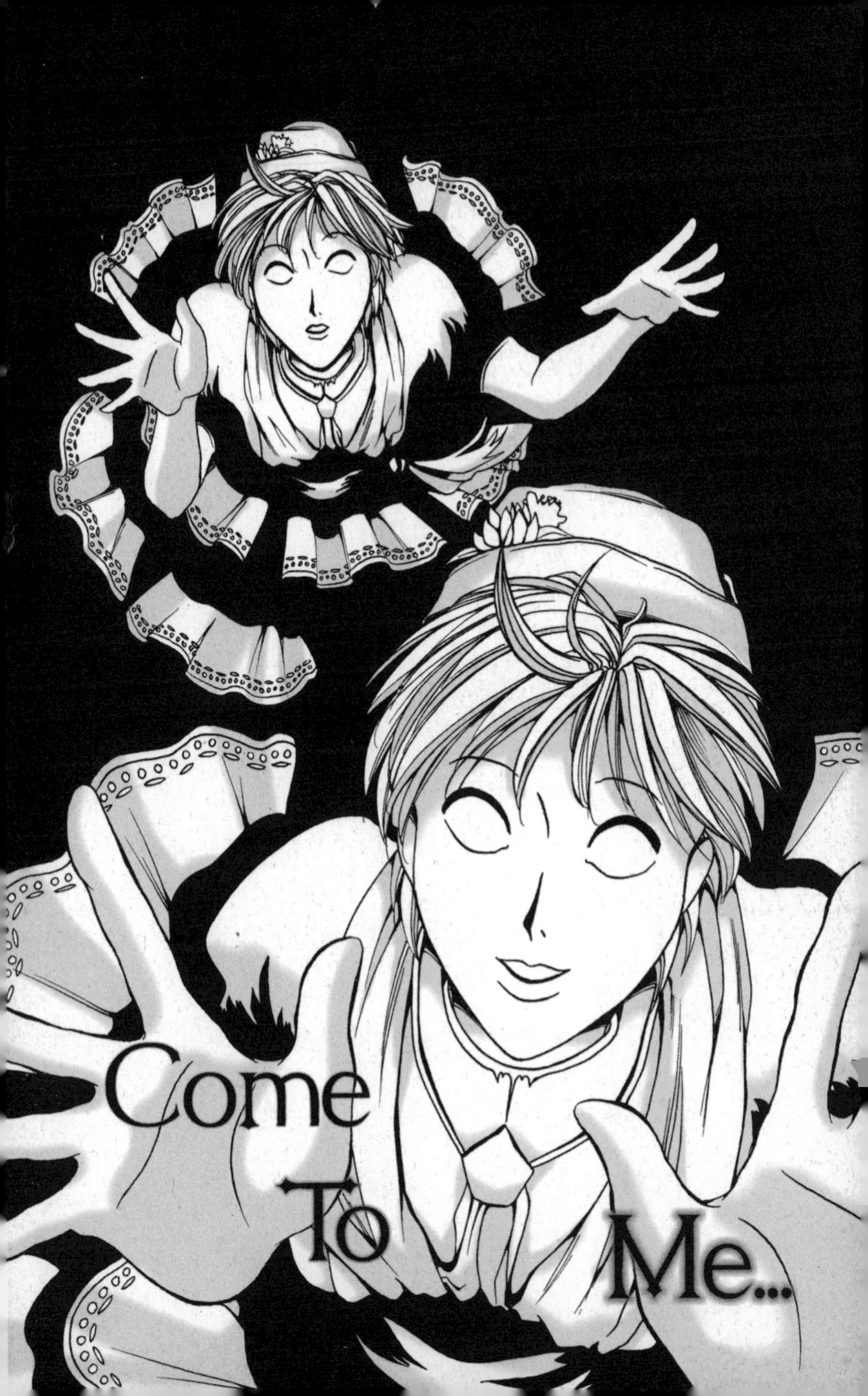
Come
To
Me...

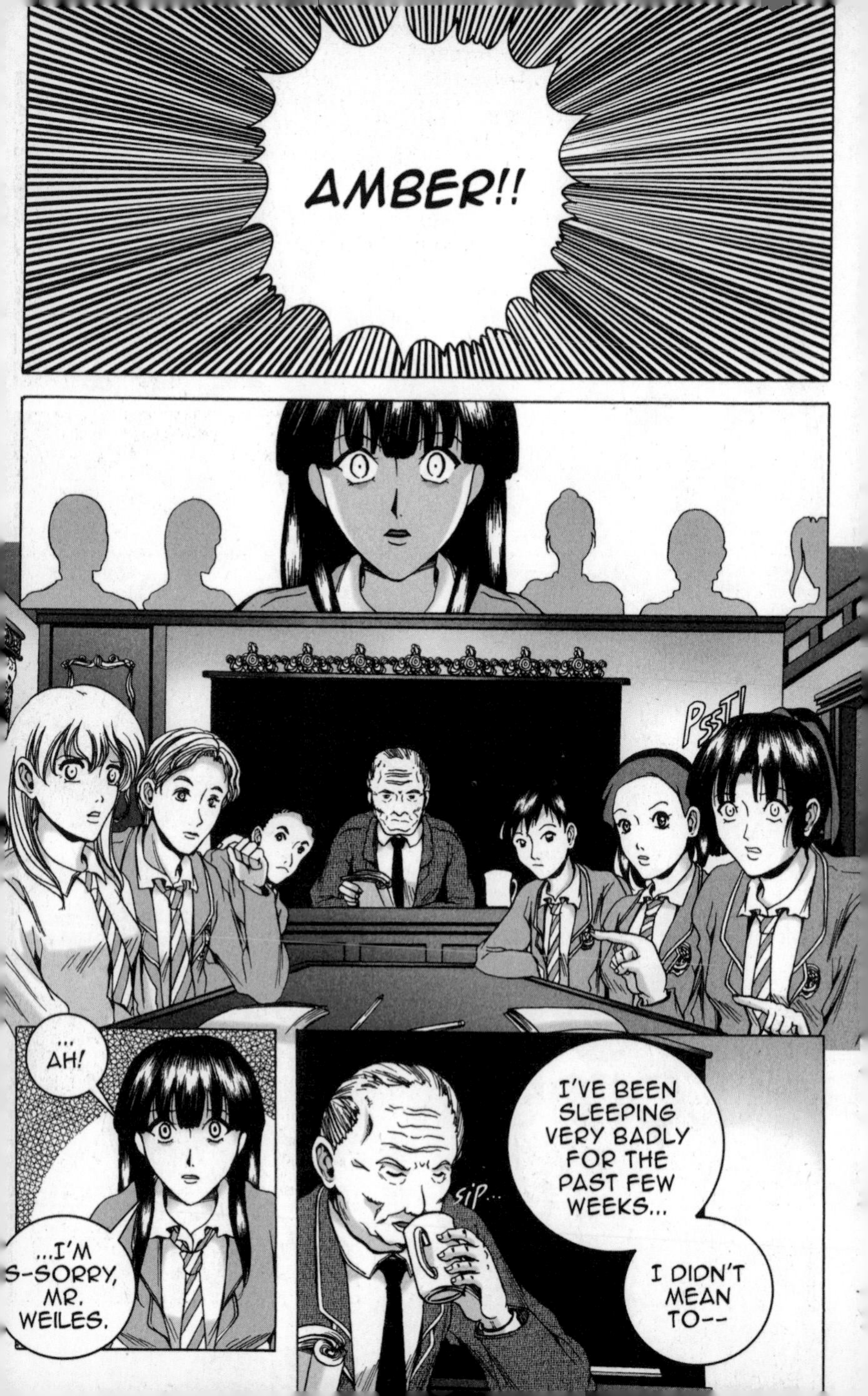
AMBER!!
PSST!
...AH!
...I'M S-SORRY, MR. WEILES.
SIP...
I'VE BEEN SLEEPING VERY BADLY FOR THE PAST FEW WEEKS...
I DIDN'T MEAN TO--

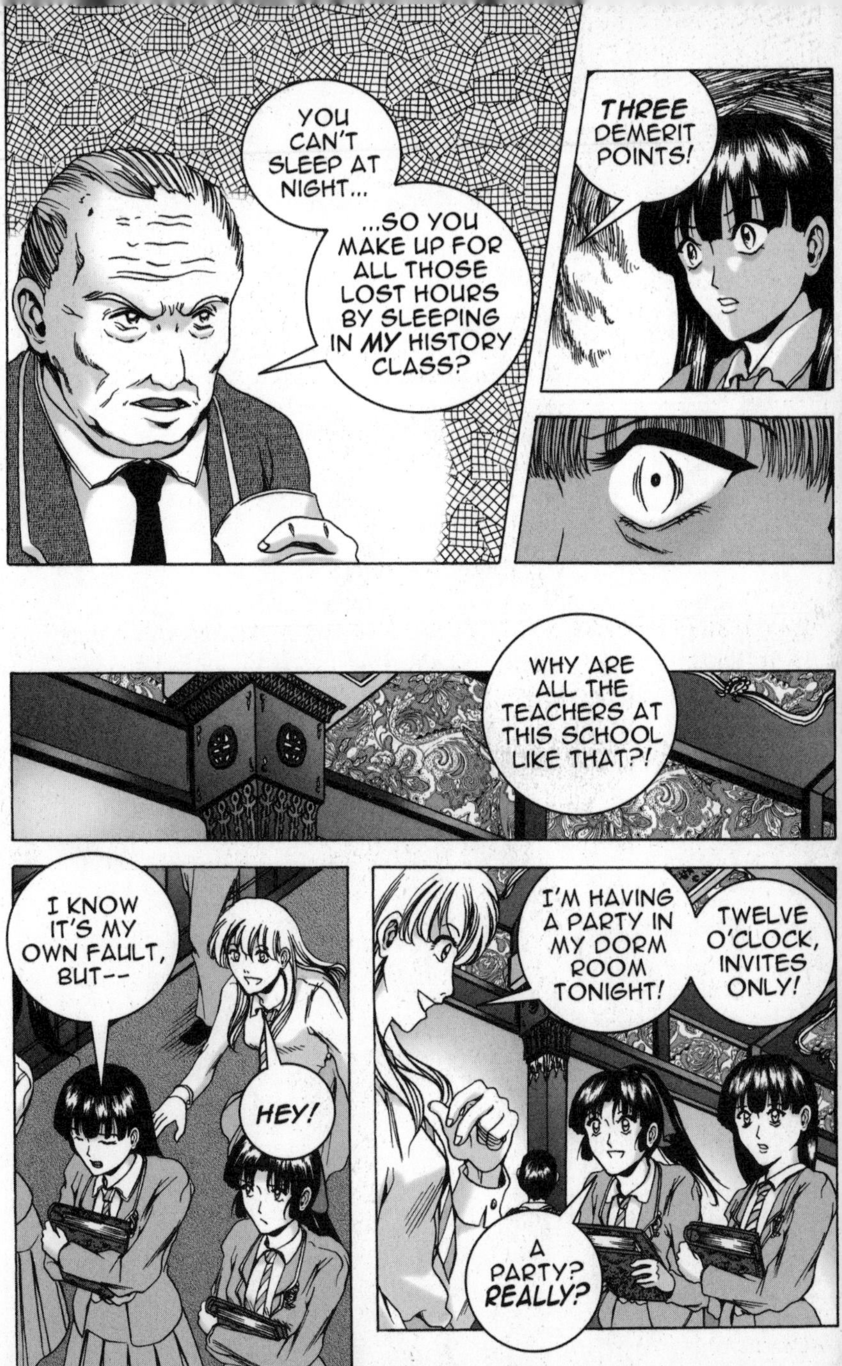
YOU CAN'T SLEEP AT NIGHT...
...SO YOU MAKE UP FOR ALL THOSE LOST HOURS BY SLEEPING IN *MY* HISTORY CLASS?
THREE DEMERIT POINTS!
WHY ARE ALL THE TEACHERS AT THIS SCHOOL LIKE THAT?!
I KNOW IT'S MY OWN FAULT, BUT--
HEY!
I'M HAVING A PARTY IN MY DORM ROOM TONIGHT!
TWELVE O'CLOCK, INVITES ONLY!
A PARTY? *REALLY?*

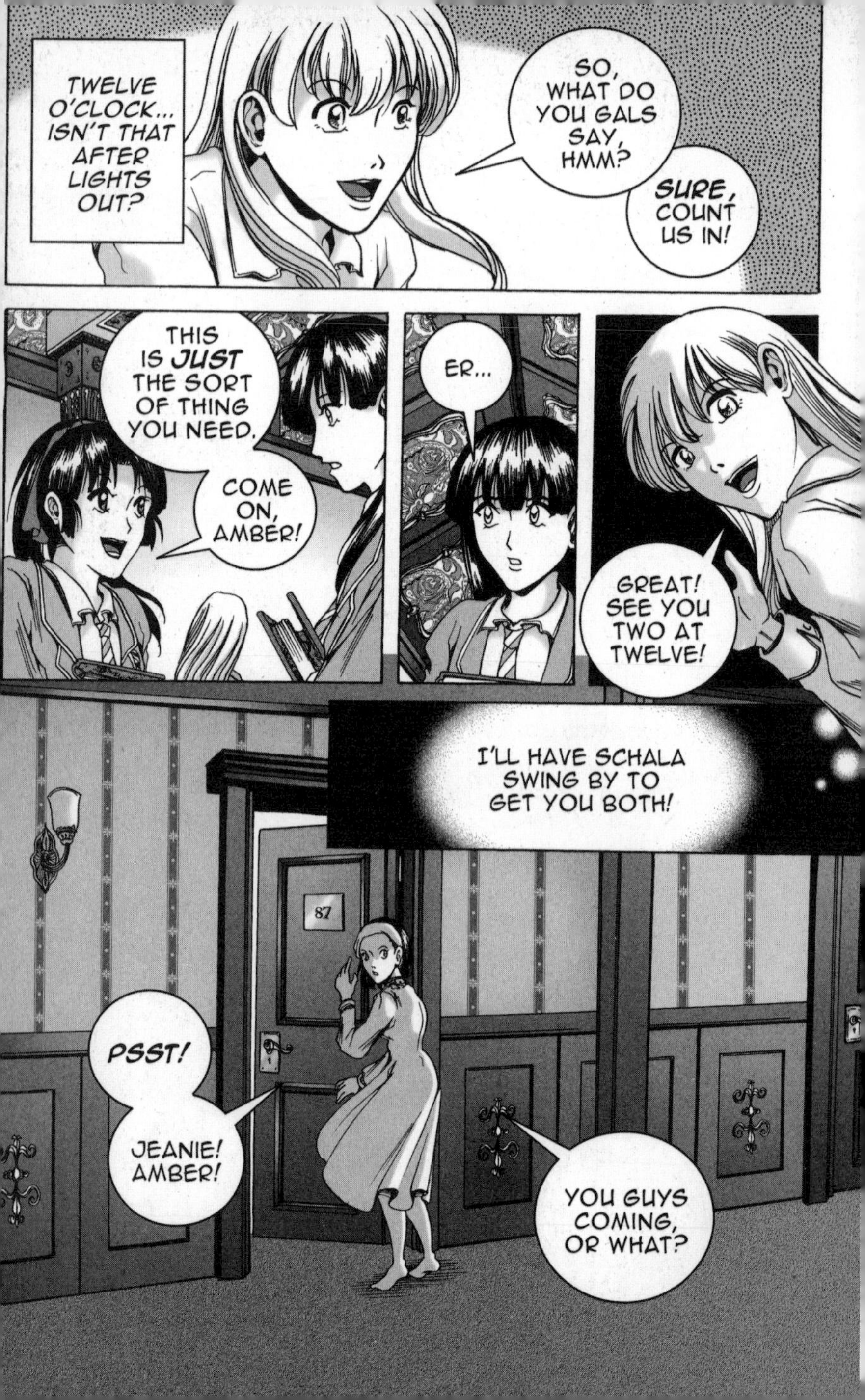
TWELVE O'CLOCK... ISN'T THAT AFTER LIGHTS OUT?
SO, WHAT DO YOU GALS SAY, HMM?
SURE, COUNT US IN!
THIS IS JUST THE SORT OF THING YOU NEED.
COME ON, AMBER!
ER...
GREAT! SEE YOU TWO AT TWELVE!
I'LL HAVE SCHALA SWING BY TO GET YOU BOTH!
87
PSST!
JEANIE! AMBER!
YOU GUYS COMING, OR WHAT?

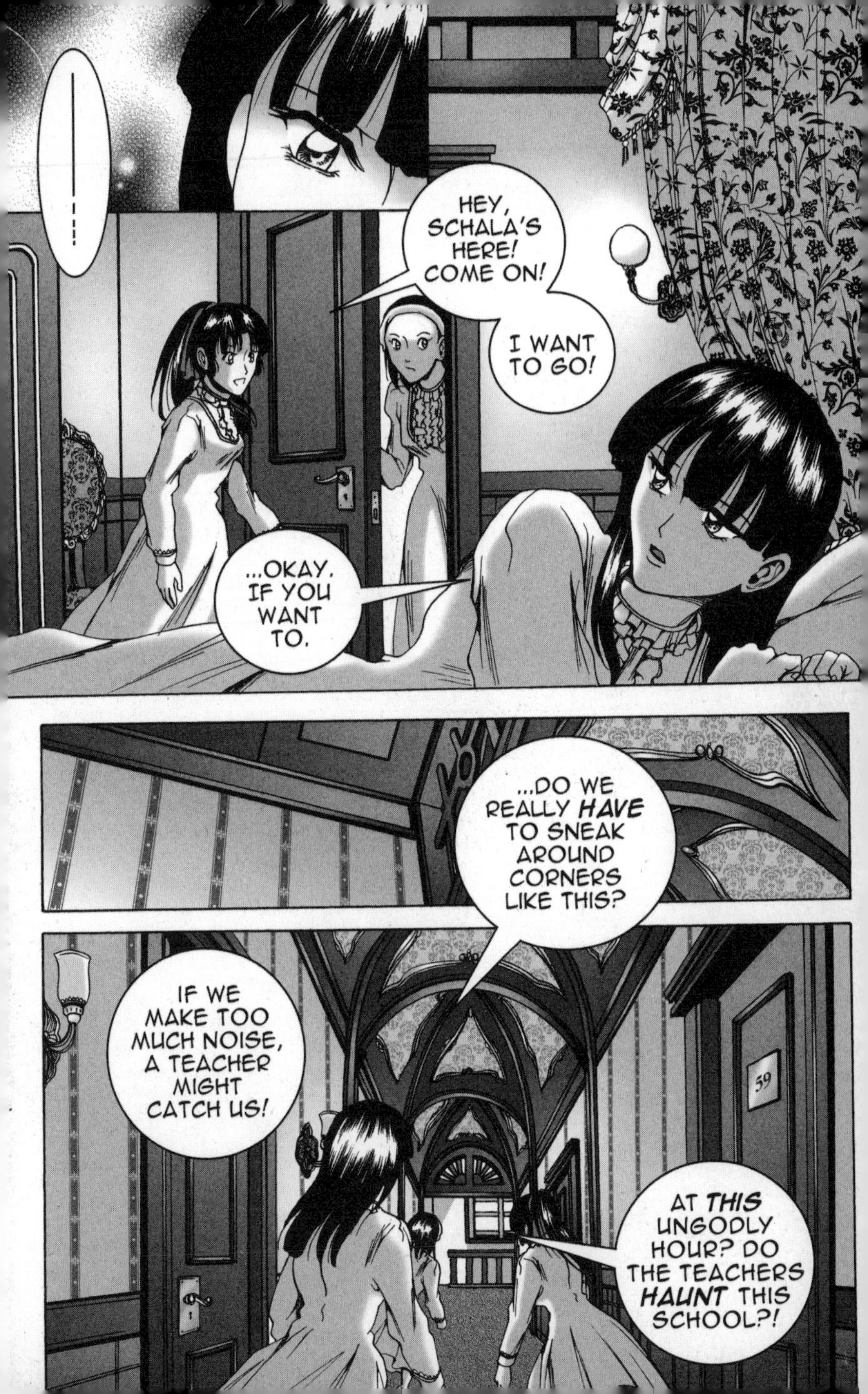
HEY, SCHALA'S HERE! COME ON!
I WANT TO GO!
...OKAY. IF YOU WANT TO.
...DO WE REALLY **HAVE** TO SNEAK AROUND CORNERS LIKE THIS?
IF WE MAKE TOO MUCH NOISE, A TEACHER MIGHT CATCH US!
AT **THIS** UNGODLY HOUR? DO THE TEACHERS **HAUNT** THIS SCHOOL?!

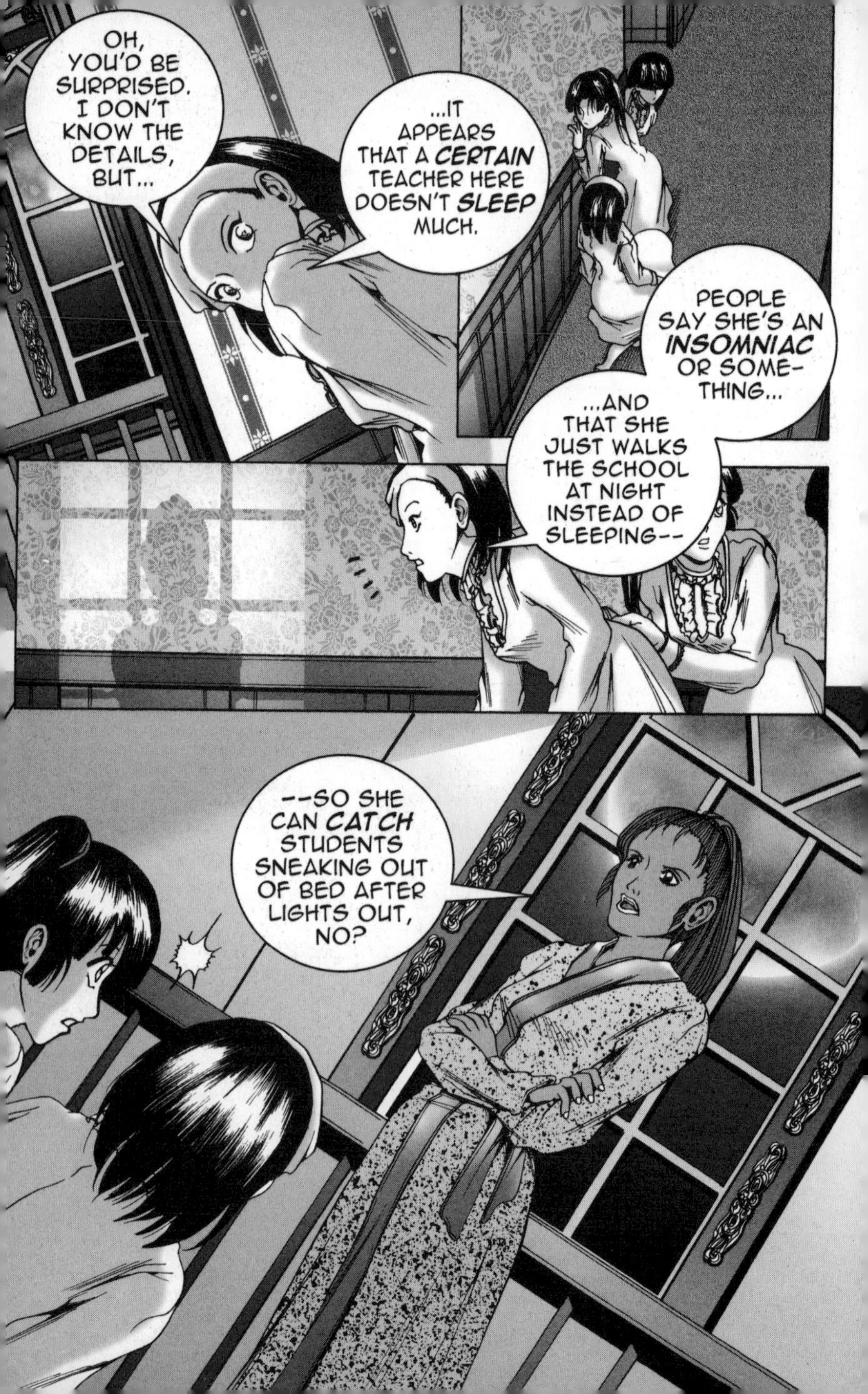
OH, YOU'D BE SURPRISED. I DON'T KNOW THE DETAILS, BUT...
...IT APPEARS THAT A CERTAIN TEACHER HERE DOESN'T SLEEP MUCH.
PEOPLE SAY SHE'S AN INSOMNIAC OR SOME-THING...
...AND THAT SHE JUST WALKS THE SCHOOL AT NIGHT INSTEAD OF SLEEPING--
--SO SHE CAN CATCH STUDENTS SNEAKING OUT OF BED AFTER LIGHTS OUT, NO?

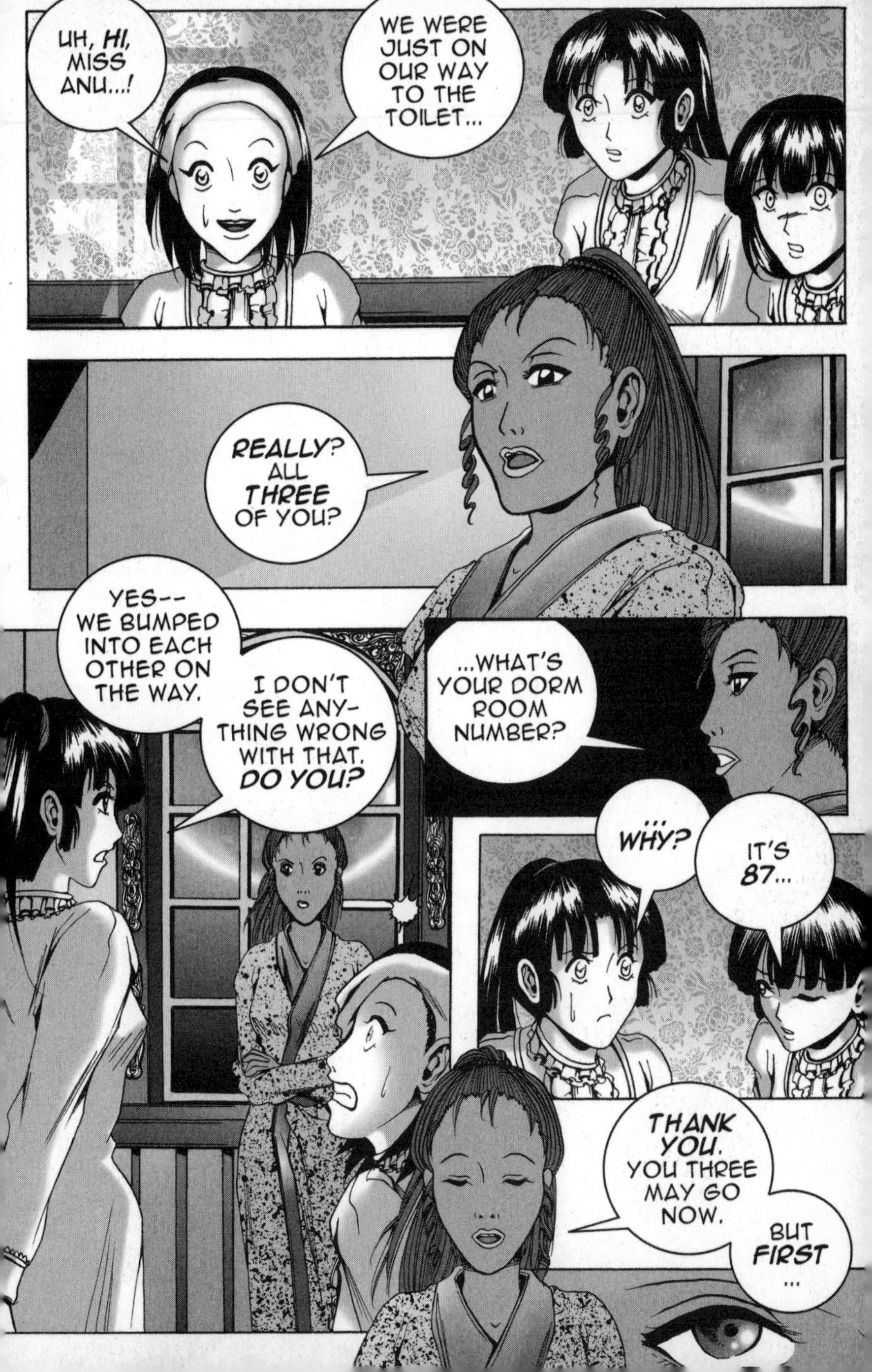
UH, *HI*, MISS ANU...!
WE WERE JUST ON OUR WAY TO THE TOILET...
REALLY? ALL *THREE* OF YOU?
YES-- WE BUMPED INTO EACH OTHER ON THE WAY.
I DON'T SEE ANY-THING WRONG WITH THAT. *DO YOU?*
...WHAT'S YOUR DORM ROOM NUMBER?
... *WHY?*
IT'S *87*...
THANK YOU. YOU THREE MAY GO NOW.
BUT *FIRST* ...

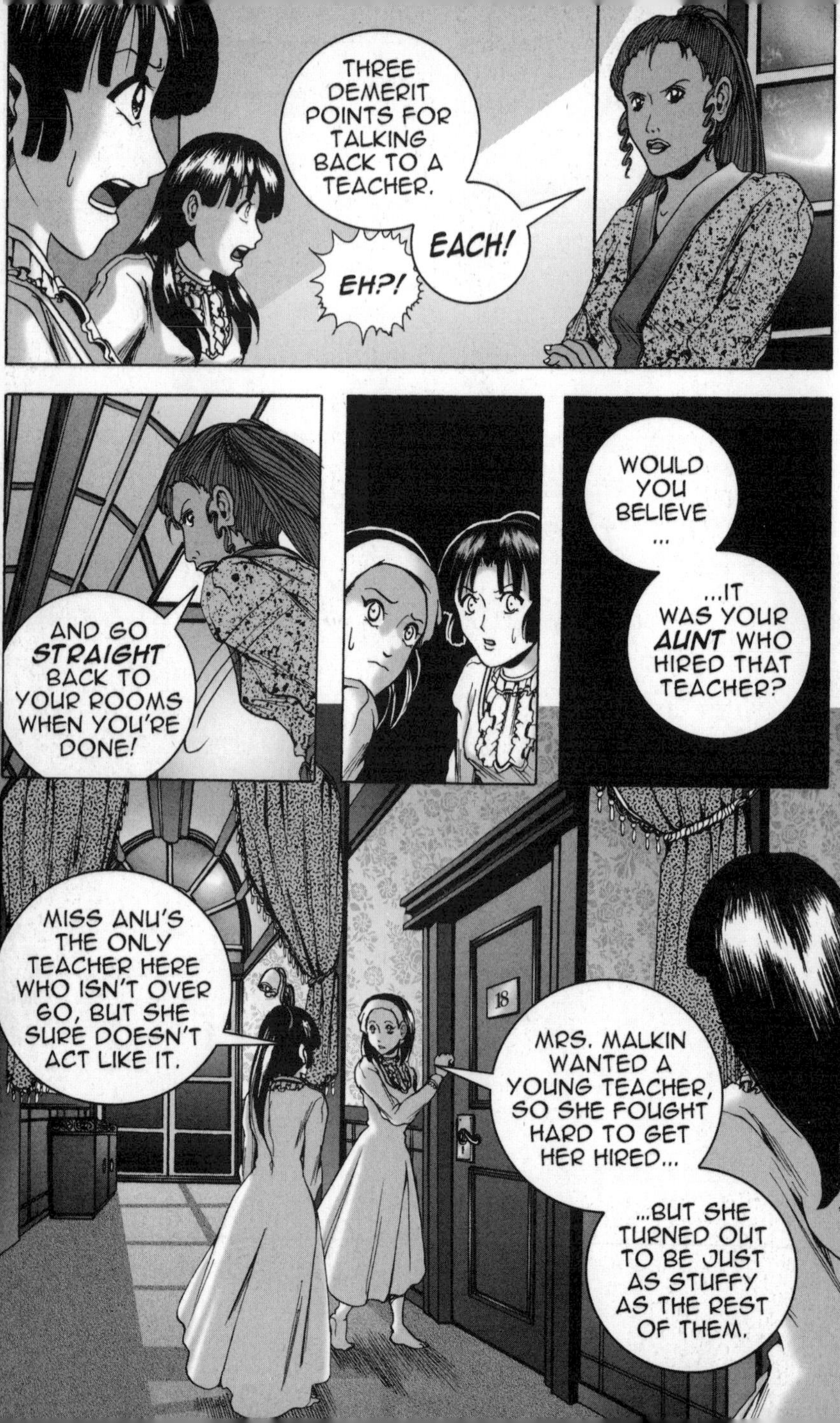
THREE DEMERIT POINTS FOR TALKING BACK TO A TEACHER.
EACH!
EH?!
AND GO STRAIGHT BACK TO YOUR ROOMS WHEN YOU'RE DONE!
WOULD YOU BELIEVE ...
...IT WAS YOUR AUNT WHO HIRED THAT TEACHER?
MISS ANU'S THE ONLY TEACHER HERE WHO ISN'T OVER 60, BUT SHE SURE DOESN'T ACT LIKE IT.
MRS. MALKIN WANTED A YOUNG TEACHER, SO SHE FOUGHT HARD TO GET HER HIRED...
...BUT SHE TURNED OUT TO BE JUST AS STUFFY AS THE REST OF THEM.
18

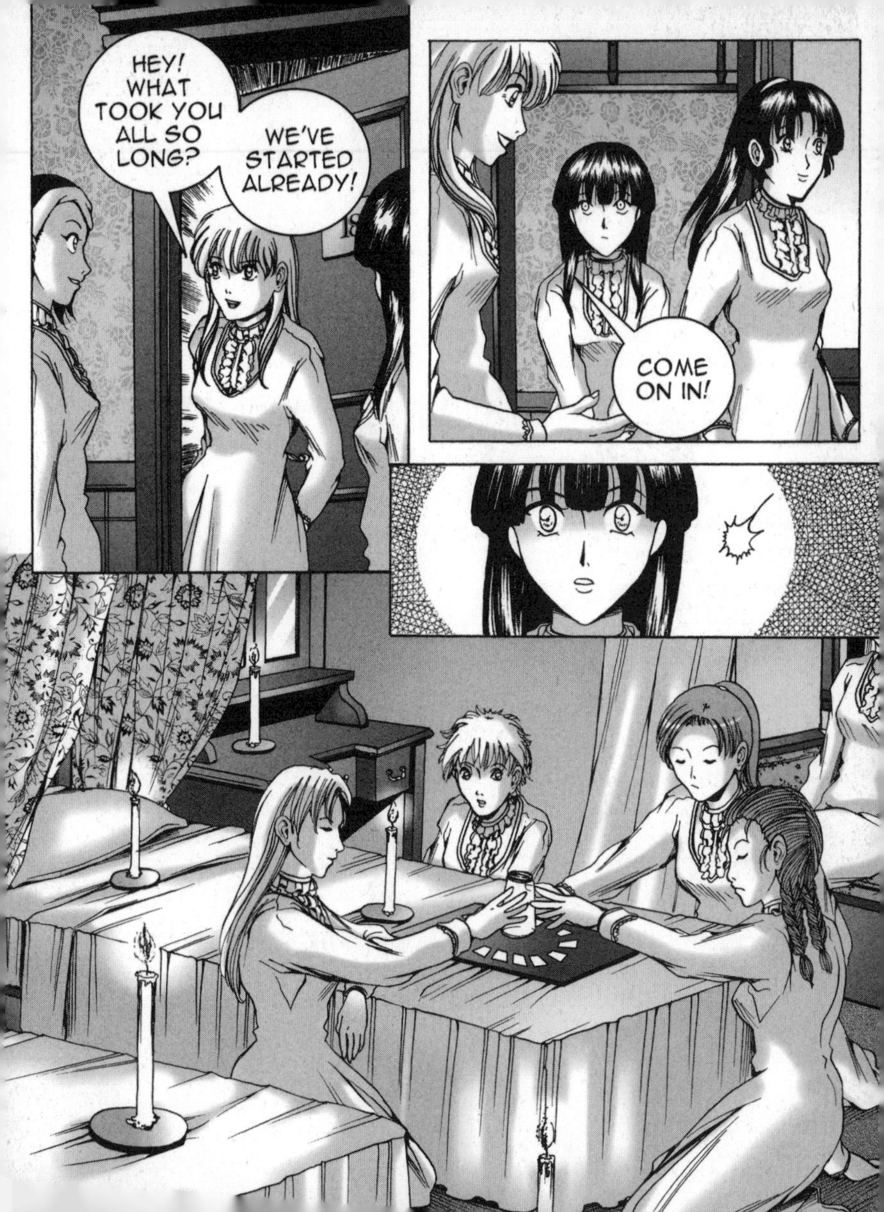
HEY! WHAT TOOK YOU ALL SO LONG?
WE'VE STARTED ALREADY!
COME ON IN!

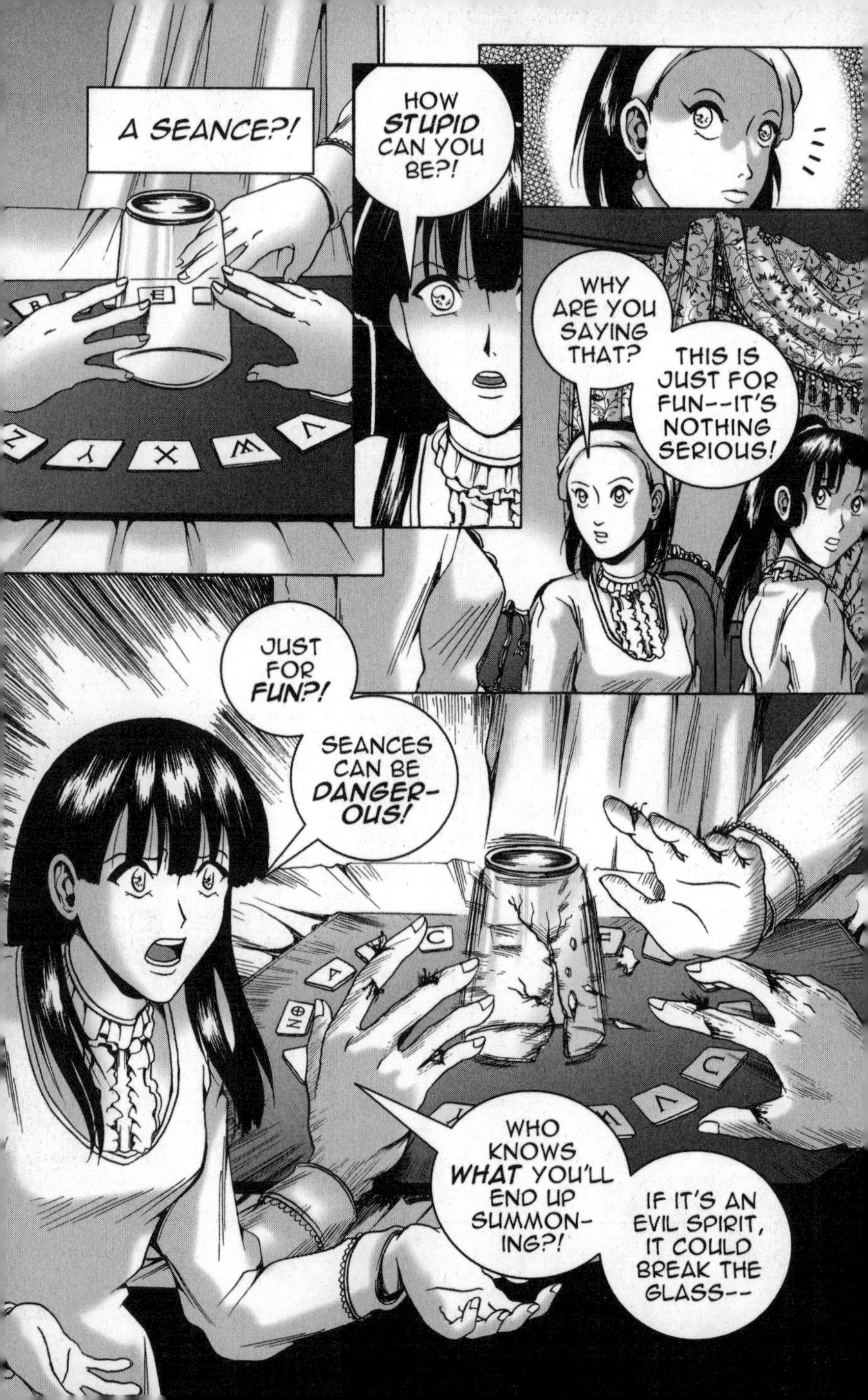
A SEANCE?!
HOW STUPID CAN YOU BE?!
WHY ARE YOU SAYING THAT?
THIS IS JUST FOR FUN--IT'S NOTHING SERIOUS!
JUST FOR FUN?!
SEANCES CAN BE DANGER-OUS!
WHO KNOWS WHAT YOU'LL END UP SUMMON-ING?!
IF IT'S AN EVIL SPIRIT, IT COULD BREAK THE GLASS--

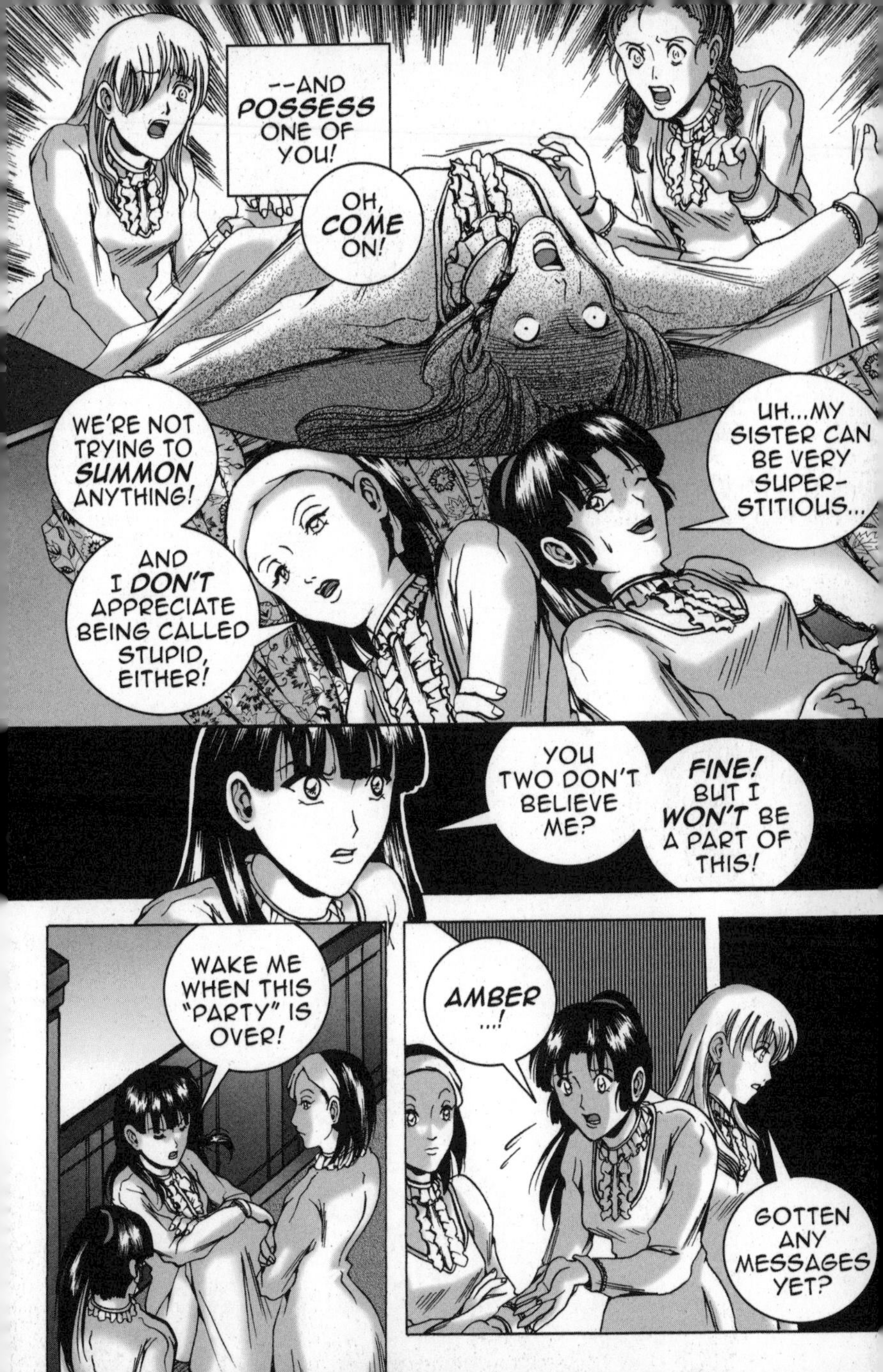
--AND POSSESS ONE OF YOU!
OH, COME ON!
WE'RE NOT TRYING TO SUMMON ANYTHING!
AND I DON'T APPRECIATE BEING CALLED STUPID, EITHER!
UH...MY SISTER CAN BE VERY SUPER-STITIOUS...
YOU TWO DON'T BELIEVE ME?
FINE! BUT I WON'T BE A PART OF THIS!
WAKE ME WHEN THIS "PARTY" IS OVER!
AMBER ...!
GOTTEN ANY MESSAGES YET?

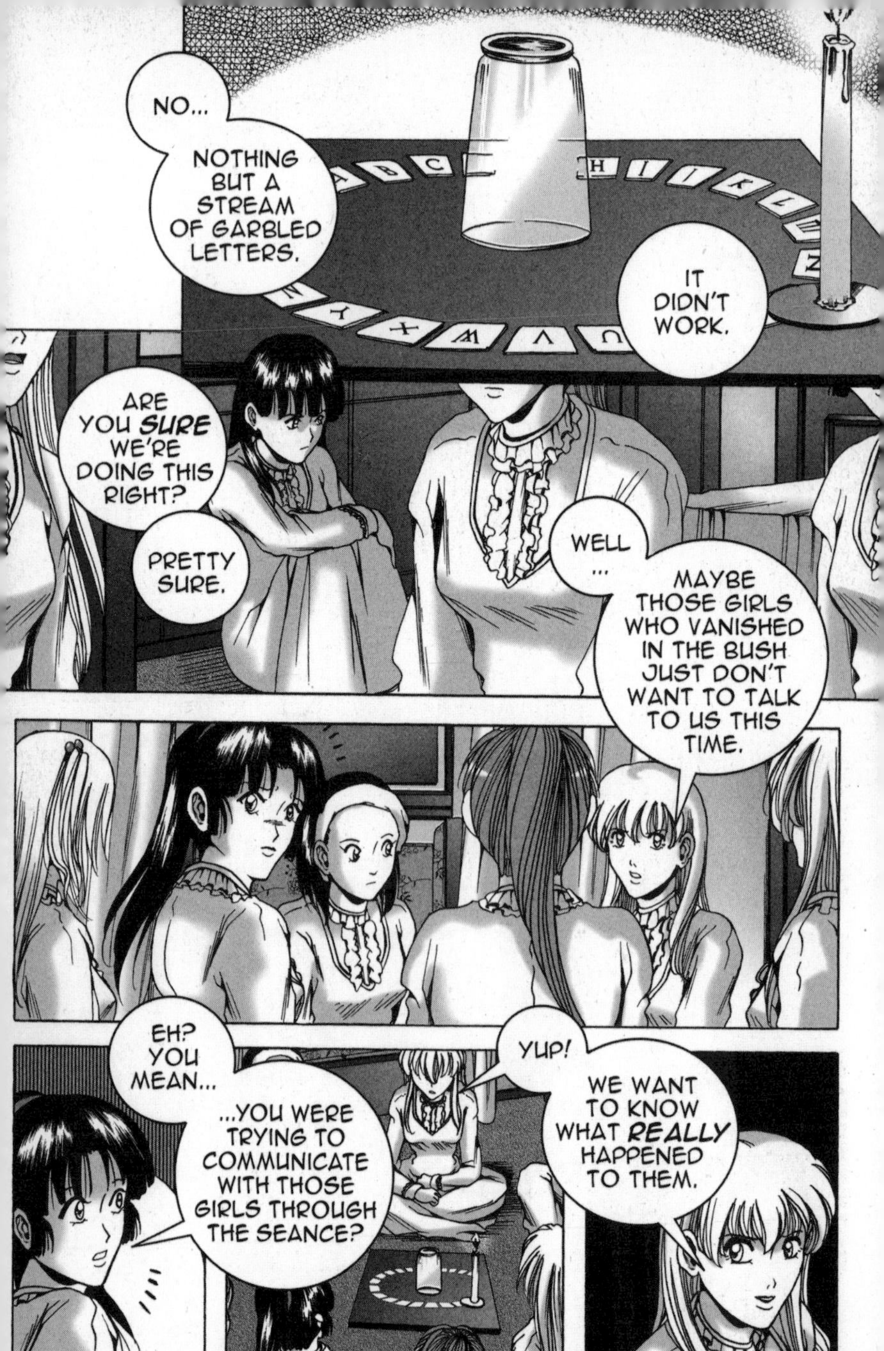
NO...
NOTHING BUT A STREAM OF GARBLED LETTERS.
IT DIDN'T WORK.
ARE YOU **SURE** WE'RE DOING THIS RIGHT?
PRETTY SURE.
WELL ...
MAYBE THOSE GIRLS WHO VANISHED IN THE BUSH JUST DON'T WANT TO TALK TO US THIS TIME.
EH? YOU MEAN...
...YOU WERE TRYING TO COMMUNICATE WITH THOSE GIRLS THROUGH THE SEANCE?
YUP!
WE WANT TO KNOW WHAT **REALLY** HAPPENED TO THEM.

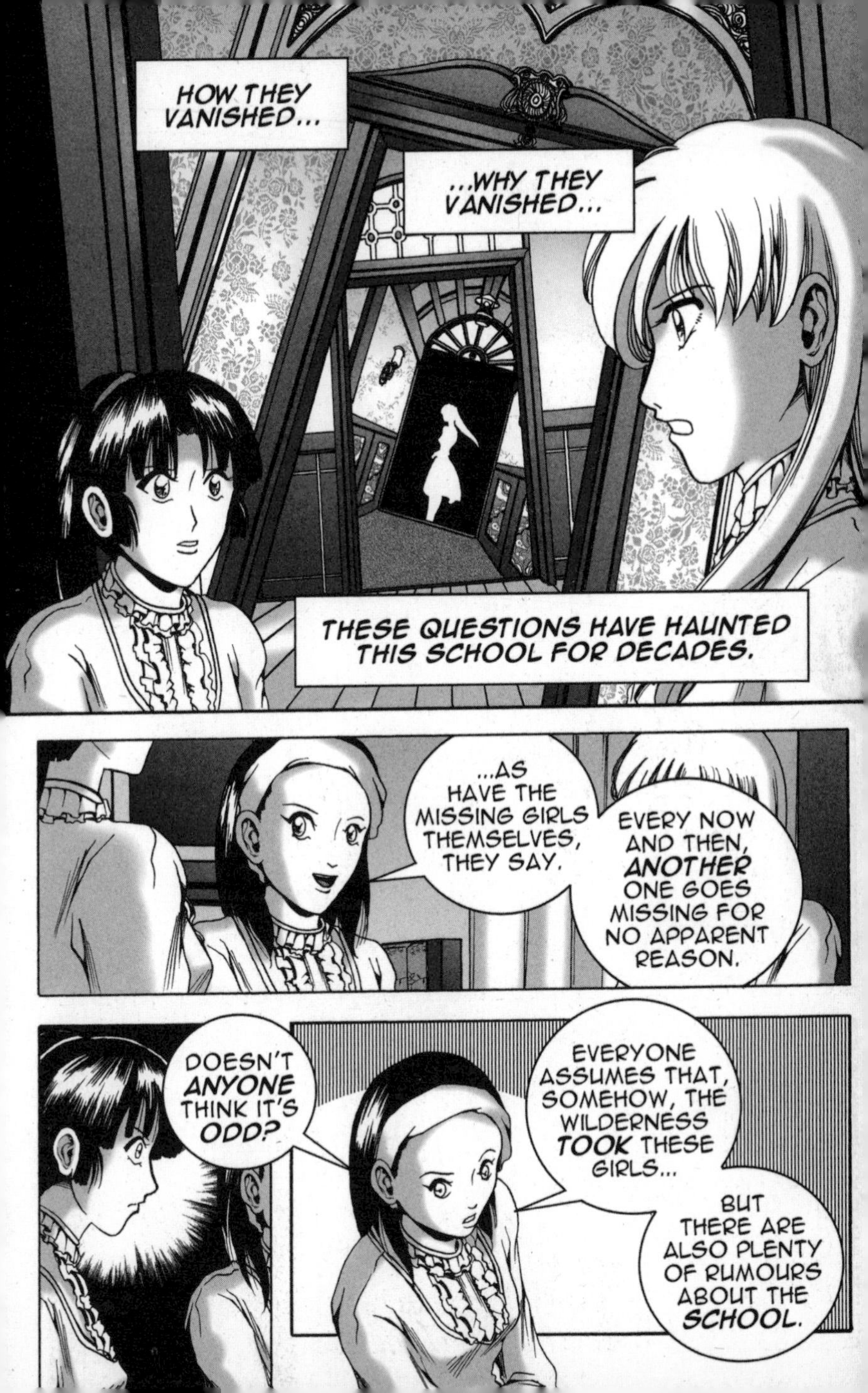
HOW THEY VANISHED...
...WHY THEY VANISHED...
THESE QUESTIONS HAVE HAUNTED THIS SCHOOL FOR DECADES.
...AS HAVE THE MISSING GIRLS THEMSELVES, THEY SAY.
EVERY NOW AND THEN, ANOTHER ONE GOES MISSING FOR NO APPARENT REASON.
DOESN'T ANYONE THINK IT'S ODD?
EVERYONE ASSUMES THAT, SOMEHOW, THE WILDERNESS TOOK THESE GIRLS...
BUT THERE ARE ALSO PLENTY OF RUMOURS ABOUT THE SCHOOL.

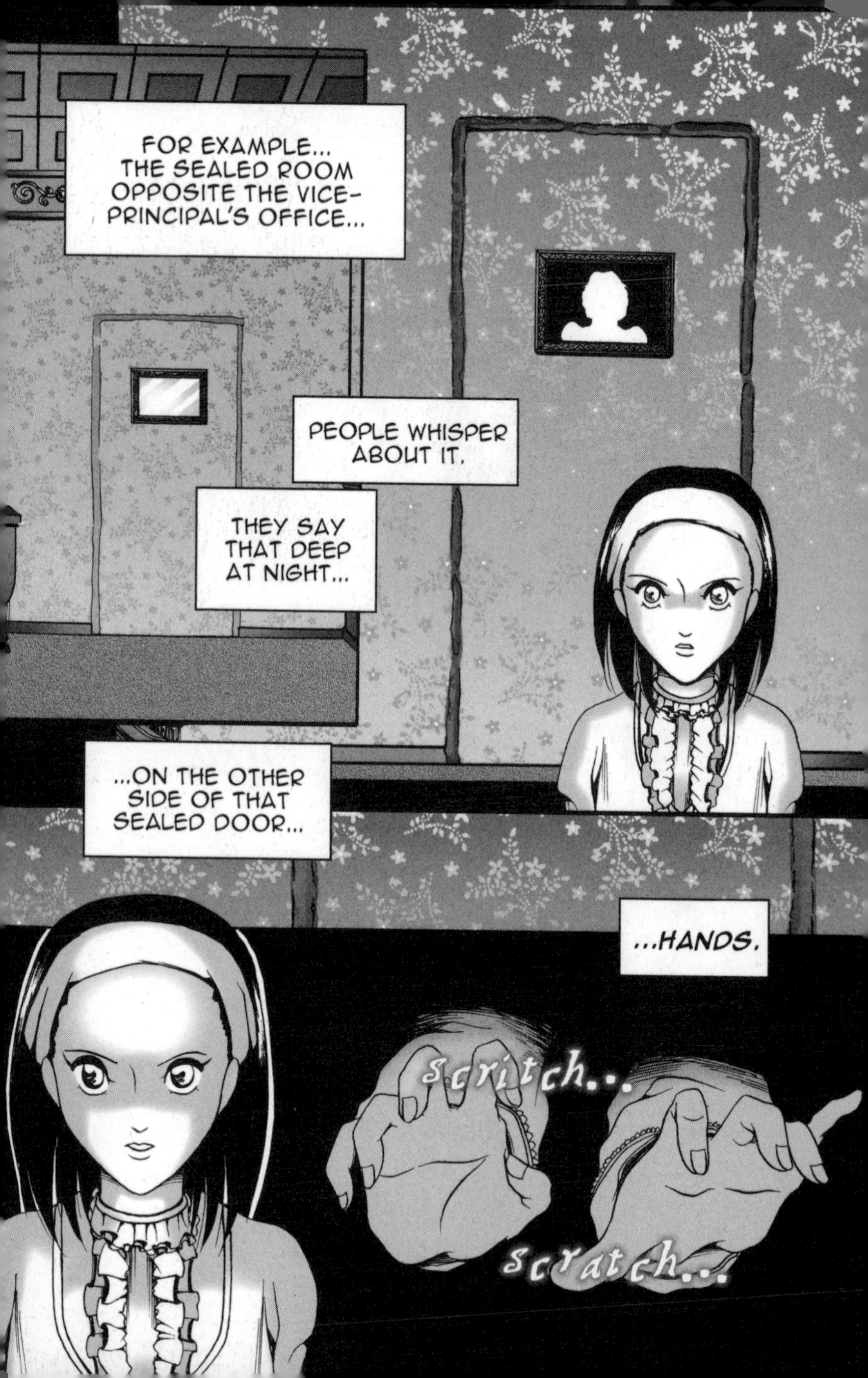
FOR EXAMPLE... THE SEALED ROOM OPPOSITE THE VICE-PRINCIPAL'S OFFICE...
PEOPLE WHISPER ABOUT IT.
THEY SAY THAT DEEP AT NIGHT...
...ON THE OTHER SIDE OF THAT SEALED DOOR...
...HANDS.
scritch...
scratch...

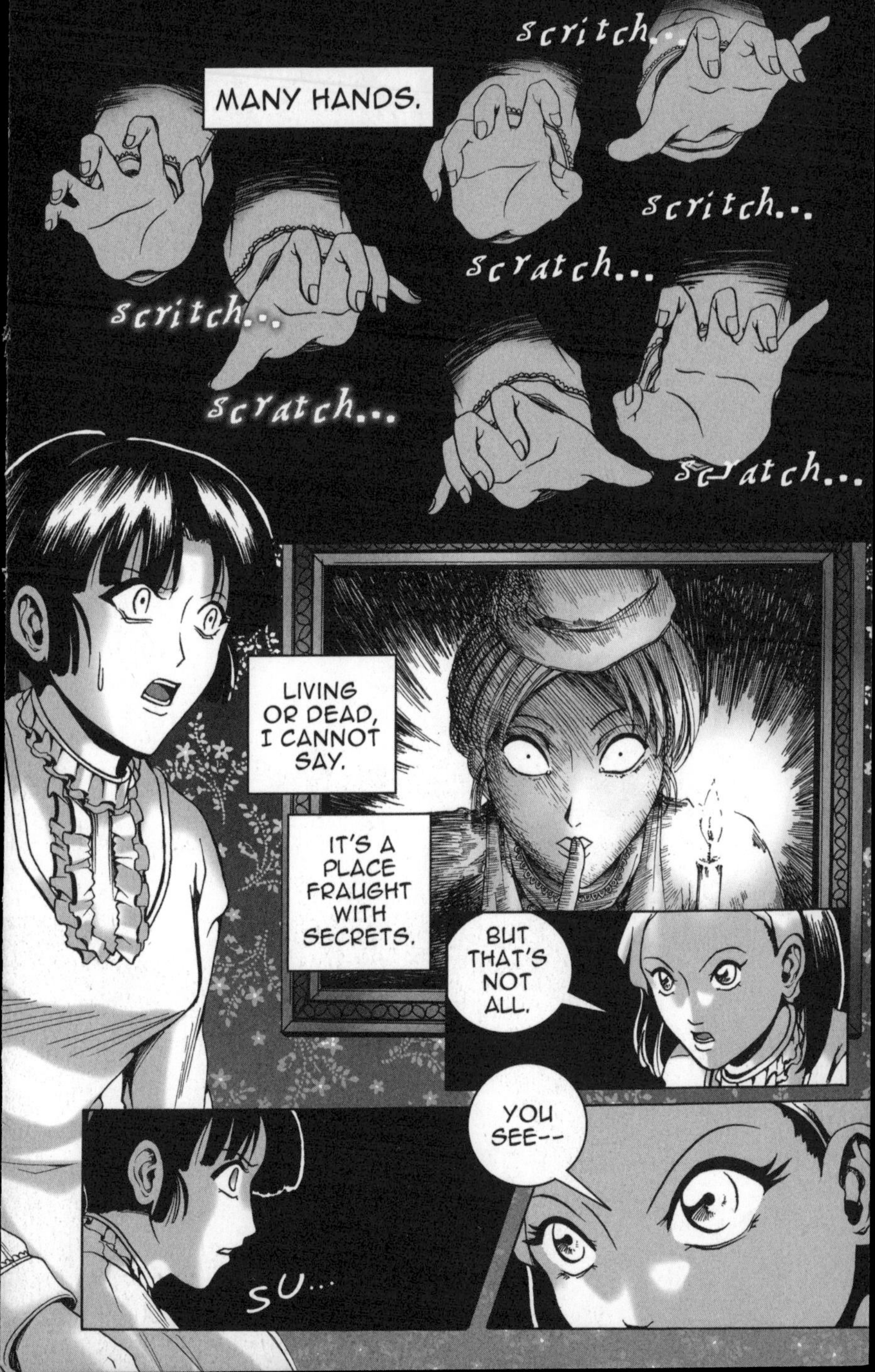
scritch...
MANY HANDS.
scritch...
scratch...
scritch...
scratch...
scratch...
LIVING OR DEAD, I CANNOT SAY.
IT'S A PLACE FRAUGHT WITH SECRETS.
BUT THAT'S NOT ALL.
YOU SEE--
SU...

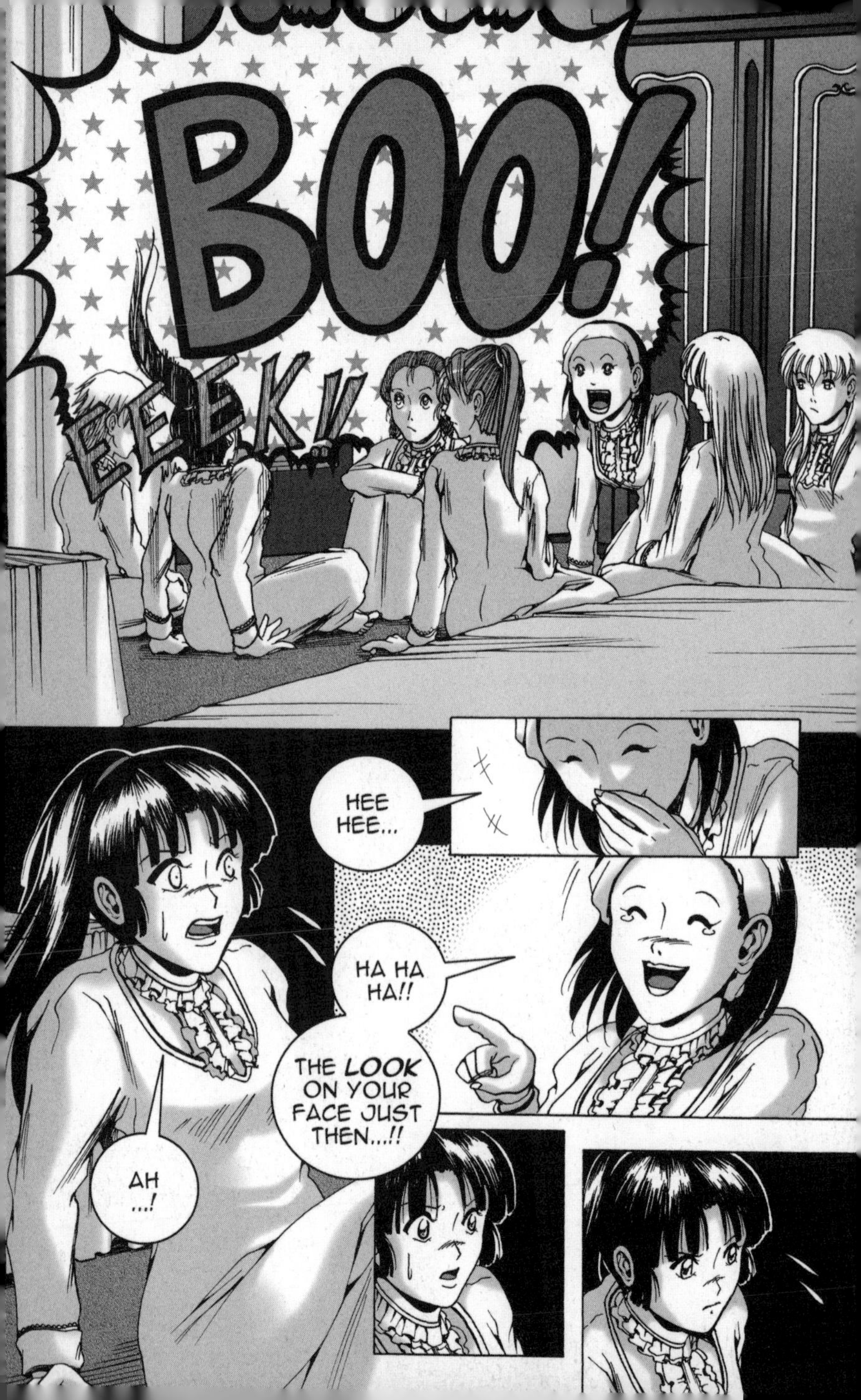
BOO!
EEEK!!
HEE HEE...
HA HA HA!!
THE LOOK ON YOUR FACE JUST THEN...!!
AH ...!

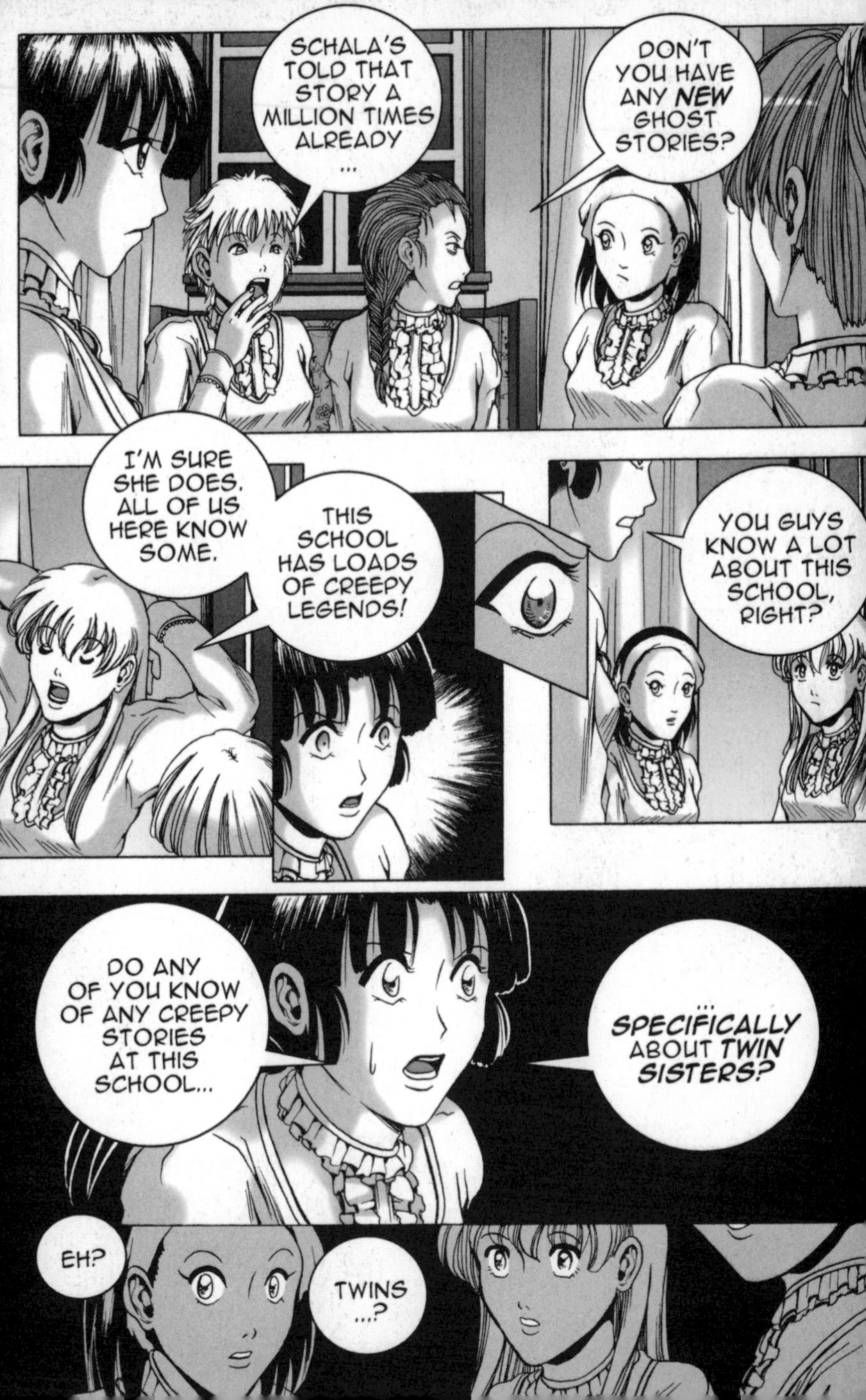
SCHALA'S TOLD THAT STORY A MILLION TIMES ALREADY ...
DON'T YOU HAVE ANY NEW GHOST STORIES?
I'M SURE SHE DOES. ALL OF US HERE KNOW SOME.
THIS SCHOOL HAS LOADS OF CREEPY LEGENDS!
YOU GUYS KNOW A LOT ABOUT THIS SCHOOL, RIGHT?
DO ANY OF YOU KNOW OF ANY CREEPY STORIES AT THIS SCHOOL...
... SPECIFICALLY ABOUT TWIN SISTERS?
EH?
TWINS ...?

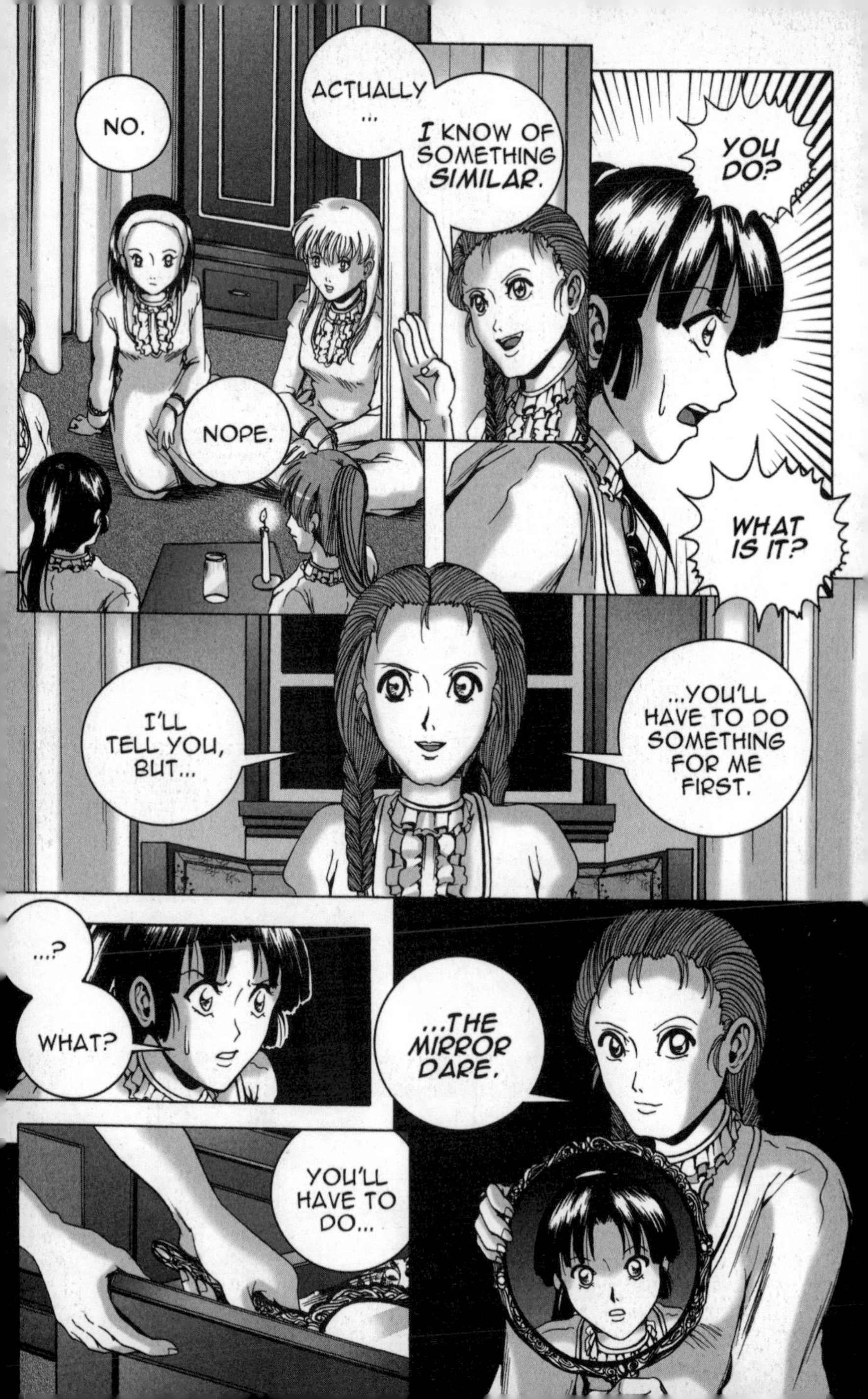
NO.
NOPE.
ACTUALLY ...
I KNOW OF SOMETHING SIMILAR.
YOU DO?
WHAT IS IT?
I'LL TELL YOU, BUT...
...YOU'LL HAVE TO DO SOMETHING FOR ME FIRST.
...?
WHAT?
YOU'LL HAVE TO DO...
...THE MIRROR DARE.

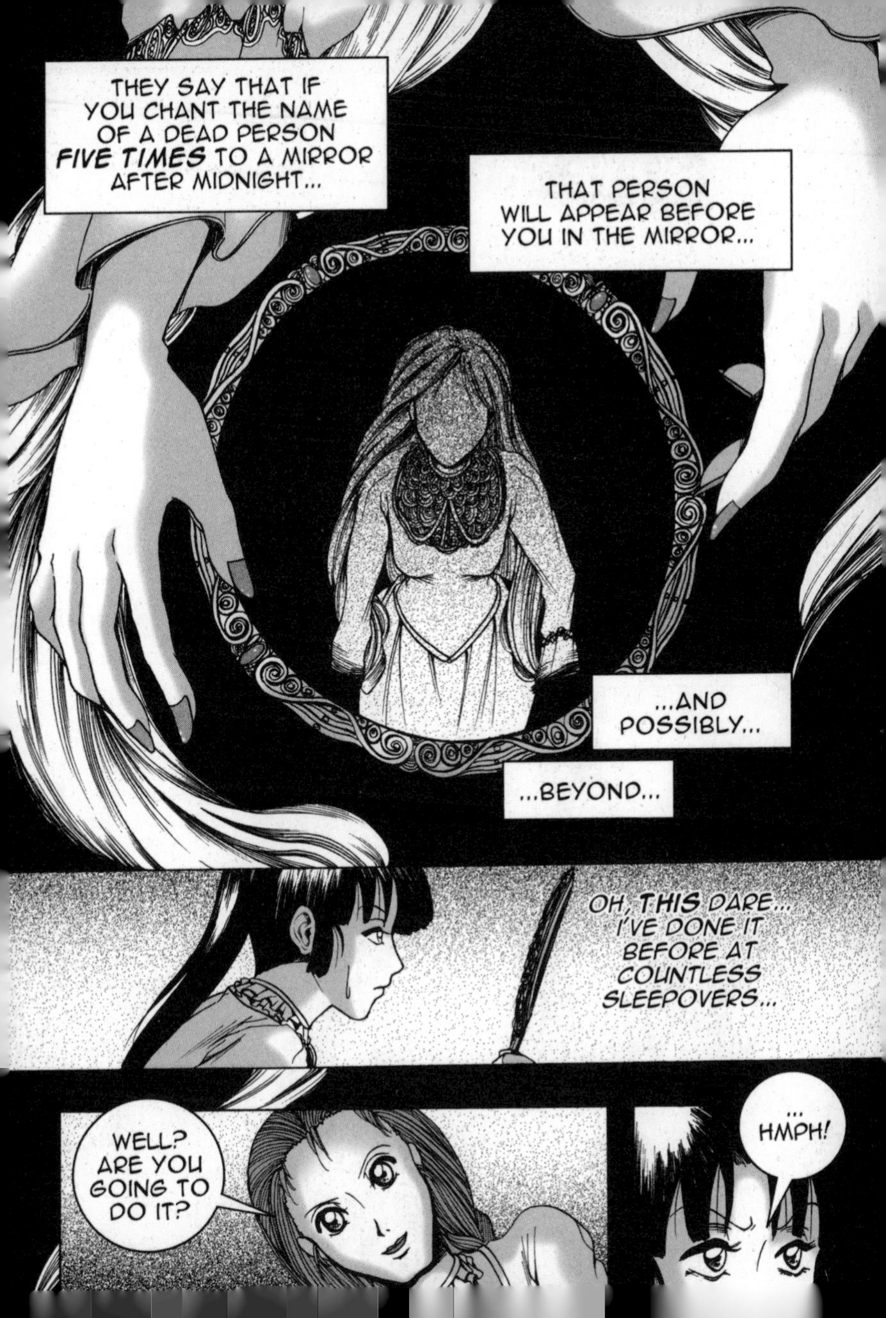
THEY SAY THAT IF YOU CHANT THE NAME OF A DEAD PERSON *FIVE TIMES* TO A MIRROR AFTER MIDNIGHT...
THAT PERSON WILL APPEAR BEFORE YOU IN THE MIRROR...
...AND POSSIBLY...
...BEYOND...
OH, **THIS** DARE... I'VE DONE IT BEFORE AT COUNTLESS SLEEPOVERS...
WELL? ARE YOU GOING TO DO IT?
... HMPH!

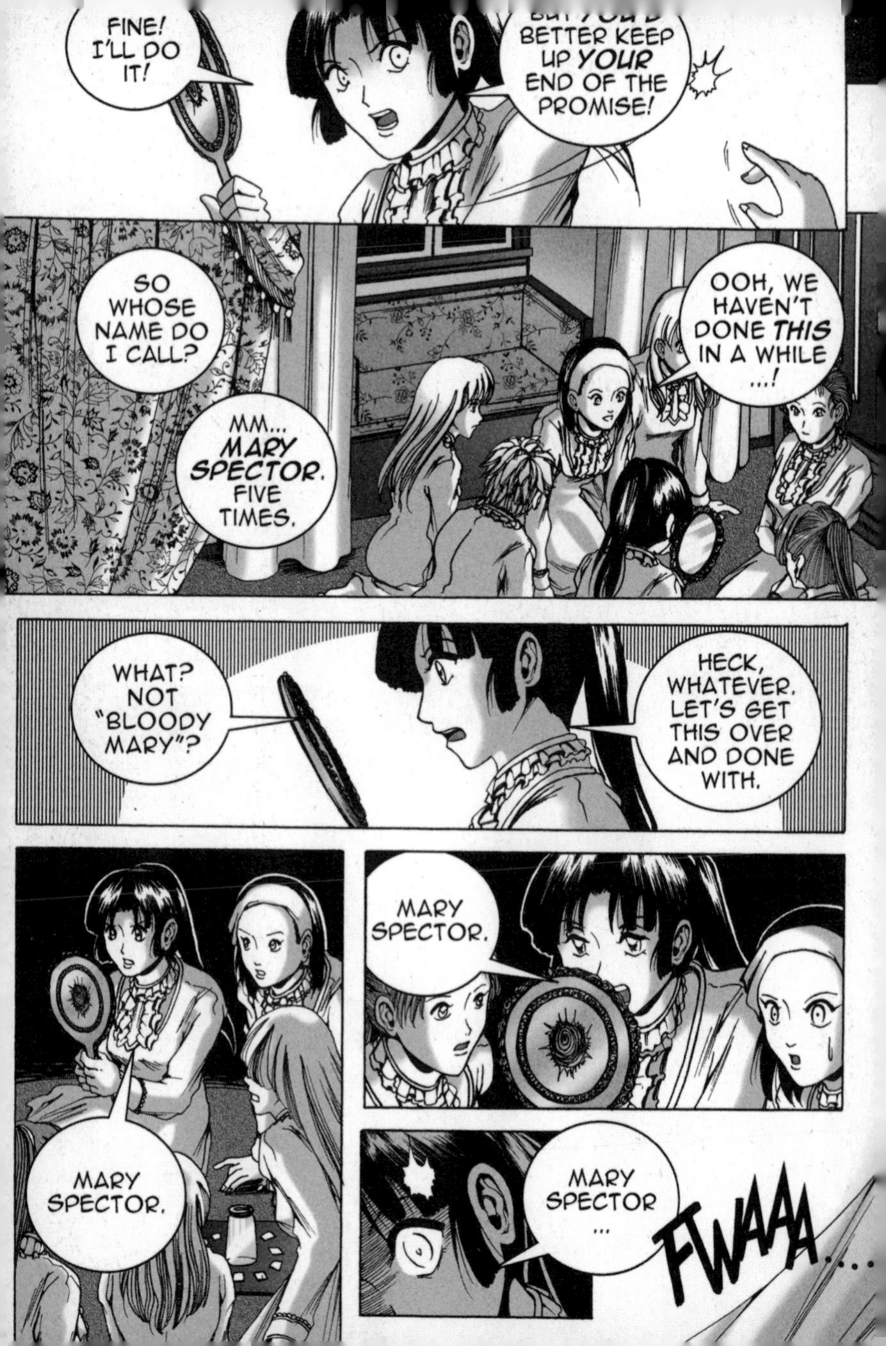
FINE! I'LL DO IT!
BETTER KEEP UP YOUR END OF THE PROMISE!
SO WHOSE NAME DO I CALL?
MM... MARY SPECTOR. FIVE TIMES.
OOH, WE HAVEN'T DONE THIS IN A WHILE ...!
WHAT? NOT "BLOODY MARY"?
HECK, WHATEVER. LET'S GET THIS OVER AND DONE WITH.
MARY SPECTOR.
MARY SPECTOR.
MARY SPECTOR ...
FWAAA....

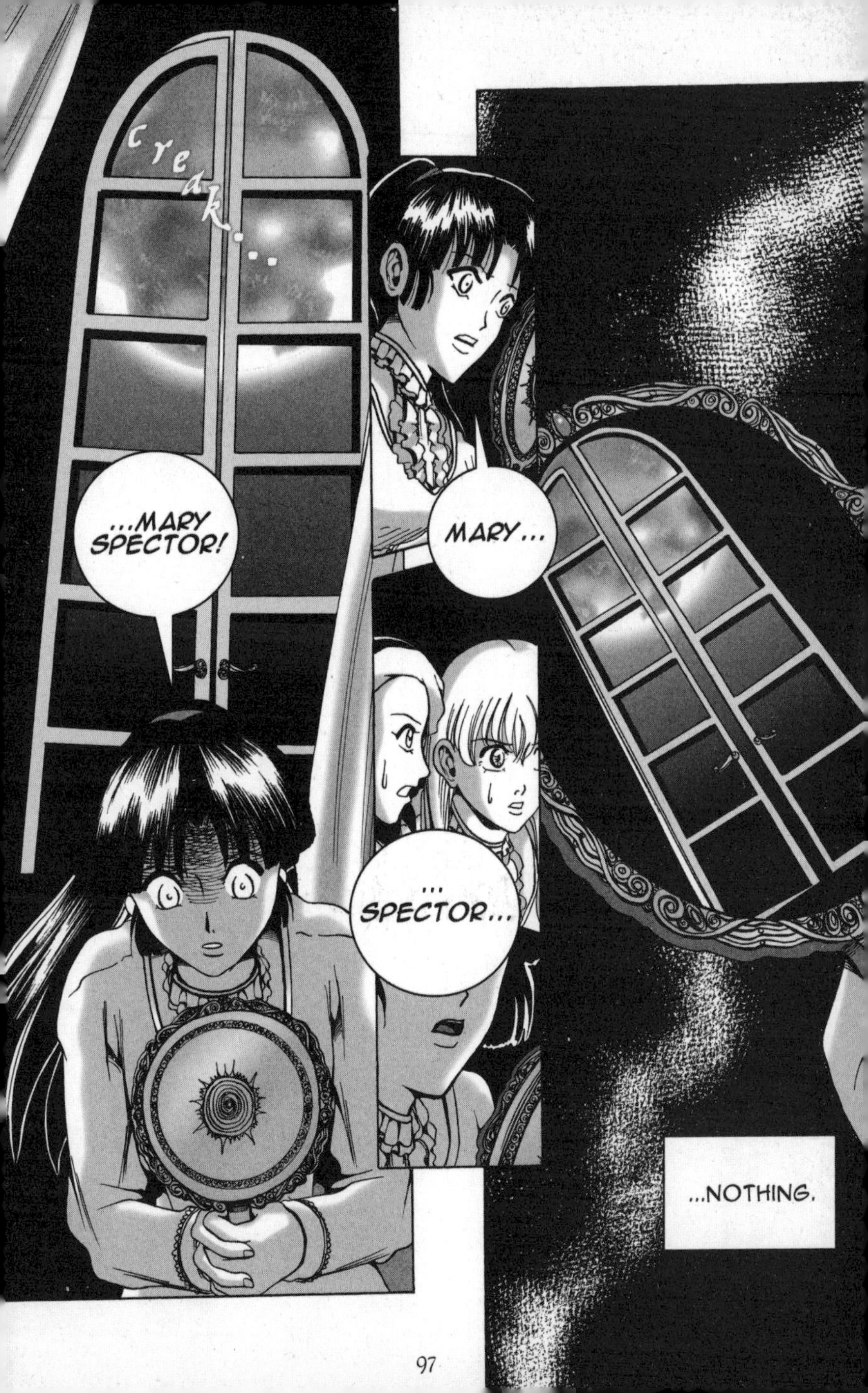
creak...
...MARY SPECTOR!
MARY...
...SPECTOR...
...NOTHING.

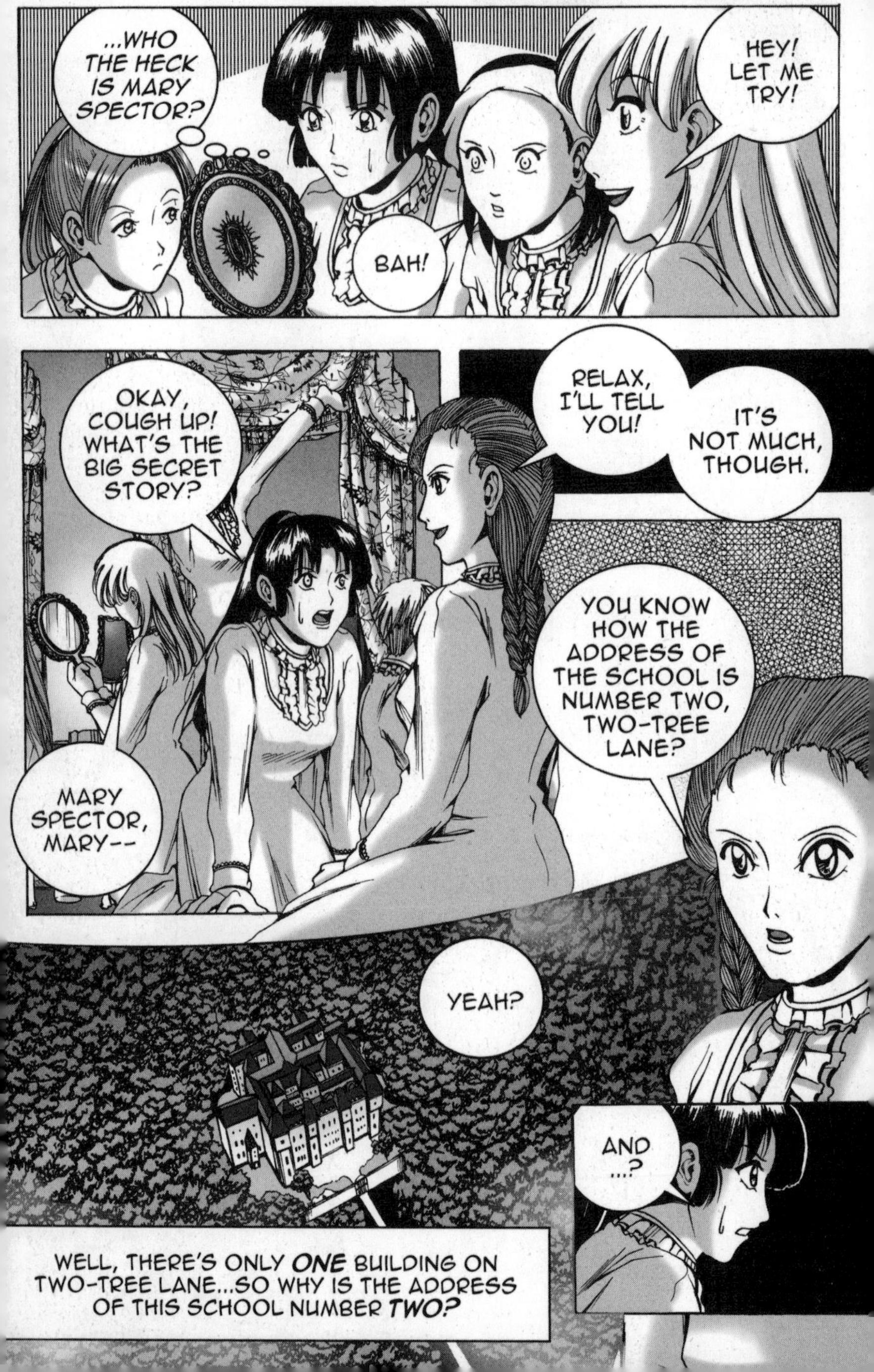
...WHO THE HECK IS MARY SPECTOR?
BAH!
HEY! LET ME TRY!
OKAY, COUGH UP! WHAT'S THE BIG SECRET STORY?
MARY SPECTOR, MARY--
RELAX, I'LL TELL YOU!
IT'S NOT MUCH, THOUGH.
YOU KNOW HOW THE ADDRESS OF THE SCHOOL IS NUMBER TWO, TWO-TREE LANE?
YEAH?
AND ...?
WELL, THERE'S ONLY *ONE* BUILDING ON TWO-TREE LANE...SO WHY IS THE ADDRESS OF THIS SCHOOL NUMBER *TWO?*

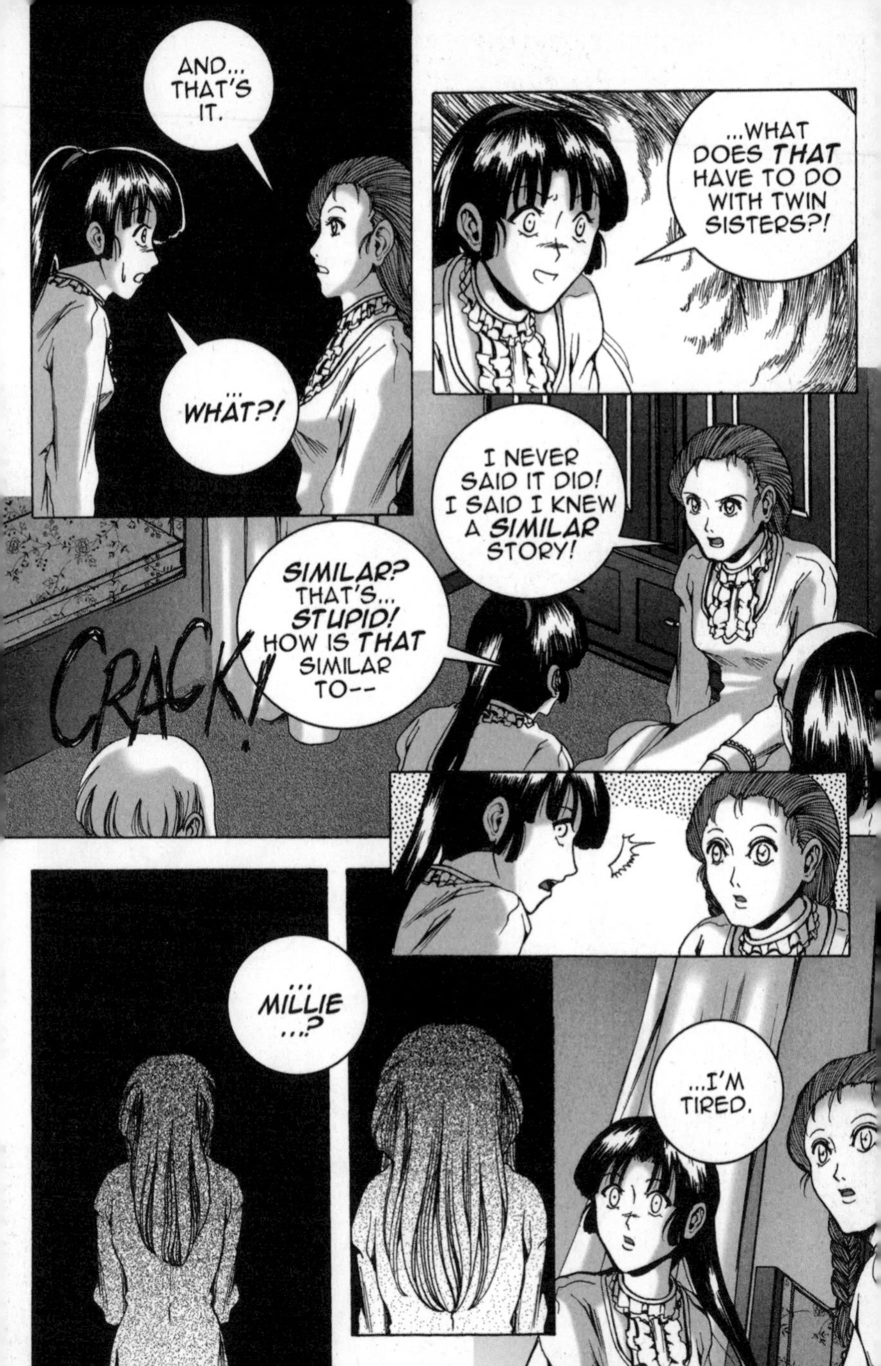
AND... THAT'S IT.
... WHAT?!
...WHAT DOES THAT HAVE TO DO WITH TWIN SISTERS?!
I NEVER SAID IT DID! I SAID I KNEW A SIMILAR STORY!
SIMILAR? THAT'S... STUPID! HOW IS THAT SIMILAR TO--
CRACK!
... MILLIE ...?
...I'M TIRED.

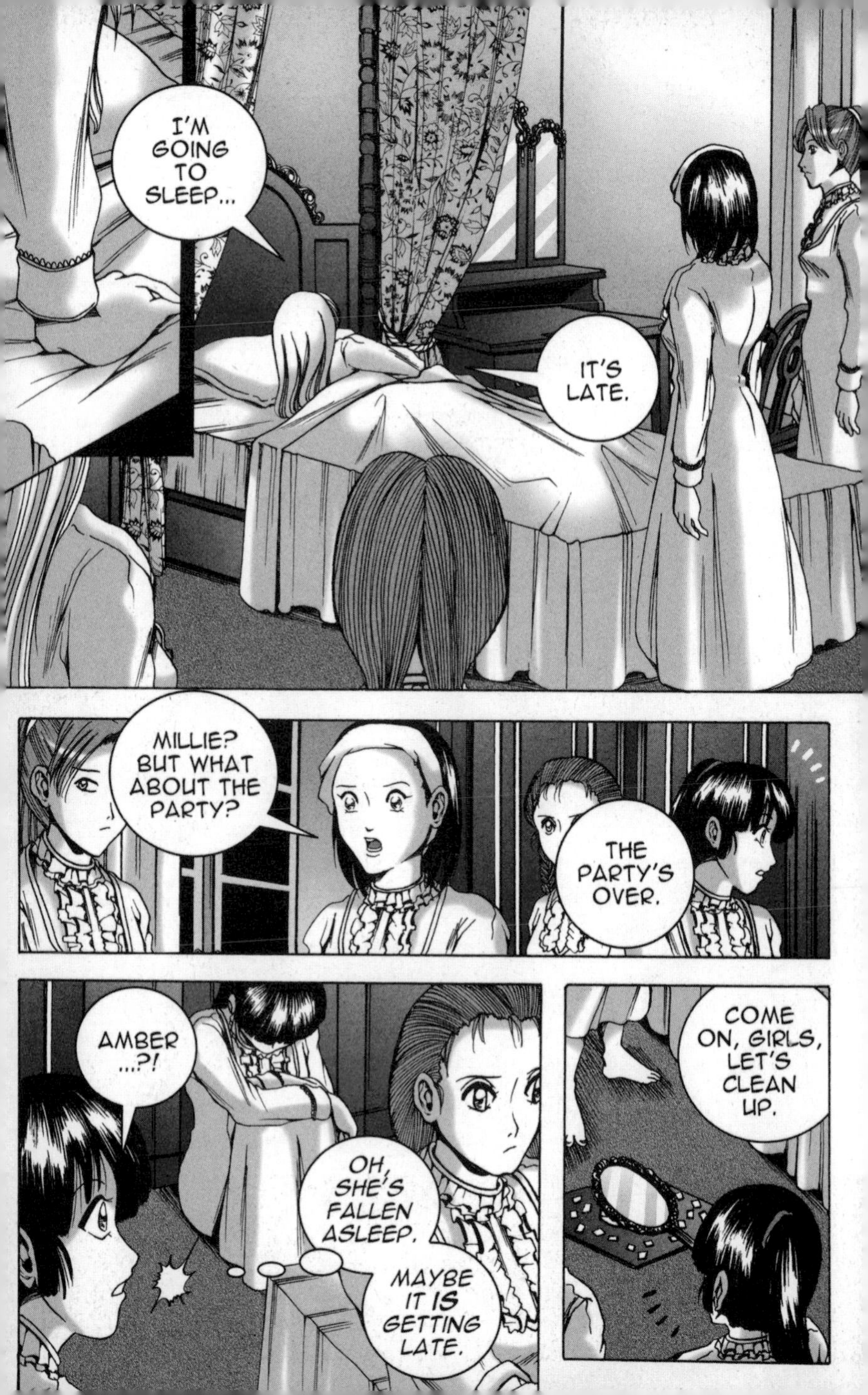
I'M GOING TO SLEEP...
IT'S LATE.
MILLIE? BUT WHAT ABOUT THE PARTY?
THE PARTY'S OVER.
AMBER ...?!
OH, SHE'S FALLEN ASLEEP.
MAYBE IT IS GETTING LATE.
COME ON, GIRLS, LET'S CLEAN UP.

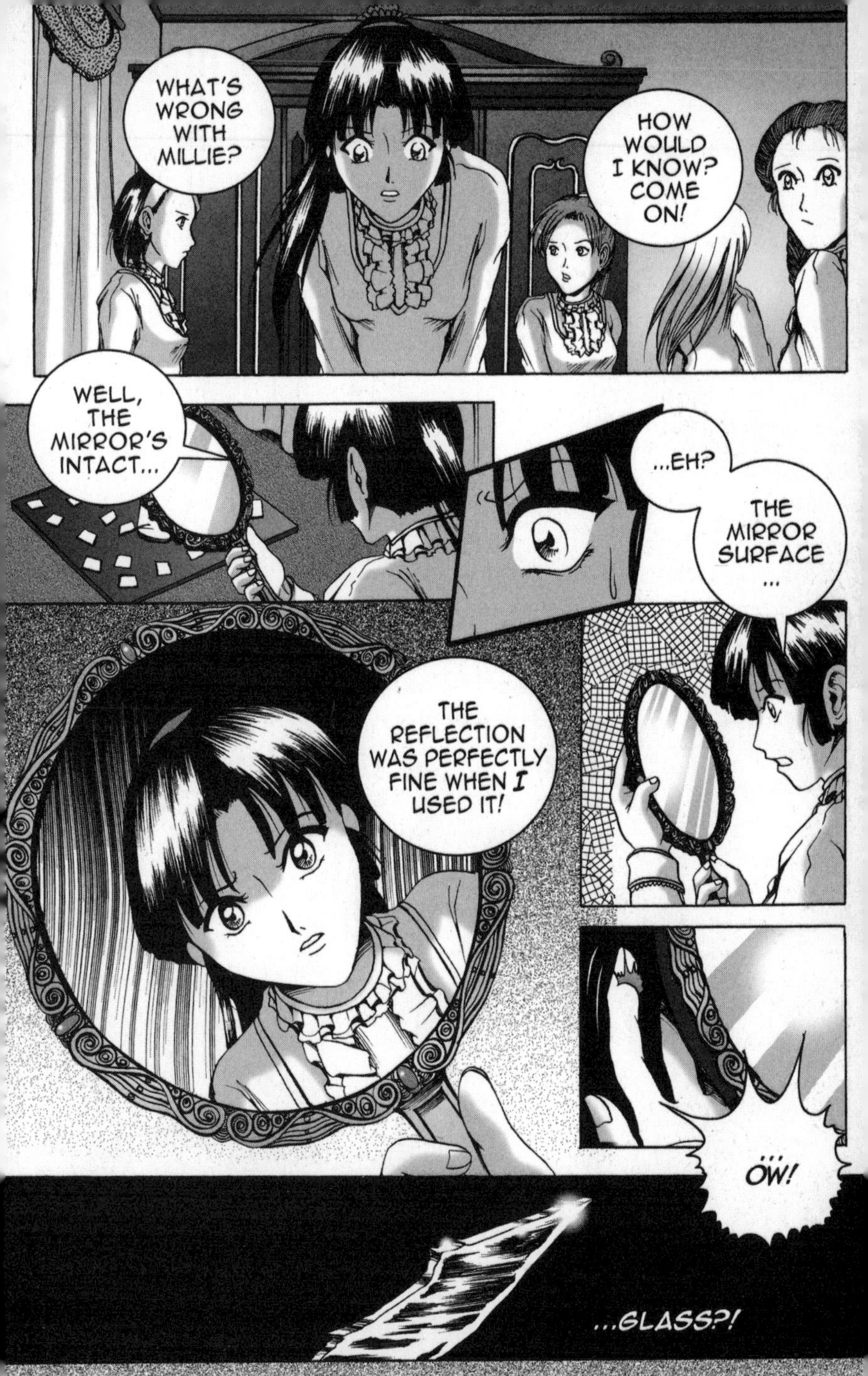
WHAT'S WRONG WITH MILLIE?
HOW WOULD I KNOW? COME ON!
WELL, THE MIRROR'S INTACT...
...EH?
THE MIRROR SURFACE ...
THE REFLECTION WAS PERFECTLY FINE WHEN I USED IT!
... ÖW!
...GLASS?!

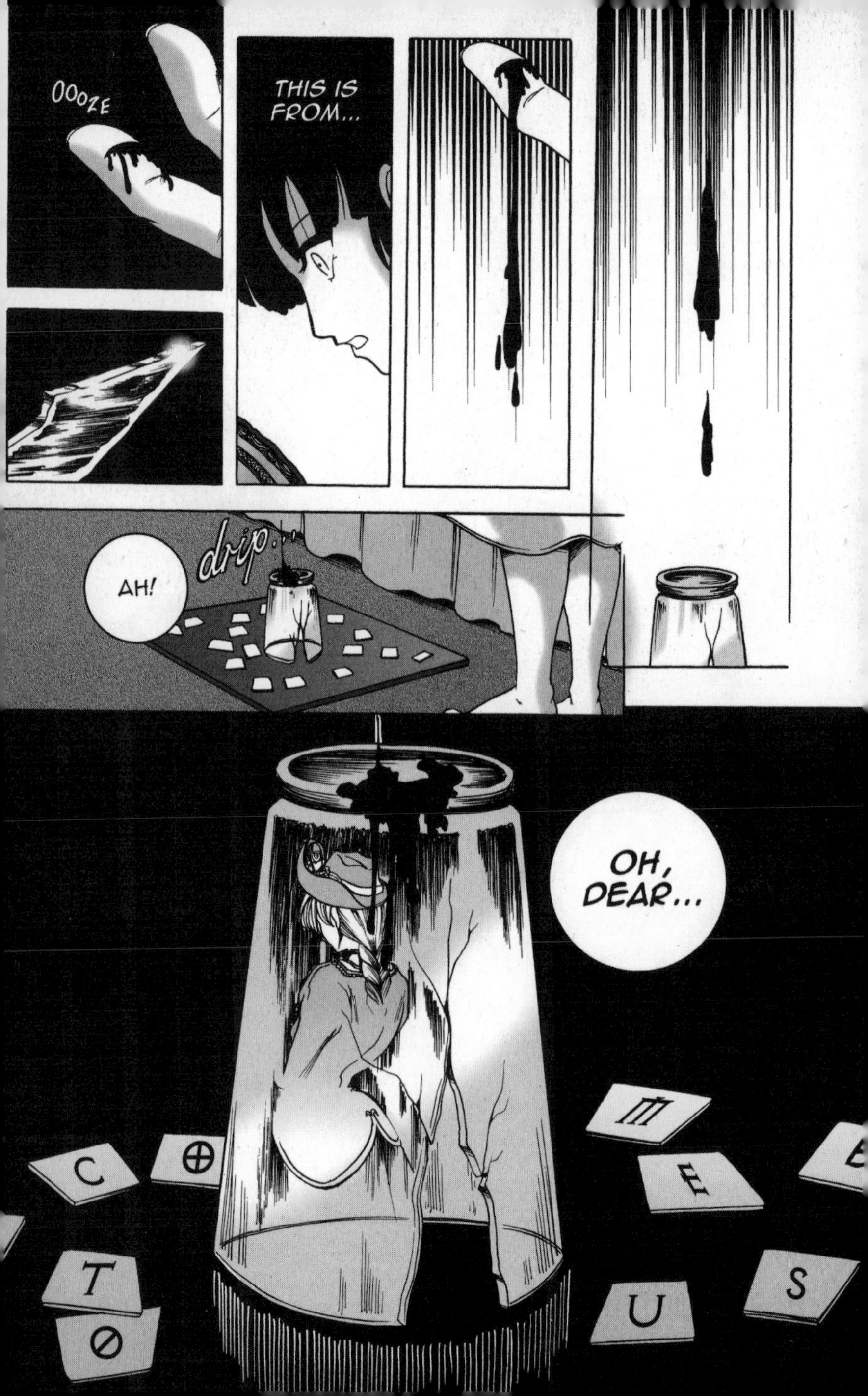
THIS IS FROM...
OOOZE
drip...
AH!
OH, DEAR...

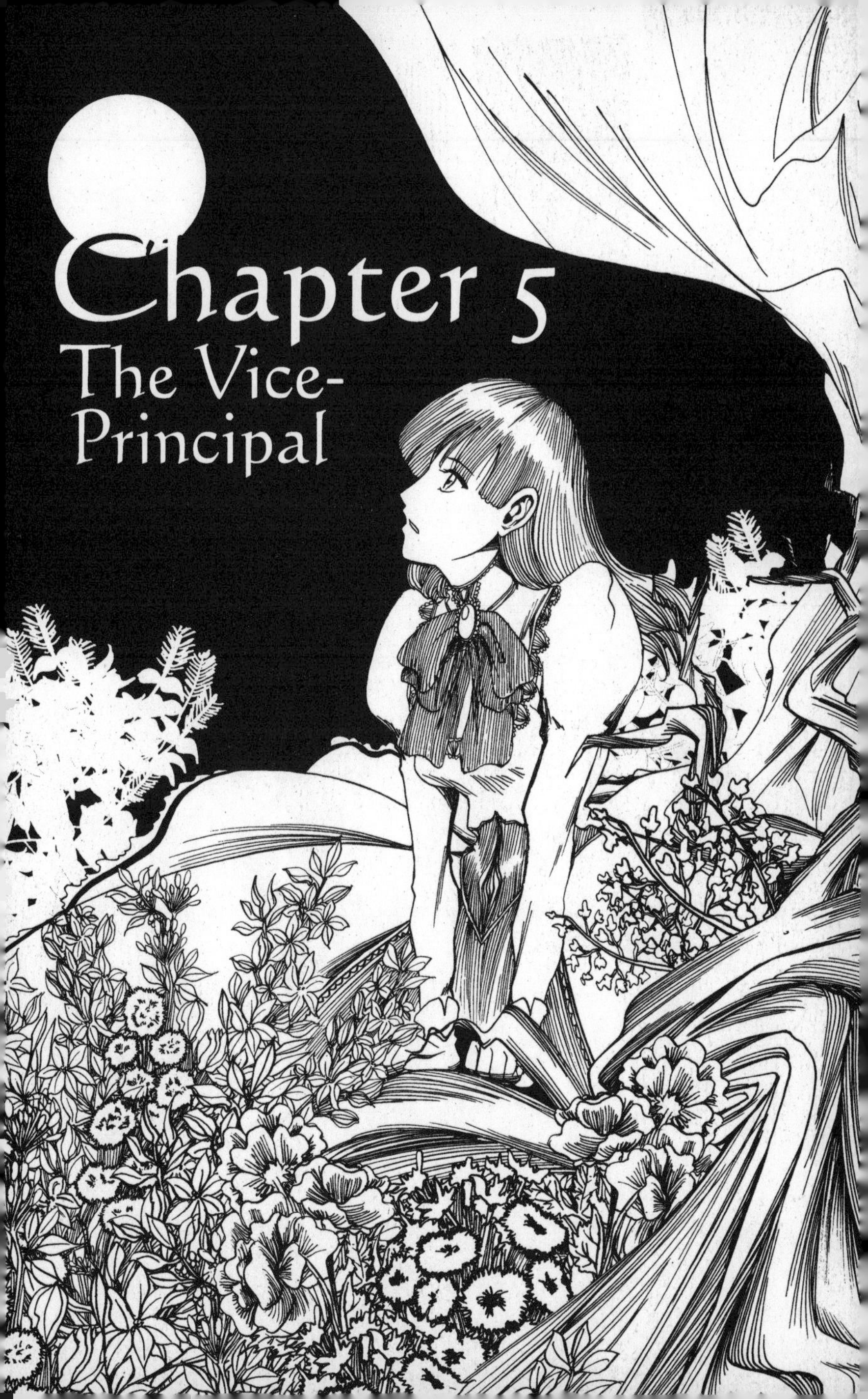
Chapter 5
The Vice-Principal

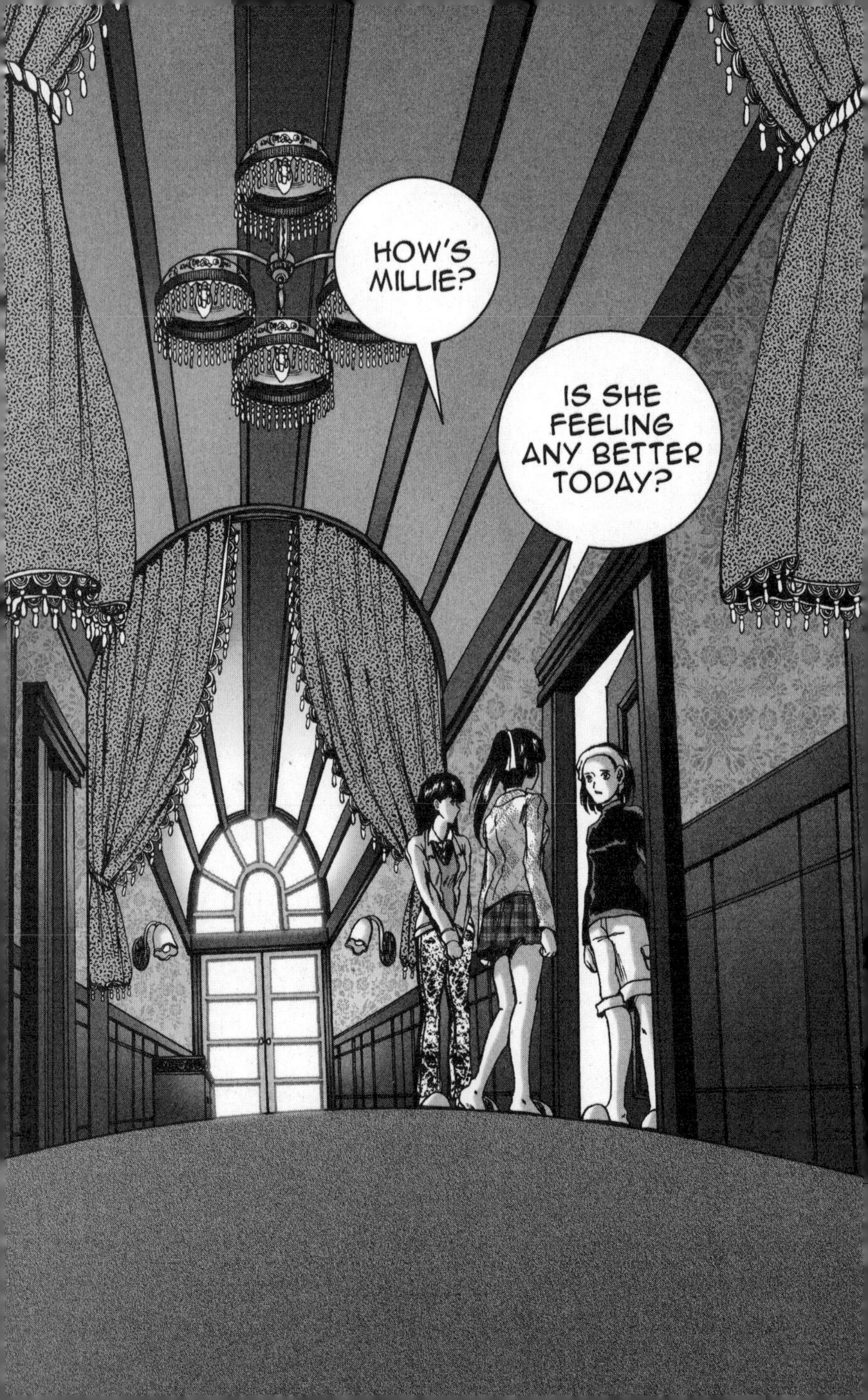
HOW'S MILLIE?
IS SHE FEELING ANY BETTER TODAY?

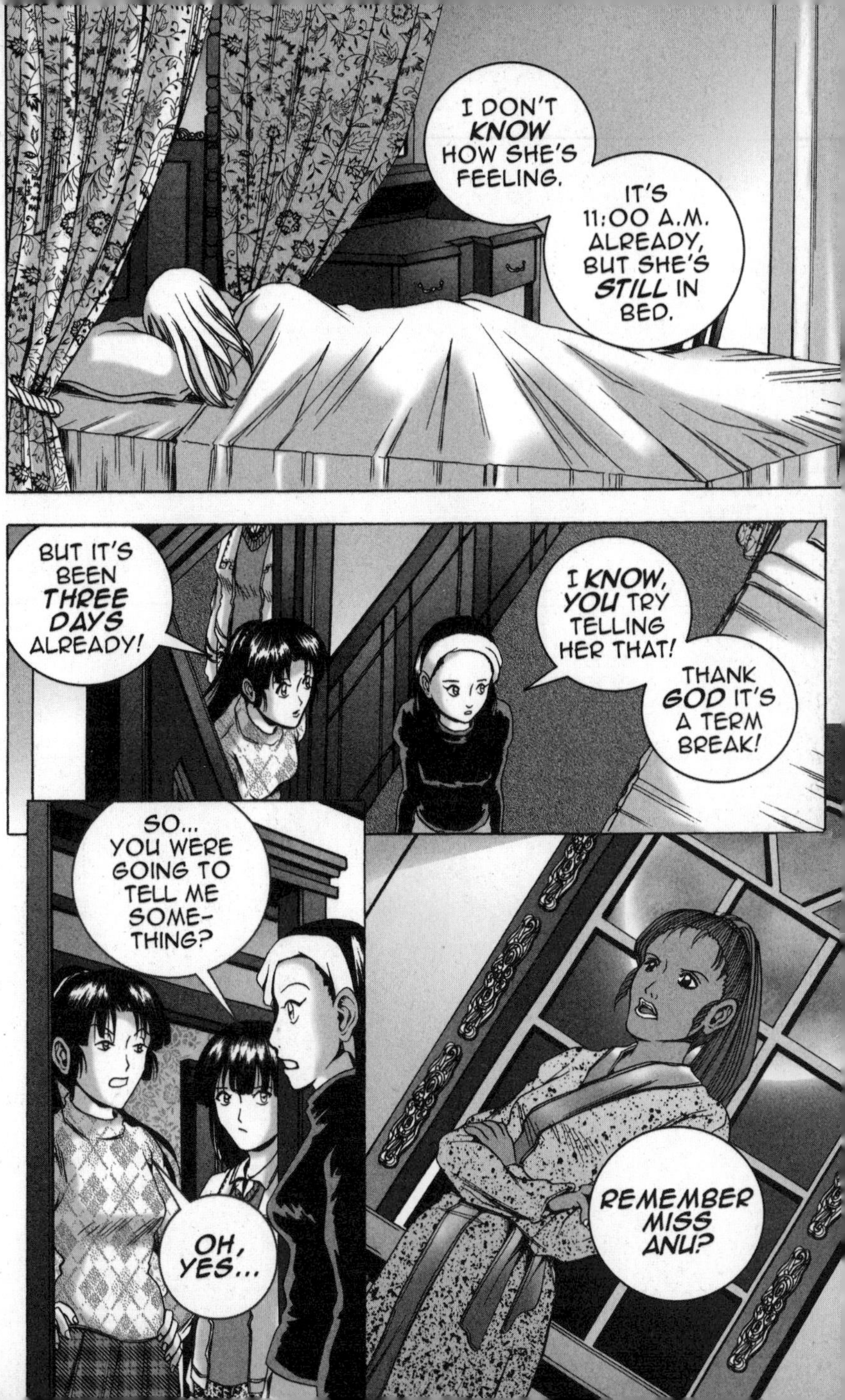
I DON'T KNOW HOW SHE'S FEELING.
IT'S 11:00 A.M. ALREADY, BUT SHE'S STILL IN BED.
BUT IT'S BEEN THREE DAYS ALREADY!
I KNOW, YOU TRY TELLING HER THAT!
THANK GOD IT'S A TERM BREAK!
SO... YOU WERE GOING TO TELL ME SOME-THING?
OH, YES...
REMEMBER MISS ANU?

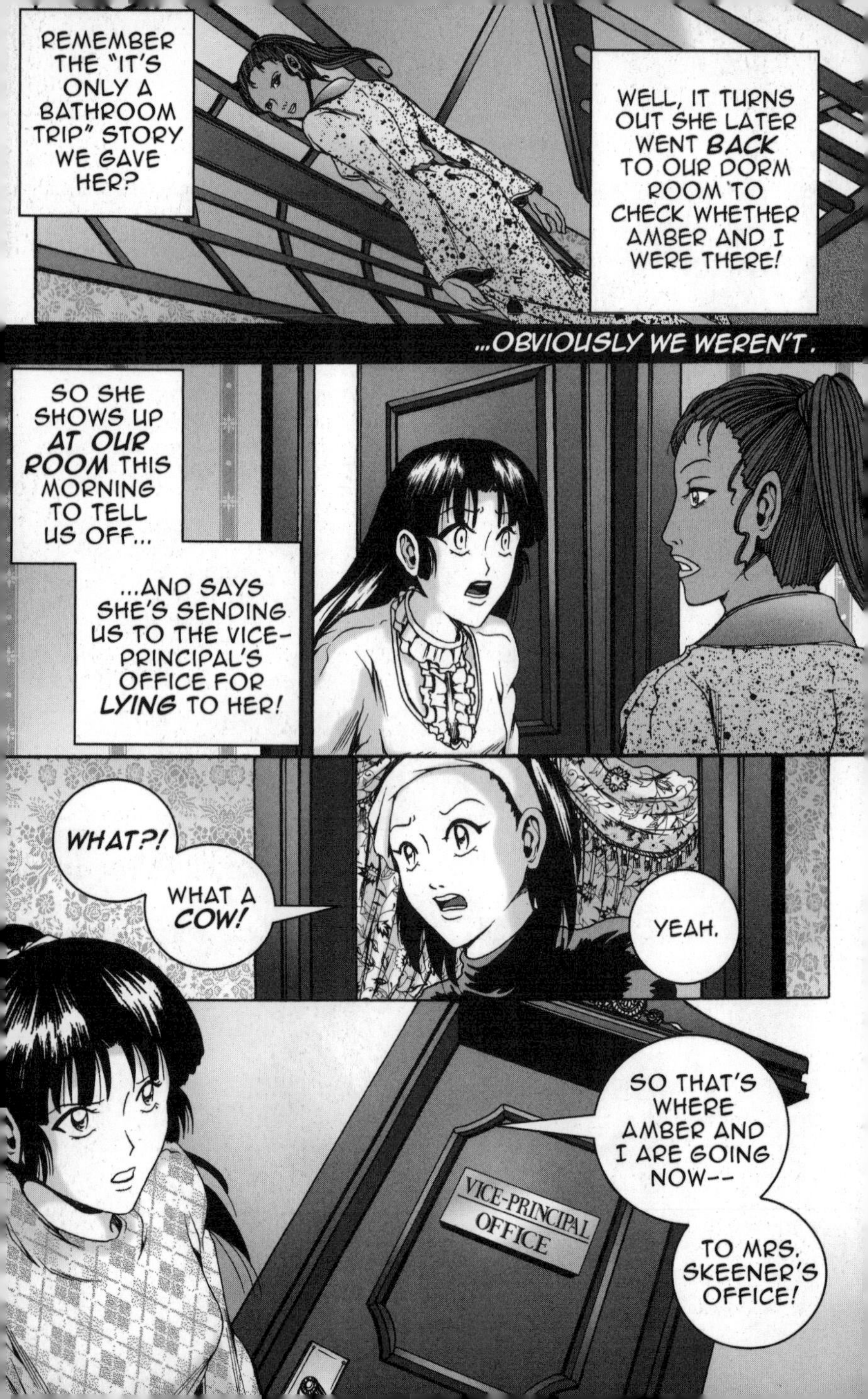
REMEMBER THE "IT'S ONLY A BATHROOM TRIP" STORY WE GAVE HER?
WELL, IT TURNS OUT SHE LATER WENT BACK TO OUR DORM ROOM TO CHECK WHETHER AMBER AND I WERE THERE!
...OBVIOUSLY WE WEREN'T.
SO SHE SHOWS UP AT OUR ROOM THIS MORNING TO TELL US OFF...
...AND SAYS SHE'S SENDING US TO THE VICE-PRINCIPAL'S OFFICE FOR LYING TO HER!
WHAT?!
WHAT A COW!
YEAH.
SO THAT'S WHERE AMBER AND I ARE GOING NOW--
TO MRS. SKEENER'S OFFICE!
VICE-PRINCIPAL OFFICE

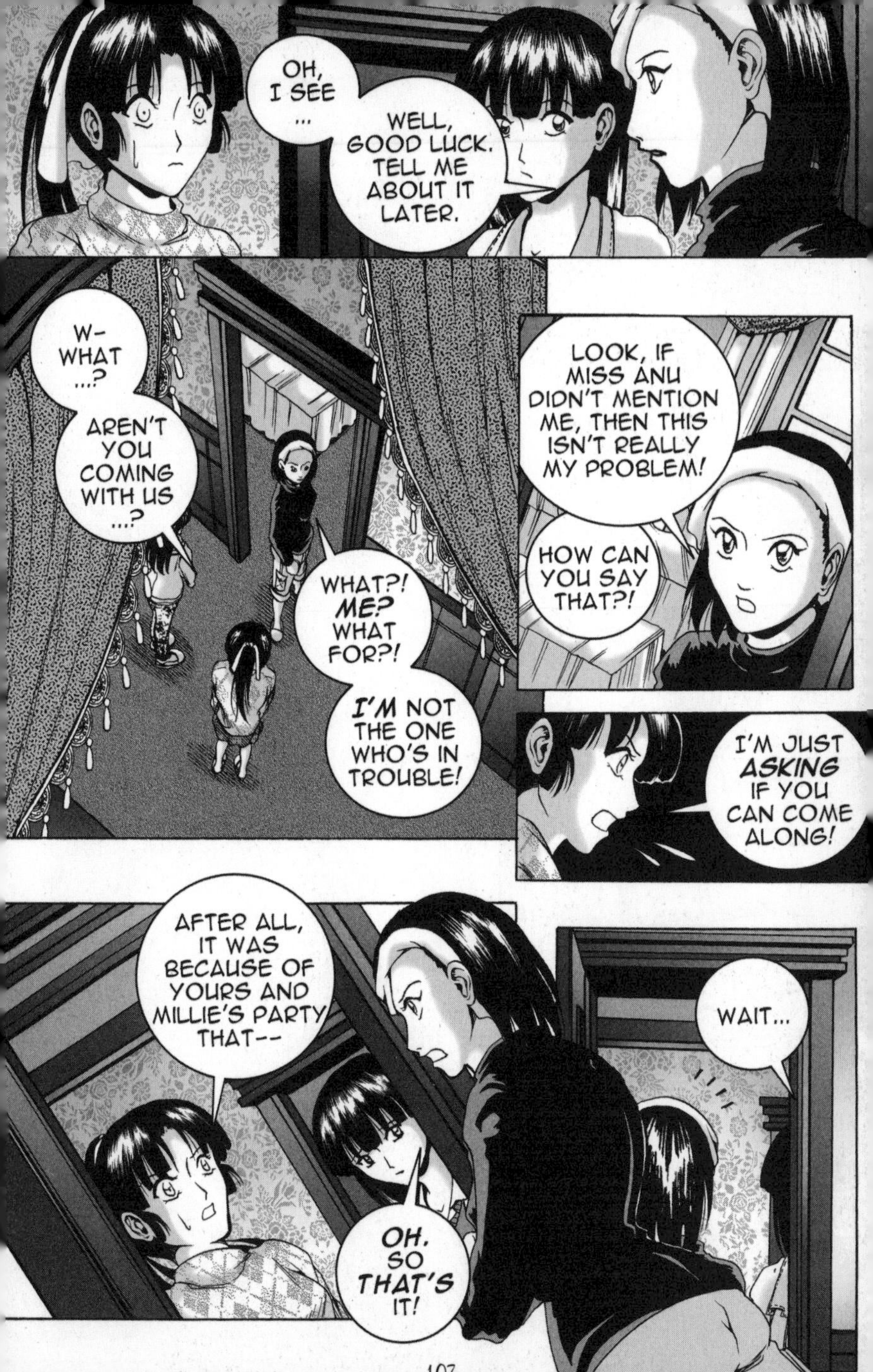
OH, I SEE ...
WELL, GOOD LUCK. TELL ME ABOUT IT LATER.
W- WHAT ...?
AREN'T YOU COMING WITH US ...?
WHAT?! *ME?* WHAT FOR?!
I'M NOT THE ONE WHO'S IN TROUBLE!
LOOK, IF MISS ANU DIDN'T MENTION ME, THEN THIS ISN'T REALLY MY PROBLEM!
HOW CAN YOU SAY THAT?!
I'M JUST *ASKING* IF YOU CAN COME ALONG!
AFTER ALL, IT WAS BECAUSE OF YOURS AND MILLIE'S PARTY THAT--
WAIT...
OH. SO *THAT'S* IT!

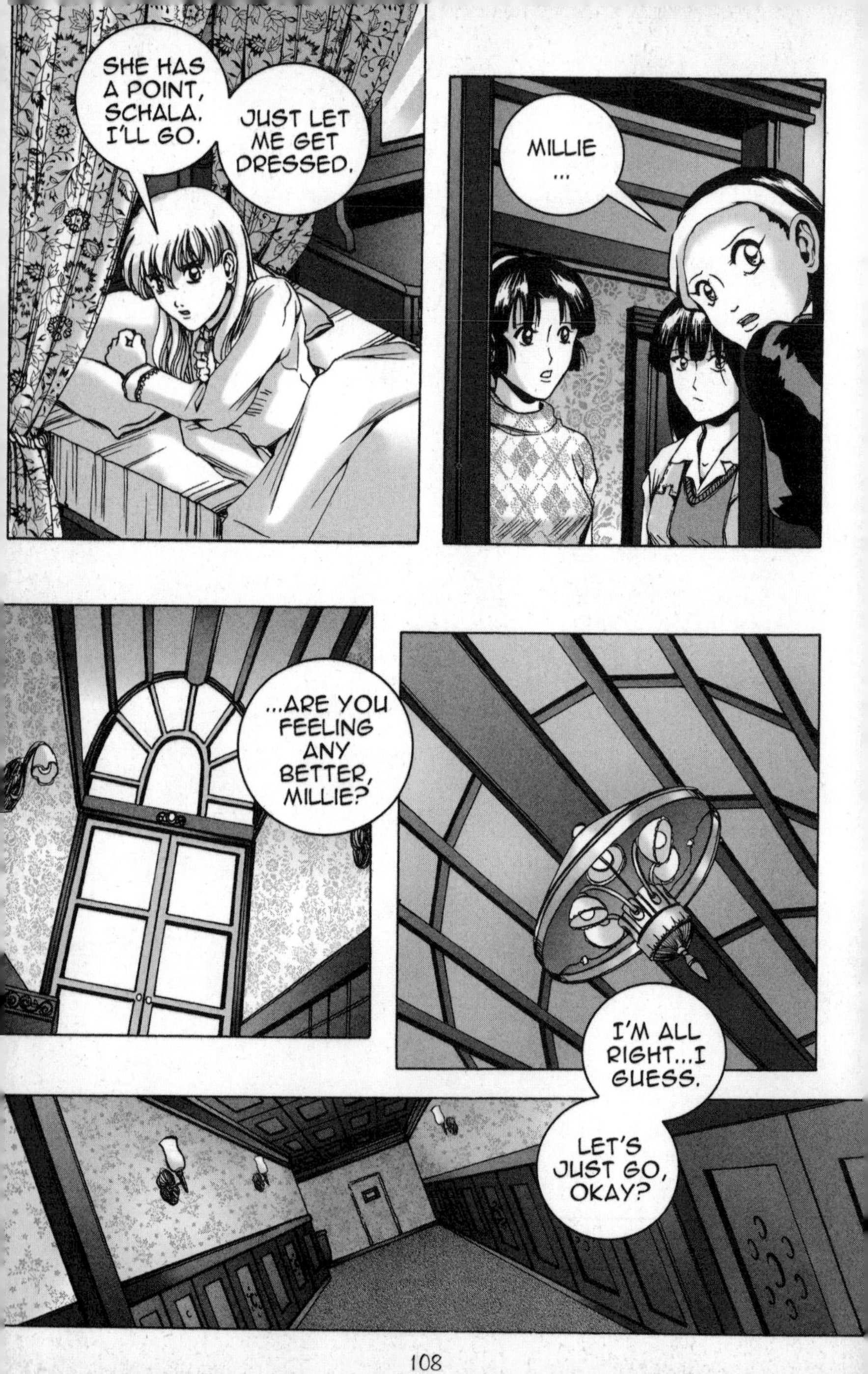
SHE HAS A POINT, SCHALA. I'LL GO.
JUST LET ME GET DRESSED.
MILLIE ...
...ARE YOU FEELING ANY BETTER, MILLIE?
I'M ALL RIGHT...I GUESS.
LET'S JUST GO, OKAY?

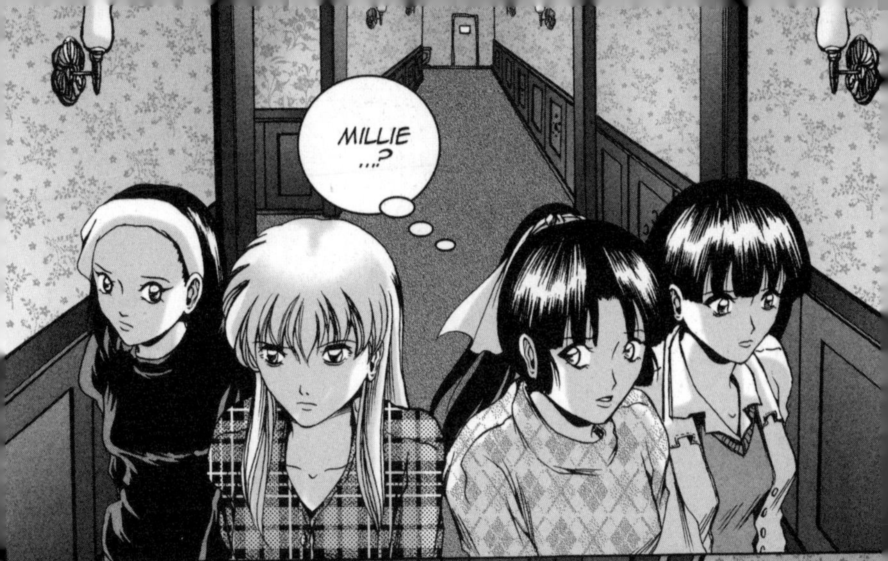
MILLIE ...?

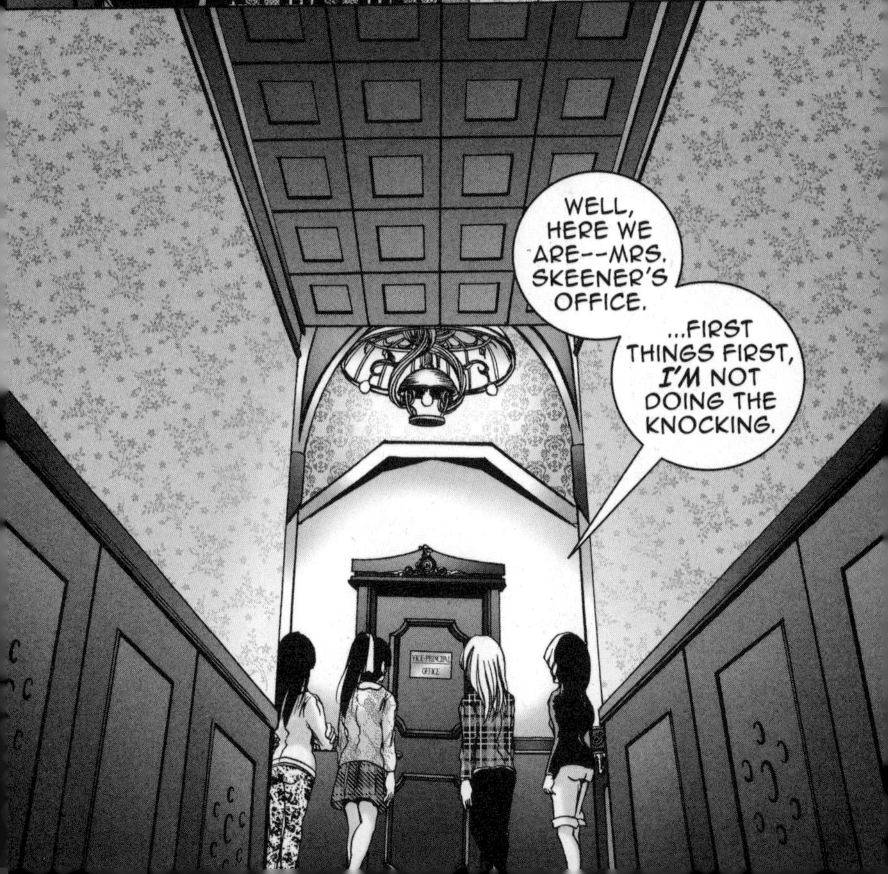
WELL, HERE WE ARE--MRS. SKEENER'S OFFICE.
...FIRST THINGS FIRST, *I'M* NOT DOING THE KNOCKING.

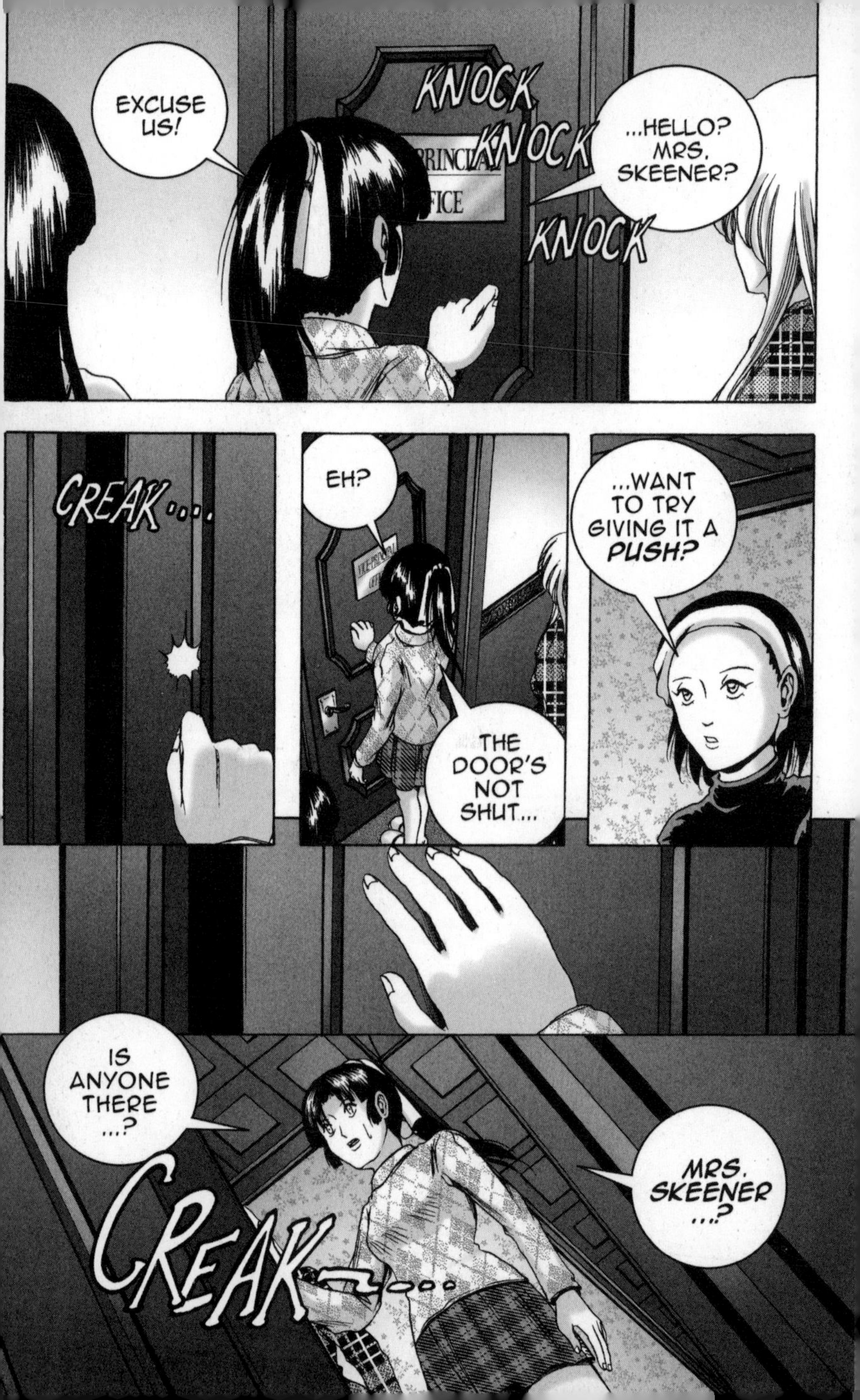
EXCUSE US!
KNOCK
KNOCK
KNOCK
...HELLO? MRS. SKEENER?
CREAK....
EH?
THE DOOR'S NOT SHUT...
...WANT TO TRY GIVING IT A PUSH?
IS ANYONE THERE ...?
CREAK...
MRS. SKEENER ...?

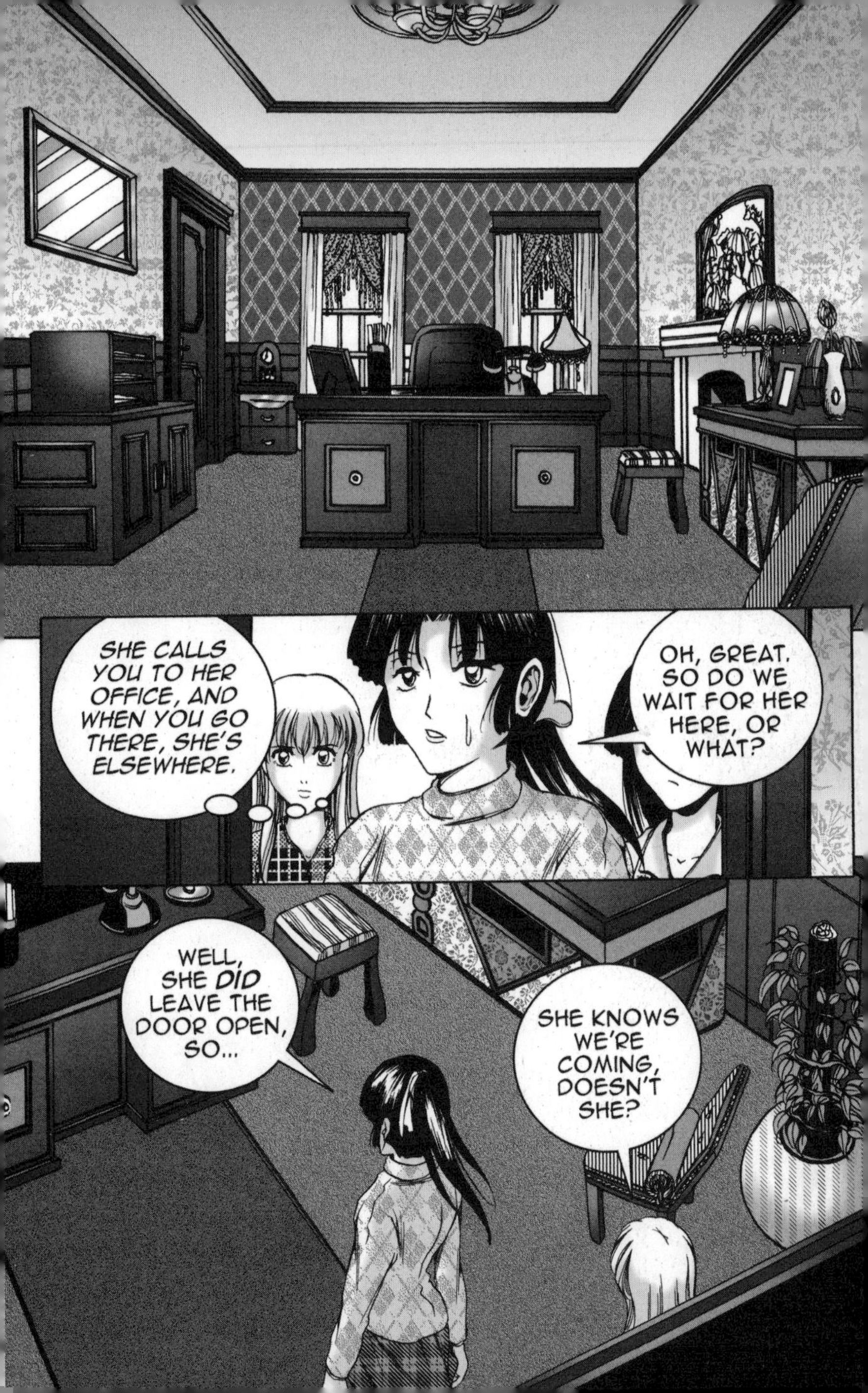
OH, GREAT. SO DO WE WAIT FOR HER HERE, OR WHAT?
SHE CALLS YOU TO HER OFFICE, AND WHEN YOU GO THERE, SHE'S ELSEWHERE.
SHE KNOWS WE'RE COMING, DOESN'T SHE?
WELL, SHE *DID* LEAVE THE DOOR OPEN, SO...

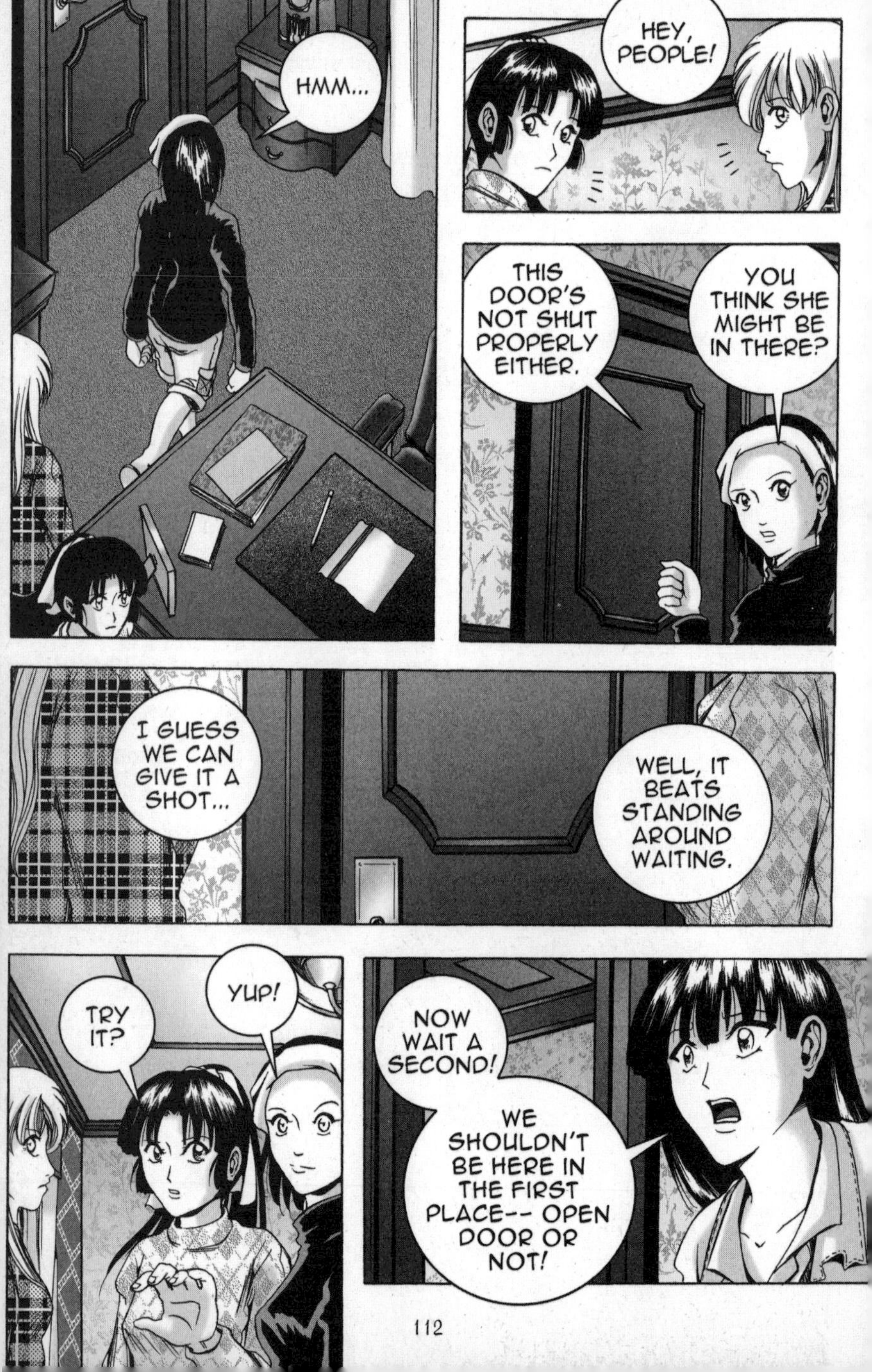
HMM...
HEY, PEOPLE!
THIS DOOR'S NOT SHUT PROPERLY EITHER.
YOU THINK SHE MIGHT BE IN THERE?
I GUESS WE CAN GIVE IT A SHOT...
WELL, IT BEATS STANDING AROUND WAITING.
TRY IT?
YUP!
NOW WAIT A SECOND!
WE SHOULDN'T BE HERE IN THE FIRST PLACE-- OPEN DOOR OR NOT!

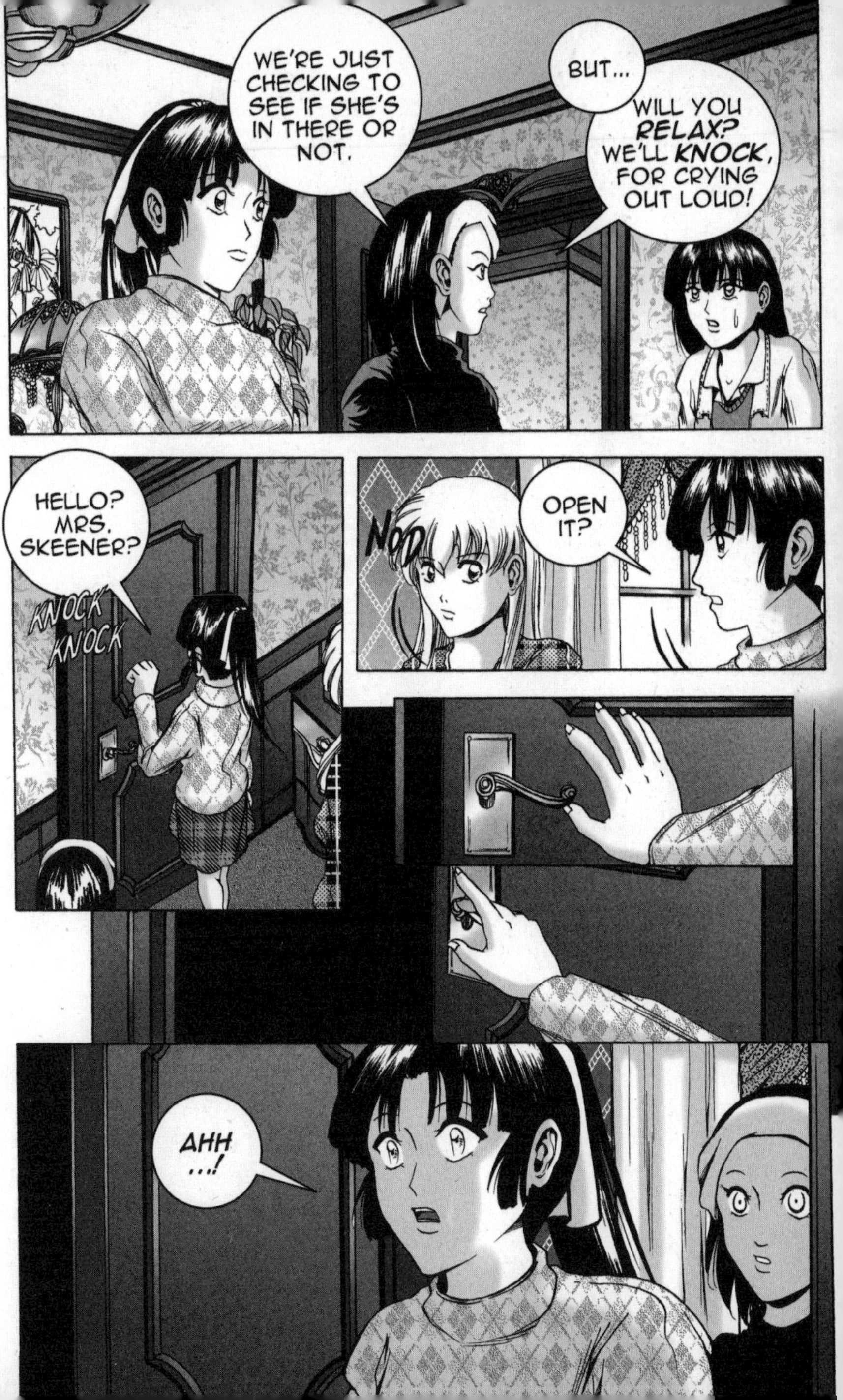
WE'RE JUST CHECKING TO SEE IF SHE'S IN THERE OR NOT.
BUT...
WILL YOU **RELAX?** WE'LL **KNOCK**, FOR CRYING OUT LOUD!
HELLO? MRS. SKEENER?
KNOCK KNOCK
NOD
OPEN IT?
AHH ...!

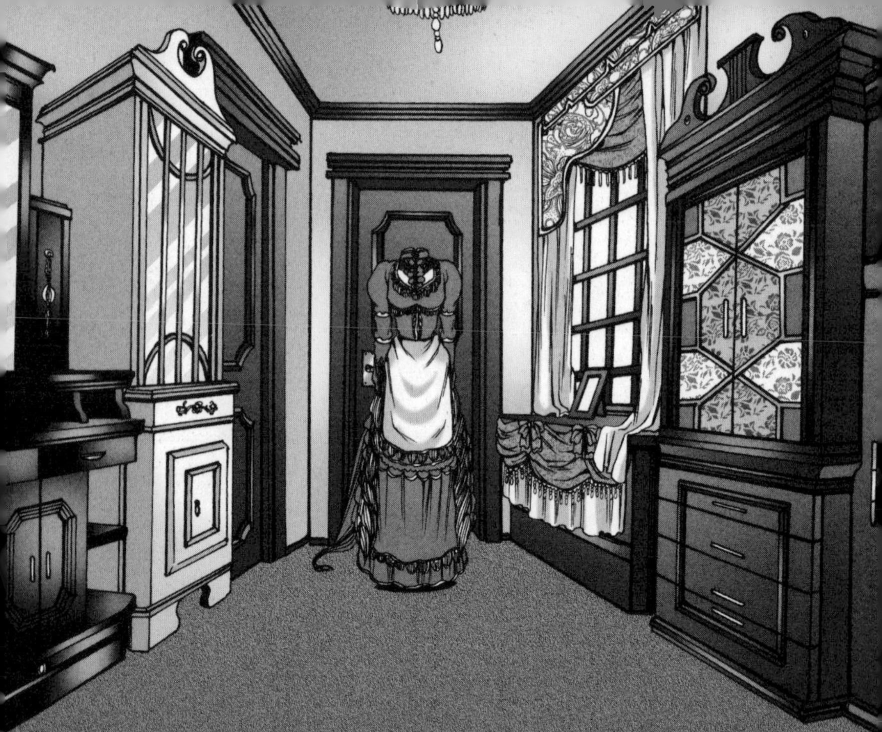
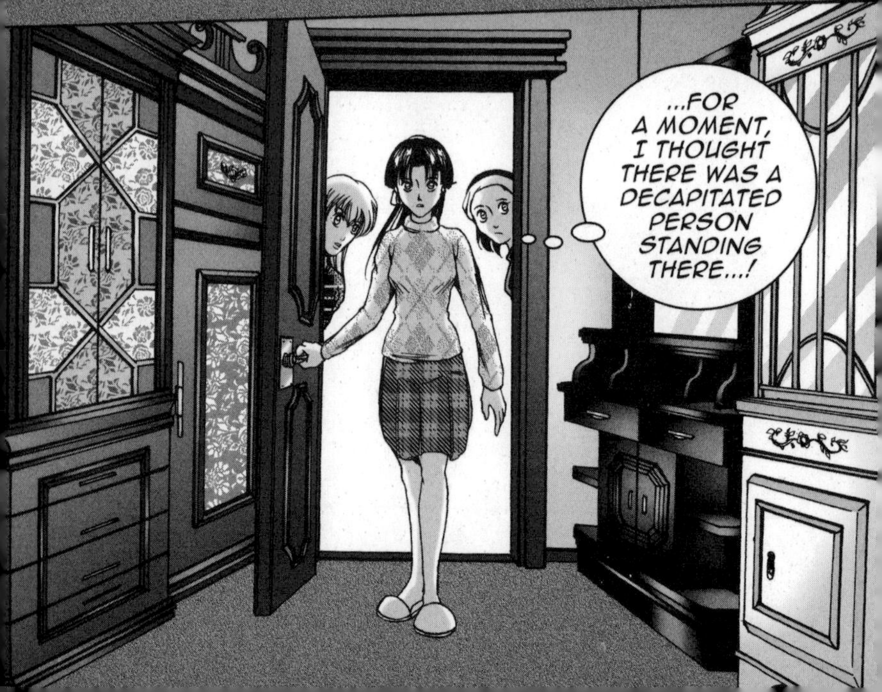
...FOR A MOMENT, I THOUGHT THERE WAS A DECAPITATED PERSON STANDING THERE...!

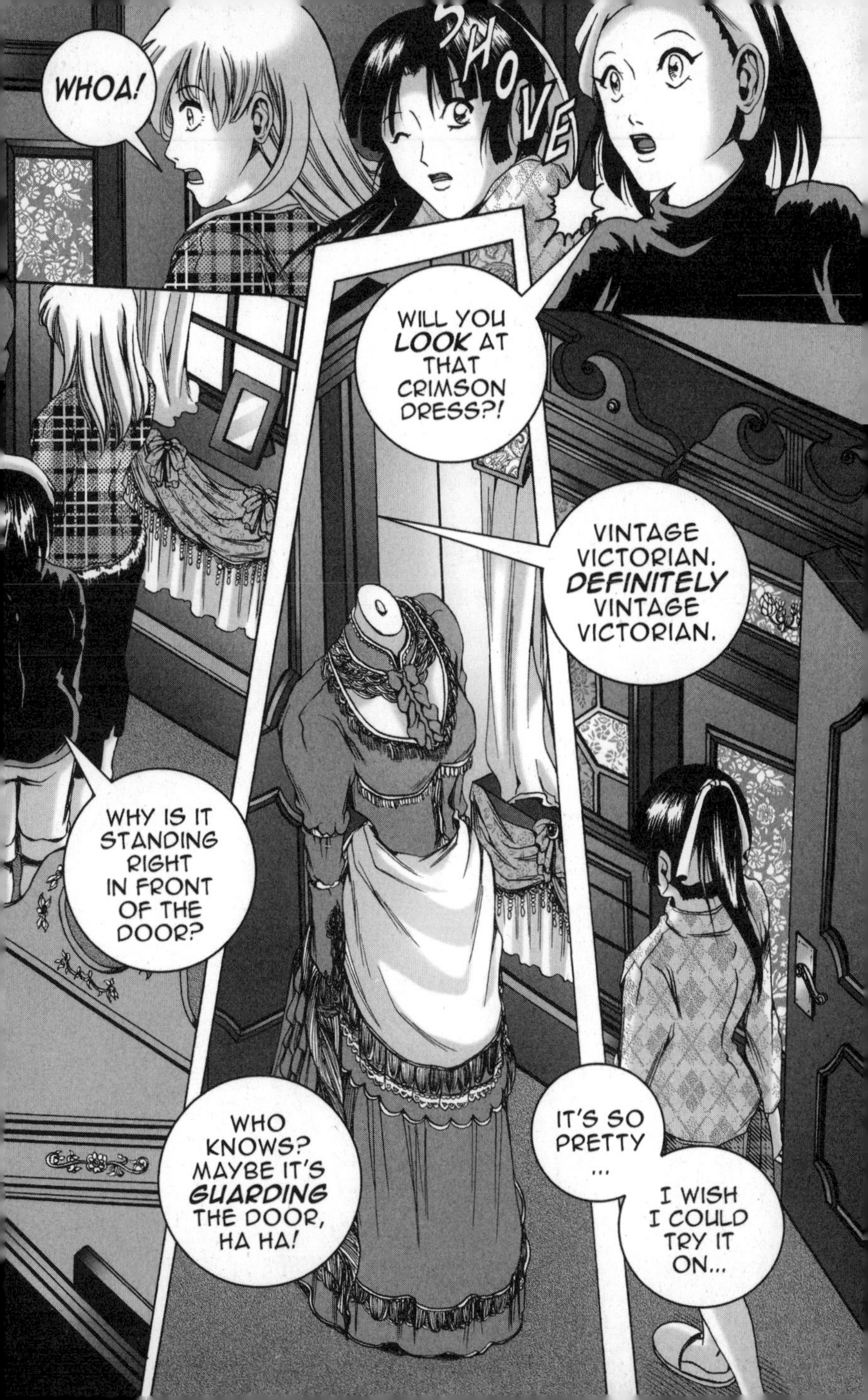
SHOVE
WHOA!
WILL YOU LOOK AT THAT CRIMSON DRESS?!
VINTAGE VICTORIAN. DEFINITELY VINTAGE VICTORIAN.
IT'S SO PRETTY ...
I WISH I COULD TRY IT ON...
WHY IS IT STANDING RIGHT IN FRONT OF THE DOOR?
WHO KNOWS? MAYBE IT'S GUARDING THE DOOR, HA HA!

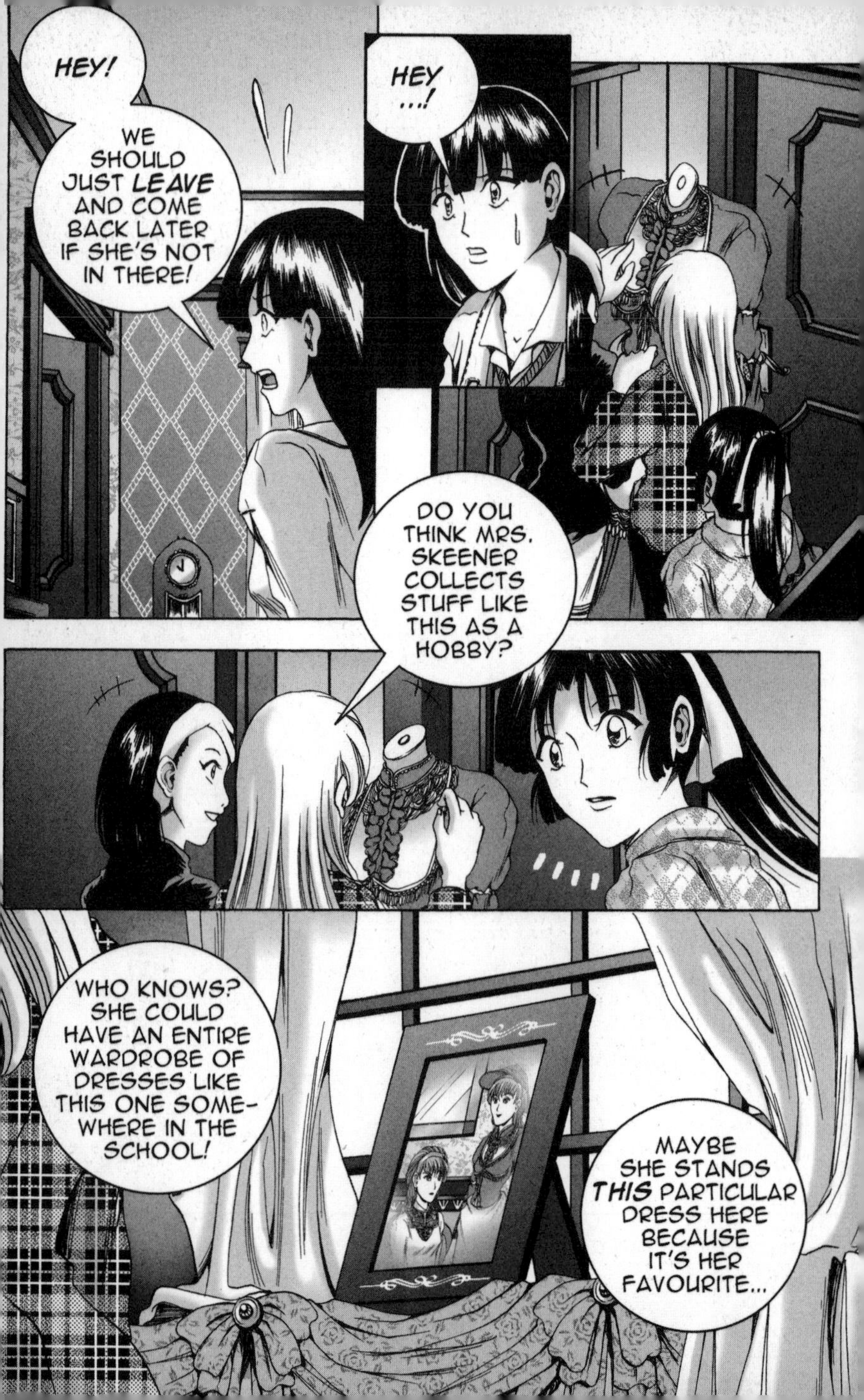
HEY!
WE SHOULD JUST LEAVE AND COME BACK LATER IF SHE'S NOT IN THERE!
HEY ...!
DO YOU THINK MRS. SKEENER COLLECTS STUFF LIKE THIS AS A HOBBY?
WHO KNOWS? SHE COULD HAVE AN ENTIRE WARDROBE OF DRESSES LIKE THIS ONE SOME-WHERE IN THE SCHOOL!
MAYBE SHE STANDS THIS PARTICULAR DRESS HERE BECAUSE IT'S HER FAVOURITE...

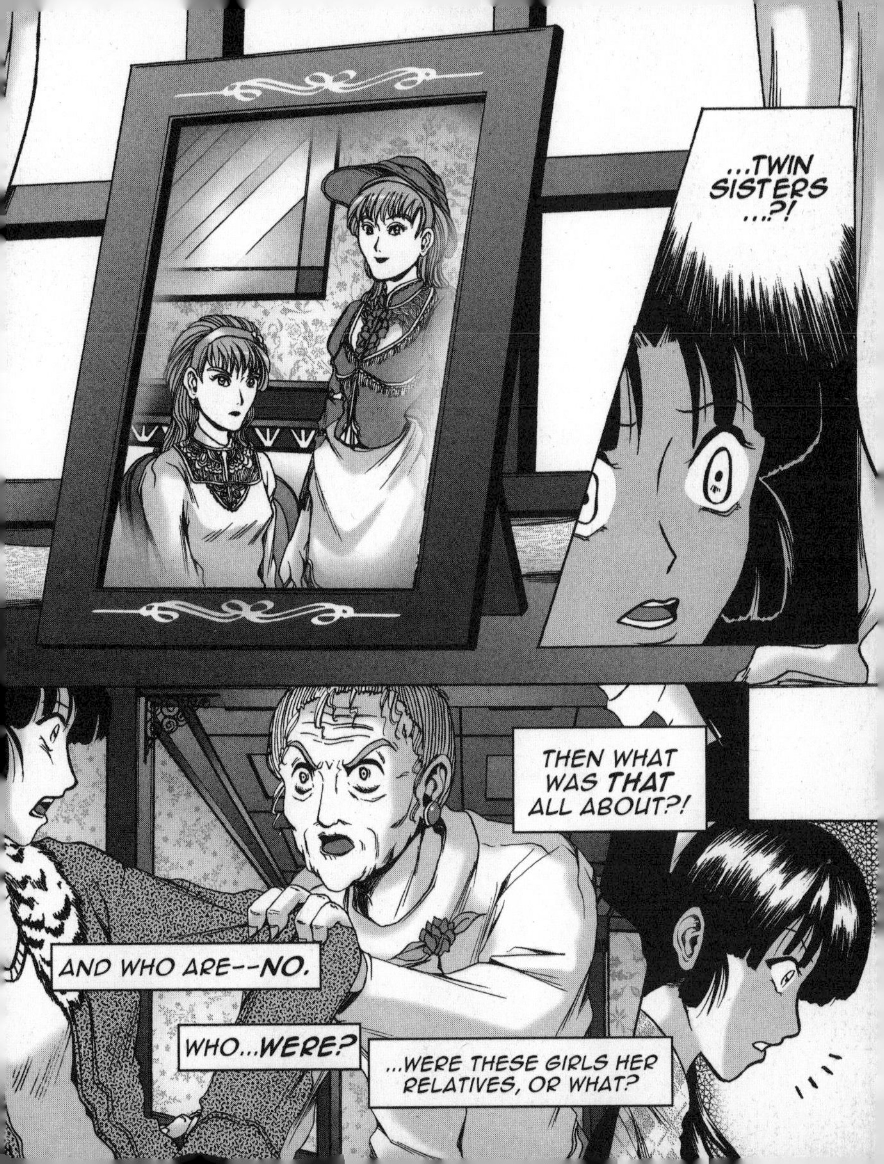
...TWIN SISTERS ...?!
THEN WHAT WAS THAT ALL ABOUT?!
AND WHO ARE--NO.
WHO...WERE?
...WERE THESE GIRLS HER RELATIVES, OR WHAT?

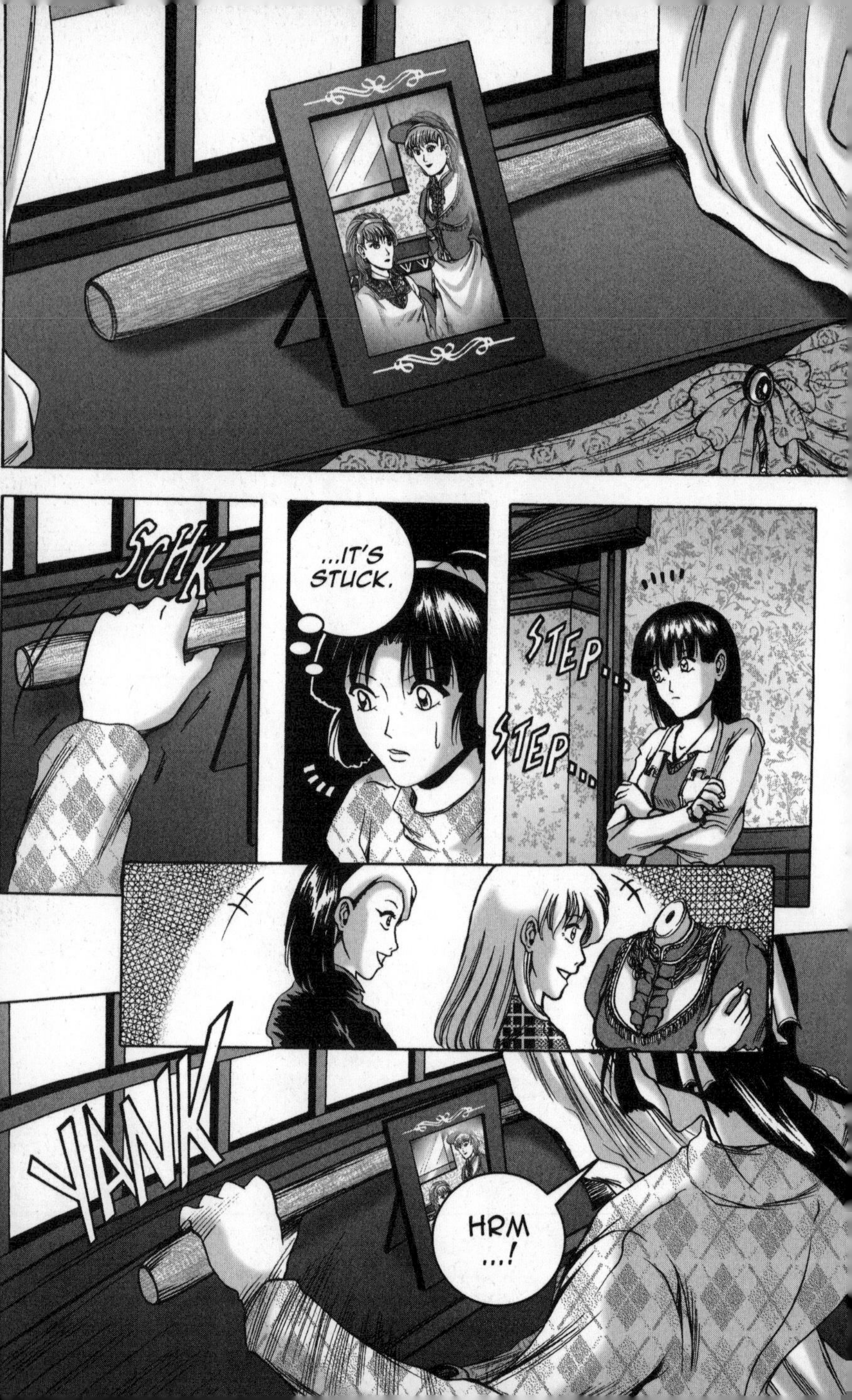
STEP...
STEP...
...IT'S STUCK.
SCHK
HRM ...!
YANK

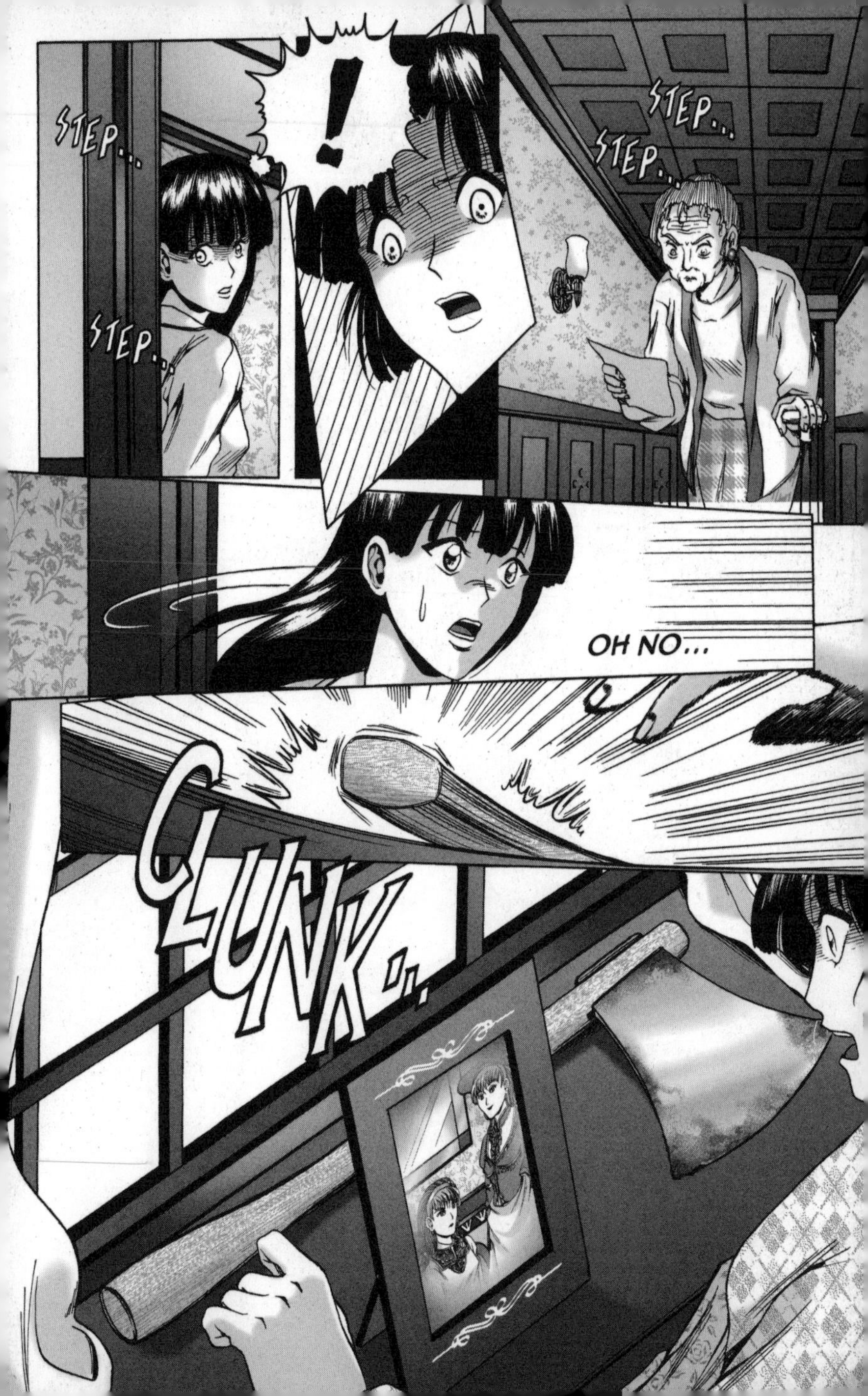
STEP...
STEP...
!
STEP...
STEP...
OH NO...
CLUNK...

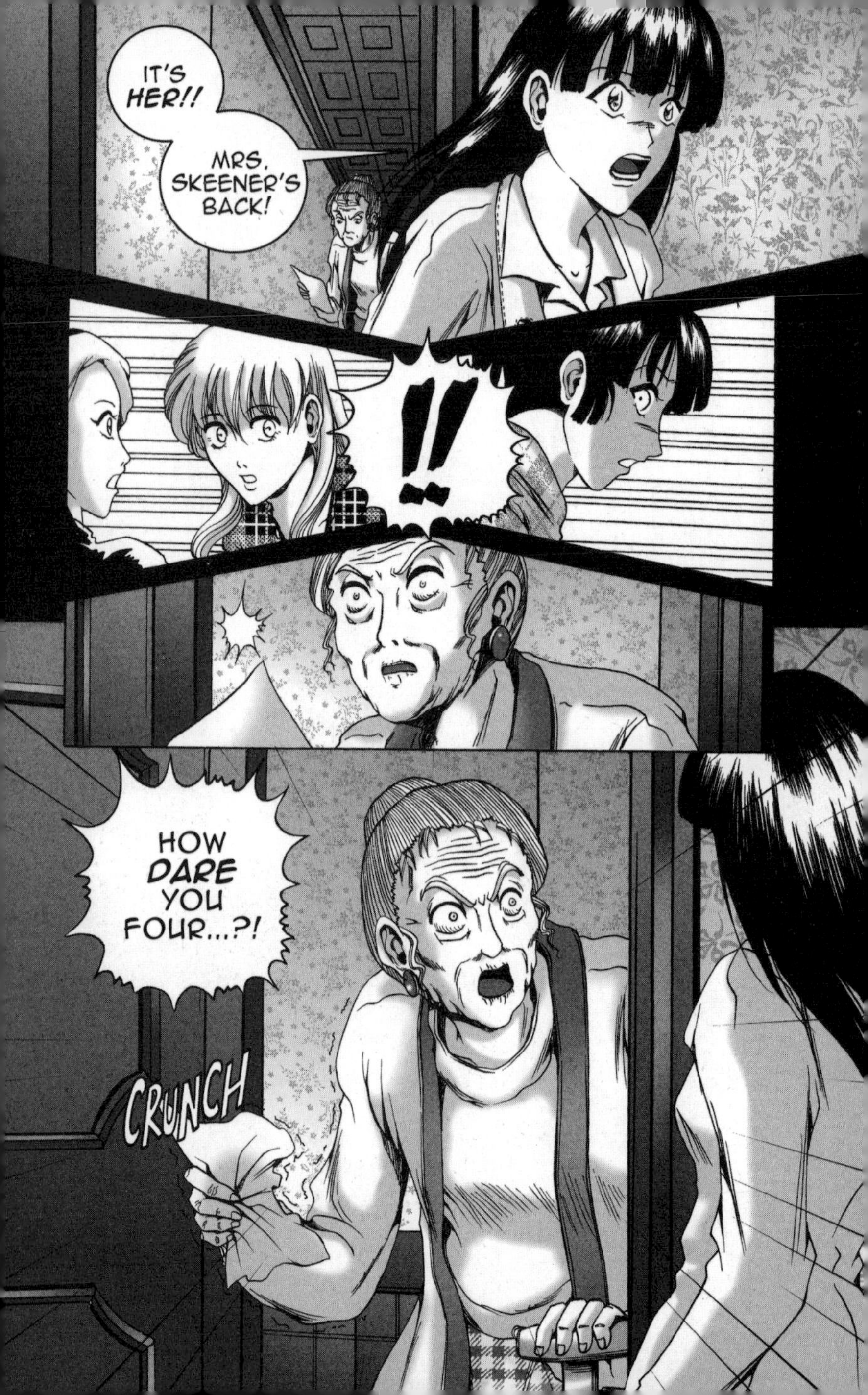
IT'S HER!!
MRS. SKEENER'S BACK!
!!
HOW DARE YOU FOUR...?!
CRUNCH

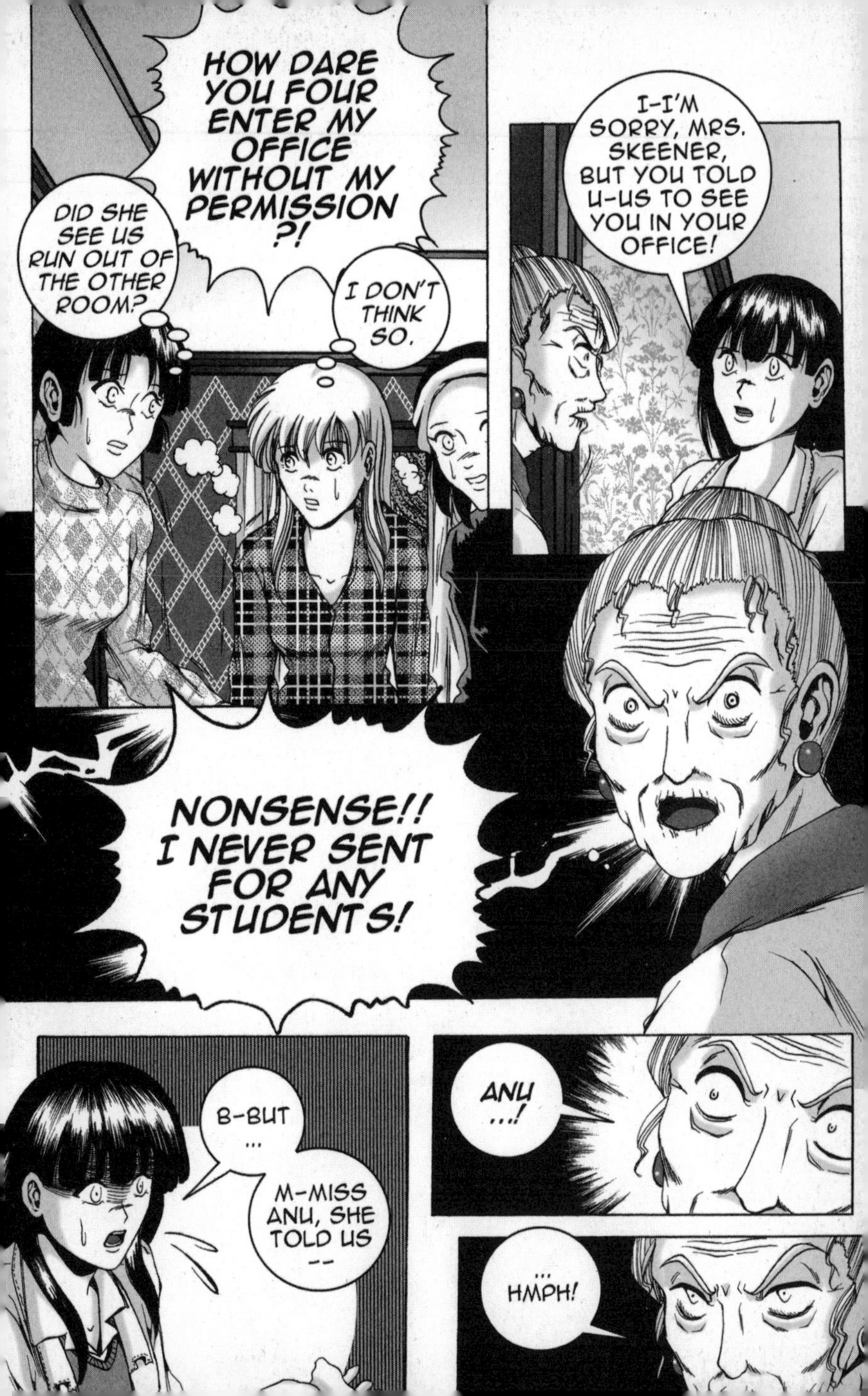
HOW DARE YOU FOUR ENTER MY OFFICE WITHOUT MY PERMISSION ?!
DID SHE SEE US RUN OUT OF THE OTHER ROOM?
I DON'T THINK SO.
I-I'M SORRY, MRS. SKEENER, BUT YOU TOLD U-US TO SEE YOU IN YOUR OFFICE!
NONSENSE!! I NEVER SENT FOR ANY STUDENTS!
B-BUT ...
M-MISS ANU, SHE TOLD US --
ANU ...!
... HMPH!

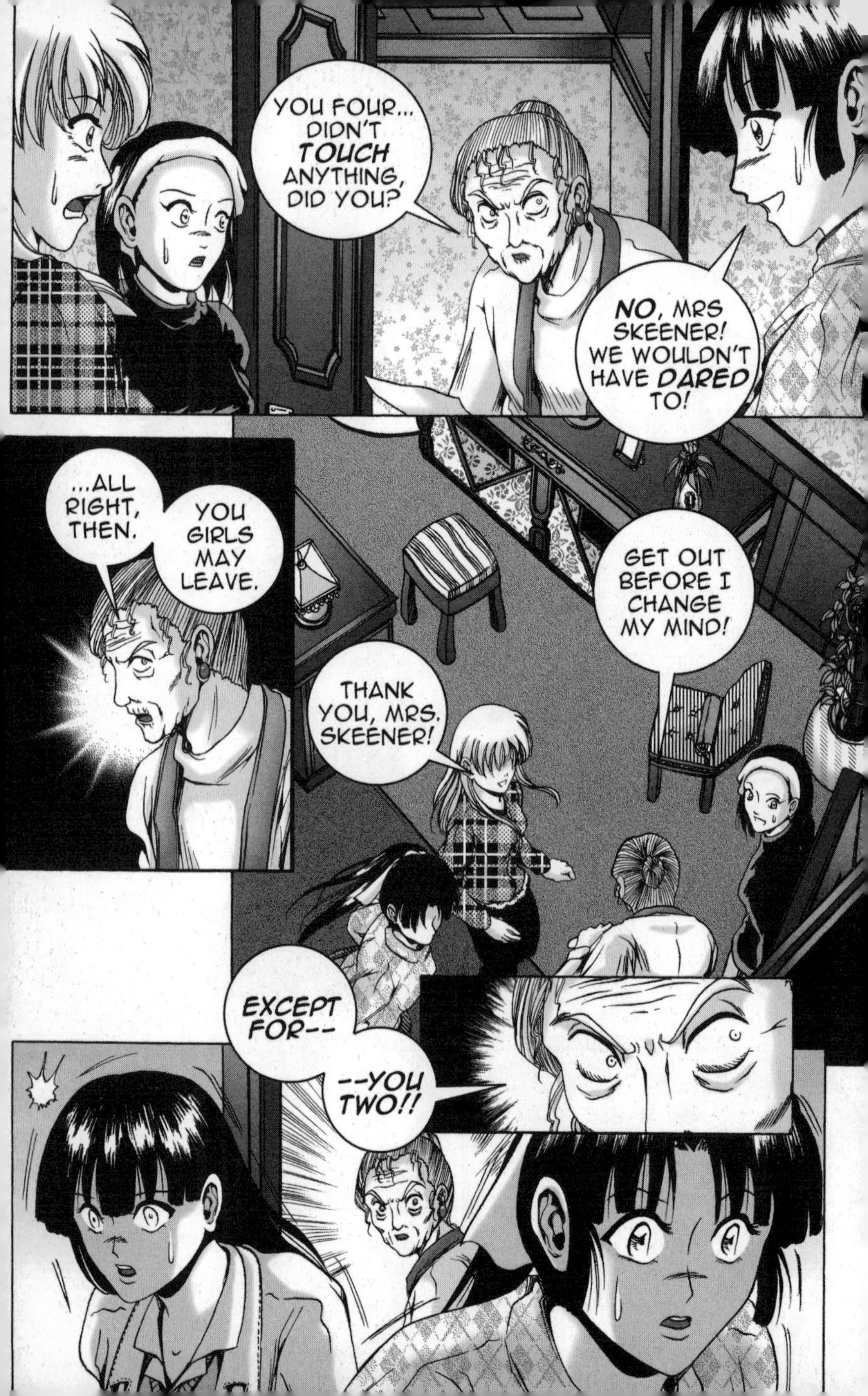
YOU FOUR... DIDN'T *TOUCH* ANYTHING, DID YOU?
NO, MRS SKEENER! WE WOULDN'T HAVE *DARED* TO!
...ALL RIGHT, THEN.
YOU GIRLS MAY LEAVE.
THANK YOU, MRS. SKEENER!
GET OUT BEFORE I CHANGE MY MIND!
EXCEPT FOR--
--YOU TWO!!

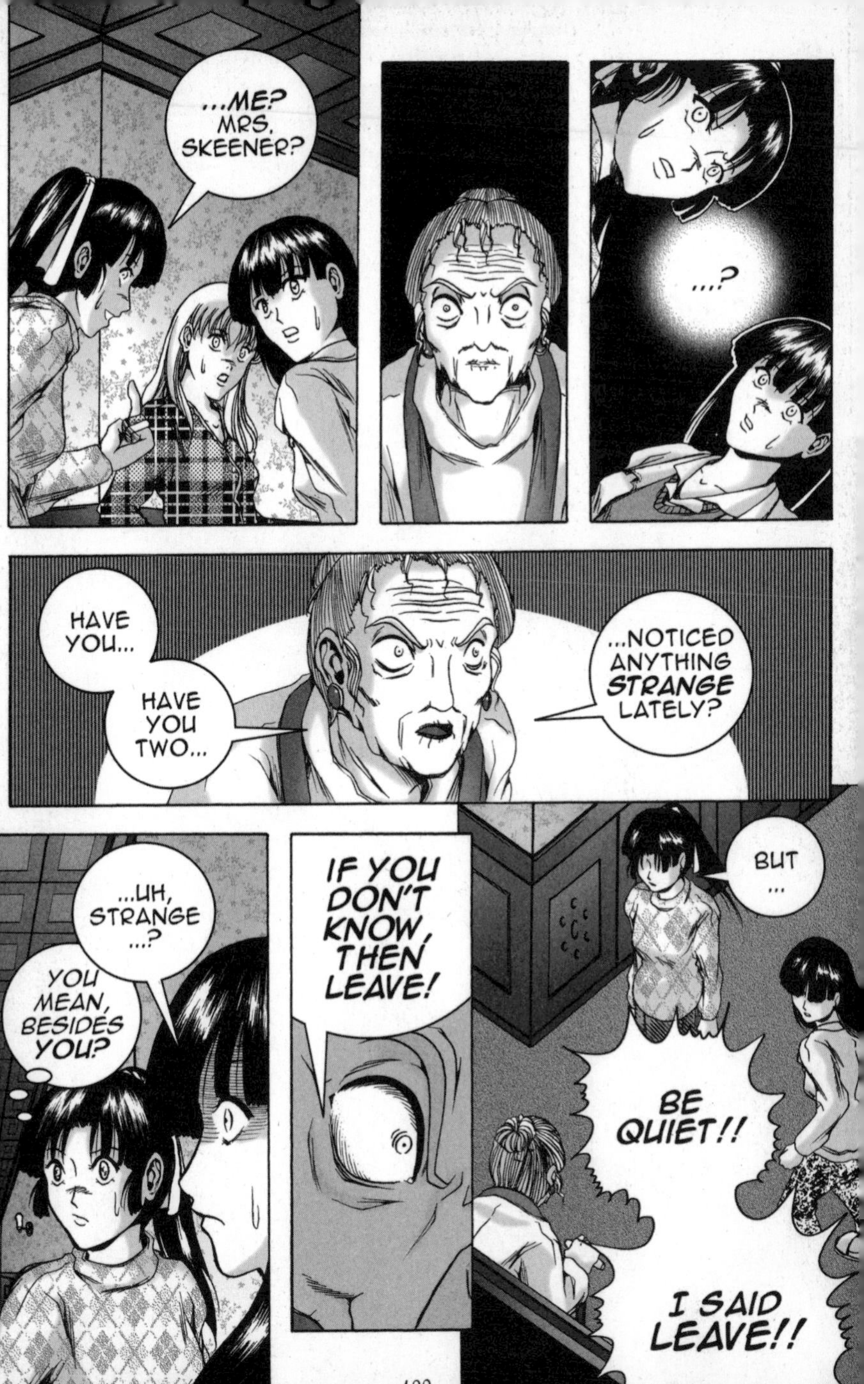
...ME? MRS. SKEENER?
...?
HAVE YOU...
HAVE YOU TWO...
...NOTICED ANYTHING STRANGE LATELY?
...UH, STRANGE ...?
YOU MEAN, BESIDES YOU?
IF YOU DON'T KNOW, THEN LEAVE!
BUT ...
BE QUIET!!
I SAID LEAVE!!

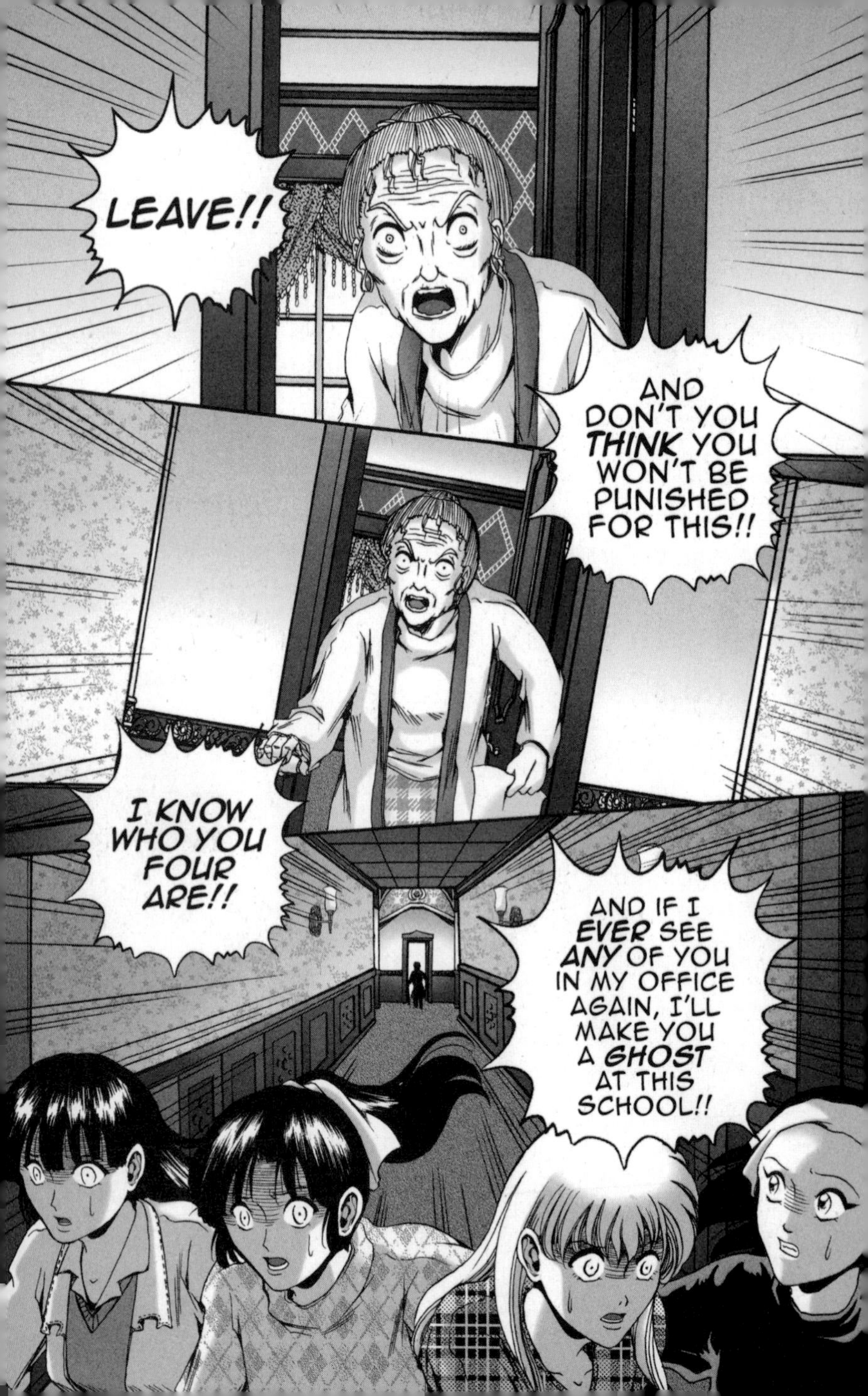
LEAVE!!
AND DON'T YOU THINK YOU WON'T BE PUNISHED FOR THIS!!
I KNOW WHO YOU FOUR ARE!!
AND IF I EVER SEE ANY OF YOU IN MY OFFICE AGAIN, I'LL MAKE YOU A GHOST AT THIS SCHOOL!!

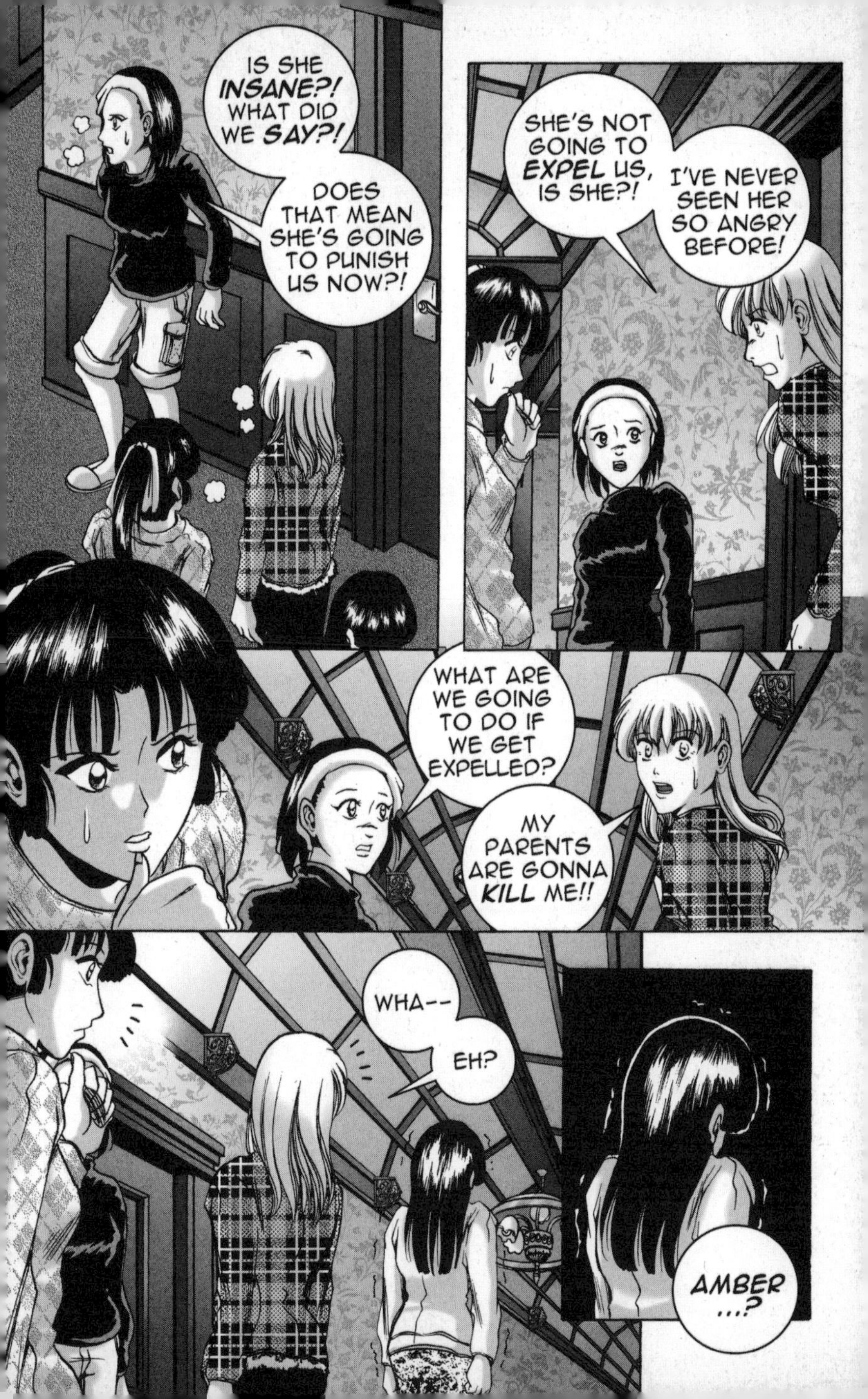
IS SHE INSANE?! WHAT DID WE SAY?!
DOES THAT MEAN SHE'S GOING TO PUNISH US NOW?!
SHE'S NOT GOING TO EXPEL US, IS SHE?!
I'VE NEVER SEEN HER SO ANGRY BEFORE!
WHAT ARE WE GOING TO DO IF WE GET EXPELLED?
MY PARENTS ARE GONNA KILL ME!!
WHA--
EH?
AMBER ...?

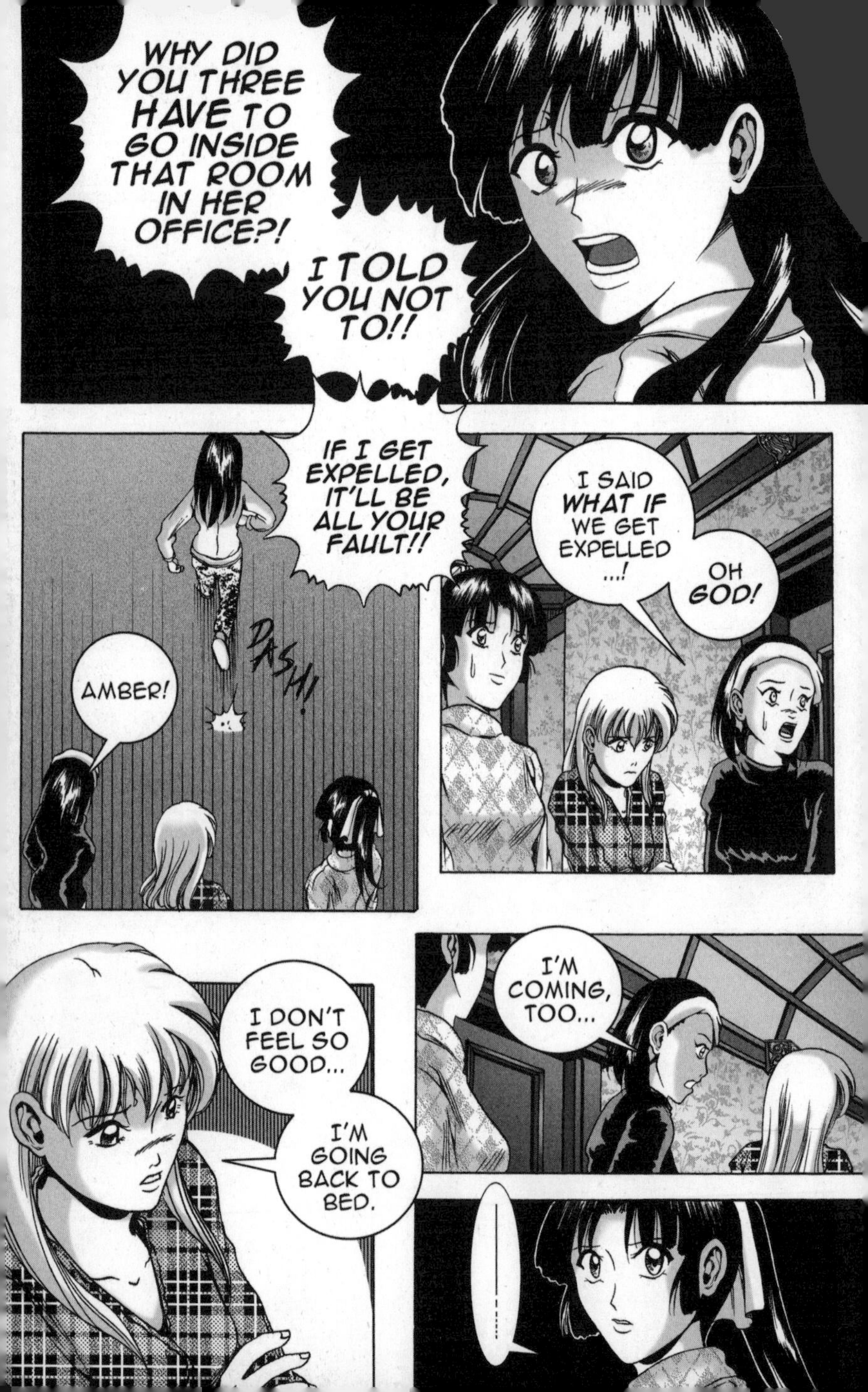
WHY DID YOU THREE HAVE TO GO INSIDE THAT ROOM IN HER OFFICE?!
I TOLD YOU NOT TO!!
IF I GET EXPELLED, IT'LL BE ALL YOUR FAULT!!
DASH!
AMBER!
I SAID WHAT IF WE GET EXPELLED ...!
OH GOD!
I DON'T FEEL SO GOOD...
I'M GOING BACK TO BED.
I'M COMING, TOO...
......

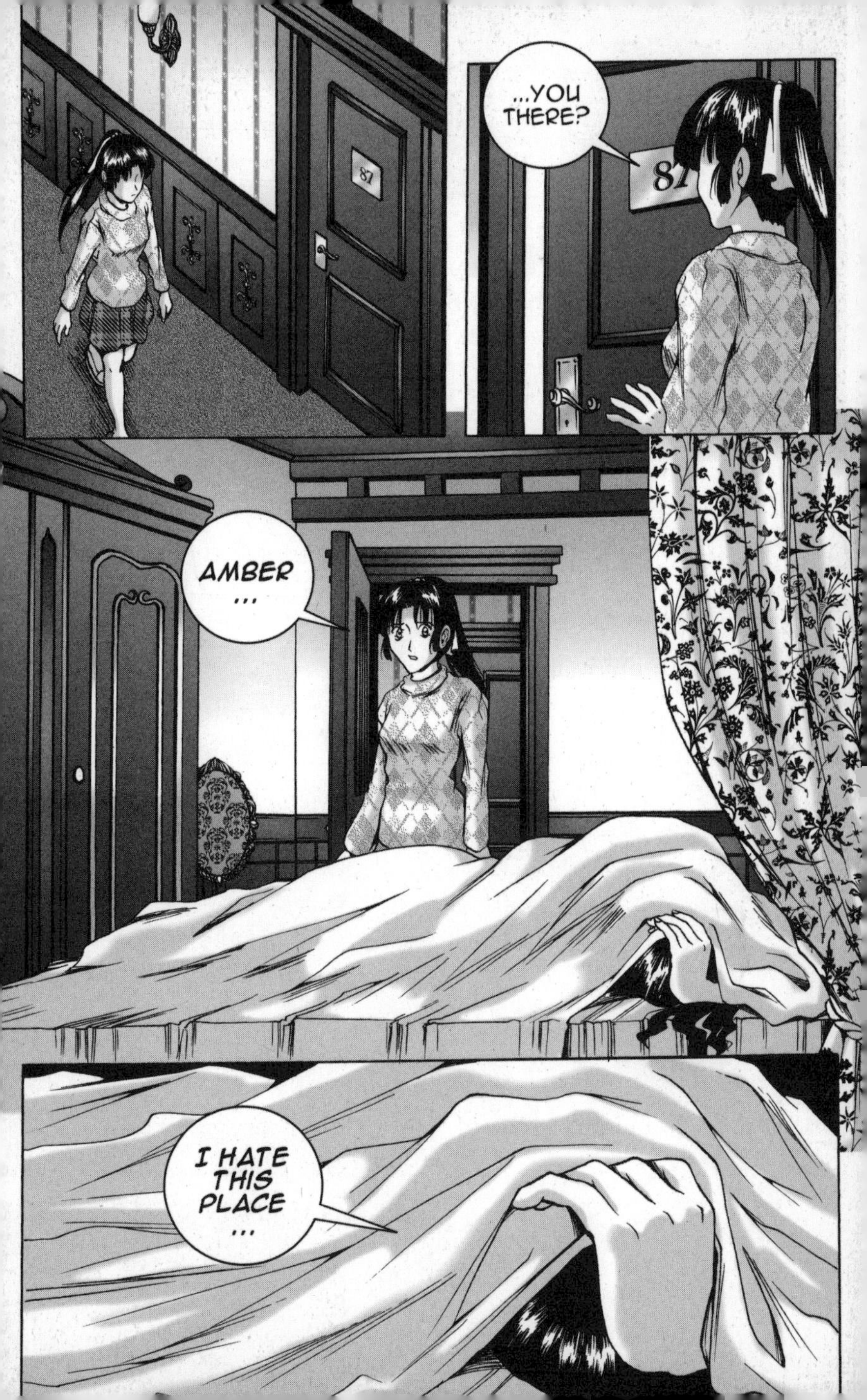
...YOU THERE?
87
AMBER ...
I HATE THIS PLACE ...

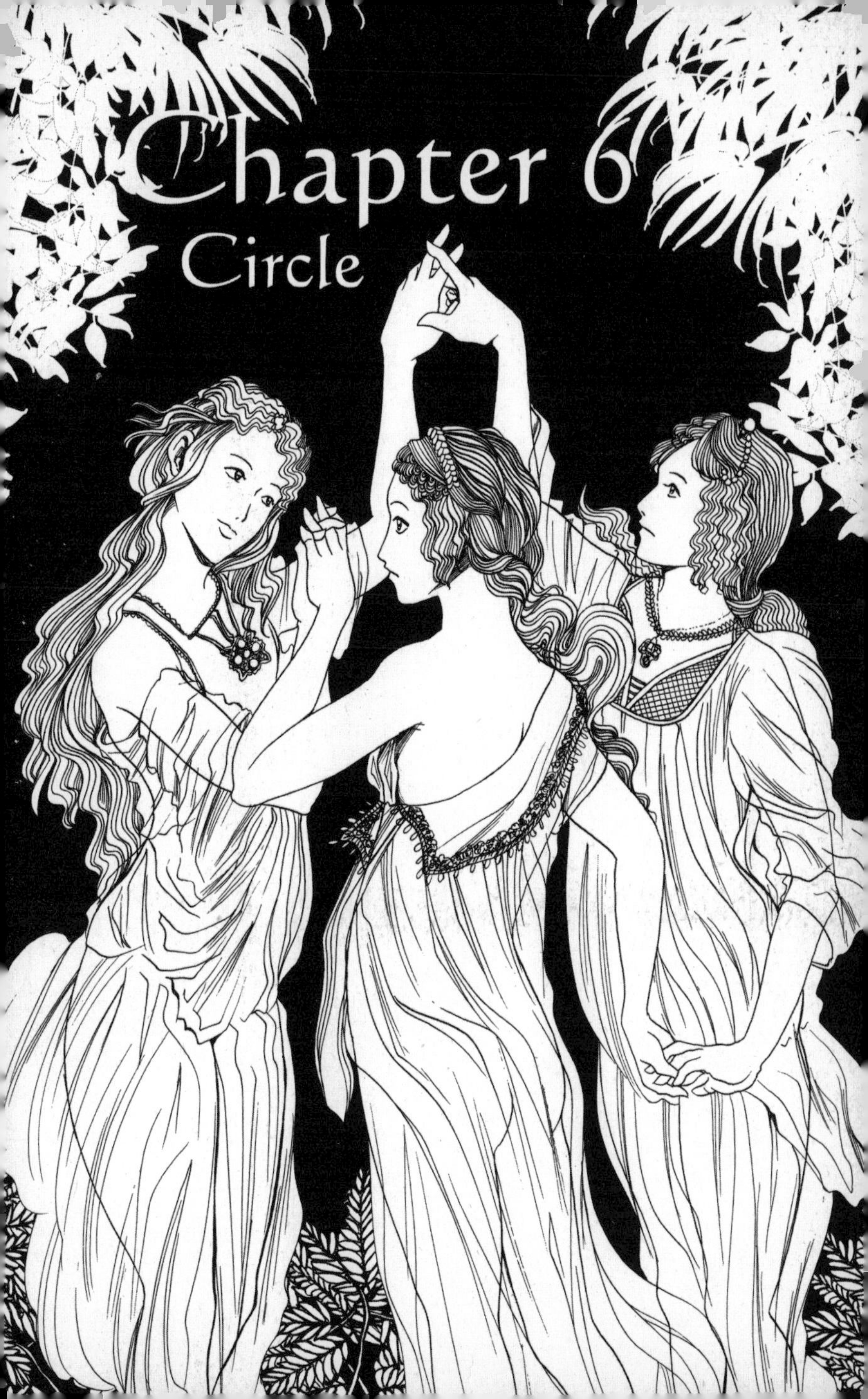
Chapter 6
Circle

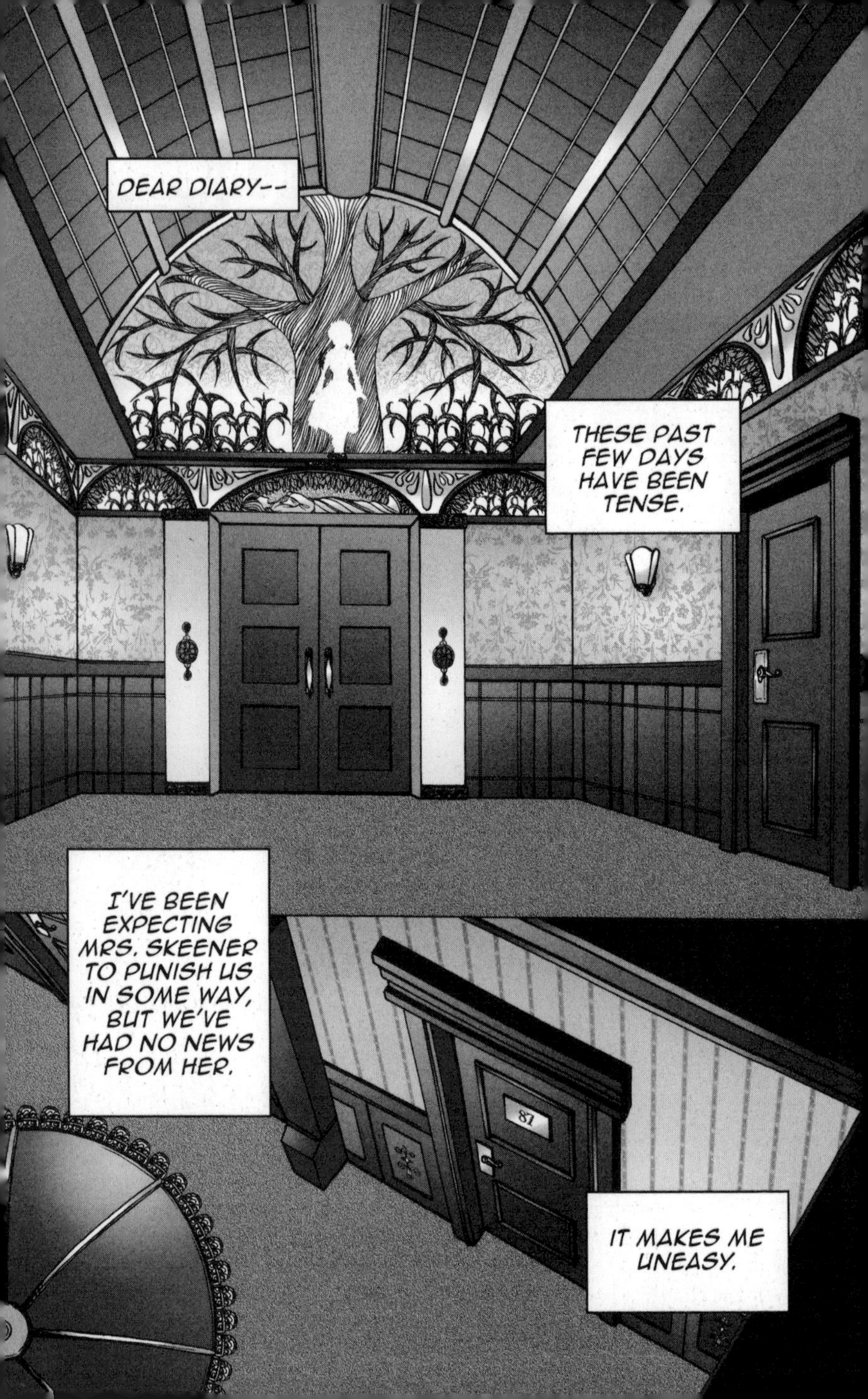
DEAR DIARY--
THESE PAST FEW DAYS HAVE BEEN TENSE.
I'VE BEEN EXPECTING MRS. SKEENER TO PUNISH US IN SOME WAY, BUT WE'VE HAD NO NEWS FROM HER.
87
IT MAKES ME UNEASY.

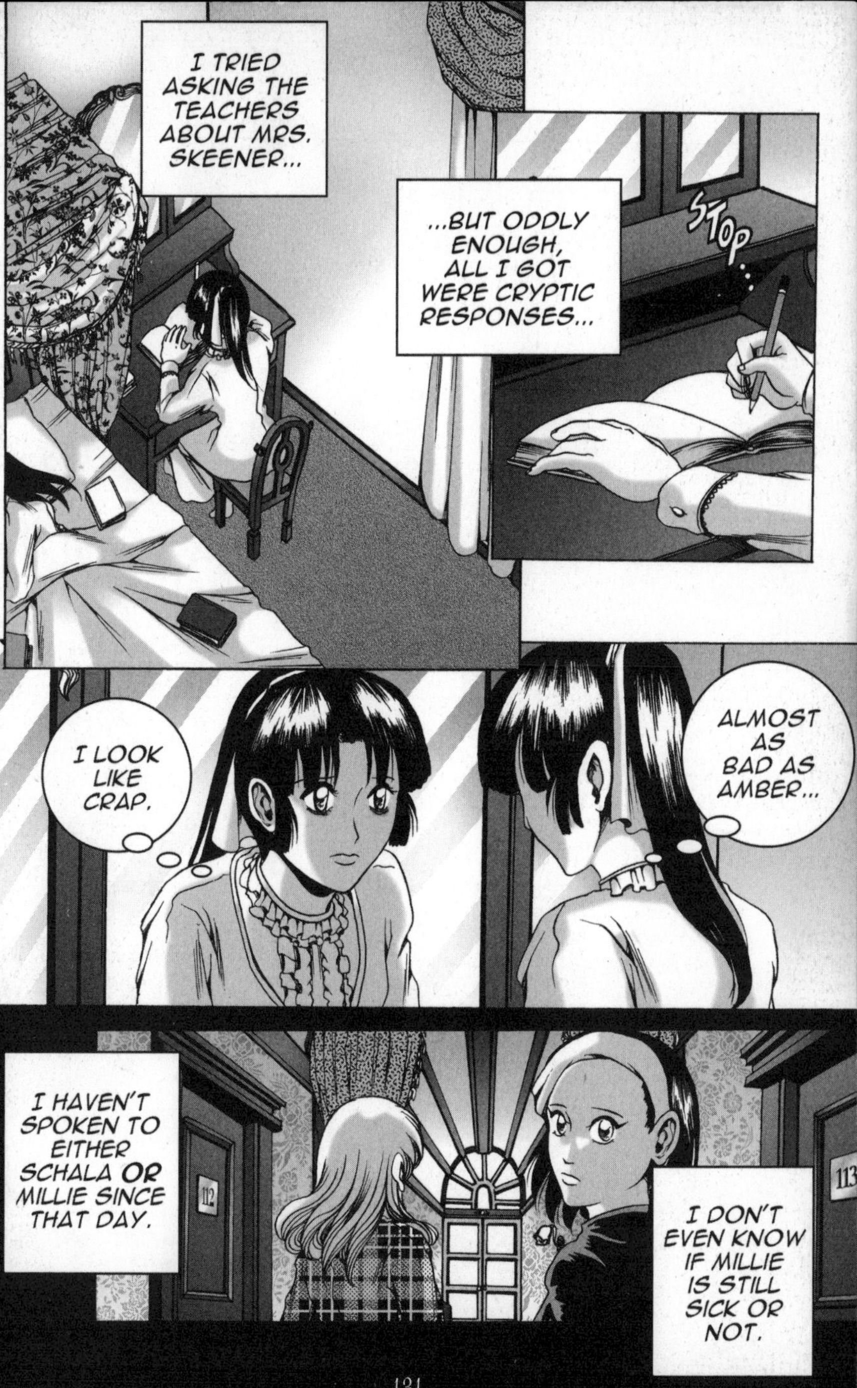
I TRIED ASKING THE TEACHERS ABOUT MRS. SKEENER...
...BUT ODDLY ENOUGH, ALL I GOT WERE CRYPTIC RESPONSES...
STOP...
I LOOK LIKE CRAP.
ALMOST AS BAD AS AMBER...
I HAVEN'T SPOKEN TO EITHER SCHALA OR MILLIE SINCE THAT DAY.
112
113
I DON'T EVEN KNOW IF MILLIE IS STILL SICK OR NOT.

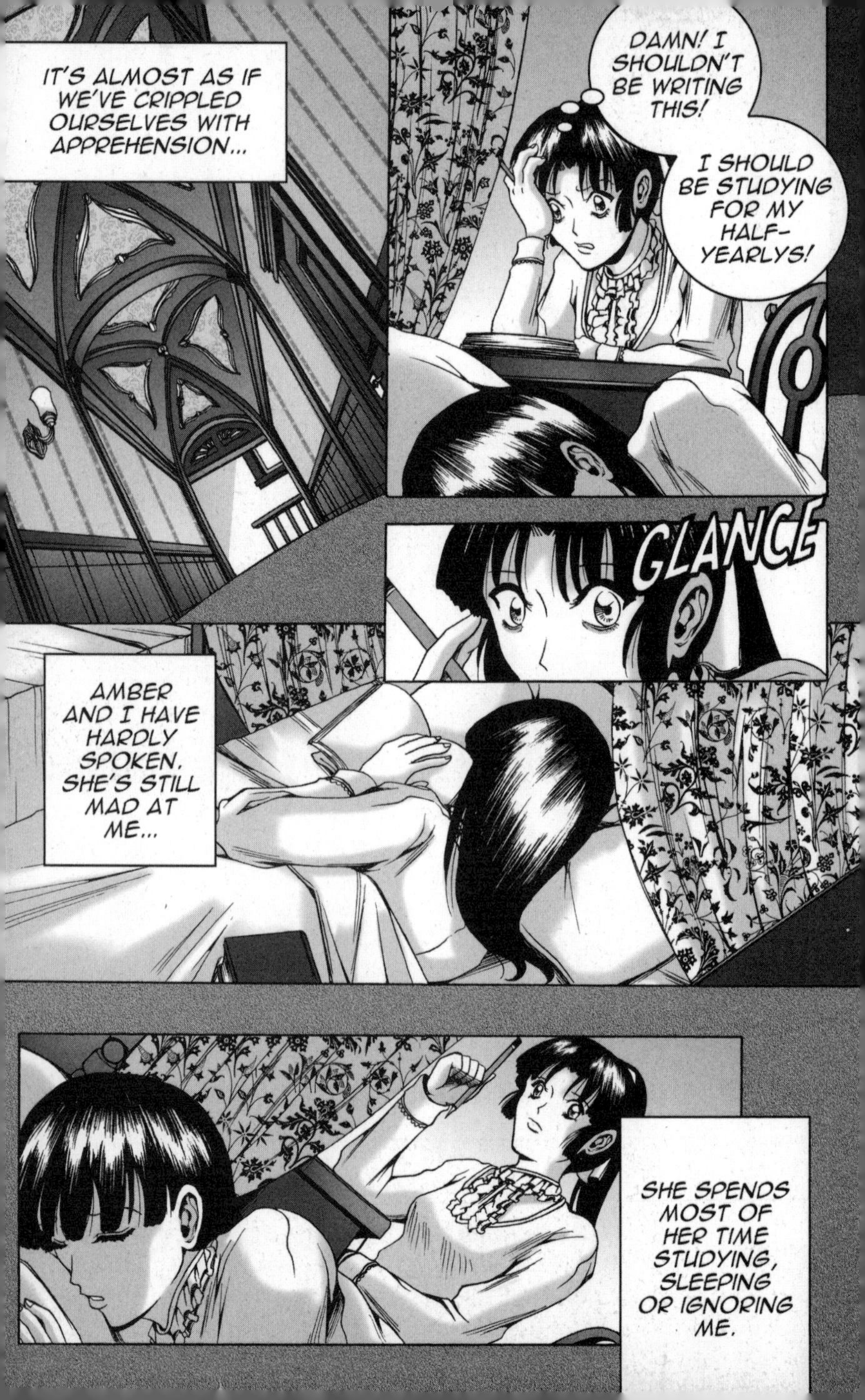
IT'S ALMOST AS IF WE'VE CRIPPLED OURSELVES WITH APPREHENSION...
DAMN! I SHOULDN'T BE WRITING THIS!
I SHOULD BE STUDYING FOR MY HALF-YEARLYS!
GLANCE
AMBER AND I HAVE HARDLY SPOKEN. SHE'S STILL MAD AT ME...
SHE SPENDS MOST OF HER TIME STUDYING, SLEEPING OR IGNORING ME.

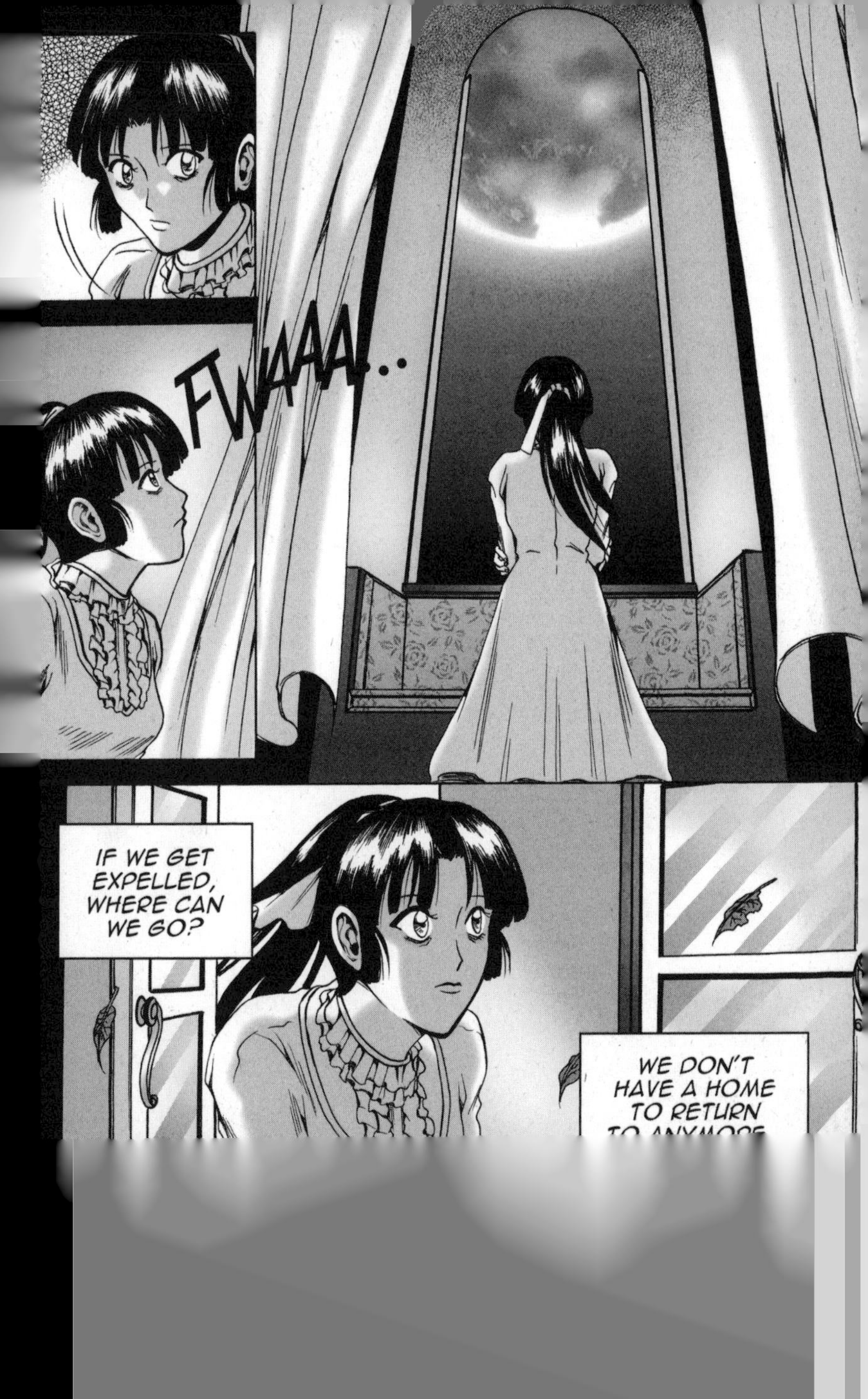
FWAAA...
IF WE GET EXPELLED, WHERE CAN WE GO?
WE DON'T HAVE A HOME TO RETURN

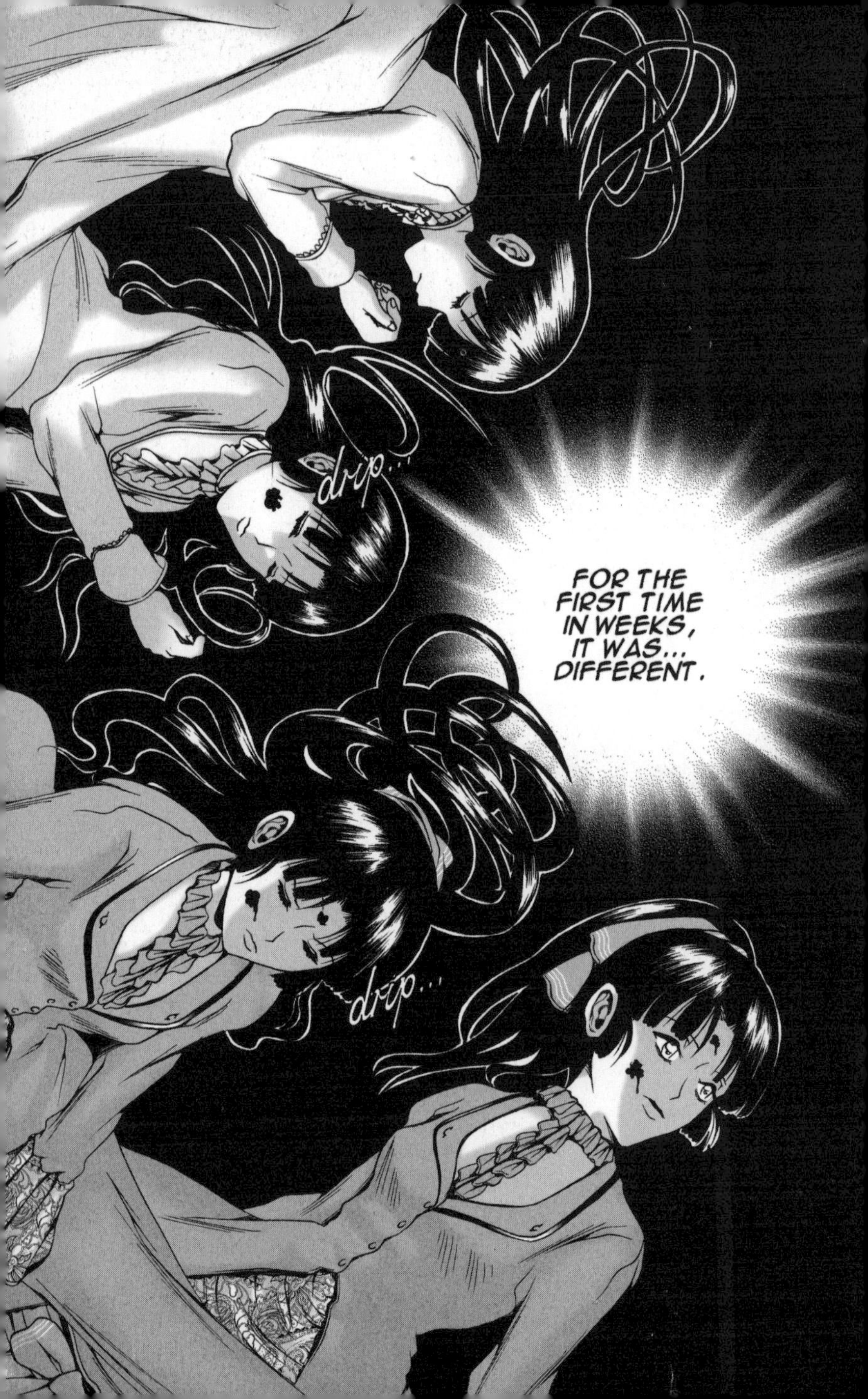
FOR THE FIRST TIME IN WEEKS, IT WAS... DIFFERENT.
drip...
drip...

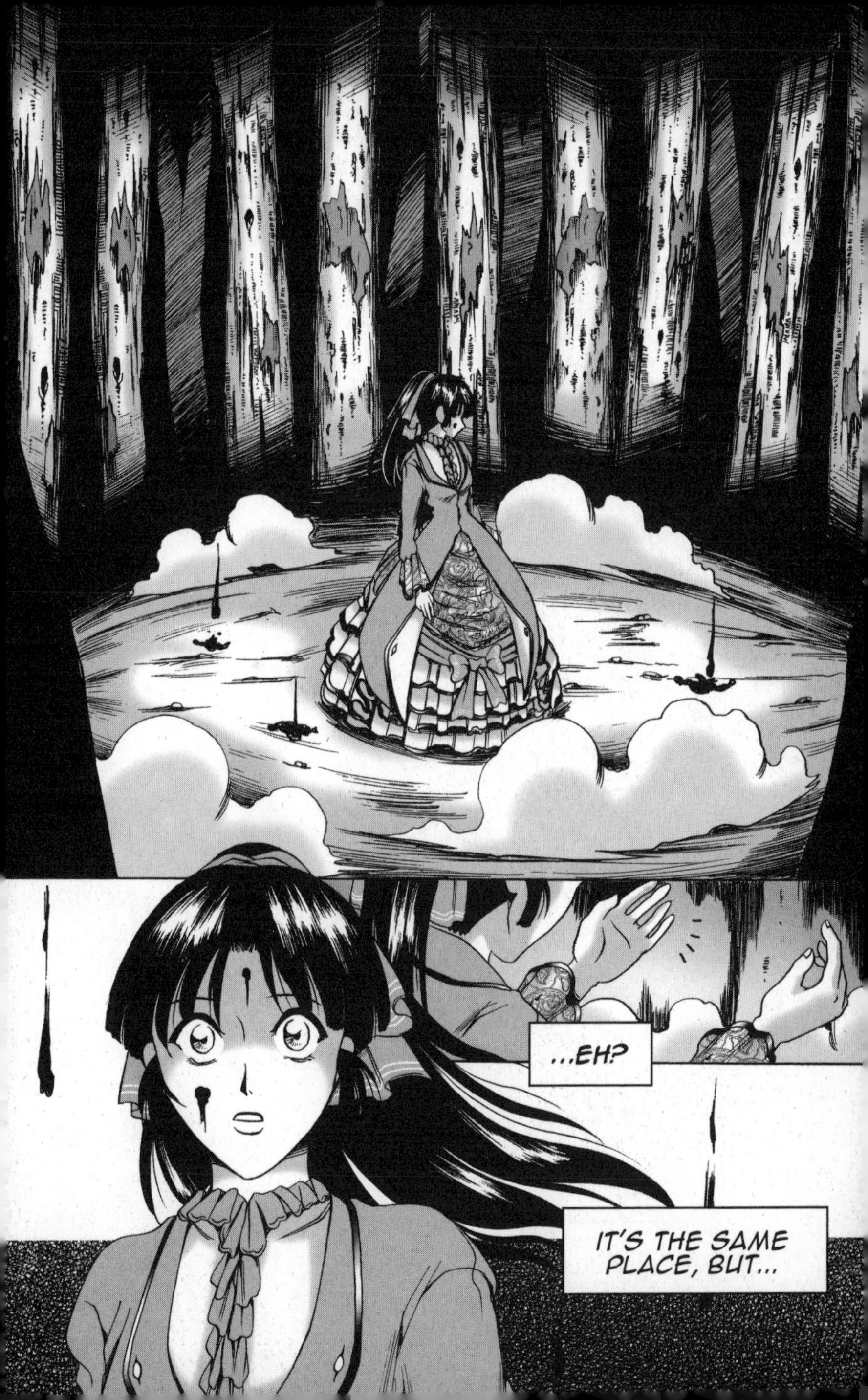
...EH?
IT'S THE SAME PLACE, BUT...

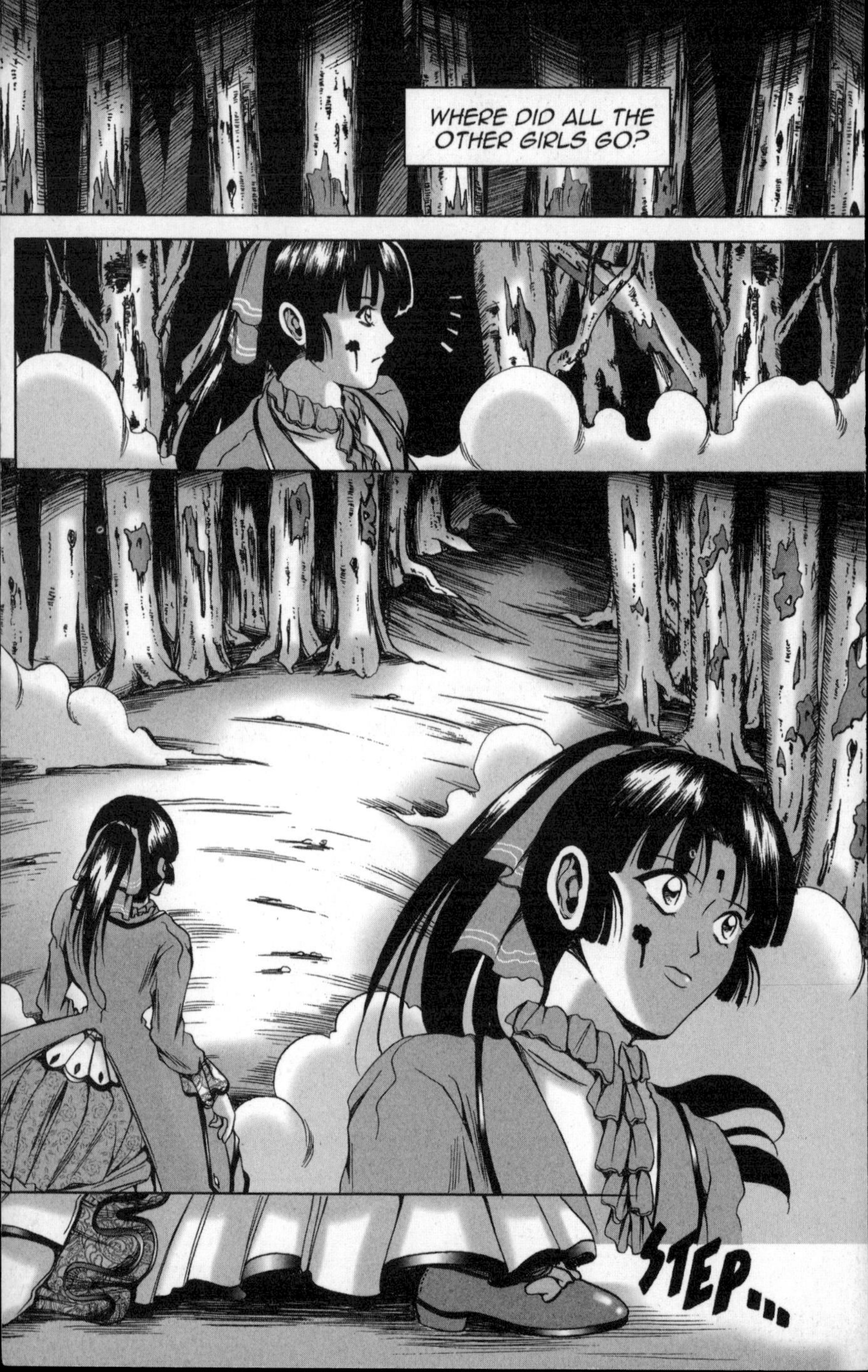
WHERE DID ALL THE OTHER GIRLS GO?
STEP...

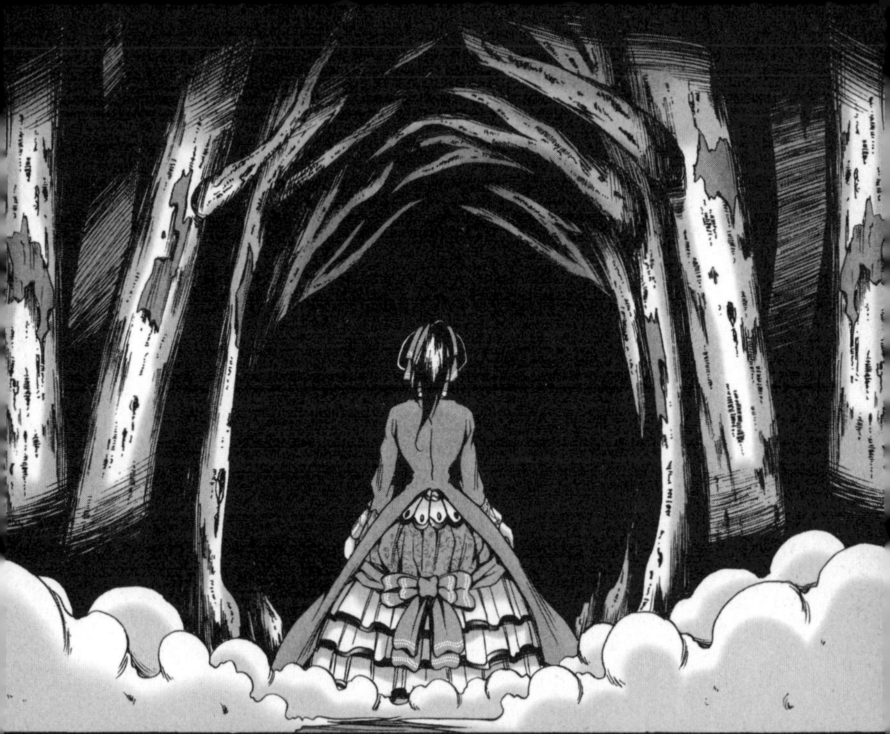

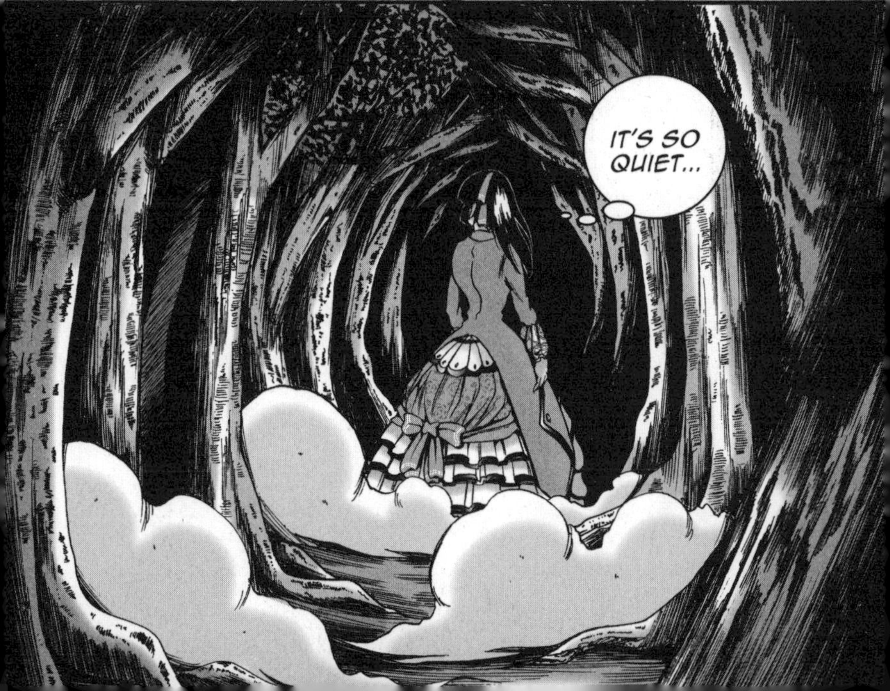
IT'S SO QUIET...

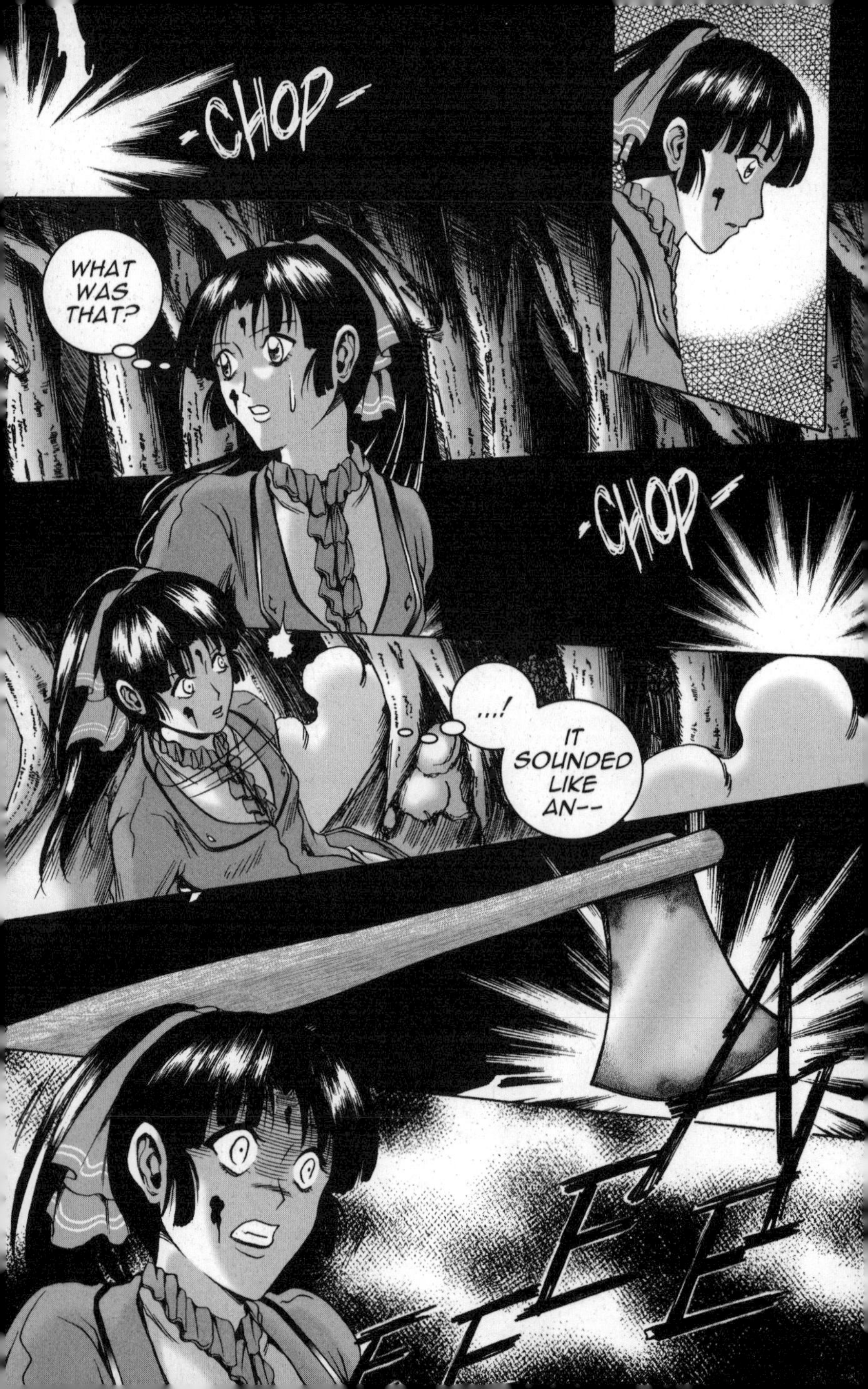
-CHOP-
WHAT WAS THAT?
-CHOP-
...!
IT SOUNDED LIKE AN--

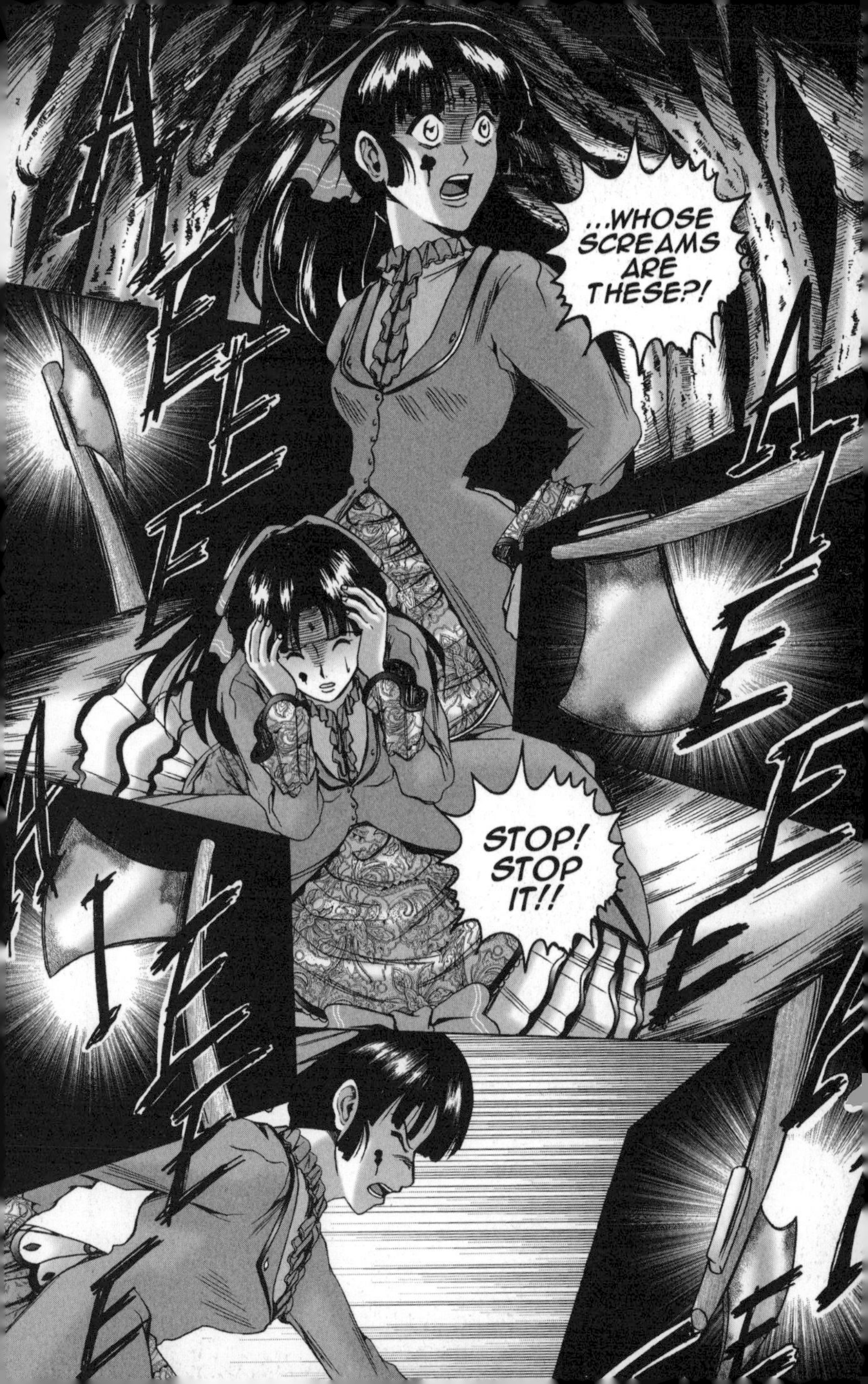
...WHOSE SCREAMS ARE THESE?!
STOP! STOP IT!!

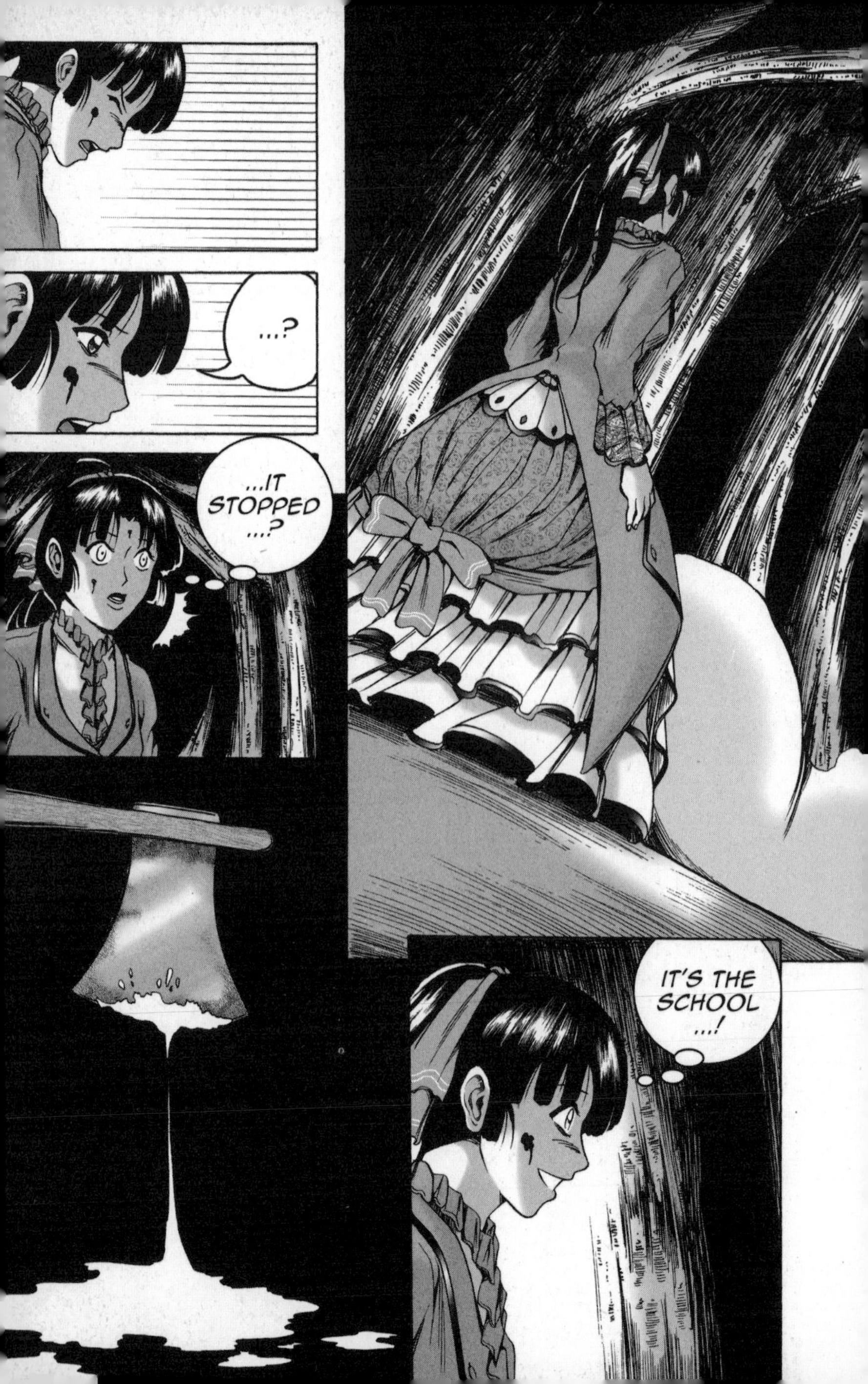
...?
...IT STOPPED ...?
IT'S THE SCHOOL ...!

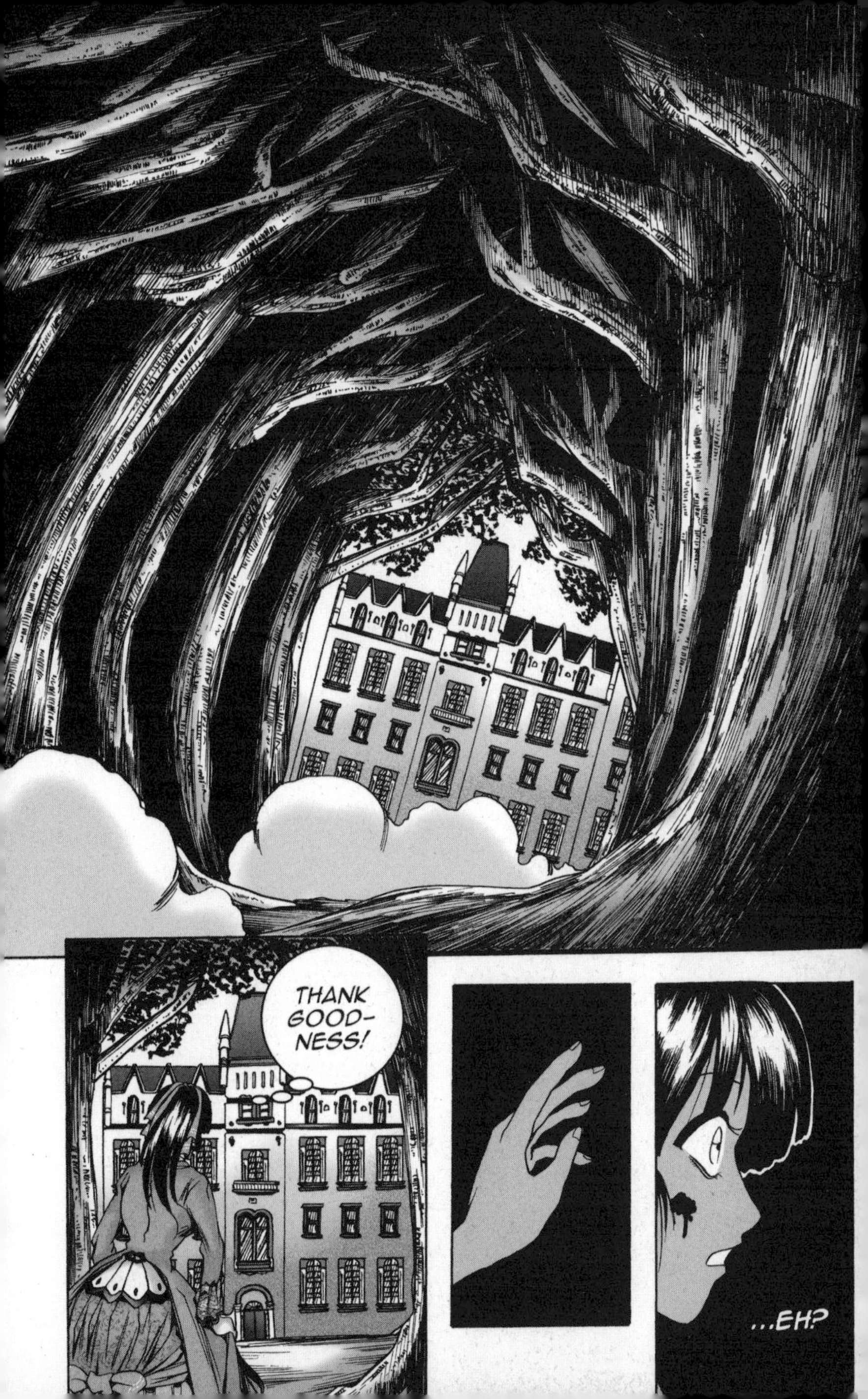
...EH?
THANK GOOD-NESS!

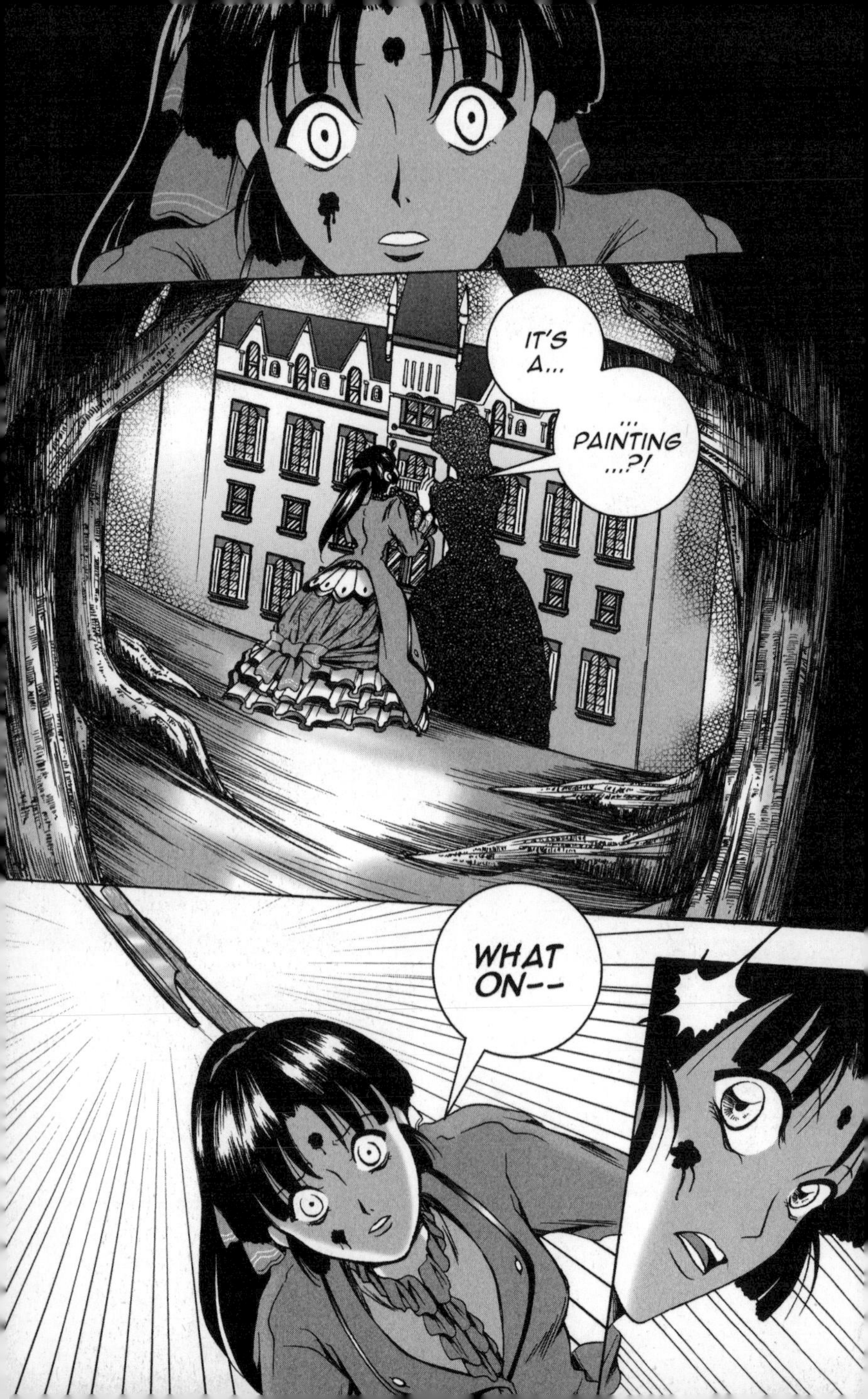
IT'S A...
... PAINTING ...?!
WHAT ON--

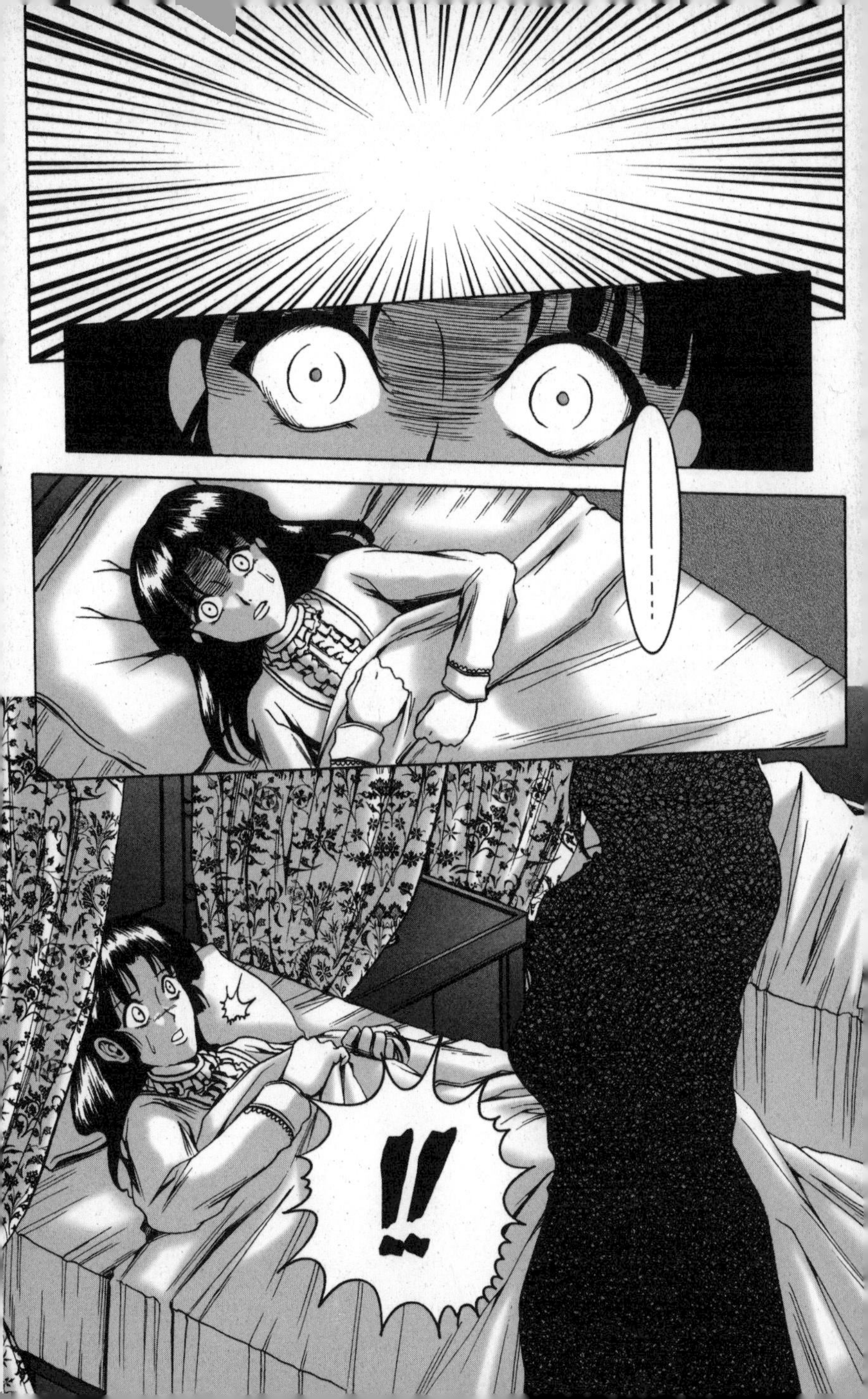
......
!!

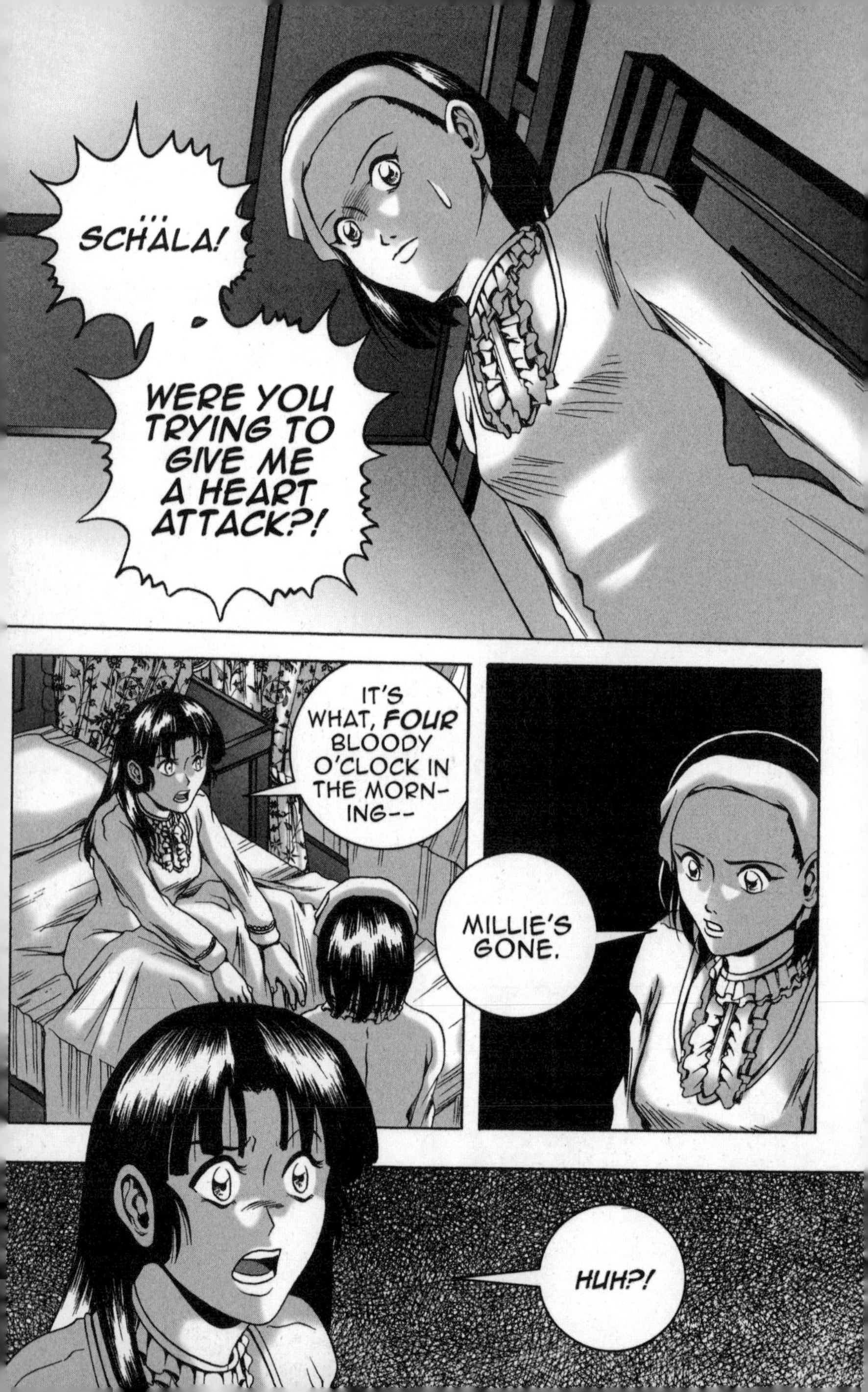
...SCHÄLA!
WERE YOU TRYING TO GIVE ME A HEART ATTACK?!
IT'S WHAT, FOUR BLOODY O'CLOCK IN THE MORN-ING--
MILLIE'S GONE.
HUH?!

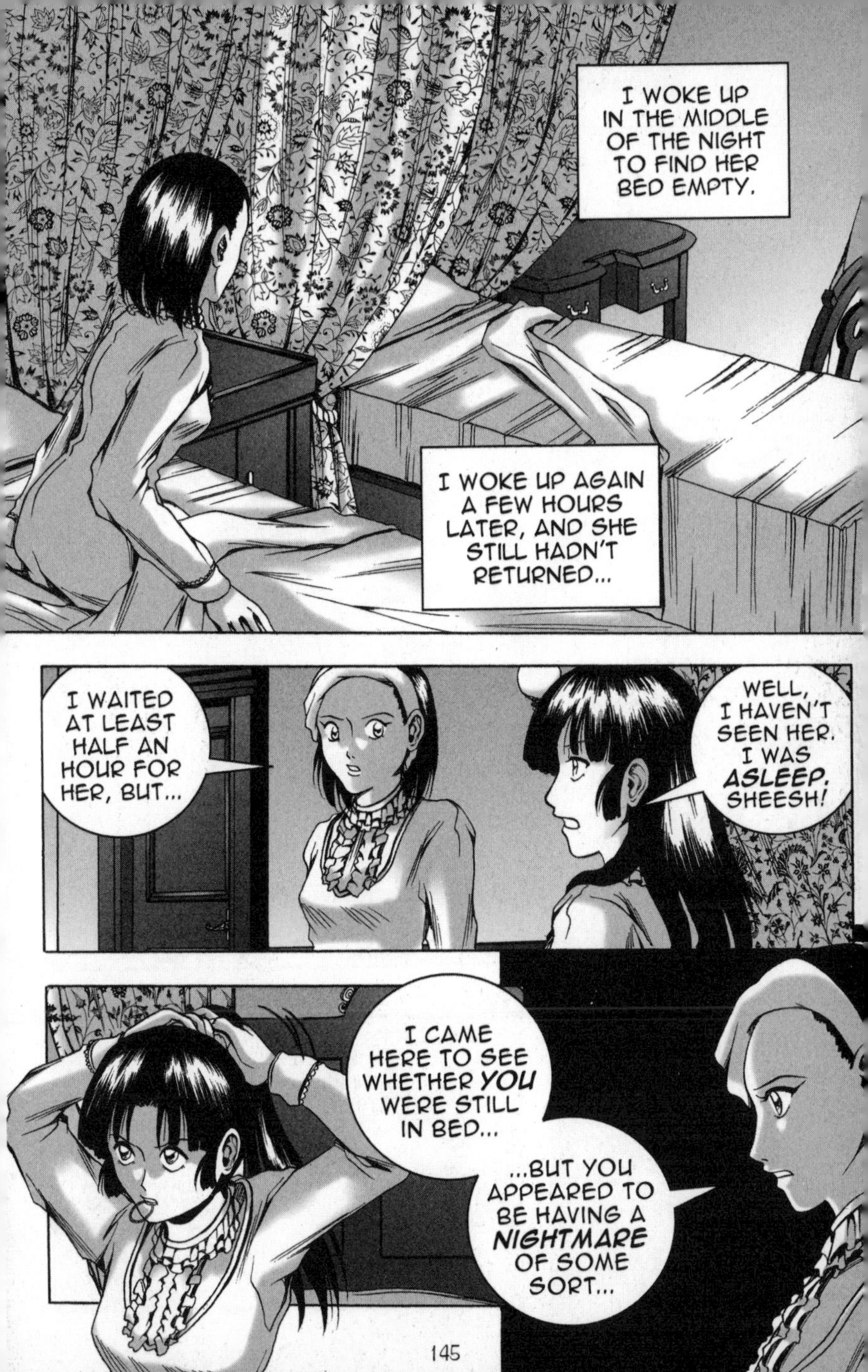
I WOKE UP IN THE MIDDLE OF THE NIGHT TO FIND HER BED EMPTY.
I WOKE UP AGAIN A FEW HOURS LATER, AND SHE STILL HADN'T RETURNED...
I WAITED AT LEAST HALF AN HOUR FOR HER, BUT...
WELL, I HAVEN'T SEEN HER. I WAS *ASLEEP*. SHEESH!
I CAME HERE TO SEE WHETHER *YOU* WERE STILL IN BED...
...BUT YOU APPEARED TO BE HAVING A *NIGHTMARE* OF SOME SORT...

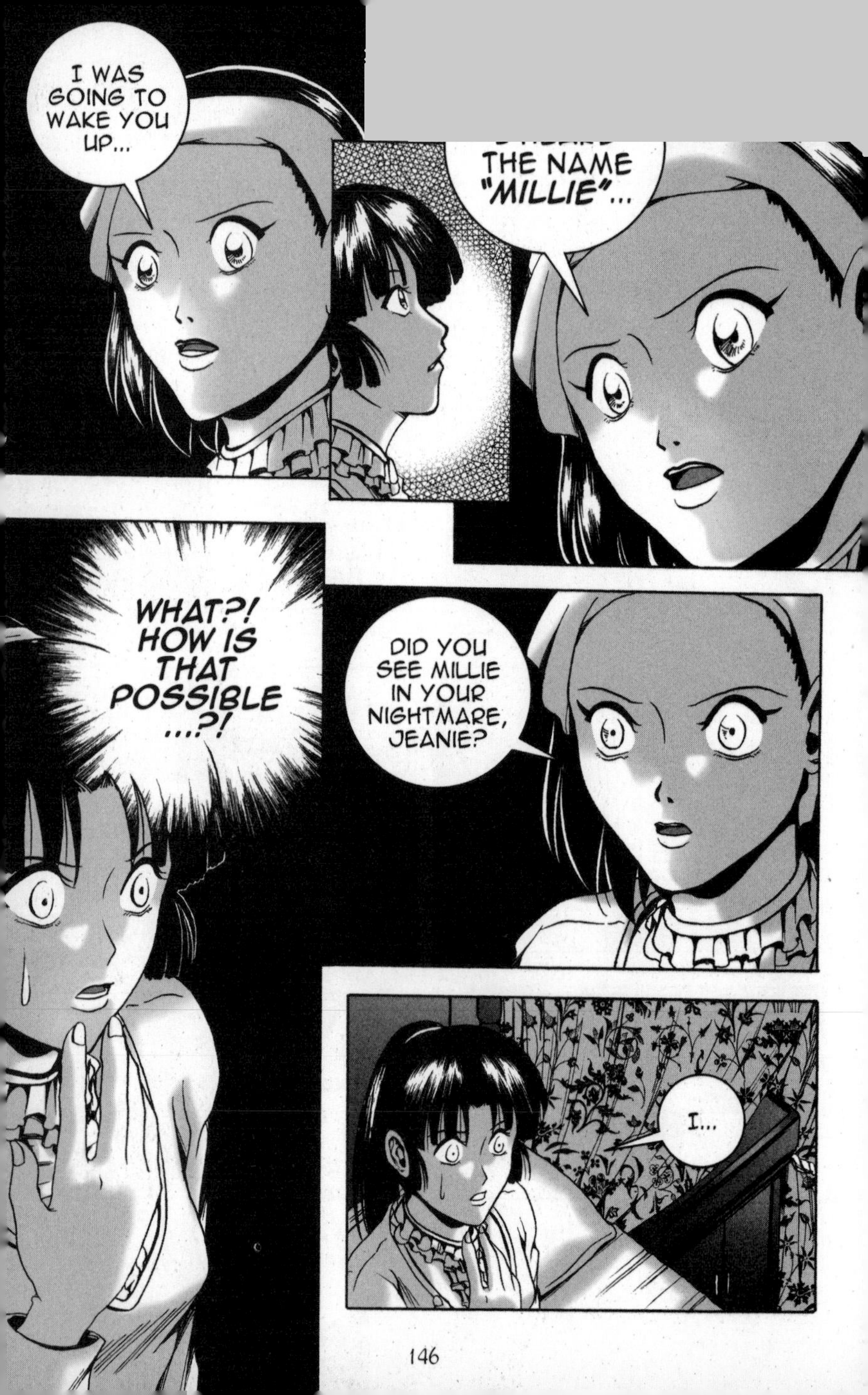
THE NAME "MILLIE"...
I WAS GOING TO WAKE YOU UP...
DID YOU SEE MILLIE IN YOUR NIGHTMARE, JEANIE?
I...
WHAT?! HOW IS THAT POSSIBLE ...?!

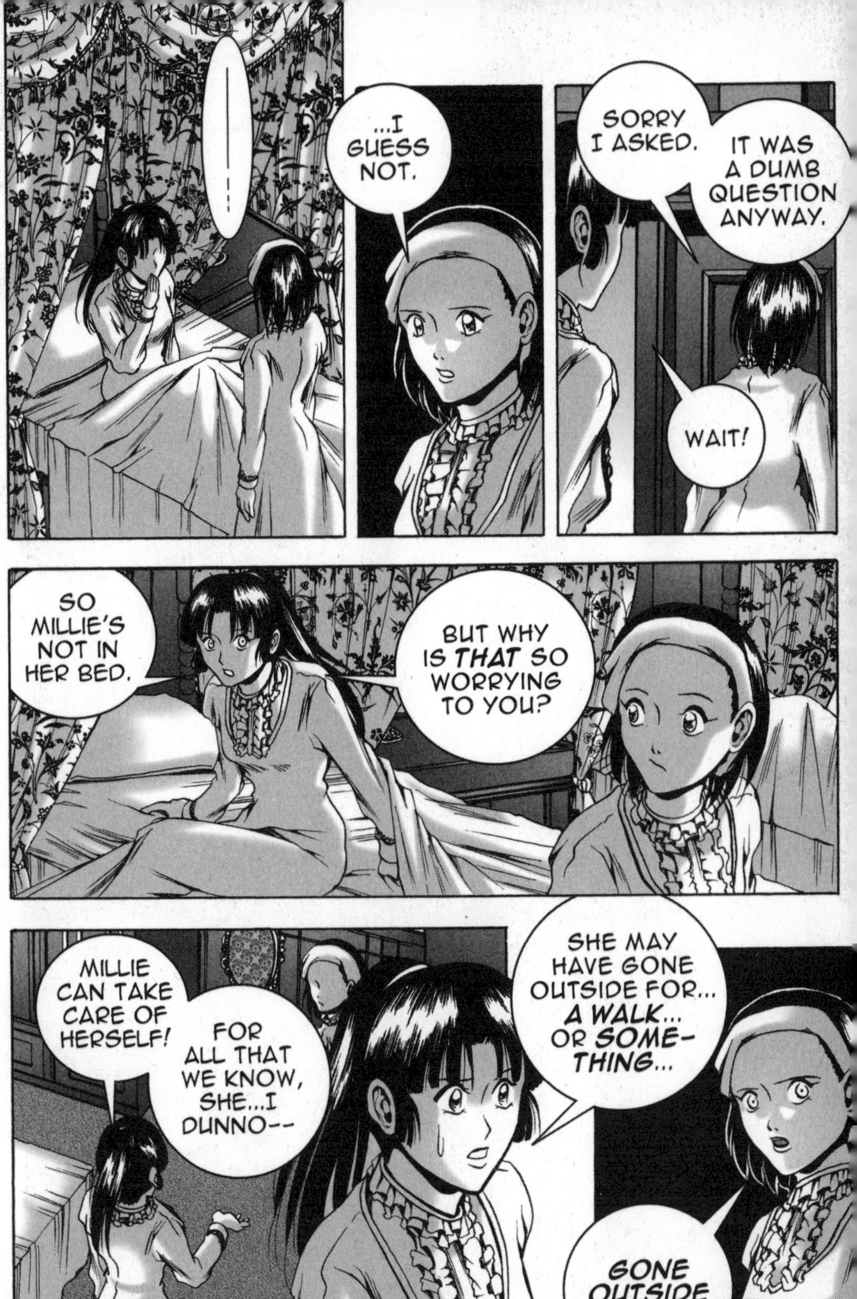
——!!
...I GUESS NOT.
SORRY I ASKED.
IT WAS A DUMB QUESTION ANYWAY.
WAIT!
SO MILLIE'S NOT IN HER BED.
BUT WHY IS *THAT* SO WORRYING TO YOU?
MILLIE CAN TAKE CARE OF HERSELF!
FOR ALL THAT WE KNOW, SHE...I DUNNO--
SHE MAY HAVE GONE OUTSIDE FOR... **A WALK**... OR **SOME-THING**...
GONE OUTSIDE ...?!

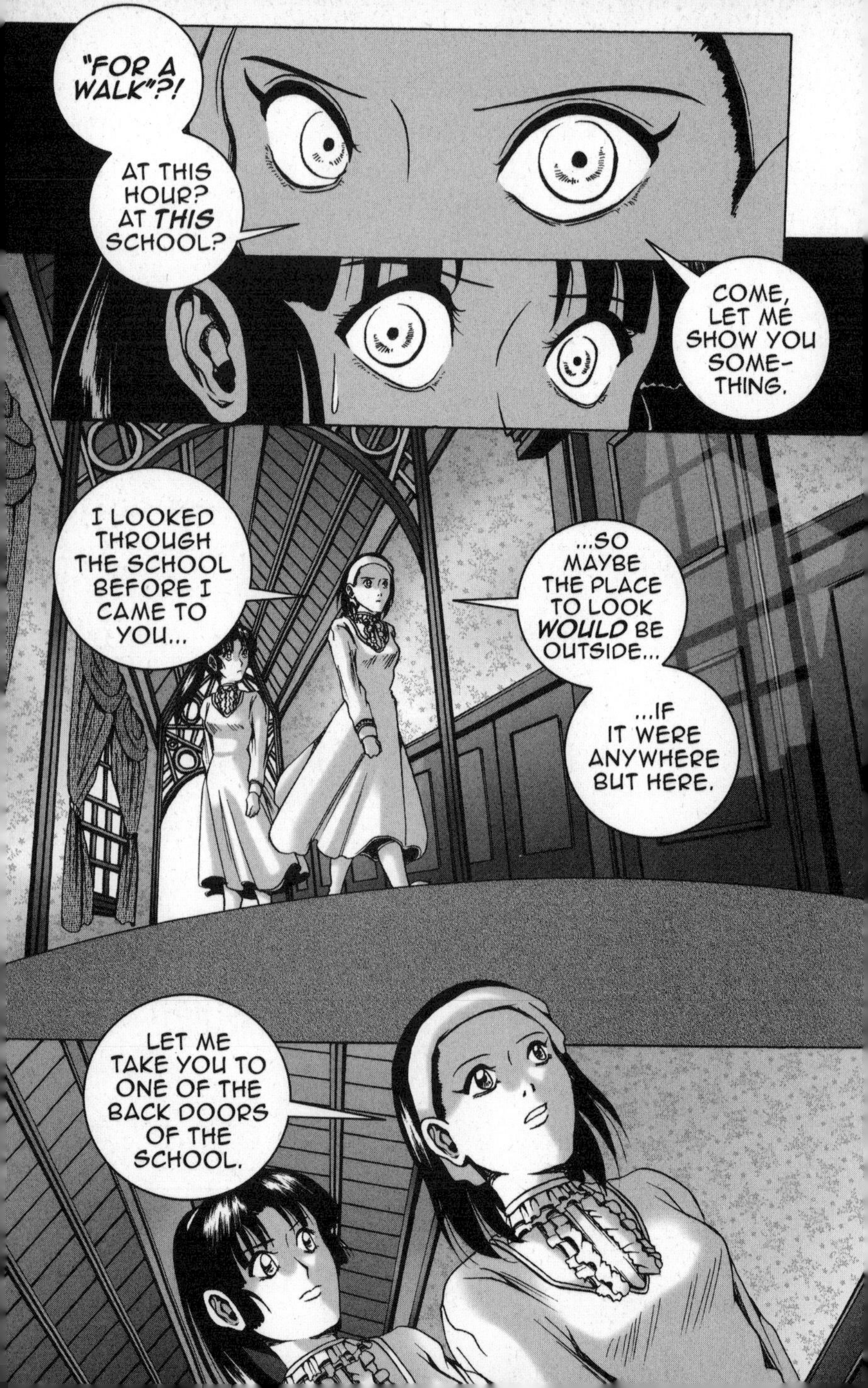
"FOR A WALK"?!
AT THIS HOUR? AT THIS SCHOOL?
COME, LET ME SHOW YOU SOME-THING.
I LOOKED THROUGH THE SCHOOL BEFORE I CAME TO YOU...
...SO MAYBE THE PLACE TO LOOK WOULD BE OUTSIDE...
...IF IT WERE ANYWHERE BUT HERE.
LET ME TAKE YOU TO ONE OF THE BACK DOORS OF THE SCHOOL.

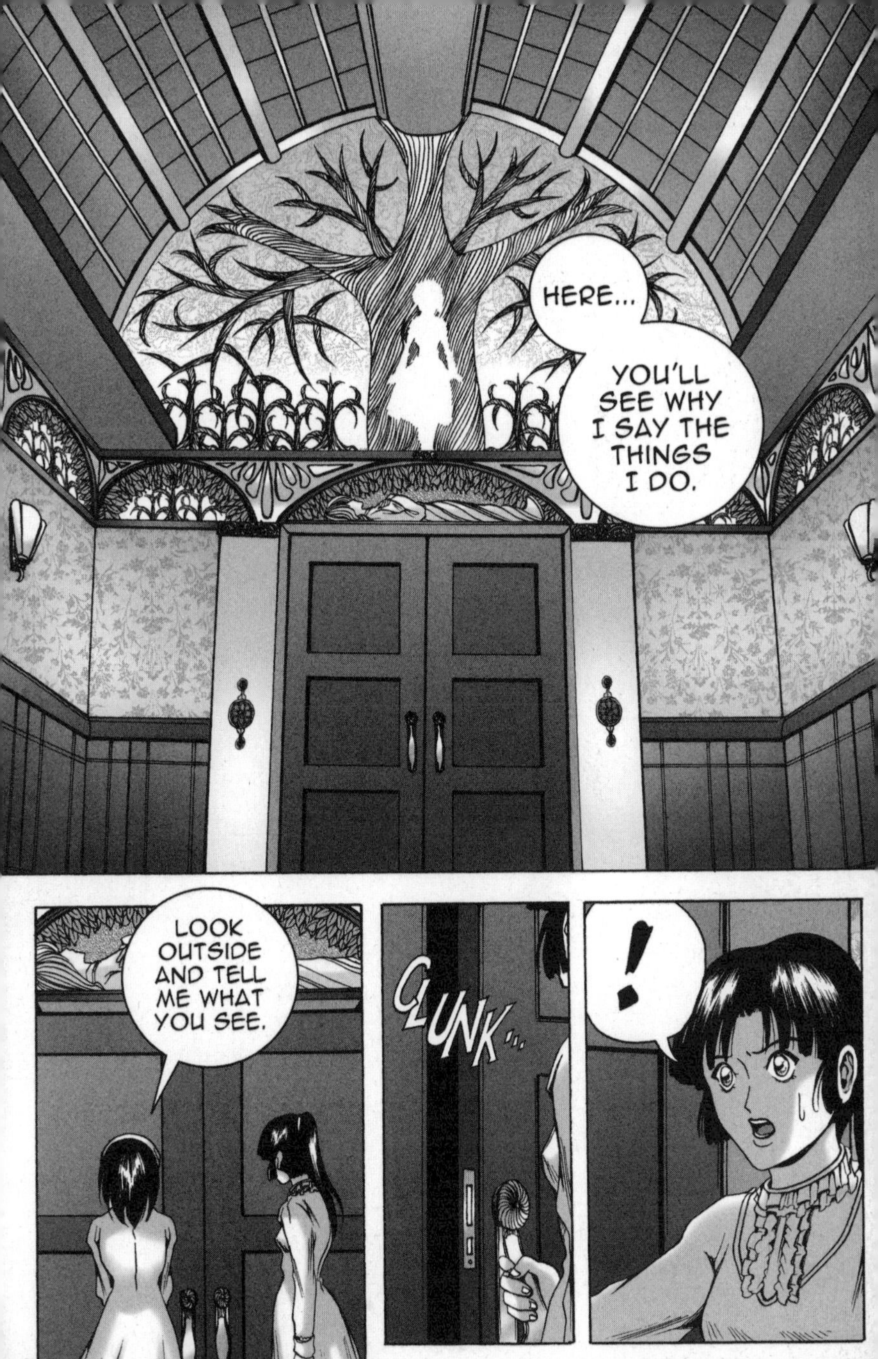
HERE...
YOU'LL SEE WHY I SAY THE THINGS I DO.
LOOK OUTSIDE AND TELL ME WHAT YOU SEE.
CLUNK...
!

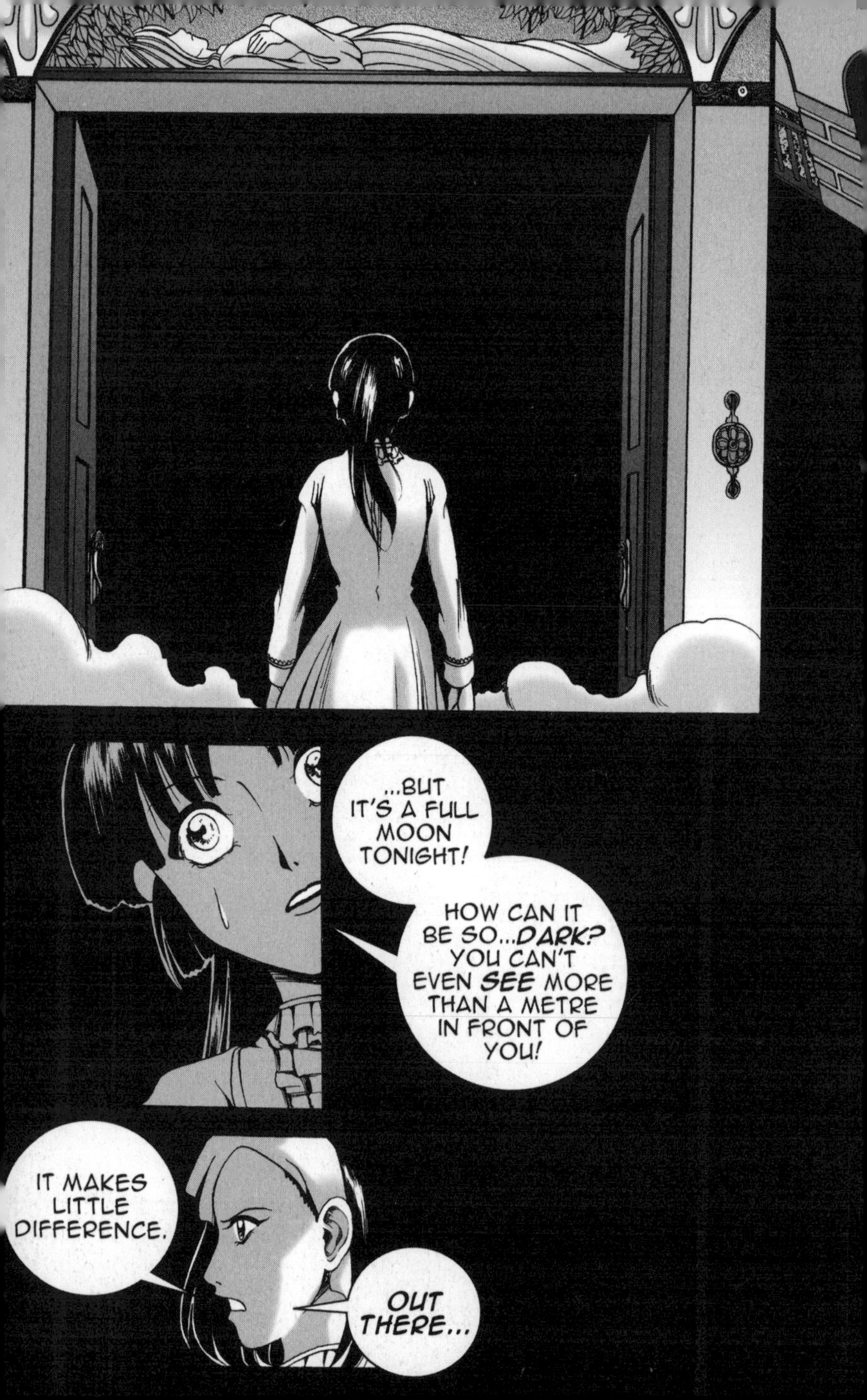
...BUT IT'S A FULL MOON TONIGHT!
HOW CAN IT BE SO...DARK? YOU CAN'T EVEN SEE MORE THAN A METRE IN FRONT OF YOU!
IT MAKES LITTLE DIFFERENCE.
OUT THERE...

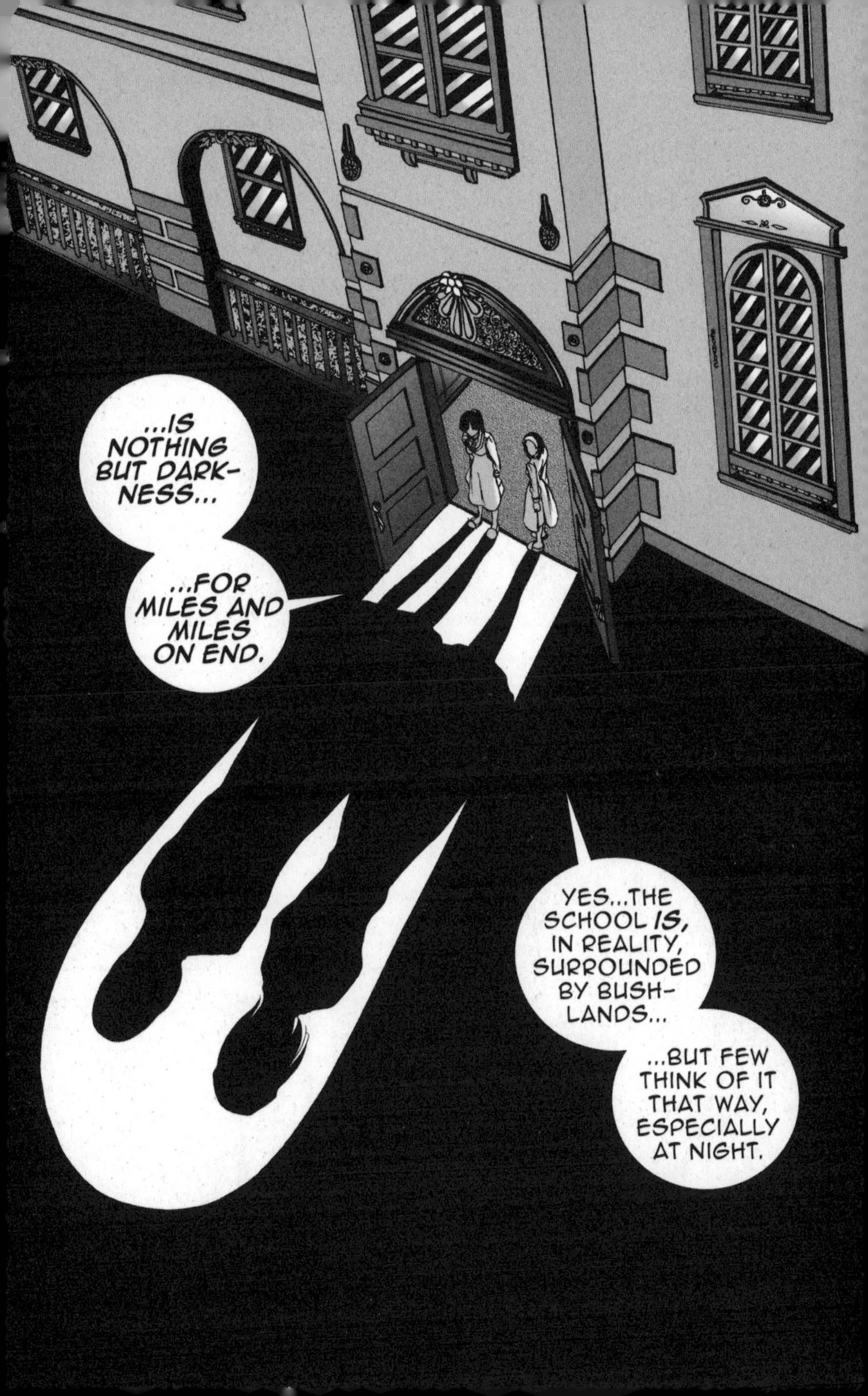
...IS NOTHING BUT DARK-NESS...
...FOR MILES AND MILES ON END.
YES...THE SCHOOL *IS*, IN REALITY, SURROUNDED BY BUSH-LANDS...
...BUT FEW THINK OF IT THAT WAY, ESPECIALLY AT NIGHT.

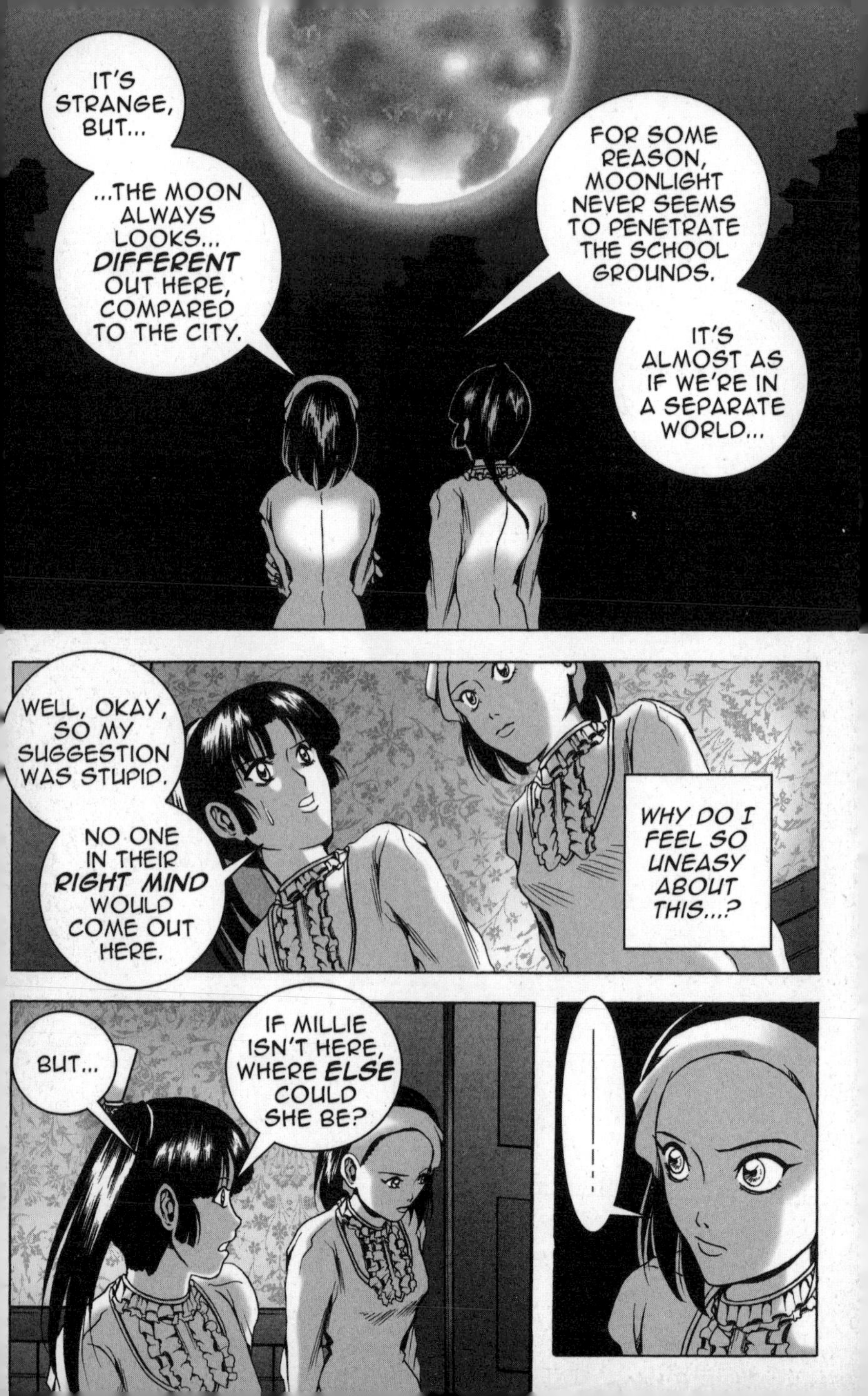
IT'S STRANGE, BUT...
...THE MOON ALWAYS LOOKS... *DIFFERENT* OUT HERE, COMPARED TO THE CITY.
FOR SOME REASON, MOONLIGHT NEVER SEEMS TO PENETRATE THE SCHOOL GROUNDS.
IT'S ALMOST AS IF WE'RE IN A SEPARATE WORLD...
WELL, OKAY, SO MY SUGGESTION WAS STUPID.
NO ONE IN THEIR *RIGHT MIND* WOULD COME OUT HERE.
WHY DO I FEEL SO UNEASY ABOUT THIS...?
BUT...
IF MILLIE ISN'T HERE, WHERE *ELSE* COULD SHE BE?
......

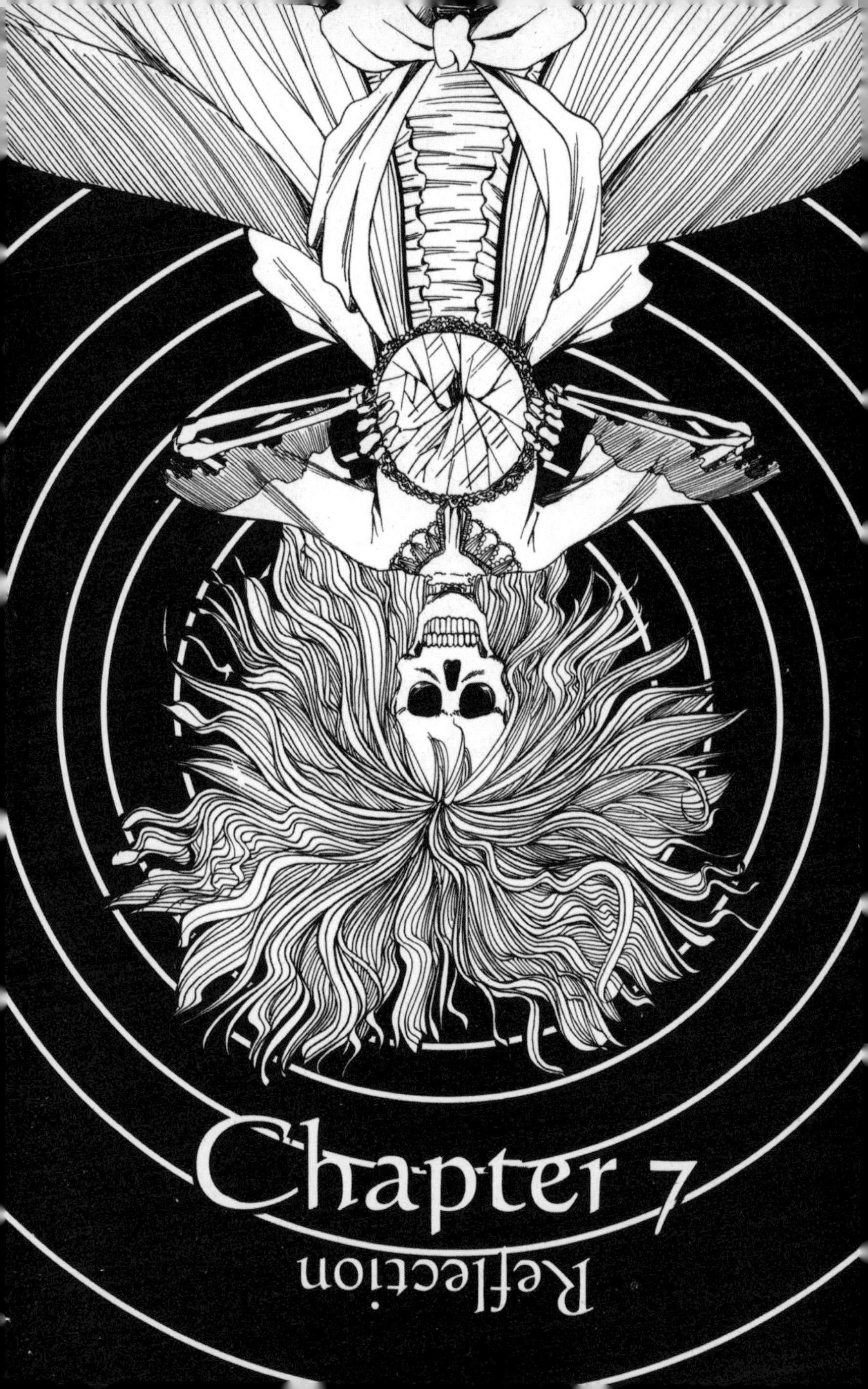

Chapter 7

Reflection

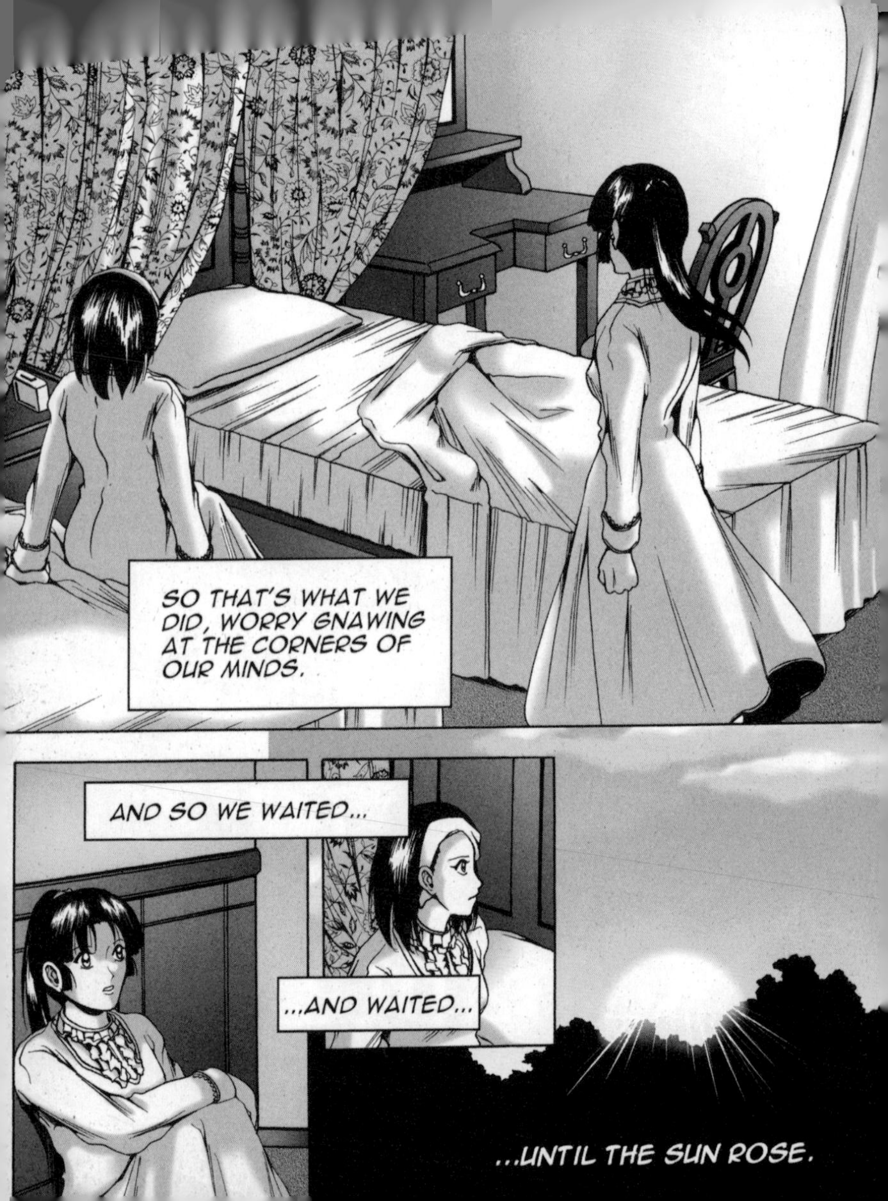
SO THAT'S WHAT WE DID, WORRY GNAWING AT THE CORNERS OF OUR MINDS.
AND SO WE WAITED...
...AND WAITED...
...UNTIL THE SUN ROSE.

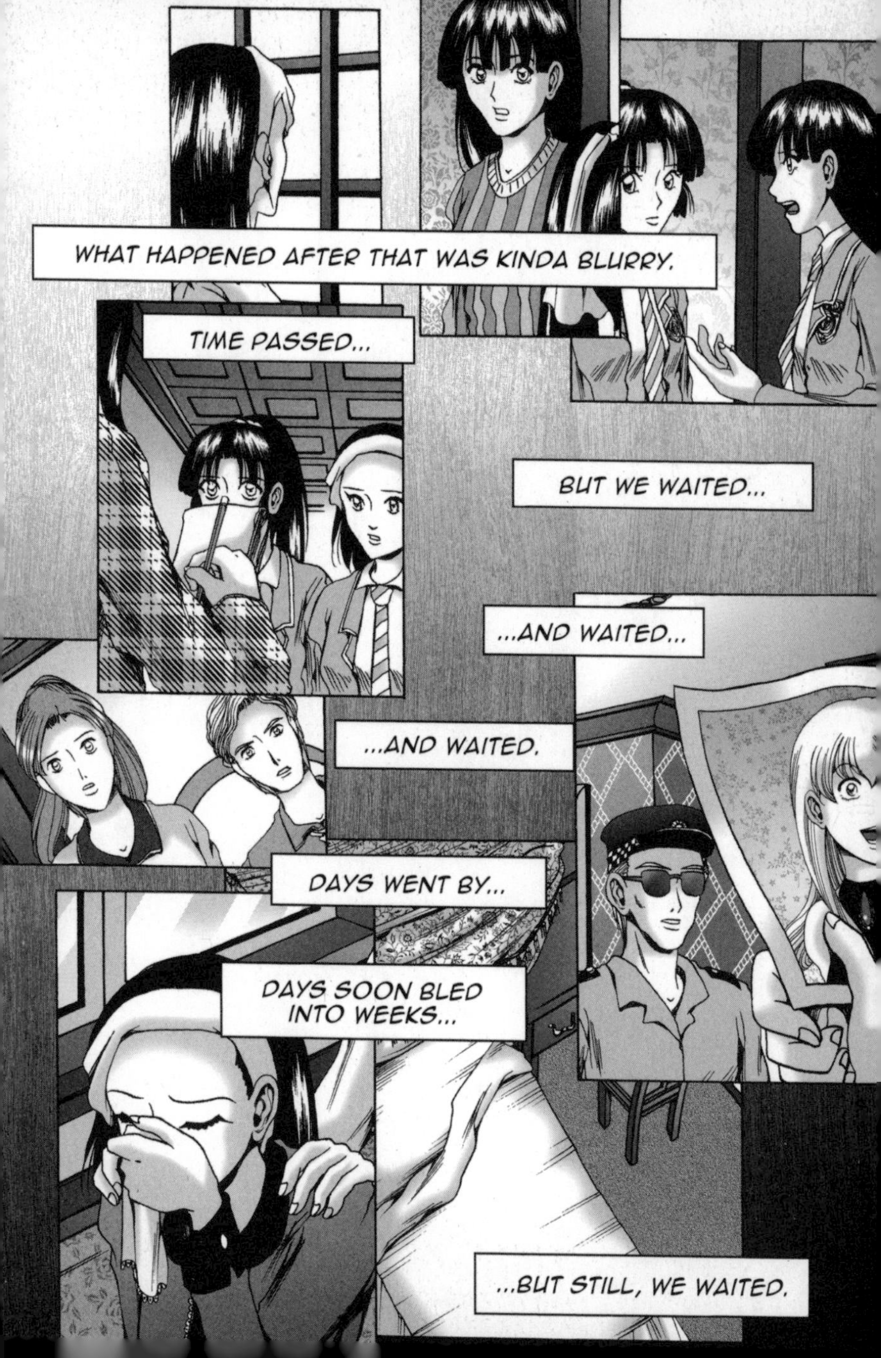
WHAT HAPPENED AFTER THAT WAS KINDA BLURRY.
TIME PASSED...
BUT WE WAITED...
...AND WAITED...
...AND WAITED.
DAYS WENT BY...
DAYS SOON BLED INTO WEEKS...
...BUT STILL, WE WAITED.

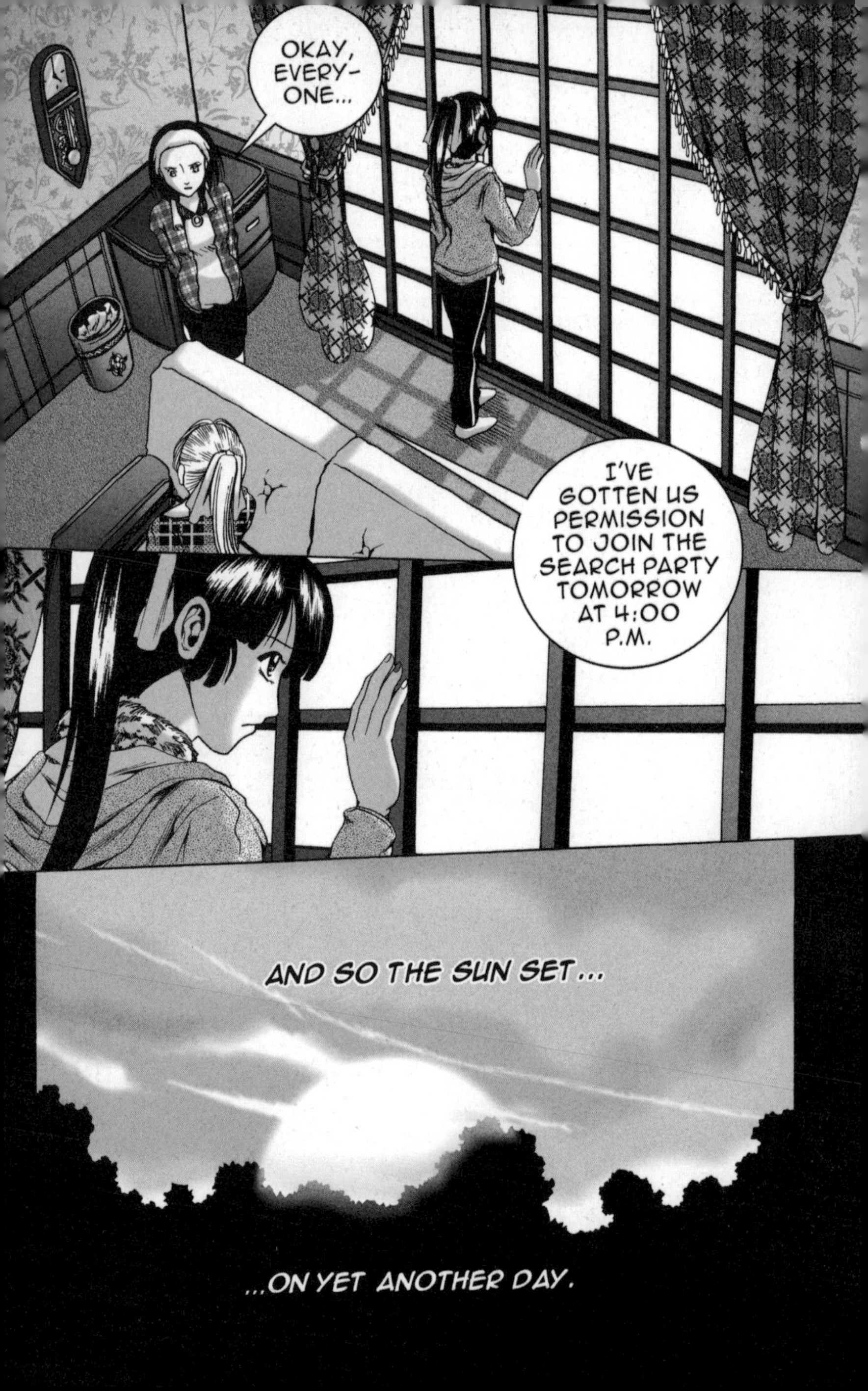
OKAY, EVERY-ONE...
I'VE GOTTEN US PERMISSION TO JOIN THE SEARCH PARTY TOMORROW AT 4:00 P.M.
AND SO THE SUN SET...
...ON YET ANOTHER DAY.

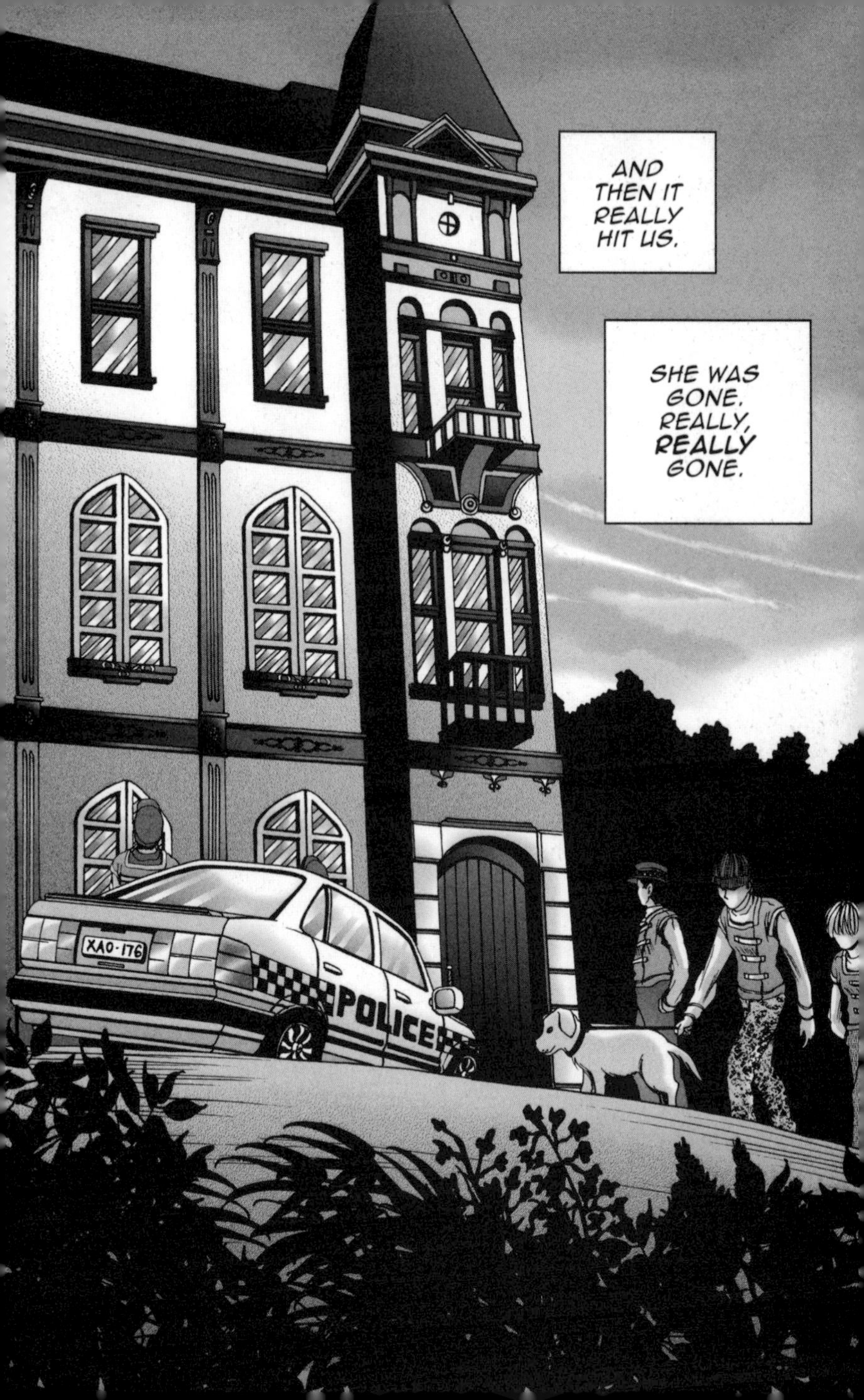
AND THEN IT REALLY HIT US.
SHE WAS GONE. REALLY, REALLY GONE.
XAO-176
POLICE

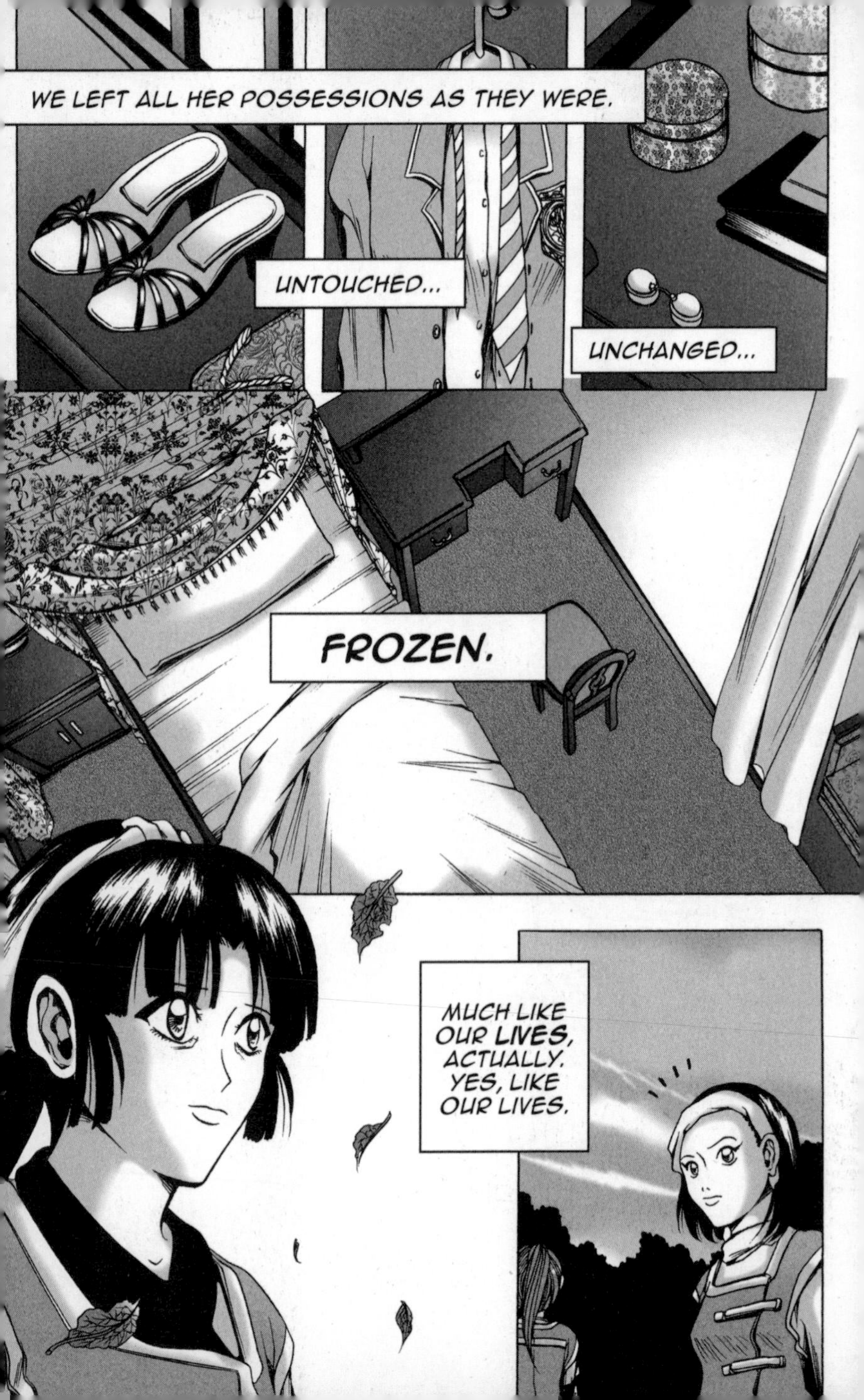
WE LEFT ALL HER POSSESSIONS AS THEY WERE.
UNTOUCHED...
UNCHANGED...
FROZEN.
MUCH LIKE OUR LIVES, ACTUALLY. YES, LIKE OUR LIVES.

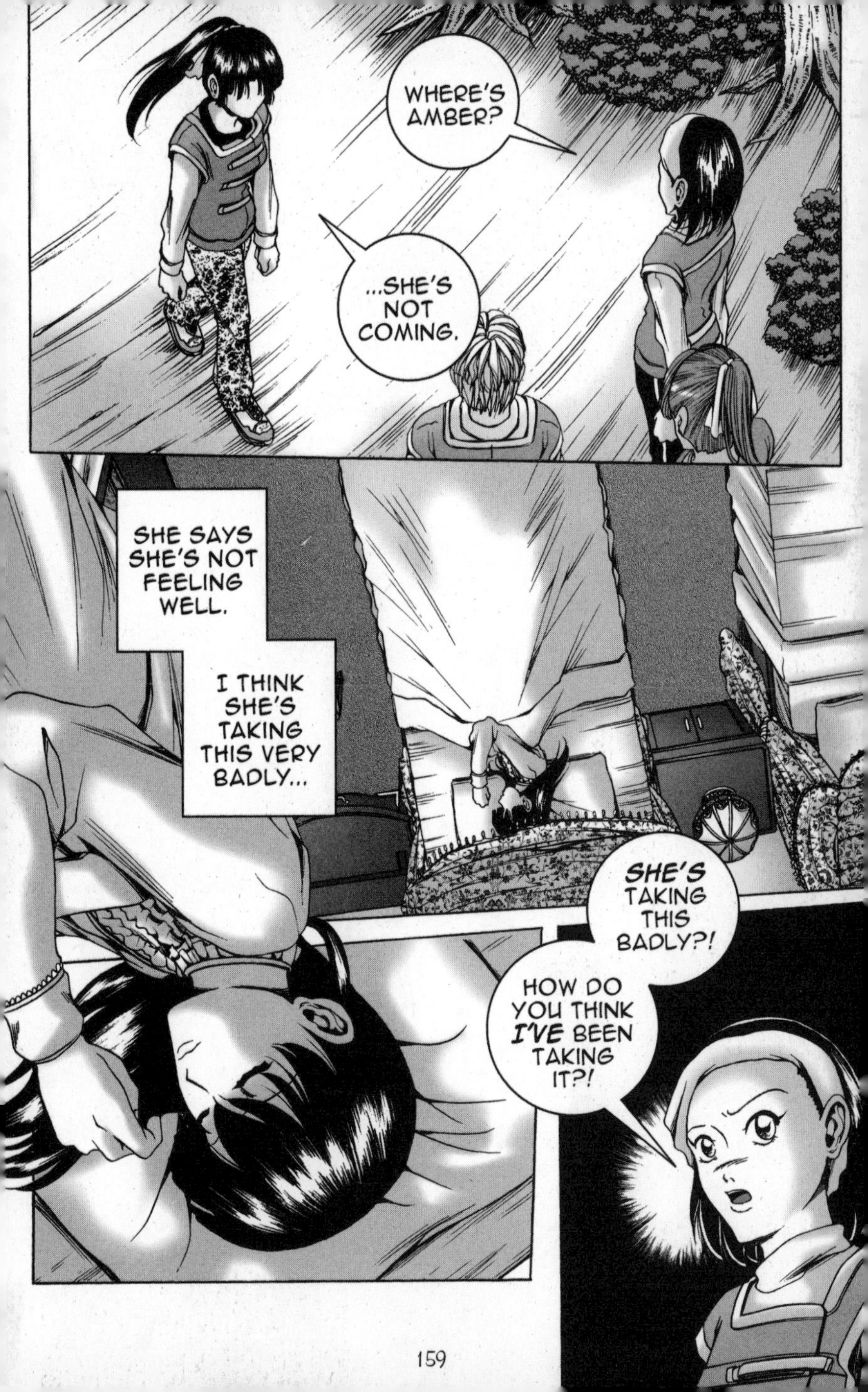
WHERE'S AMBER?
...SHE'S NOT COMING.
SHE SAYS SHE'S NOT FEELING WELL.
I THINK SHE'S TAKING THIS VERY BADLY...
SHE'S TAKING THIS BADLY?!
HOW DO YOU THINK I'VE BEEN TAKING IT?!

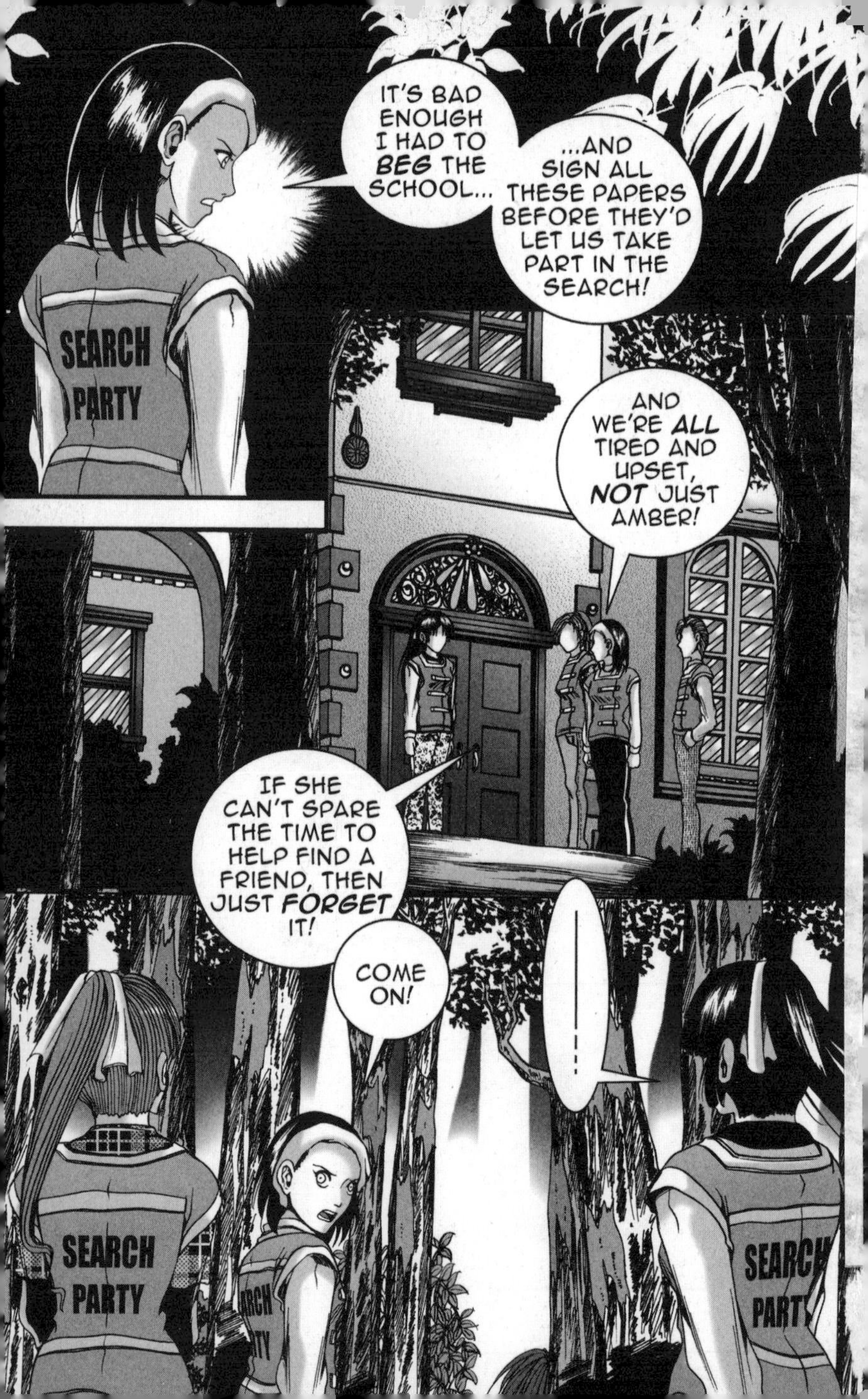
IT'S BAD ENOUGH I HAD TO BEG THE SCHOOL...
...AND SIGN ALL THESE PAPERS BEFORE THEY'D LET US TAKE PART IN THE SEARCH!
SEARCH PARTY
AND WE'RE ALL TIRED AND UPSET, NOT JUST AMBER!
IF SHE CAN'T SPARE THE TIME TO HELP FIND A FRIEND, THEN JUST FORGET IT!
COME ON!
...
SEARCH PARTY
SEARCH PARTY

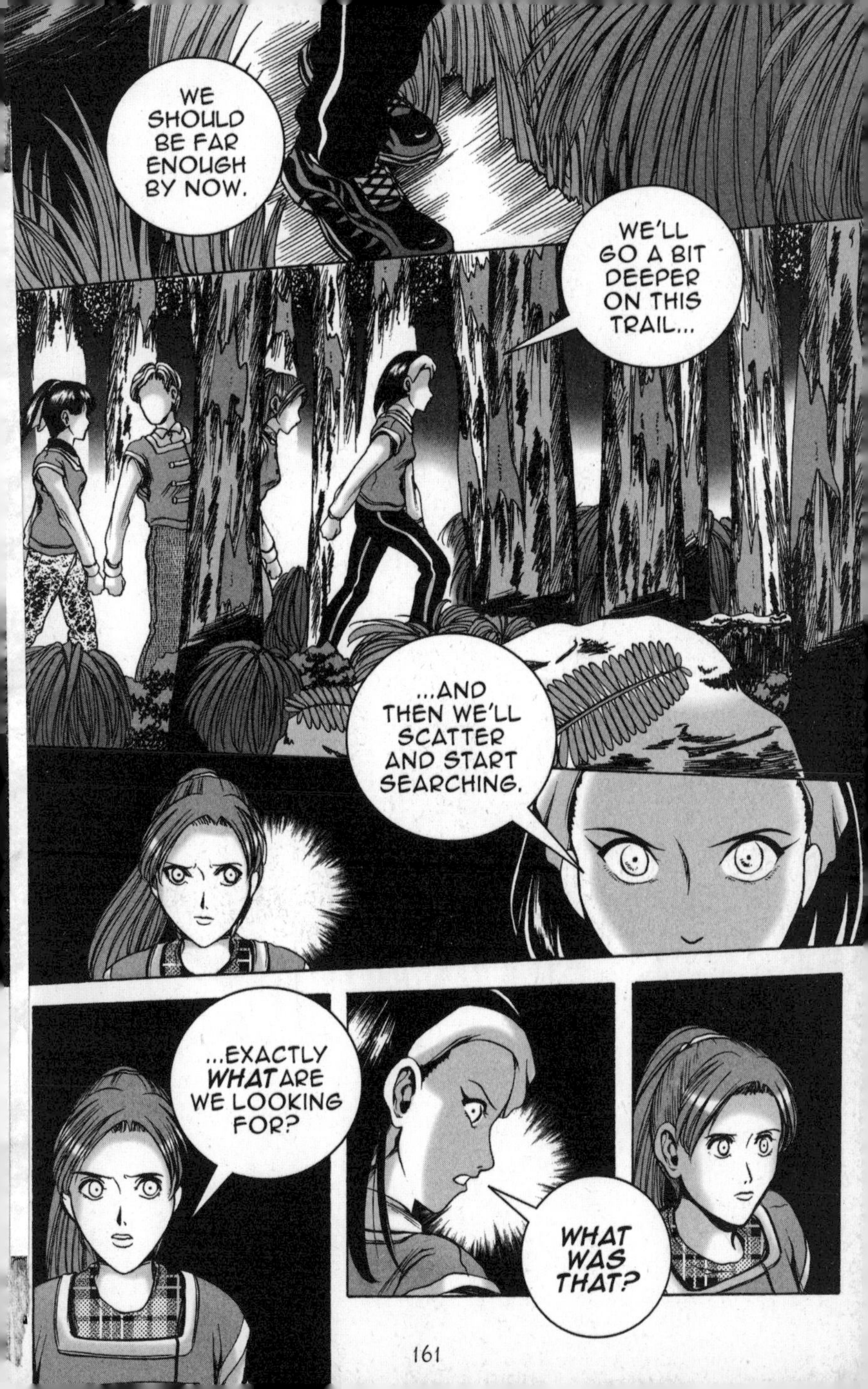
WE SHOULD BE FAR ENOUGH BY NOW.
WE'LL GO A BIT DEEPER ON THIS TRAIL...
...AND THEN WE'LL SCATTER AND START SEARCHING.
...EXACTLY *WHAT* ARE WE LOOKING FOR?
WHAT WAS THAT?

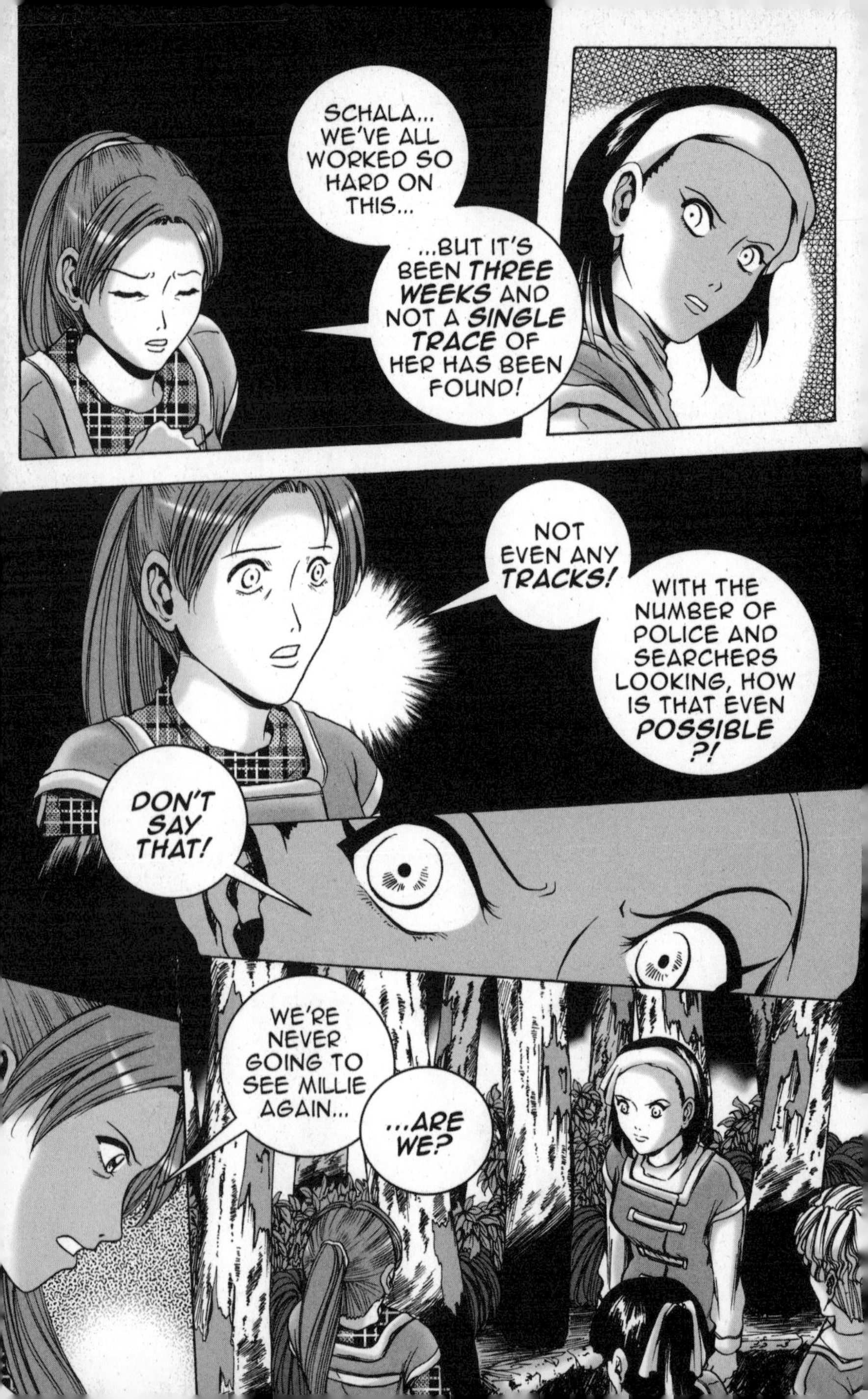
SCHALA... WE'VE ALL WORKED SO HARD ON THIS...
...BUT IT'S BEEN *THREE WEEKS* AND NOT A *SINGLE TRACE* OF HER HAS BEEN FOUND!
NOT EVEN ANY *TRACKS!*
WITH THE NUMBER OF POLICE AND SEARCHERS LOOKING, HOW IS THAT EVEN *POSSIBLE* ?!
DON'T SAY THAT!
WE'RE NEVER GOING TO SEE MILLIE AGAIN...
...ARE WE?

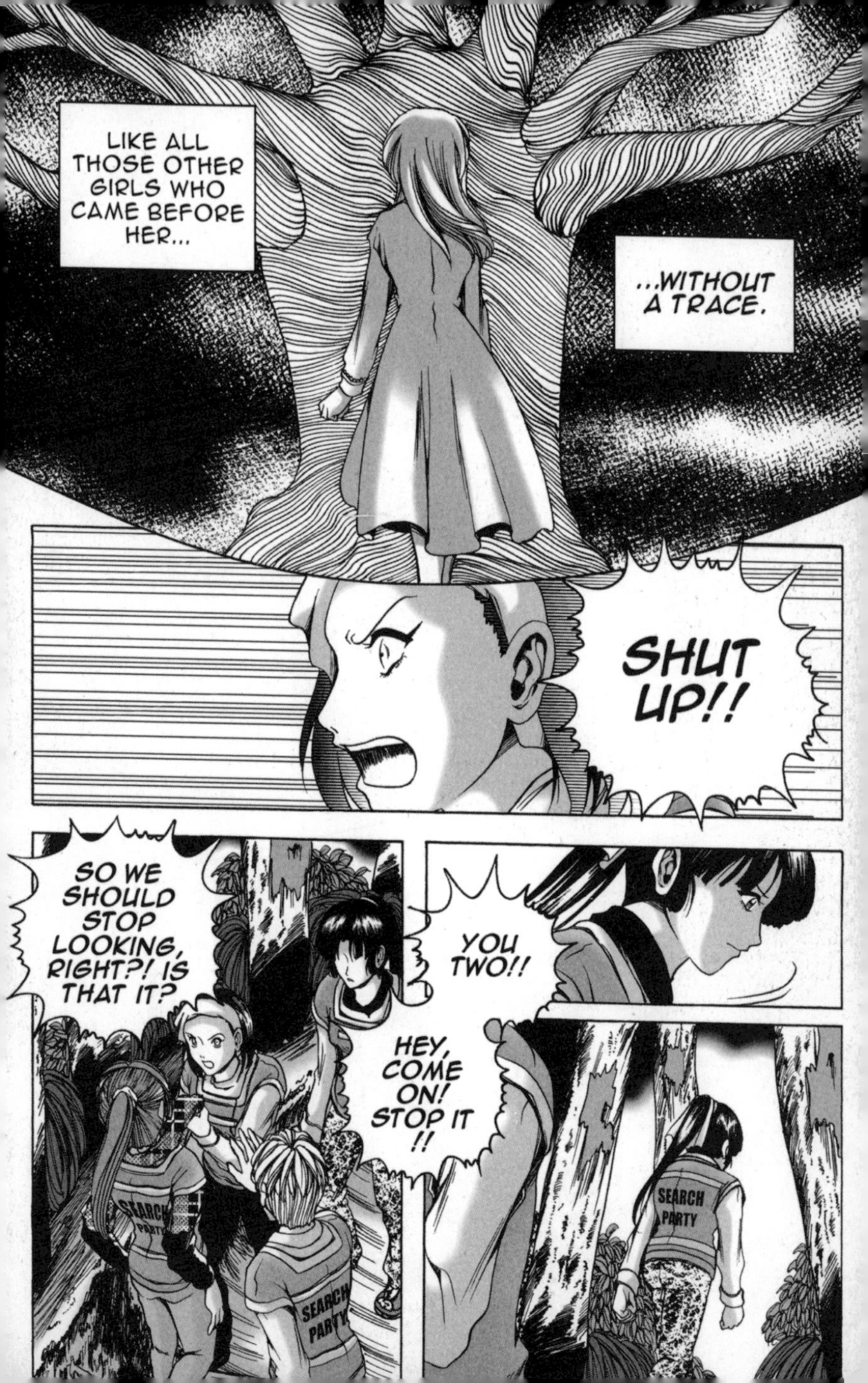
LIKE ALL THOSE OTHER GIRLS WHO CAME BEFORE HER...
...WITHOUT A TRACE.
SHUT UP!!
SO WE SHOULD STOP LOOKING, RIGHT?! IS THAT IT?
SEARCH PARTY
SEARCH PARTY
HEY, COME ON! STOP IT !!
YOU TWO!!
SEARCH PARTY

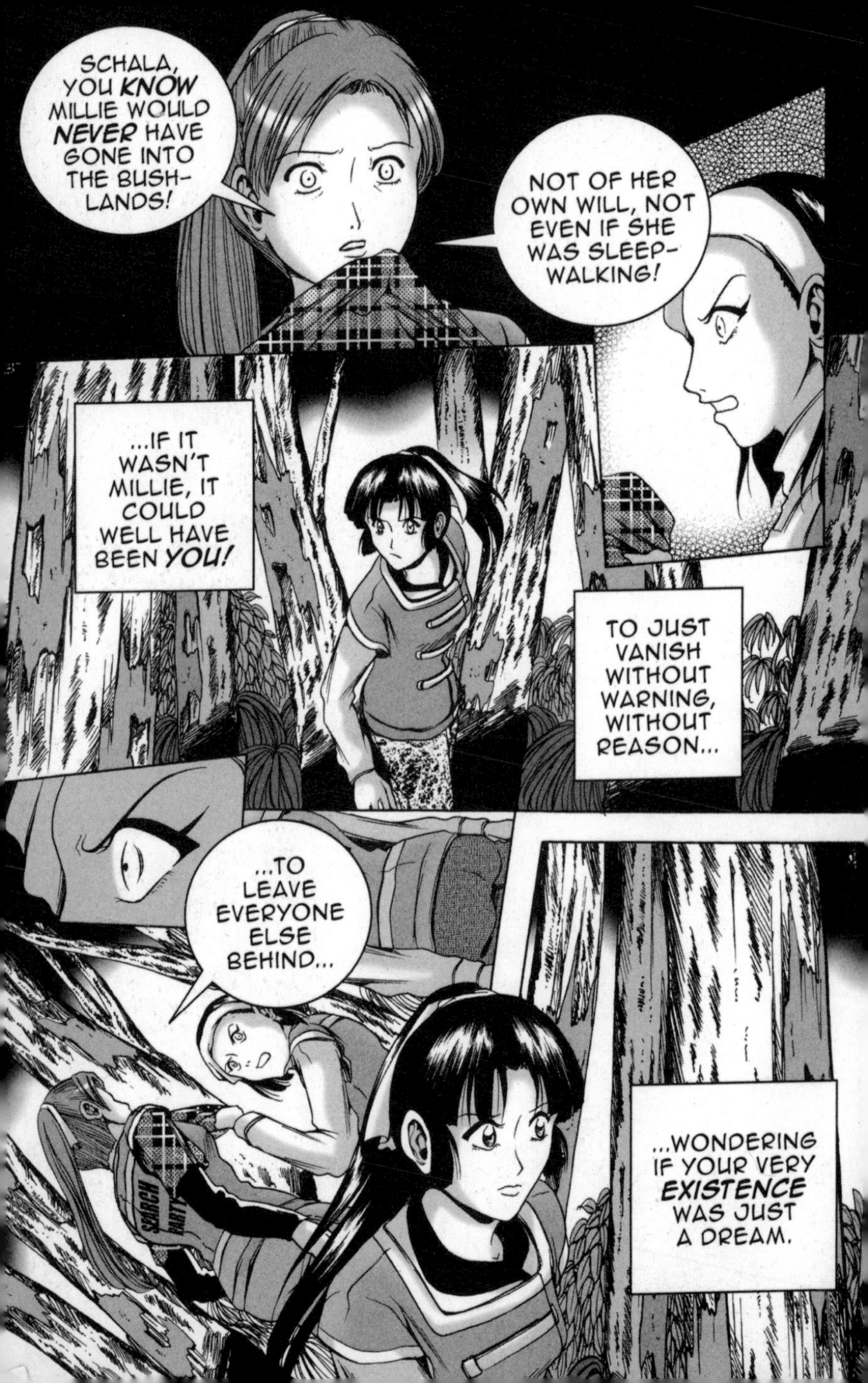
SCHALA, YOU *KNOW* MILLIE WOULD *NEVER* HAVE GONE INTO THE BUSH-LANDS!
NOT OF HER OWN WILL, NOT EVEN IF SHE WAS SLEEP-WALKING!
...IF IT WASN'T MILLIE, IT COULD WELL HAVE BEEN *YOU!*
TO JUST VANISH WITHOUT WARNING, WITHOUT REASON...
...TO LEAVE EVERYONE ELSE BEHIND...
SEARCH PARTY
...WONDERING IF YOUR VERY *EXISTENCE* WAS JUST A DREAM.

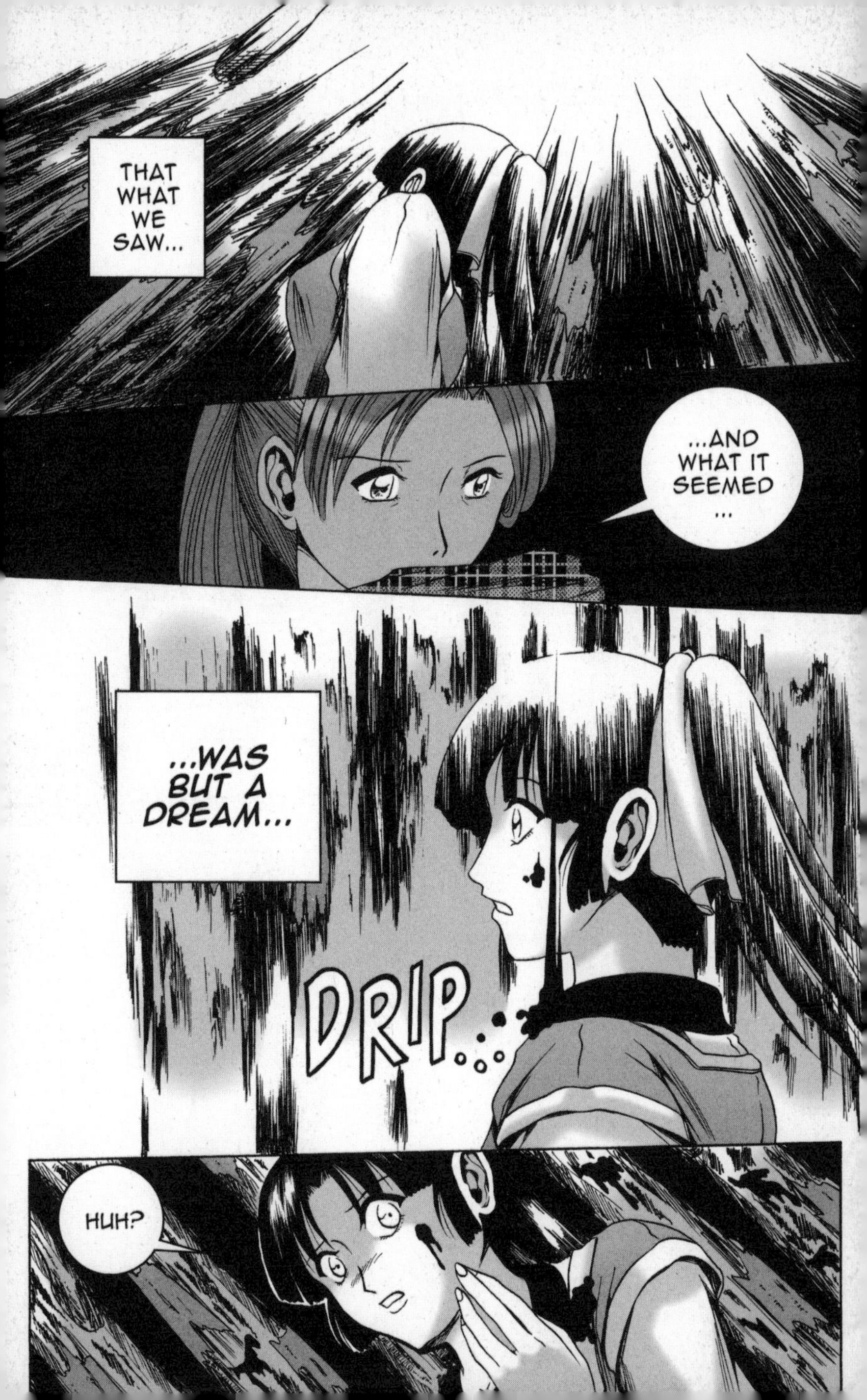
THAT WHAT WE SAW...
...AND WHAT IT SEEMED ...
...WAS BUT A DREAM...
DRIP...
HUH?

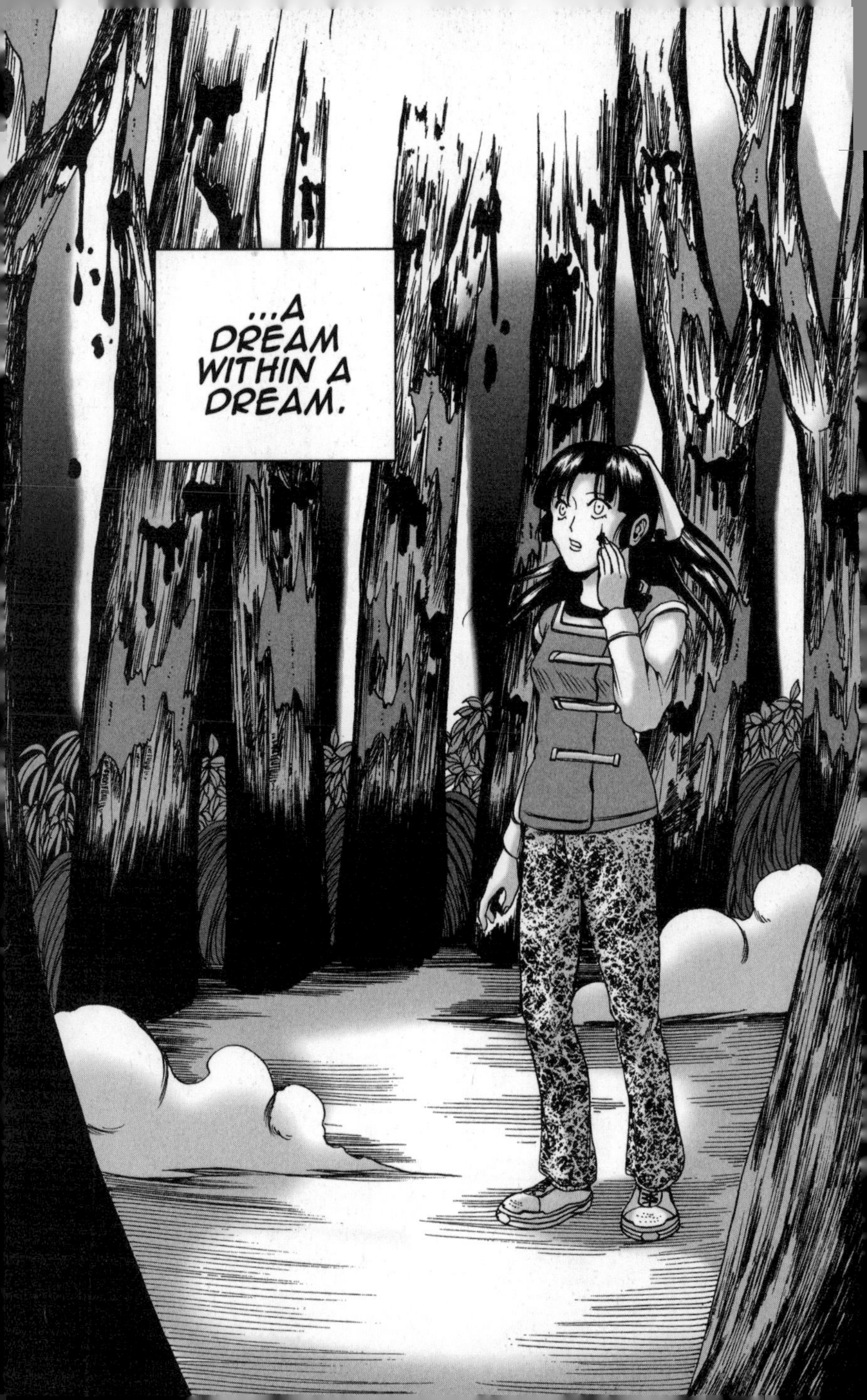
...A DREAM WITHIN A DREAM.

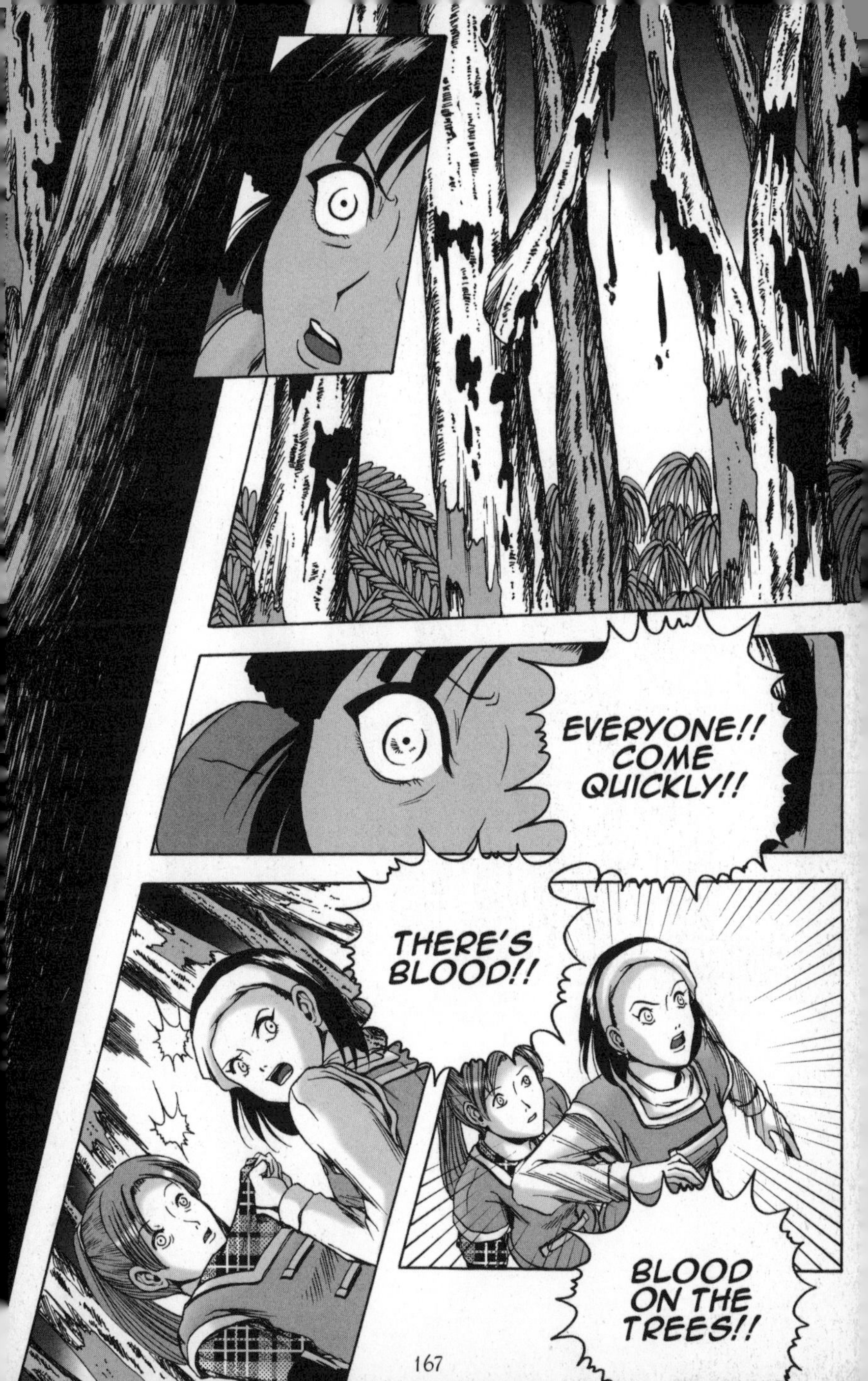
EVERYONE!! COME QUICKLY!!
BLOOD ON THE TREES!!
THERE'S BLOOD!!

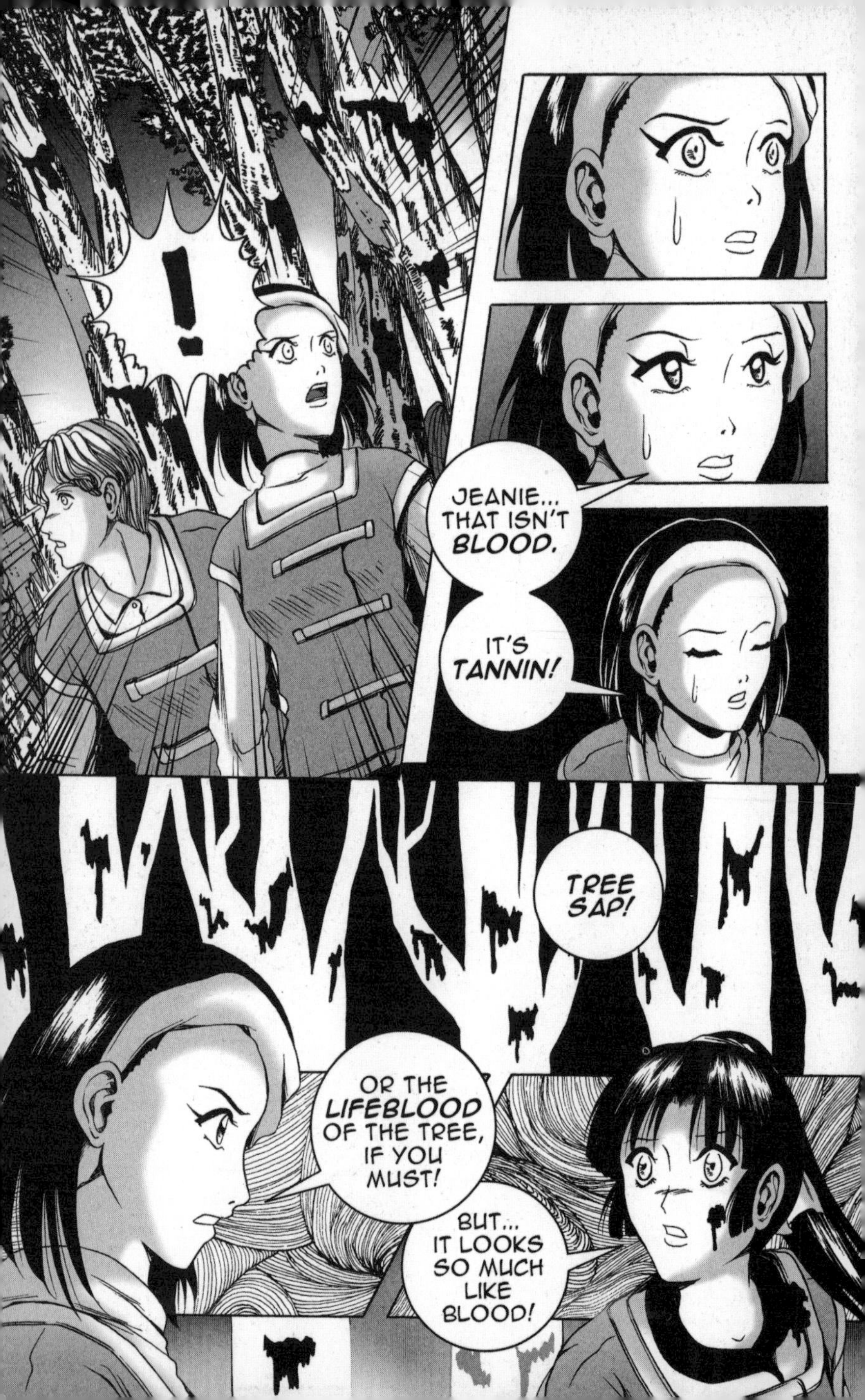
JEANIE... THAT ISN'T BLOOD.
IT'S TANNIN!
!
TREE SAP!
OR THE LIFEBLOOD OF THE TREE, IF YOU MUST!
BUT... IT LOOKS SO MUCH LIKE BLOOD!

AND IT LOOKS SO MUCH LIKE MY DREAM, TOO...
YEAH.
THAT'S WHY THEY CALL THIS TYPE OF EUCALYPTUS "WEEPING TREES."
PEOPLE SAY THEY'RE ACTUALLY THE LOST SOULS OF THOSE WHO VANISHED IN THE BUSH--TURNED INTO TREES.
OTHERS, THOUGH, SAY THAT THE TREES TEND TO GROW WHERE PEOPLE HAVE DIED... PERHAPS BY MURDER.

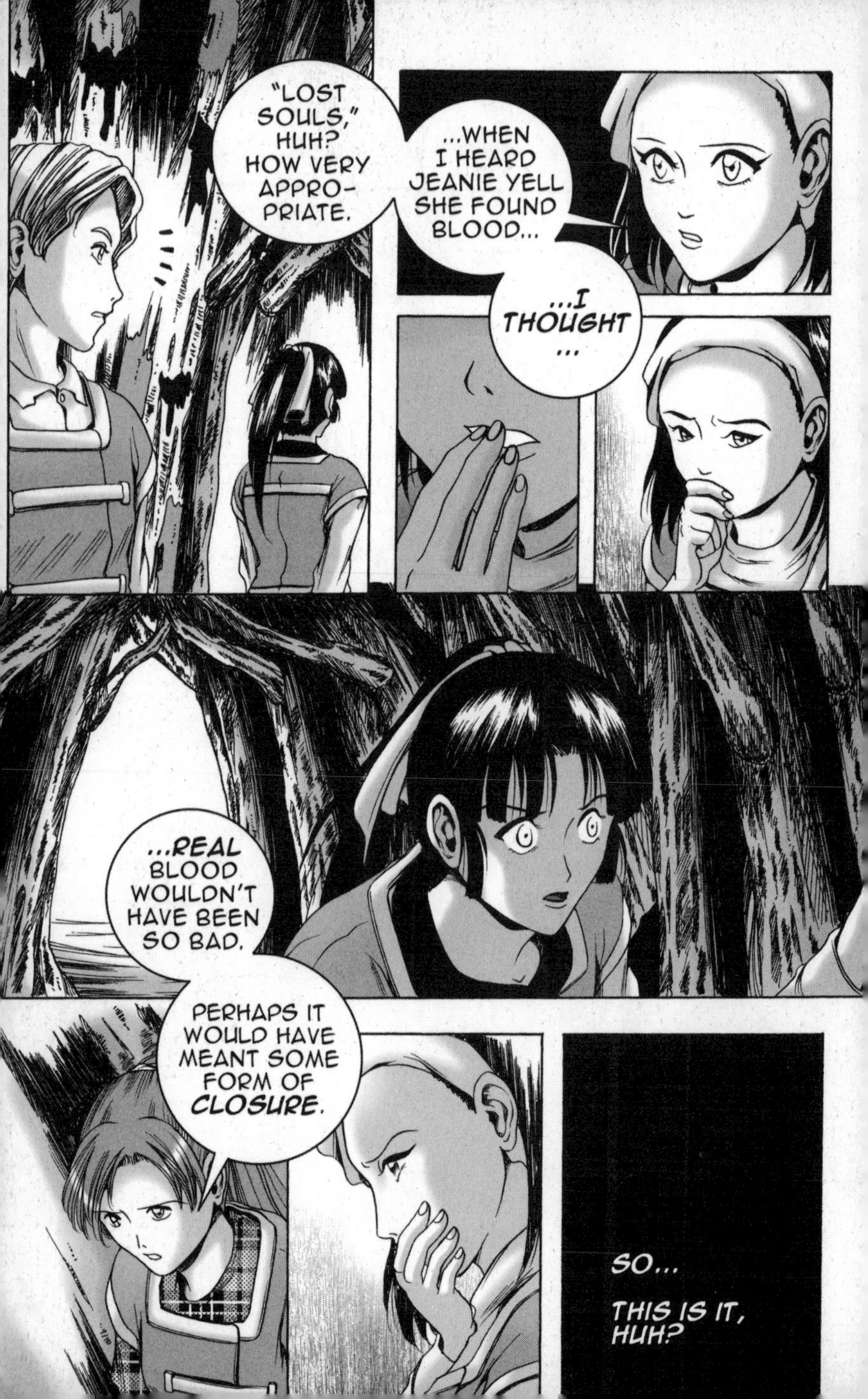
"LOST SOULS," HUH? HOW VERY APPROPRIATE.
...
...WHEN I HEARD JEANIE YELL SHE FOUND BLOOD...
...I THOUGHT...
...REAL BLOOD WOULDN'T HAVE BEEN SO BAD.
PERHAPS IT WOULD HAVE MEANT SOME FORM OF CLOSURE.
SO...
THIS IS IT, HUH?

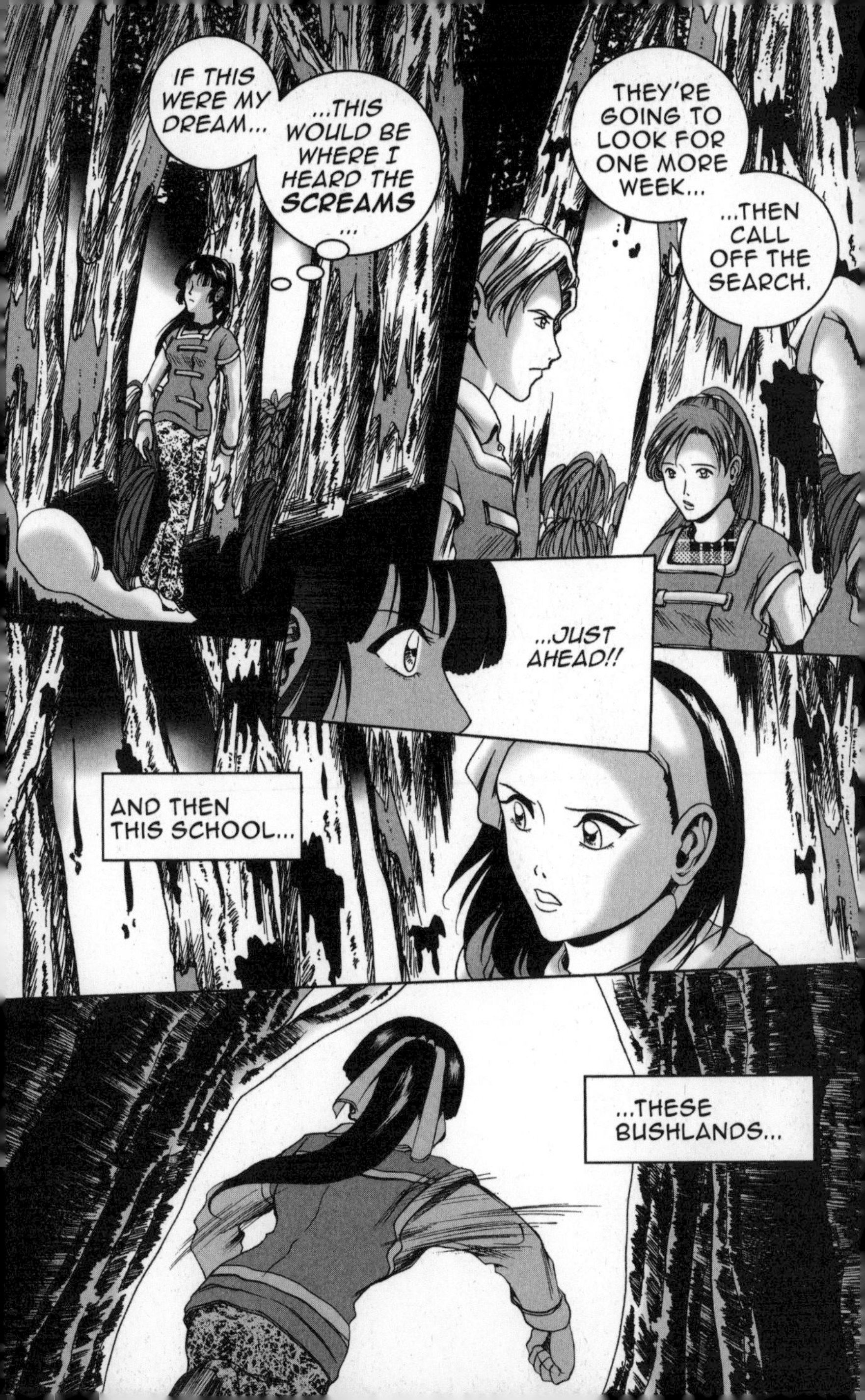
THEY'RE GOING TO LOOK FOR ONE MORE WEEK...
...THEN CALL OFF THE SEARCH.
IF THIS WERE MY DREAM...
...THIS WOULD BE WHERE I HEARD THE SCREAMS ...
...JUST AHEAD!!
AND THEN THIS SCHOOL...
...THESE BUSHLANDS...

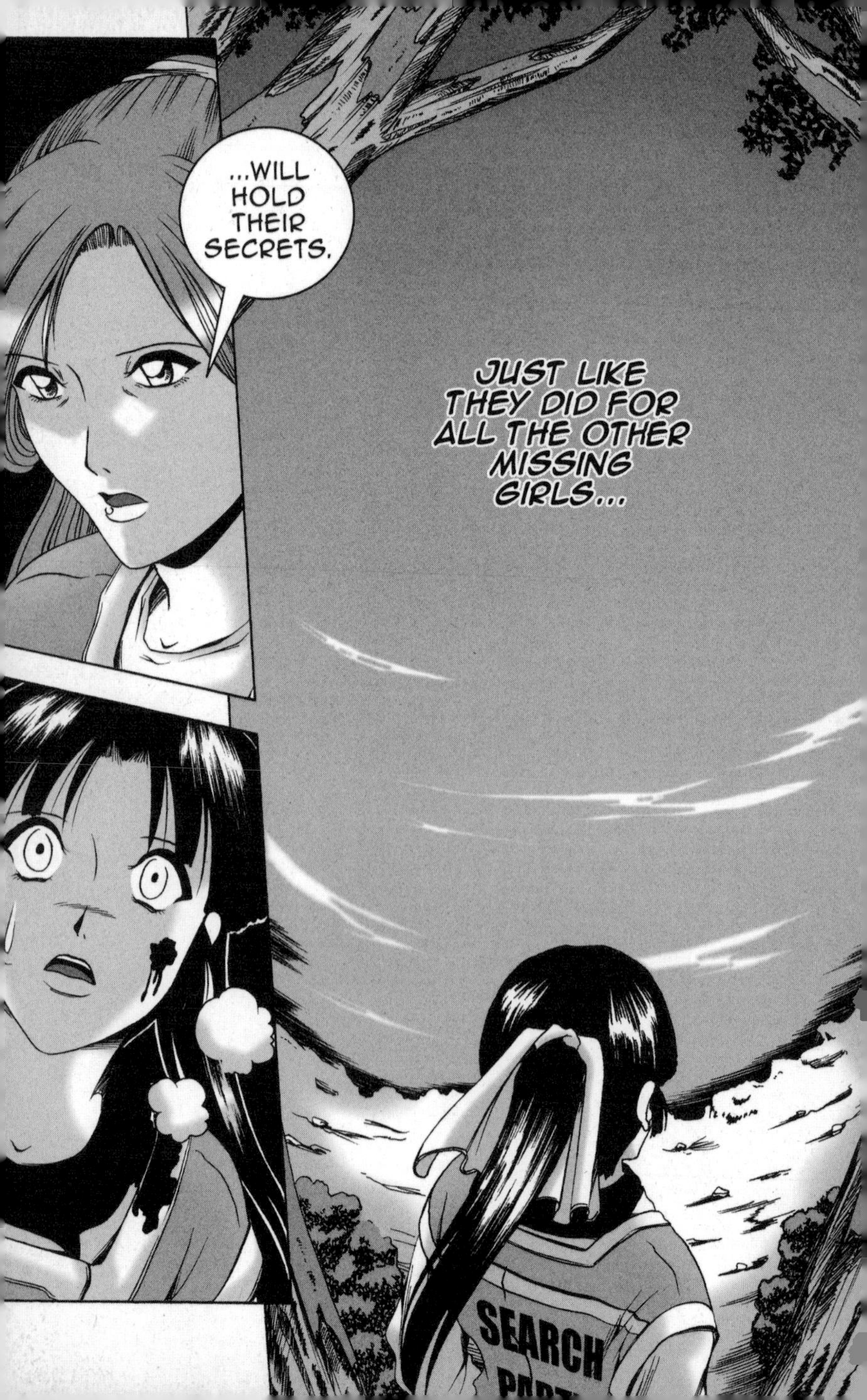
...WILL HOLD THEIR SECRETS.
JUST LIKE THEY DID FOR ALL THE OTHER MISSING GIRLS...
SEARCH

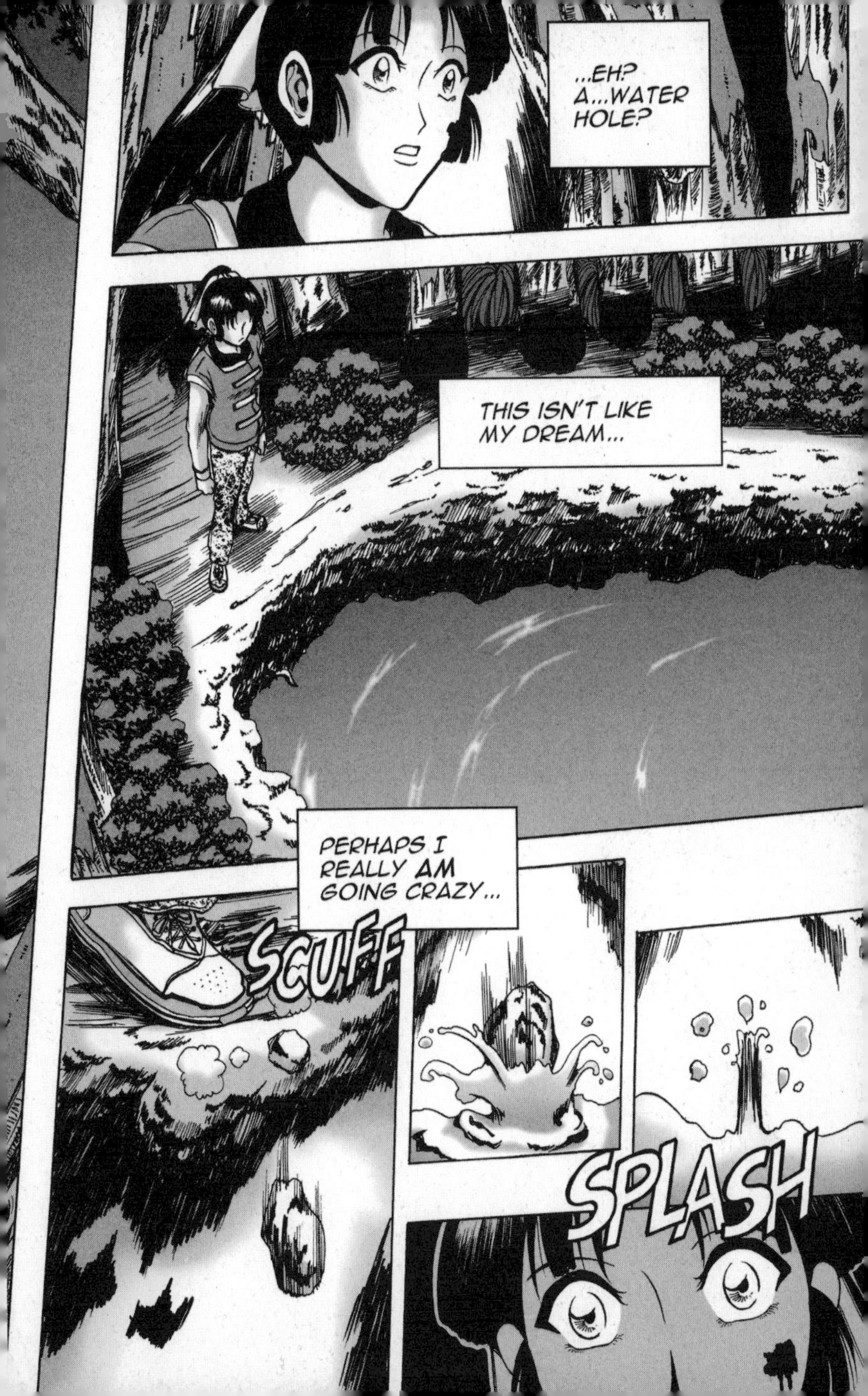
...EH?
A...WATER
HOLE?
THIS ISN'T LIKE
MY DREAM...
PERHAPS I
REALLY AM
GOING CRAZY...
SCUFF
SPLASH

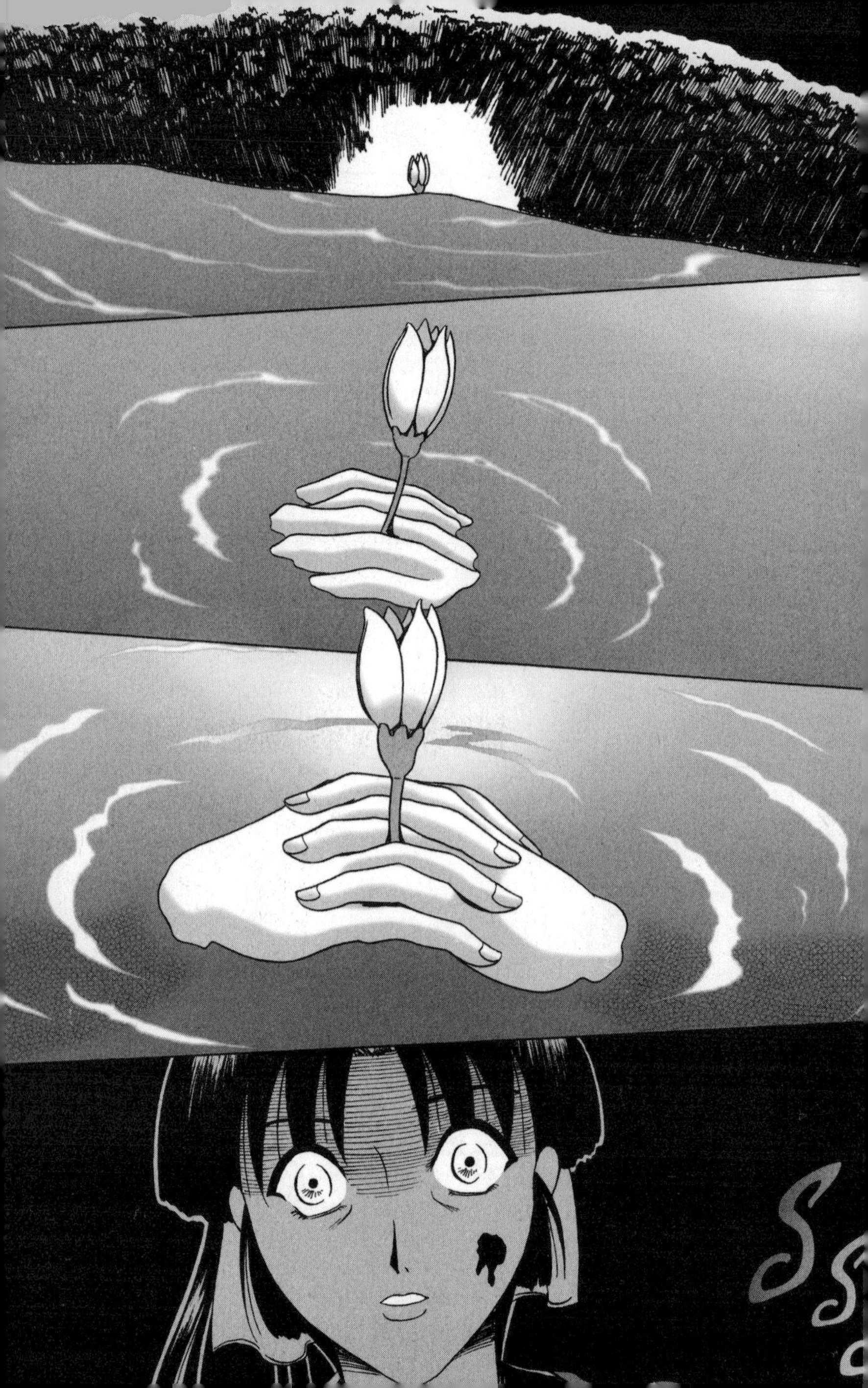

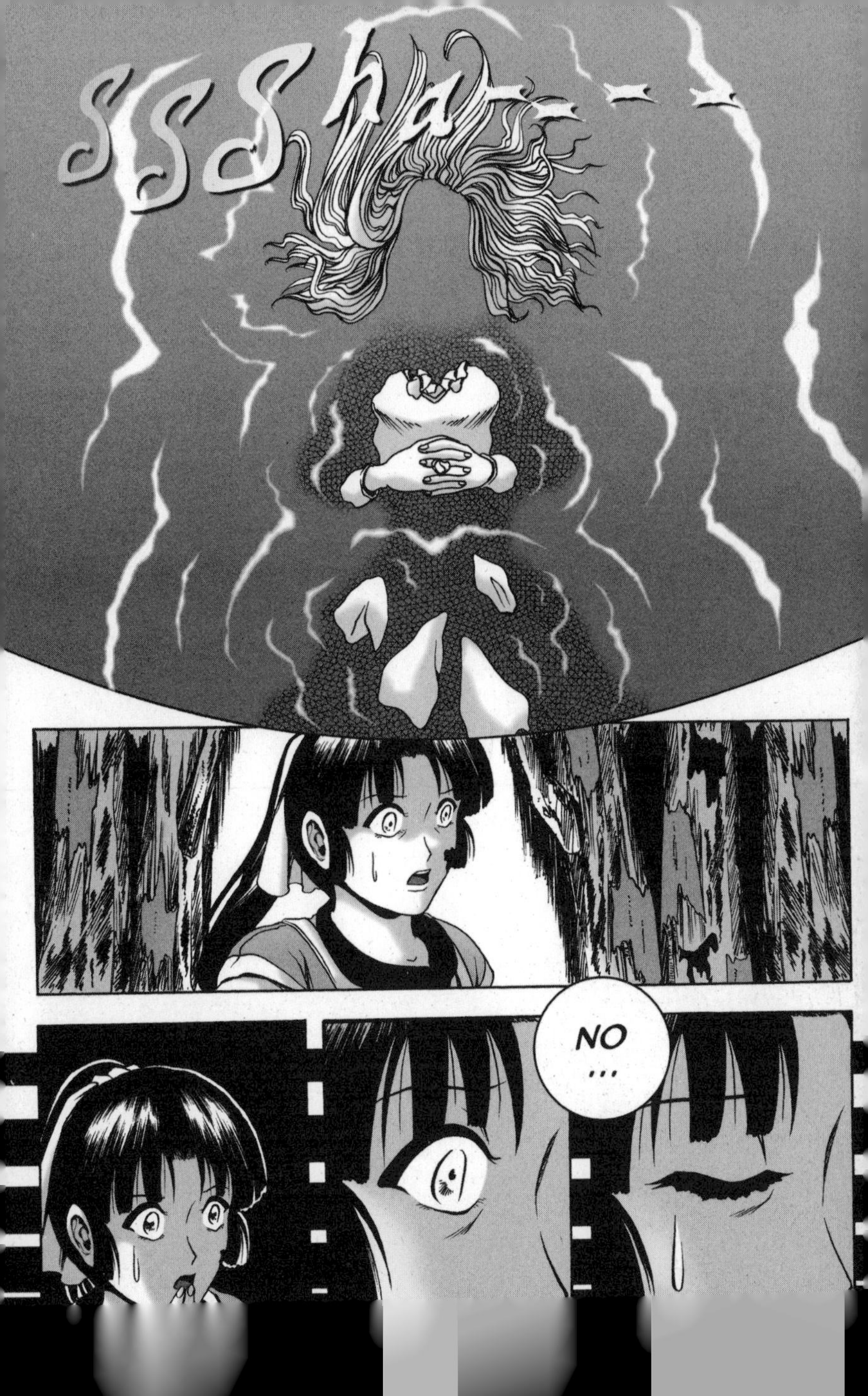
SSSha---
NO
...

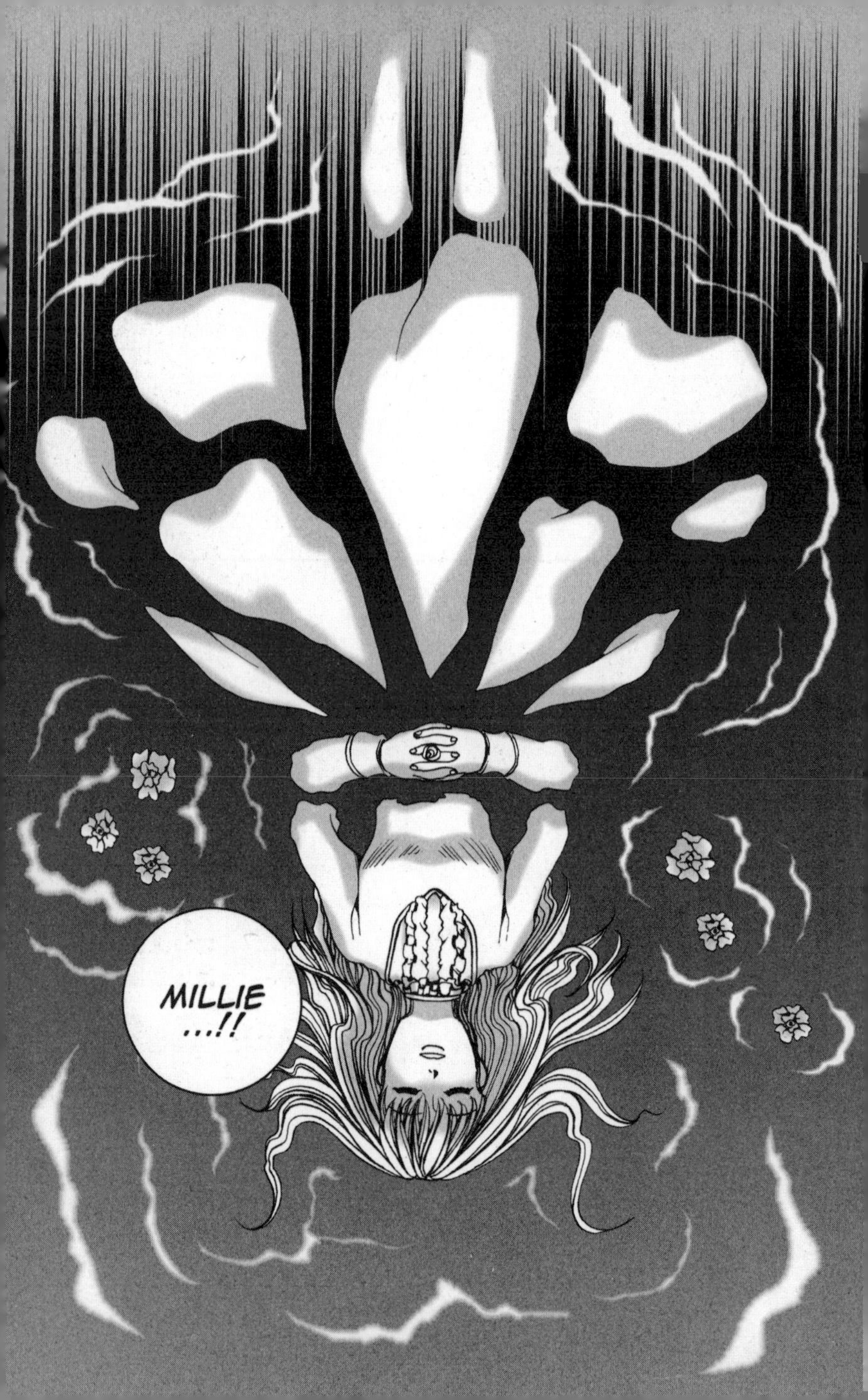
MILLIE ...!!

To Be Continued In...

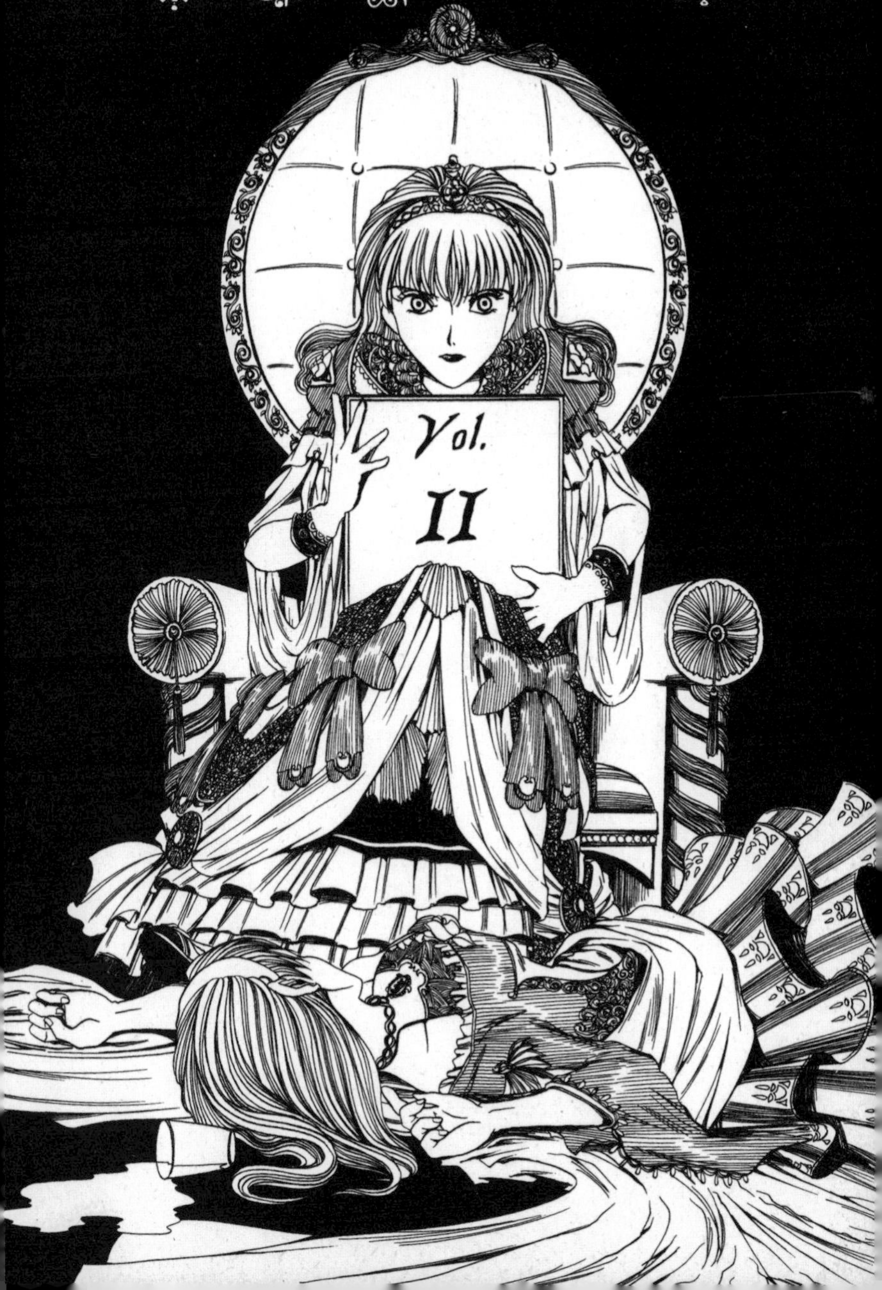
Vol.
II

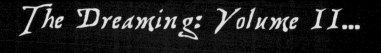

The Dreaming: Volume II...

With Millie's death, the school grinds completely to a halt.
As many students return home, fearful rumours are
whispered in the halls, and a dark, ominous cloud seems to
descend upon the school. Unable to leave and still plagued by
her dreams, Jeanie attempts to discover more about the other
missing girls. As she begins to delve into the history of the
school, she realizes just how dark and disturbing its past
really is...

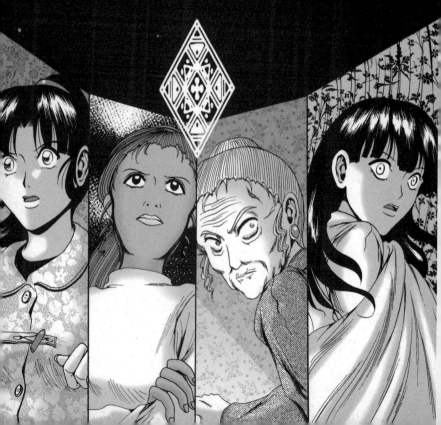

The Inspiration for "The Dreaming"

Australia has many stories involving schoolgirls vanishing into the bush. Perhaps the most famous one is a 1967 novel by Joan Lindsay called *Picnic at Hanging Rock*, later made into a movie. The book caused quite a stir when first released, as readers believed the events described in the book were true. This was unlikely, but the story captured the public imagination—largely because such stories often have some basis in fact.

However, my inspiration for *The Dreaming* doesn't really come from this book. It comes more directly from a former classmate of mine, class of '97, who vanished in the Tasmanian wilderness while trekking from one point to another. She was alone, and wasn't following any trails, but had made the trip before, so her disappearance wasn't due to inexperience—or suicide. They found her camping gear, all set up for the night, but despite searching everywhere for miles around, they found no trace of her. Months later, she was pronounced "missing, presumed dead."

I wonder what happened to her sometimes. Did she run into someone else out there, in the middle of nowhere? Did she fall into some hidden crevice, and the earth just swallowed her up? Perhaps, when I wrote this story, I was trying to explain something that really has no explanation.

Thousands of people go missing every year, in many countries, for no discernable reason most of the time. Most of these people are never seen again, and what happens to them remains an unsolved mystery. What are the chances it could be someone you know...or you?

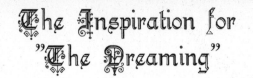

Amber and Jeanie hail from an earlier pitch of mine to TOKYOPOP—*TwinSide*, which can be found at *www.queeniechan.com*. It was a romantic comedy, but hey...things change.

Truth is, they have an even earlier incarnation, in a short story I drew for a competition, called *Twins* (also on my site). I often build long stories from my short stories, and vice versa. It's a good way of establishing the characters and their world before a longer story. *Twins* is nothing like *The Dreaming*, but you may find the girls still retain some remnants of their old personalities.

NT
QLD
WA
SA
NSW
VIC
TAS

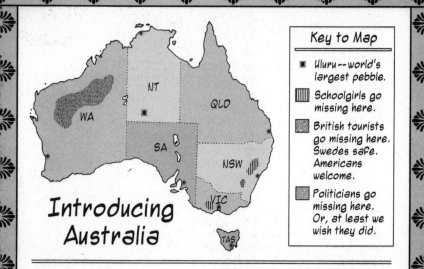

Key to Map

- Uluru--world's largest pebble.
- Schoolgirls go missing here.
- British tourists go missing here. Swedes safe. Americans welcome.
- Politicians go missing here. Or, at least we wish they did.

Introducing Australia

Australia is a rather young country, with a history of about 200 years. It was first "discovered" in 1770 by an English fella called Captain James Cook, who recognised its excellent potential as a convict dumping ground. There were already native Aborigines living here, but they were regarded merely as part of the local wildlife and thus ignored (the lucky ones, that is).

Over time, the country became independent and formed a federation of states. They are New South Wales, Victoria, Queensland, South Australia, Northern Territory, Western Australia, Tasmania and the Australian Capital Territory. Naturally, the country has long stopped importing criminals, though many criminals still work in the government.

AUSTRALIA

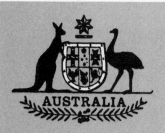

This is the esteemed Australian coat-of-arms, flanked by the Kangaroo and the Emu. Come to think of it, we shoot and eat both these animals.

BET YOU DIDN'T KNOW...

For a multi-cultural country, Australia has one of the world's leading diasporas--5% of the total population. 1 million Aussies live and work overseas.

Multiple Choice Question: The Australian outback is crawling with:

a) sheep and other cattle
b) serial killers
c) foreign tourists convinced they're experiencing the "real" Australia
d) all of the above

Answer: (d)

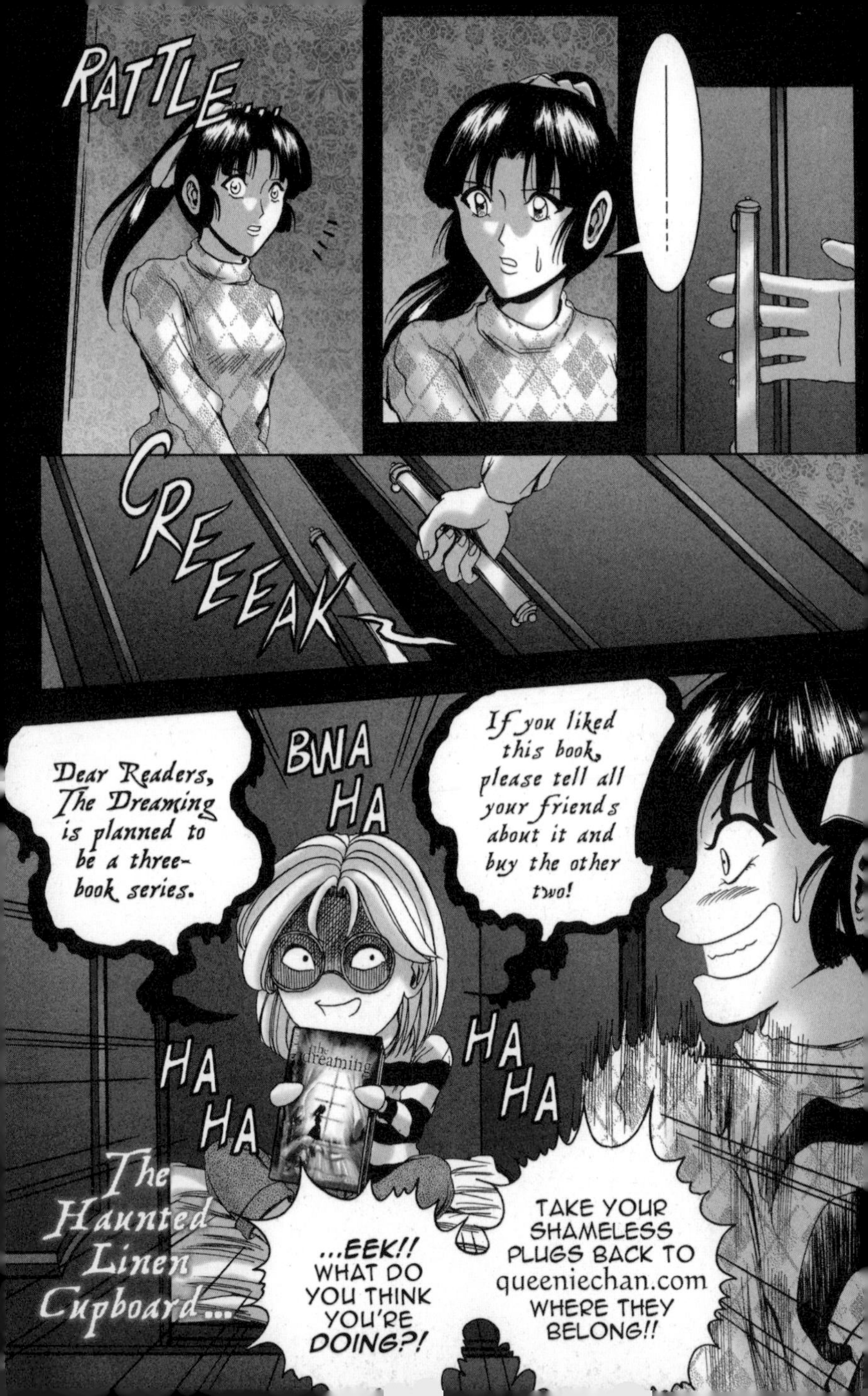
RATTLE...
…
CREEEAK
Dear Readers, The Dreaming is planned to be a three-book series.
BWA HA
If you liked this book, please tell all your friends about it and buy the other two!
HA HA
HA HA
The Haunted Linen Cupboard...
...EEK!! WHAT DO YOU THINK YOU'RE DOING?!
TAKE YOUR SHAMELESS PLUGS BACK TO queeniechan.com WHERE THEY BELONG!!

Locker No. 246

By Sarah Ferrick

AN ECCENTRIC GIRL AND HER FRUSTRATED BEST FRIEND
FORM THE HEART OF THIS DARKLY HUMOROUS STORY,
WRITTEN AND ILLUSTRATED BY ONE OF TOKYOPOP'S
FORMER RISING STARS OF MANGA WINNERS. SARAH
FERRICK'S SHORT MANGA IS THE FIRST IN AN ONGOING
SERIES OF ORIGINAL BACKUP FEATURES THAT WILL BE
EXCLUSIVE TO TOKYOPOP'S ORIGINAL MANGA. ENJOY!

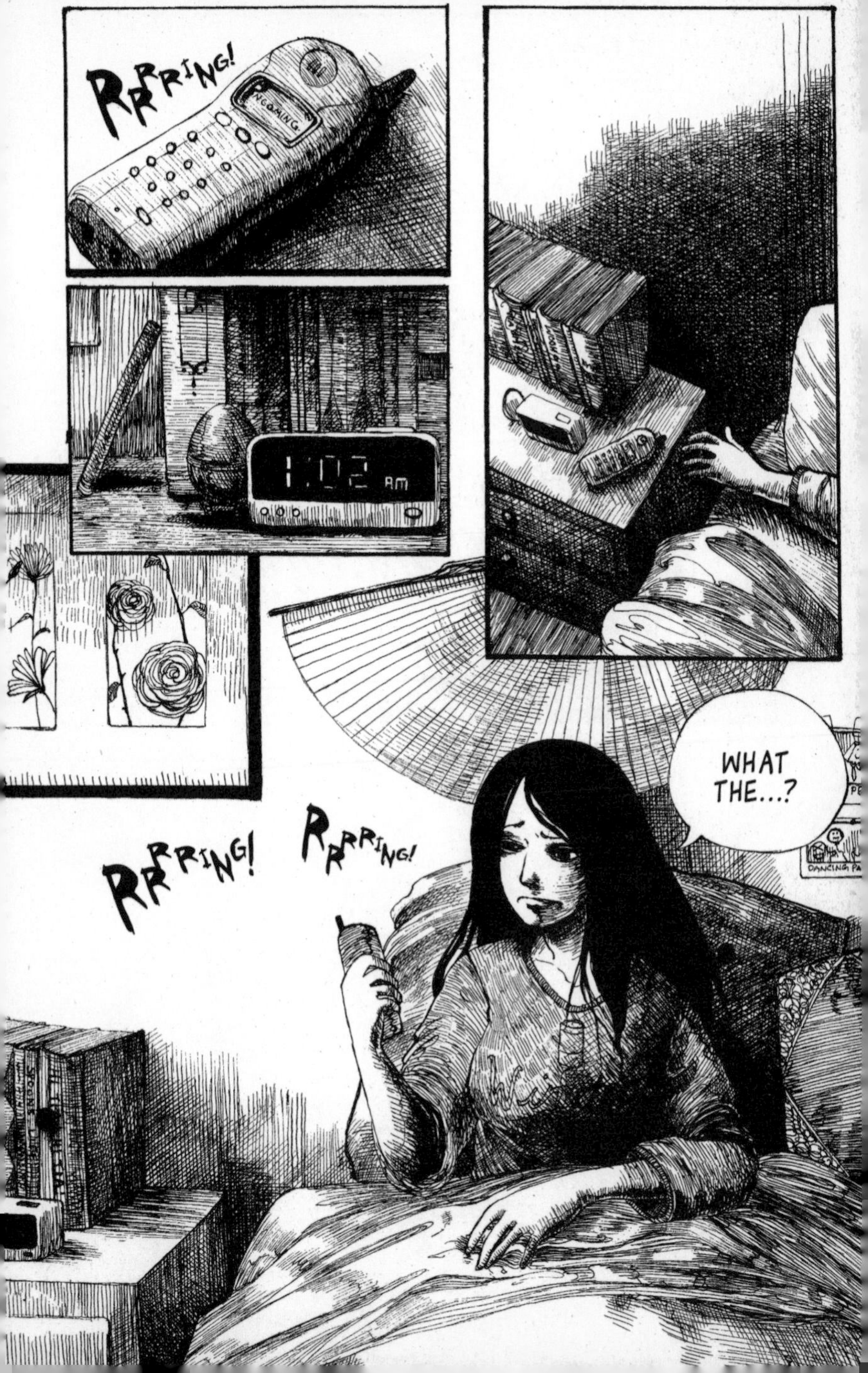
RRRRING!
INCOMING
1:02 AM
RRRRING!
RRRRING!
WHAT THE...?

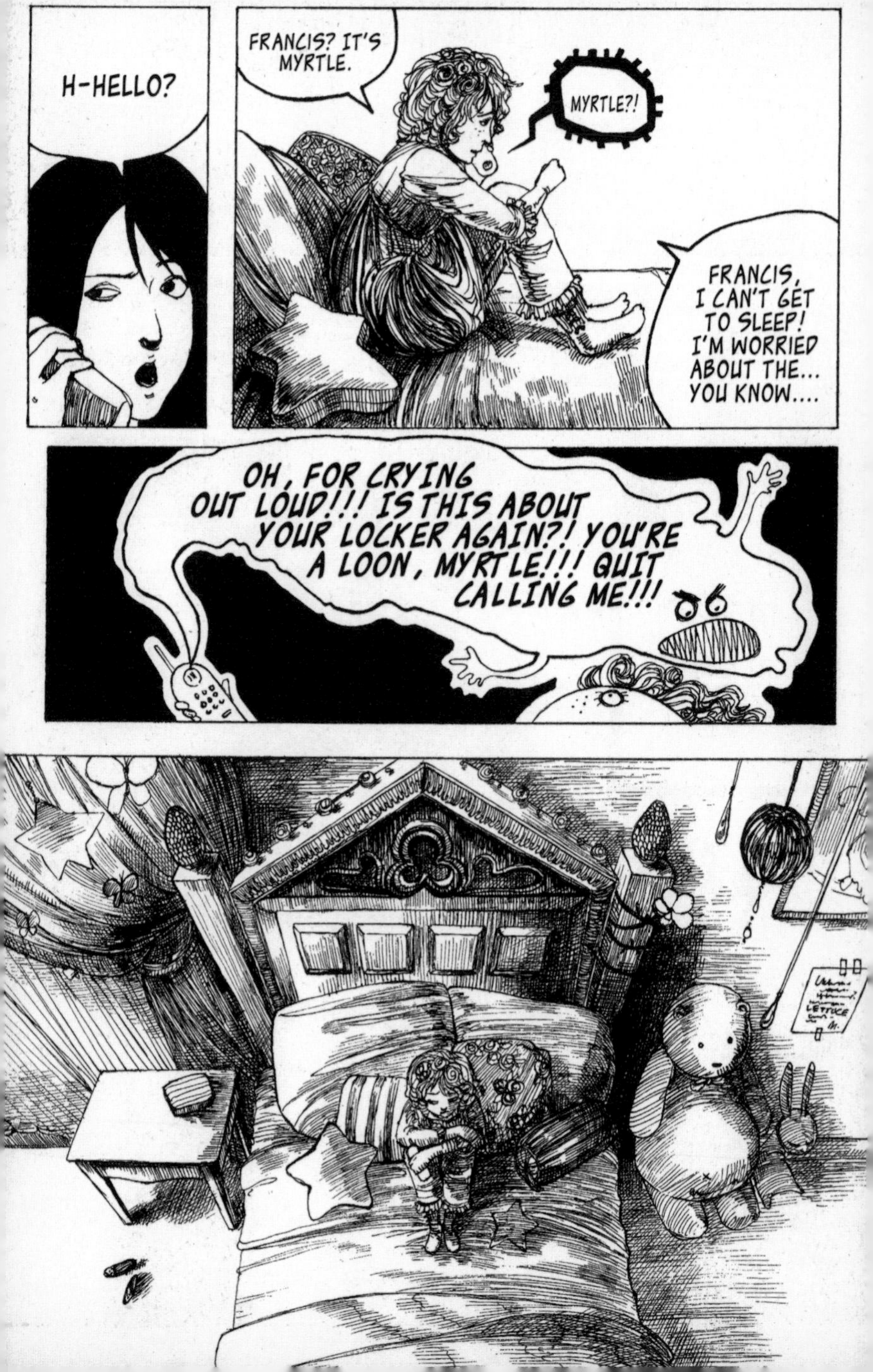
H-HELLO?
FRANCIS? IT'S MYRTLE.
MYRTLE?!
FRANCIS, I CAN'T GET TO SLEEP! I'M WORRIED ABOUT THE... YOU KNOW....
OH, FOR CRYING OUT LOUD!!! IS THIS ABOUT YOUR LOCKER AGAIN?! YOU'RE A LOON, MYRTLE!!! QUIT CALLING ME!!!
LETTUCE

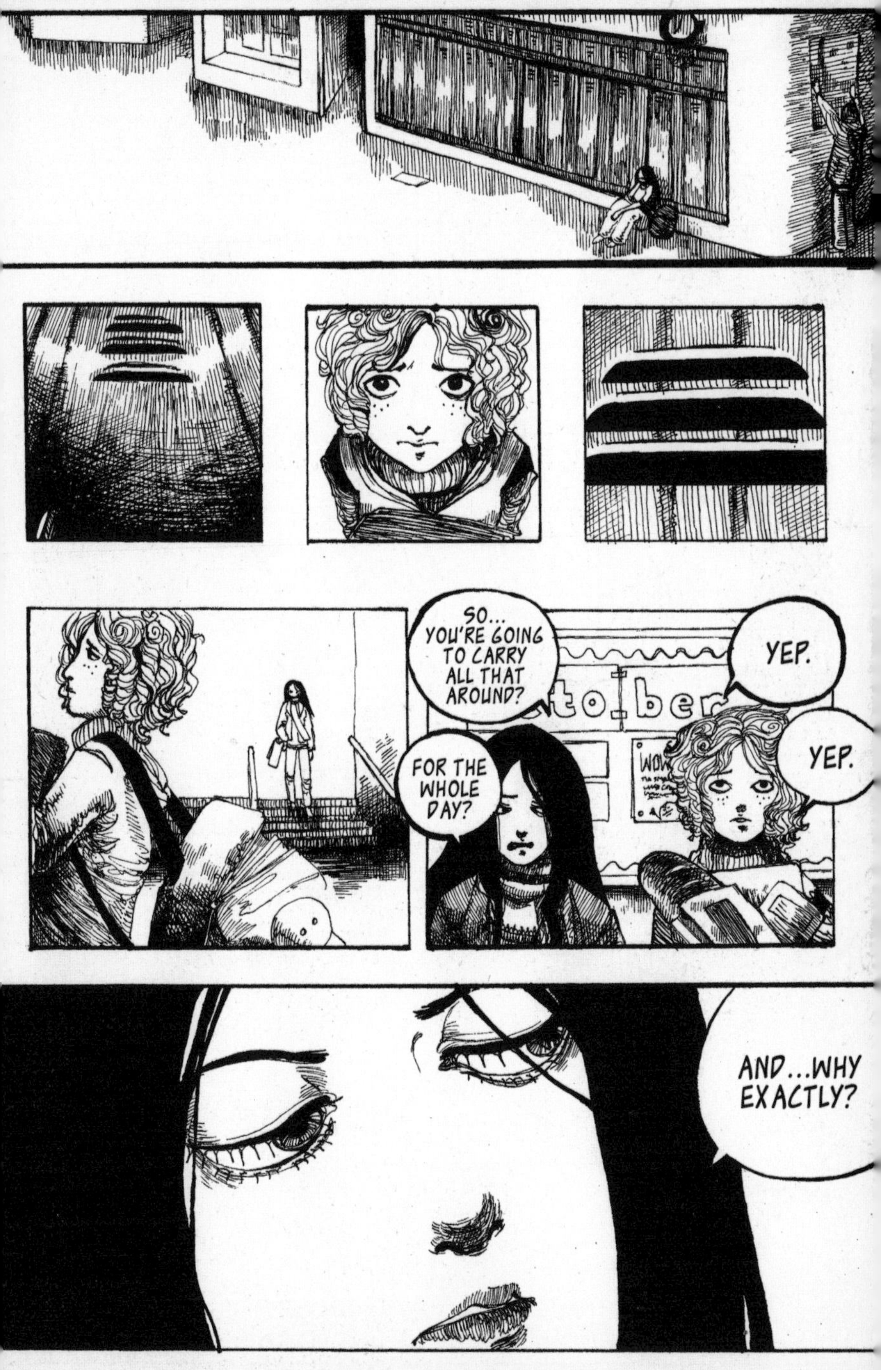
SO... YOU'RE GOING TO CARRY ALL THAT AROUND?
YEP.
FOR THE WHOLE DAY?
YEP.
AND...WHY EXACTLY?

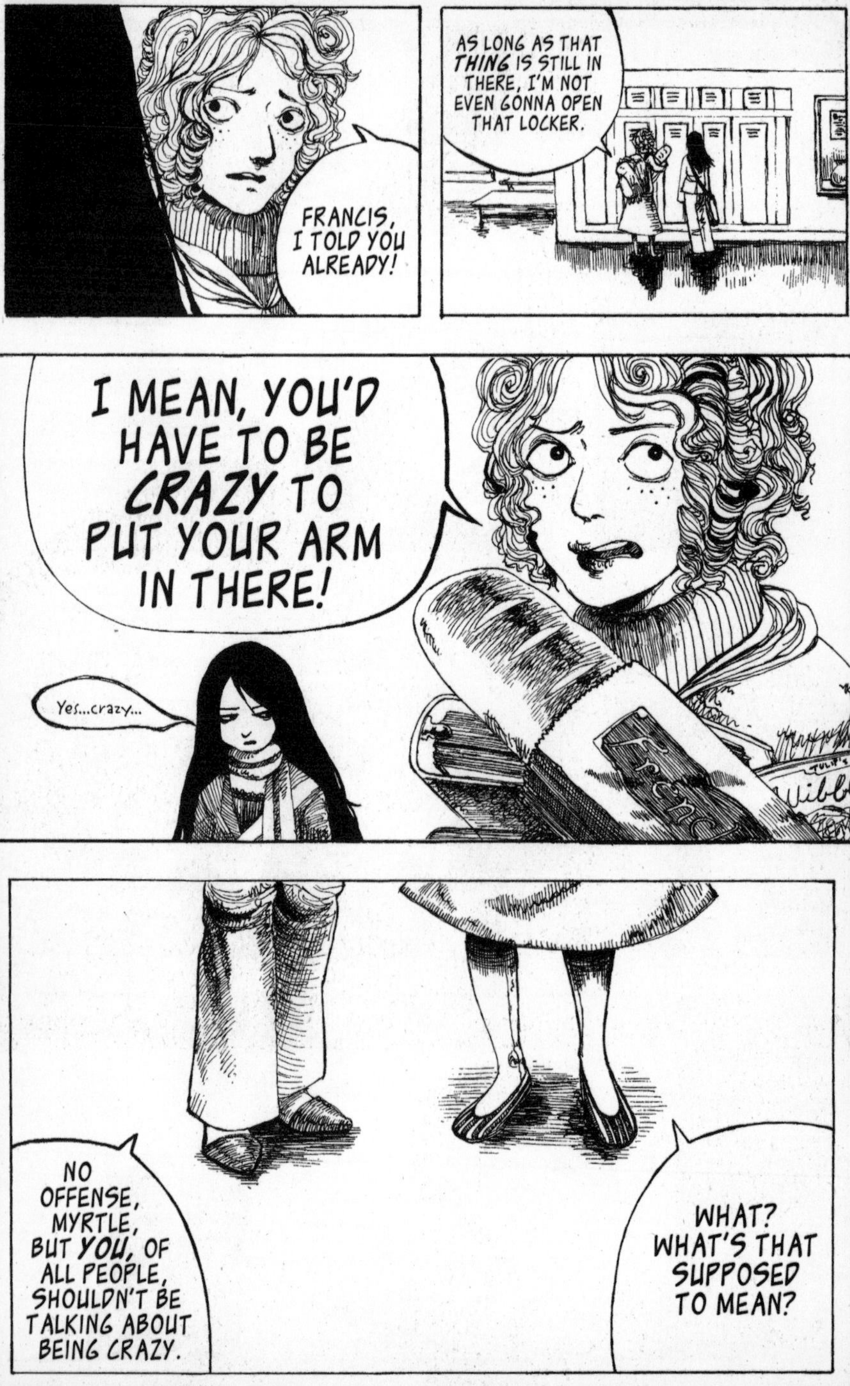
FRANCIS, I TOLD YOU ALREADY!
AS LONG AS THAT *THING* IS STILL IN THERE, I'M NOT EVEN GONNA OPEN THAT LOCKER.
I MEAN, YOU'D HAVE TO BE *CRAZY* TO PUT YOUR ARM IN THERE!
Yes...crazy...
NO OFFENSE, MYRTLE, BUT *YOU*, OF ALL PEOPLE, SHOULDN'T BE TALKING ABOUT BEING CRAZY.
WHAT? WHAT'S THAT SUPPOSED TO MEAN?

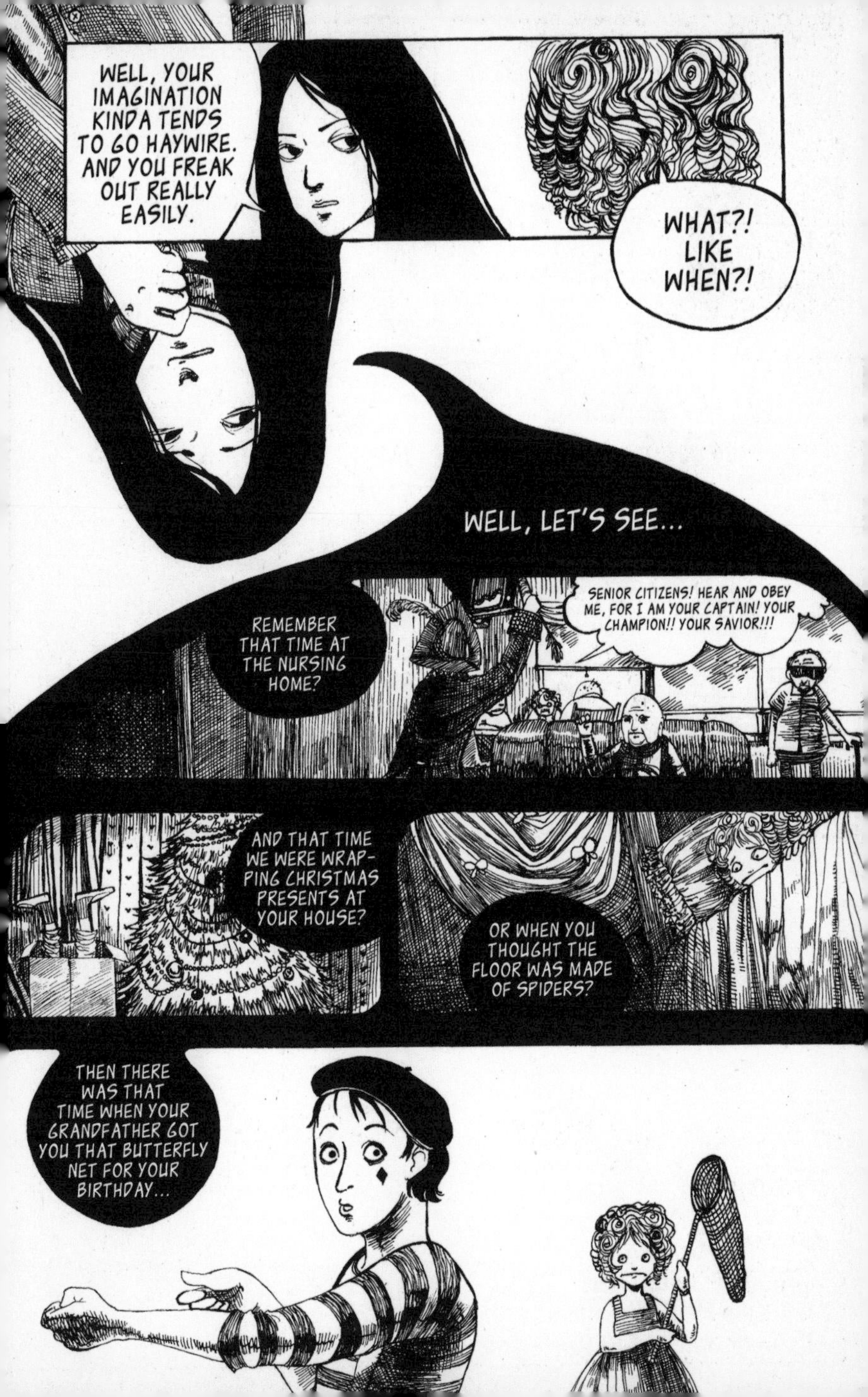
WELL, YOUR IMAGINATION KINDA TENDS TO GO HAYWIRE. AND YOU FREAK OUT REALLY EASILY.
WHAT?! LIKE WHEN?!
WELL, LET'S SEE...
REMEMBER THAT TIME AT THE NURSING HOME?
SENIOR CITIZENS! HEAR AND OBEY ME, FOR I AM YOUR CAPTAIN! YOUR CHAMPION!! YOUR SAVIOR!!!
AND THAT TIME WE WERE WRAP-PING CHRISTMAS PRESENTS AT YOUR HOUSE?
OR WHEN YOU THOUGHT THE FLOOR WAS MADE OF SPIDERS?
THEN THERE WAS THAT TIME WHEN YOUR GRANDFATHER GOT YOU THAT BUTTERFLY NET FOR YOUR BIRTHDAY...

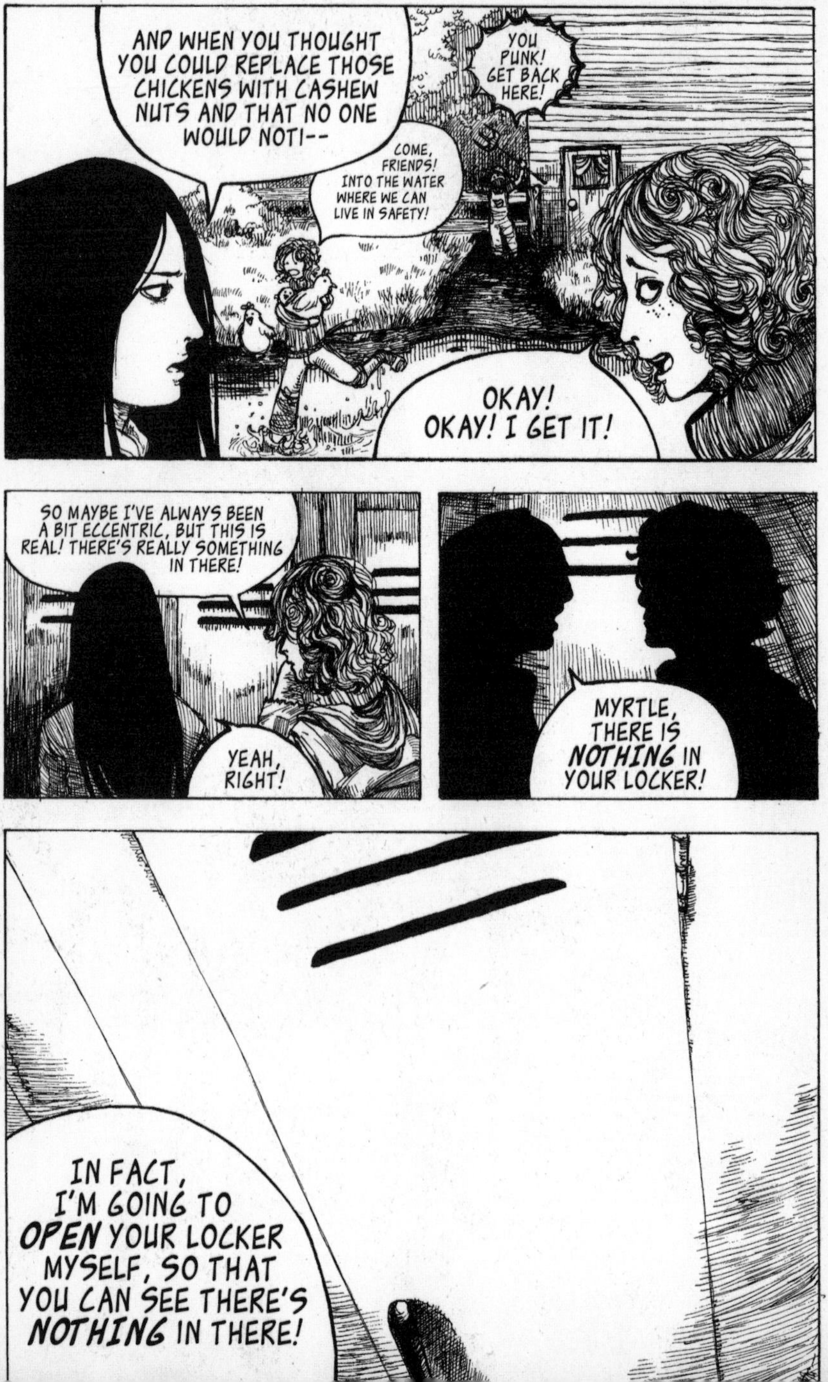
AND WHEN YOU THOUGHT YOU COULD REPLACE THOSE CHICKENS WITH CASHEW NUTS AND THAT NO ONE WOULD NOTI--
YOU PUNK! GET BACK HERE!
COME, FRIENDS! INTO THE WATER WHERE WE CAN LIVE IN SAFETY!
OKAY! OKAY! I GET IT!
SO MAYBE I'VE ALWAYS BEEN A BIT ECCENTRIC, BUT THIS IS REAL! THERE'S REALLY SOMETHING IN THERE!
YEAH, RIGHT!
MYRTLE, THERE IS NOTHING IN YOUR LOCKER!
IN FACT, I'M GOING TO OPEN YOUR LOCKER MYSELF, SO THAT YOU CAN SEE THERE'S NOTHING IN THERE!

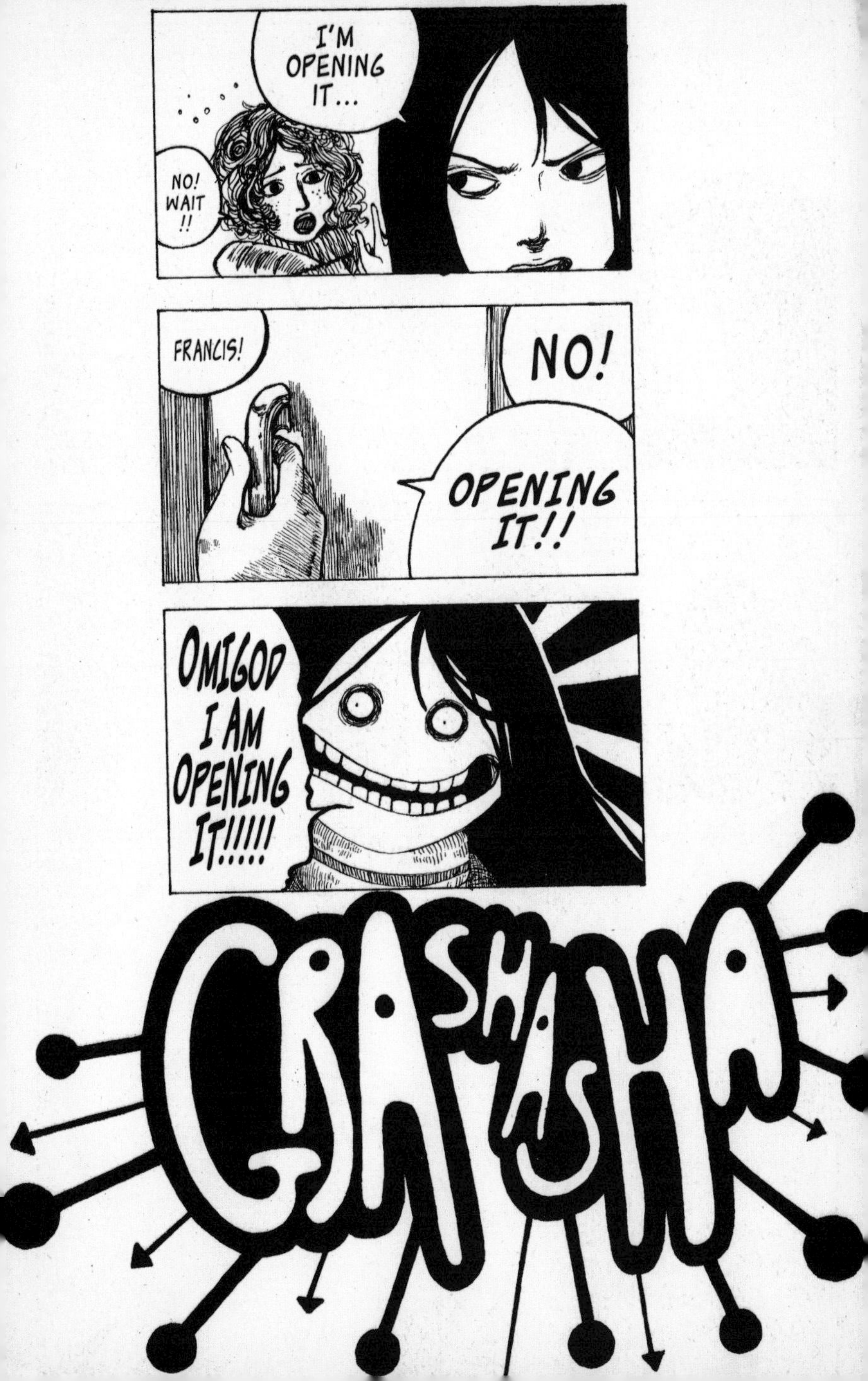
I'M OPENING IT...
NO! WAIT !!
FRANCIS!
NO!
OPENING IT!!
OMIGOD I AM OPENING IT!!!!!!
CRASHA SHASHA

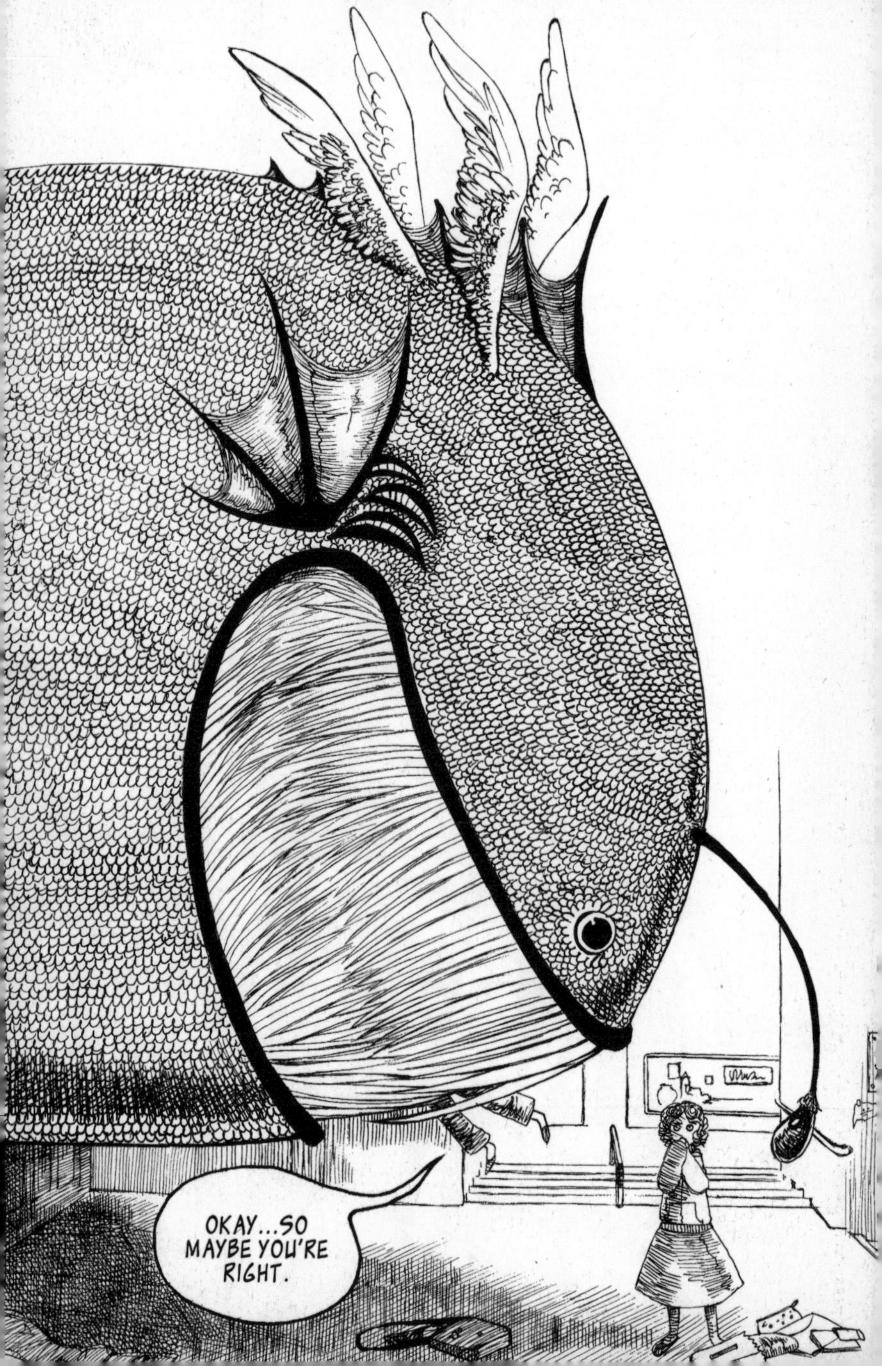
OKAY...SO MAYBE YOU'RE RIGHT.

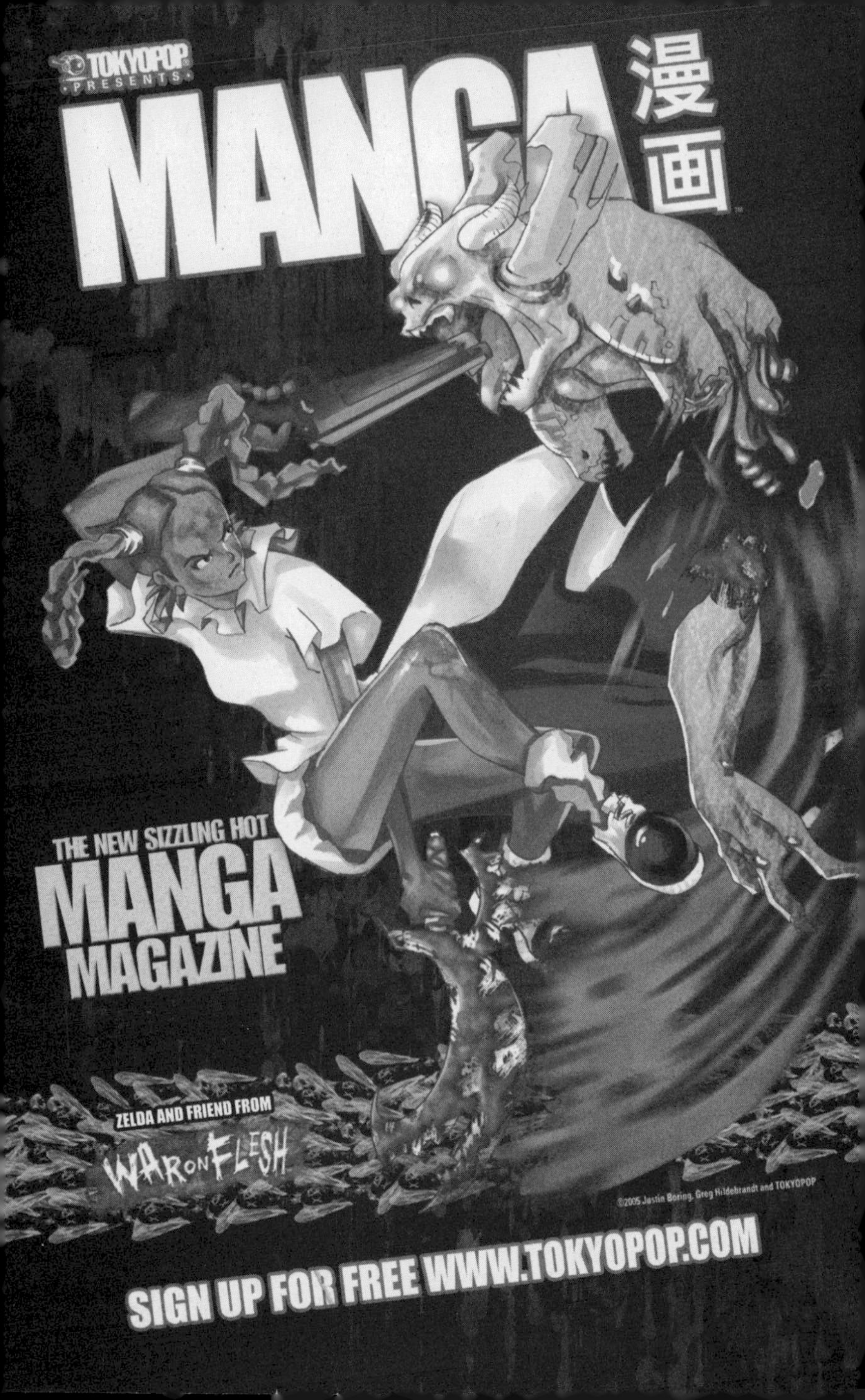
TOKYOPOP PRESENTS
MANGA 漫画™
THE NEW SIZZLING HOT
MANGA
MAGAZINE
ZELDA AND FRIEND FROM
WAR ON FLESH
©2005 Justin Boring, Greg Hildebrandt and TOKYOPOP
SIGN UP FOR FREE WWW.TOKYOPOP.COM

WWW.TOKYOPOP.COM/SHOP

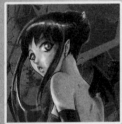

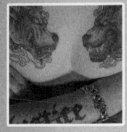